JAVA™
PROGRAMMING

Douglas Downing, Ph.D.
Seattle Pacific University

BARRON'S

Acknowledgments

This book would not be possible without the support of my wife Lori; and with help from Robert Downing for reviewing the manuscript; Mark Yoshimi for introducing me to Java; Melody Covington for typesetting the manuscript with TeX; Alec Hill and Seattle Pacific University for their support; the sponsors of the annual JavaOne conference; and editor Lynne Vessie at Barron's Educational Series, Inc.

About the Author

Douglas Downing teaches economics and quantitative methods and is undergraduate program chair for the School of Business and Economics at Seattle Pacific University. He earned a B.S. and Ph.D. at Yale University, and has written 14 books on math and computers.

Trademarks

Java is a trademark of Sun Microsystems, Inc. Windows is a trademark of Microsoft, Inc. This book is published by Barron's Educational Series, Inc. independently of these (or any other) company.

All inquiries should be addressed to:
Barron's Educational Series, Inc.
250 Wireless Boulevard
Hauppauge, New York 11788
http://www.barronseduc.com

Library of Congress Catalog No. 98-43741

International Standard Book No. 0-7641-0752-6

Library of Congress Cataloging-in-Publication Data
Downing, Douglas.
    Java™ programming, the easy way / Douglas Downing.
       p.   cm. — (The easy way)
    Includes bibliographical references and index.
    ISBN 0-7641-0752-6 (paperback)
    1. Java (Computer program language)   I. Title.   II. Series.
QA76.73.J38D68   1999
005.13'3–dc21   98-43741
                                     CIP

PRINTED IN THE UNITED STATES OF AMERICA
9 8 7 6 5 4 3 2 1

CONTENTS

10   Graphics   136

11   Files   172

12   Mathematical Operations   190

13   Windows Programming: Mouse Clicks and Buttons   210

APPENDICES

PREFACE

A computer will be glad to do many tasks that you would rather not do. Also, because it can work very fast, it can do many tasks that would be impossible without computers because they would take too long. The only requirement is that the computer needs to receive clear-cut instructions. These instructions must be written in a *computer programming language*. Learning a computer language is a bit like learning a foreign language, but it is easier because there are not as many words to learn.

There are several programming languages in common use. Java is one of the newest of these; it was released by Sun Microsystems in 1995. Java is designed to work with the Internet/World Wide Web, and it has many other advantages as well. Because it is a new language, the designers were able to take advantage of the experience programmers have had with previous languages.

Java is an object-oriented programming language. That means that you solve a problem by thinking of relevant objects and determining their characteristics and their behavior. The programming process involves creating Java objects that represent the behavior of their real-world counterparts. After you have written the program for an object, you can use that object while you are creating other objects, but you don't have to think of the internal details of an object while you are using it elsewhere. One of the biggest difficulties with computer programming is the inability of the human mind to keep track of too many things at once. Therefore, any method we can find that reduces the number of things we need to think of at once will amplify our power as programmers; you will learn how Java allows you to do this.

Java is full of different options. It can be very confusing while you are first learning the language if all of the options are placed in front of you at once. This book follows a careful sequence of presenting information. Not all of the options are presented to you at the beginning. The focus is on practical programs that you can quickly learn how to write, modify, and use. In particular, abstract concepts come later, after you have experience with some basic building blocks.

Sometimes an idea must make an appearance before we are ready to explain it. This works because you can include a feature in your program by copying it even if you do not yet fully understand how it works. This book contains cross-references where appropriate so you know where to find more information about a topic.

To learn about additional features of Java that are not covered in this book, you can check Sun's Java web page (*http://www.javasoft.com*).

One big advantage of Java is that it is platform independent. That means that you can write the same Java programs whether you are working with Windows, a Macintosh, UNIX, or something else. However, the exact process of executing a Java program will depend on the specific system you are using. Examples of system-dependent implementation in this book will apply to Windows 95/98/NT, since that is such a common platform.

There is only one way to learn computer programming: practice. The book includes many exercises that give suggested computer programming applications. The exercises near the beginning of the book ask you to write short programs. Suggested answers to many of these exercises are on the disc accompanying the book.

You don't need to know much mathematics to learn the general ideas of computer programming, although you do need to know some algebra and trigonometry to understand some of the programs, particularly in Chapters 12 and 18.

This book comes with a disc that contains the Java 2 Software Development Kit version 1.2 (Java SDK), which is provided free by Sun Microsystems. The disc also contains the source code for the example programs in this book along with some other examples. Look on the disc for the file *about_the_disc.html* for more information about the contents of the disc. The disc also contains a program that you can use to help you write Java programs—that is, you specify an outline of the program, and the code generator program will turn it into Java code.

For up to date information, see the web page for this book at *http://www.spu.edu/~ddowning/cpjava.html*

You are now about to embark on the journey of learning computer programming.

CHAPTER 1

INTRODUCTION TO JAVA PROGRAMMING

1.1 Computers and Programming Languages

If you like to do a lot of boring work yourself, this book is not for you. If, however, you're like me, you would much rather have somebody else do the boring work for you. The ideal boring work servant would be able to do routine tasks very quickly, without making mistakes and without complaining. The servant wouldn't have to be very creative because we would give all the instructions. Unfortunately, people don't really fit this description. If, however, we could build a *machine* to do the work, then we would be in good shape. We would also need to decide how to give instructions for our machine. The hardware without the instructions is like a helper who can't understand a word you say.

The machine that can do this work is a computer. You are probably familiar with using computers for applications such as word processing, spreadsheets, or games. You are likely familiar with a computer that uses a version of Windows, such as Windows NT, Windows 98, or Windows 95. Or, you may have worked with Macintosh computers. As you were using the computer, you may have been wondering: How did the computer learn how to do these tasks in the first place? How can I get the computer to do even more than the tasks included in the software that's already there? In order to answer these questions, you need to understand *computer programs*. Learning how to write computer programs will greatly increase your ability to get computers to do what you need them to do.

We will pretend that we are starting from scratch, making our own list of computer instructions. In each chapter we will face a new problem, and then we will figure out what instructions we would like the computer to understand. When we are finished, we will have created a whole new type of language called a *computer programming language*. Fortunately, we don't really have to start from scratch. There are many different computer programming languages available. The language that we will develop in this book is called Java. Java is a very new language as far as computer languages go; it was only introduced in 1995. Because the developers of Java (at a company called Sun Microsystems) could learn from the experience people had using earlier languages, they were able to design a language that makes it easier to write programs, and that is still a very powerful language able to solve a wide variety of different problems. We'll be seeing some of these features of Java later on.

One reason Java has become popular is that Java programs can enhance pages on the World Wide Web. Most web browsers in common use can understand Java, so you can include Java programs on your web page and anyone anywhere in the world can use your program. A Java program that appears on the World Wide Web is called an *applet*. The other type of Java program is called an *application*. In order to run a Java application, you first need to load it on your computer, and then you need to call a command to execute the program. In this book we will describe both Java applets and Java applications; see Chapter 3 for more information about the difference between them.

Another important advantage of Java is that it is designed so that a program can be written once and run anywhere that has a Java system (called a *virtual machine*) on it. This means that if you write a Java program intending it to work for Windows, you're guaranteed it will also work on a Macintosh or on a system using the Unix operating system. (Well, almost guaranteed. There are still some features that will vary from machine to machine; for example, not all monitors can produce the same set of colors, so programs will look different on different monitors.)

Java is an *object-oriented* computer programming language. This provides a very powerful way to arrange programs as collections of objects that consist of data and the instructions that process these data. We're not going to talk about object-oriented programming immediately in this book, because you need to learn some basic concepts of what programs can do before you can begin to appreciate the power of object-oriented programming. You can look ahead to Chapter 9 to see more about what this means.

This book assumes that you are new to computer programming, or, at least that you're new to Java. This book can also help you become familiar with Java if you have used other programming languages before.

1.2   Arithmetic Calculation: 2 + 2

First, we'll use our computer for arithmetic calculations. You probably are familiar with performing calculations on a pocket calculator. We will see that a computer can function as a sophisticated calculator. We need symbols to stand for arithmetic operations: + for plus, − for minus, an asterisk, *, for multiplication, and a slash, /, for division. (A computer keyboard usually does not have a multiplication symbol (×), but even if it did that symbol could be confused with the letter x, so the asterisk is a better multiplication symbol.) The slash, /, is a good symbol for division, since division can be represented as a fraction: 12/3 means 12 divided by 3, which is the same as the fraction $\frac{12}{3}$.

To start with a simple calculation, we'll have the computer add 2 plus 2. We would like the instructions to be as simple as possible, something like $2 + 2$.

To turn this into a Java program, however, we need to add some Java words and symbols (called *code*). We need to tell the computer that this is a Java program, that it needs to calculate $2 + 2$, and that it needs to display the result of the calculation instead of keeping the answer to itself.

The complete Java program looks like this:

```
class additionexample {

/*method*/ public static void main (String args[ ]) {
System.out.println(2+2);
} /*end main*/

} /*end additionexample*/
```

The expression "$2 + 2$" is in the middle of some other code. The next section explains these other parts.

1.3   Ten Basic Features of Java

1. Each Java program includes the word **class** at (or very near) the beginning. We'll see the significance of this later, when we see that the ability to create classes makes Java a very powerful object-oriented programming language. For now, all you need to know is that every Java program is itself a class.

2. The expression additionexample is the name of our program. Each program needs to have a name that should briefly describe what the program does. Also, the program needs to be typed into a text file with the same name as the program, plus the extension "java." For our example, the program file would be named *additionexample.java*.

3. Braces are used to mark the beginning and ending of blocks of Java code. Note the left brace, {, after "additionexample" to mark the beginning of the code for the program, and the right brace, }, that marks the end of the code in the last line of the program.

4. The computer will execute the instructions that are given without worrying about why it is being told to do so. However, people also need to read computer programs and understand what they do and why they do it. It is much easier for human readers to follow a program if it contains additional explanatory notes, called *comments*. In Java, a comment begins with the symbols /* and ends with the symbols */. The computer will ignore any text that is included between the comment symbols, so you can type whatever you want there. However, your comments should be designed

so they are helpful for people who will be reading the program. Our program contains three comments: the /*method*/ comment identifies the beginning of the method called **main**; /*end main*/ identifies the end of that method; and /*end additionexample*/ identifies the end of the program. In this book, we will usually put a /*method*/ comment to identify the beginning of a method, and we will often put a comment following a right brace, }, to indicate what that brace is marking the end of. Your Java programs will contain many right braces. Since the brace itself does not make clear what it is ending, it helps to have a comment to explain.

You can also create a comment in Java by using two slashes, //. When you do this, all characters to the right of the slashes until the end of the line will be ignored. In this book we will prefer the /* */ form because it makes it clear where the comment ends.

5. The action in a Java program occurs in a block of code called a _method_. (The terms _procedure_, _subroutine_, or _function_ are also used for the same concept.) Our program contains only one method. Since it does not return a value, it includes the word **void**. (Later, we'll learn about methods that do return values, which begin by identifying the type of the value that is returned. Also, we'll put off explaining the words **public** and **static** until later.) The name of our method is **main**. Every Java application program has one **main** method. (However, a Java applet is slightly different; see page 25.) The main method has to be called **main**, but we can create our own names for most of the other methods that we write. Also note the opening and closing parentheses, ( ), after the name of the method. The expression **String args[ ]** represents the _parameters_ of the method. The **main** method will always include **String args[ ]** as a parameter; later, we'll see other methods with different parameters. At the end of this line is the left brace, {, to mark the beginning of the code for the **main** method; note the right brace, }, later in the program that marks the end of the method.

6. The words **System.out.println** are used to display text on the screen. This is a command that directs the computer to present the _output_ of the program to us. It would do no good if the computer calculated the result but then never told anyone.

At first glance this command seems odd, since the word "print" implies that the results are sent to a printer. This oddity exists for historical reasons; you will just have to get used to the idea that **System.out.println** means to display on the screen, not the printer. (See page 259 for information on how actually to print something with Java.) We will use **System.out.println** often during the first few chapters of this book; however, if you are used to Windows programs you will be disappointed with **System.out.println**, since it presents its output in a simple text window rather than in a full-featured graphics window. Most of the output in the programs we will write after Chapter 10 will appear in a graphics window. This makes our programs more powerful, but it is slightly more complicated to do this, which is why we are delaying it until later.

After the computer displays the output from **System.out.println**, it will put the output from the next **System.out.println** on a new line. This is not an issue for this simple program, which only has one output statement, but it will become important later on. If you don't want the computer to move to a new line after it has completed the output, then use **System.out.print** instead of **System.out.println** (see page 48).

7. In Java, semicolons, ;, are used to mark the end of each statement. Our program has only one statement:

System.out.println(2+2);

8. In some cases, a computer language requires you to use the exact words that it expects. For our example, **class**, **public**, **static**, **void**, **main**, **String**, **System**, **out**, and **println** are specific Java words. As we will see later, in other cases we can make up our own words to include in our program. If you are new to a programming language, it can sometimes be difficult to tell from a program listing which are the programming language words and which are the words created by the author of the program. To make it easier, this book will put all of the Java words in boldface when they appear in program listings. This means that if you are typing the program yourself, you need to spell these words exactly as they appear. When a word is not in boldface, you can change it to whatever you want. See Appendix A for more information about Java words.

Note, however, that the boldface appears only for the printing of this book; if you type a program yourself, or copy it from the CD-ROM, that is, without using boldface, then the keywords will appear the same as all of the other words.

There is also one other exception: Java words will not appear in boldface in this book if they are in comments, since comments are never mandatory; you can change the text in a comment any way you like.

We are not going to explain all of the Java words in this chapter, but all will be made clear later. Learning a programming language is a challenge because there is much to learn and you cannot learn it all at once; you need to learn things in a reasonable sequence. Fortunately, you can use some of these keywords in your early programs just by mimicry (that is, by simply copying them) without understanding exactly what they mean yet.

9. A very important feature you need to know about Java is that it is case sensitive. This means that it treats uppercase letters and lowercase letters differently, so you must be very careful to make sure that you follow the right capitalization pattern. For example, **System.out.println** needs to be typed exactly as shown. The computer will not recognize the command if you type SYSTEM.OUT. PRINTLN or System.Out.Println, or any other variation with the same letters but a different capitalization pattern.

When you are creating your own names, you are free to use whatever capitalization pattern you like, but you must be consistent and always type the name in the same way. For example, if you create a variable *time*, then you must always type it *time* and never *TIME* or *Time*. You could if you wanted create three variables: *time*, *TIME*, and *Time*, which would be treated by the computer as three totally separate variables. However, this is strongly recommended against because it is guaranteed to cause considerable confusion. In general, it is probably best to use mostly lowercase letters.

10. The way you arrange your lines of code doesn't matter. For example, our program could also be written like this:

```
class additionexample{public static void main(String
args []){System.out.println(2+2);}}
```

This version is shorter, because it fits on two lines. It is harder for a person to read, however, because it is condensed so much, so the previous version of the program is preferred.

1.4   Compiling and Running a Java Program

A Java program needs to be typed on your computer as a text file. To do this, you need to use a text editor. The Notepad program in Windows will work. You can also use a word processor; however, you need to be sure to save the file as a text file instead of as a normal word processing document. (Word processing document files contain special codes used by the word processor that will not work in a Java program.) Our example program needs to be saved in a file with the name *additionexample.java*.

Once the program has been written, we need to tell the computer to execute it. Even though the Java language itself is platform independent, meaning that the text of the program is the same no matter what computer we are using, the actual process of executing the program will inevitably depend on the particular machine you are using.

We need to make sure that we have a Java system installed on our machine. There are several Java systems we can choose from. For now, we will assume that we are using a computer running Microsoft Windows 95, 98, or NT, and that we are using the Java Development Kit (JDK), which is available for free from Sun Microsystems, Inc. It is included on the disc that comes with this book. (See the disc for more information about using the JDK.) You can also obtain the JDK directly from Sun Microsystems at this web address: *http://www.javasoft.com*.

If the JDK is already installed, then actually running the program is easy. It requires two steps: first the program is *compiled*, and then the program is *executed*.

1. Move to the MS-DOS command prompt. In Windows 98/95/NT, do this by choosing the Start Menu; then the Programs Menu; and then clicking on MS-DOS. You will see a symbol on the screen (called a *prompt*) that will look something like this:

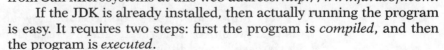

```
C:
```

This assumes that drive C is your hard drive. Change to the directory where you stored the file *additionexample.java*. To make sure that your program file is present, type this command:

```
dir additionexample.java
```

Now, type this command:

```
javac additionexample.java
```

The expression "javac" is short for Java compiler. Compiling a program means translating it from the original form you typed (called the *source code*) to a different form. Compilers for other programming languages translate a program into the *machine language* for the computer being used. However, this means they aren't very *portable* (that is, they run only on the machine for which they have been compiled). The Java compiler translates the program into a special code called *Java bytecode*. The advantage of the bytecode is that it is the same for all platforms. The disadvantage is that the bytecode itself cannot run directly on the computer (unless your computer has a *Java chip*, which is a microprocessor that uses Java bytecode as its machine language). The bytecode needs to be executed by a program called the *Java Virtual Machine*, or JVM. It is called "virtual" because it acts as if it were a computer whose machine language is Java bytecode, even though it really is running on a machine with a microprocessor such as a Pentium that uses a different machine language. A Java applet is executed by the Java virtual machine contained in the web browser. A Java application is executed by a program (that comes with the JDK) containing the JVM.

When the compiler is finished with our program, we will see the C: prompt again. If we now type the command

```
dir additionexample.*
```

we will see that there is now a file called *additionexample.class* in addition to our original file *additionexample.java*. A file with extension *.class* is a file of Java bytecodes. Don't try to look at this file with your text editor.

2. In order to execute the program, type this command:

```
java additionexample
```

Note that this command is similar to our previous command, except that the command is "java," not "javac," and we don't include an extension after the name of the file.

After we type our command, the screen will look like this:

```
C:javac additionexample.java
C:java additionexample
4
```

The 4 is the result of our 2 + 2 calculation. Admittedly, this has been a lot of work to find the result for one simple calculation, but we have nevertheless achieved an important milestone: writing our first Java program. The rest of the book will show the many ways in which the power of Java allows you to write programs that accomplish a wide variety of tasks.

CHAPTER 2

CALCULATIONS

2.1 Subtraction, Multiplication, and Division

Here are some other examples of calculation problems that we might wish to solve:

- subtraction: If you hand the cashier a ten dollar bill for a four dollar purchase, your change is $10 - 4 = 6$.

- multiplication: If you have three boxes each containing 16 books, you have $3 \times 16 = 48$ books.

- division: If a baseball player has 34 hits in 94 at-bats, you can find the batting average by dividing $34.0/94.0 = .362$. (See page 19 for why we write 34.0/94.0 instead of 34/94.)

We can also add up several numbers at once. For example, if we need to find the total amount we have spent on groceries for the last seven weeks, we can add up the weekly amounts like this:

$$34 + 50 + 35 + 66 + 34 + 37 + 41 = 297$$

If we want to find the average weekly amount spent on groceries, we need to add up the numbers and then divide:

$$(34 + 50 + 35 + 66 + 34 + 37 + 41)/7 = 42.428571$$

Note that we must put the numbers being added in parentheses, since that will tell the computer to do the additions first, and then the division.

When the computer comes to an expression with both additions and multiplications, it will do the multiplications first, and then the additions. Therefore, $20 - 3 * 4$ will result in $20 - 12 = 8$.

Divisions will be done before subtractions, so $20 - 60/4$ will result in $20 - 15 = 5$.

When an expression contains both additions and subtractions, the computer will do the operations in order from left to right, so $14 - 6 + 4$ will result in $8 + 4 = 12$.

9

If an expression contains both multiplications and divisions, the computer will do the operations in order from left to right, so $90/3 * 4$ will result in $30 * 4 = 120$.

Here's an expression with all four operations:

$$600 - 50 + 120/4 * 5$$

The division will be done first, giving the result

$$600 - 50 + 30 * 5$$

Next comes the multiplication:

$$600 - 50 + 150$$

Next comes the subtraction:

$$550 + 150$$

Finally, the addition is done; the result is 700.

This order corresponds to the way that normal algebraic notation works.

You can change the order of operation by using parentheses. For example, in the expression $2 + 3 * 4$, the computer will perform the multiplication first, so the result will be $2 + 12 = 14$. In the expression $(2 + 3) * 4$, the computer will perform the addition first, so the result will be $5 * 4 = 20$. In general, any calculation inside parentheses will be done before any other calculations outside the parentheses.

2.2   Including Output Labels

It is not very much help if the computer performs our calculation and displays the result on the screen but fails to label the result. Fortunately, in Java it is easy to include a label; simply include the text you want to appear within double quotation marks, "like this." Then, include a plus sign, +, after the label and before the calculation.

Here is a program that calculates the batting average for 34 hits in 94 at-bats and displays the result on the screen:

```
class calculationexample {

/*method*/ public static void main(String args[ ]) {
System.out.println("Batting Average="+(34.0/94.0));
} /*end main*/
} /*end calculationexample*/
```

Here is the output:

```
Batting Average=0.3617021276595745
```

The plus sign performs two roles in Java. When it is included between two numbers, it represents addition, as we would expect. However, it means something slightly different in an expression such as

```
"Batting Average="+(34.0/94.0)
```

The expression "Batting Average" is called a *character string*, or *string*. A string is any group of characters. When a plus sign comes after a string, it represents *concatenation*, which means simply "join together." Therefore, the computer will display the string "Batting Average=" followed immediately by the result of the calculation 34.0/94.0. We'll see more about operations on strings in Chapter 7. For now, all you need to know is that you use a plus sign to separate items when you have more than one item included in a System.out.println statement.

There still remains one annoying feature with the output of this program. Even though the computer is trying to be helpful by expressing the answer as precisely as possible, we don't usually want to see all of those decimal places. Therefore, we will need to work out a way to round off numbers to a specified number of decimal places (see pages 16 and 90).

2.3   Variables of Type double (Real Numbers)

Suppose you throw a baseball straight up, and you need to know how high it will be at any time. The height will be given by this formula:

$$-0.5 \times 9.8 \times t^2 + 25t + 1.2$$

In the formula, the height is measured in meters, t is the time measured in seconds since the ball was thrown, the initial speed of the ball is 25 meters per second, and the initial height of the ball is 1.2 meters.

Suppose we need to calculate the height of our baseball exactly 2.0436 seconds after launch. We can use this expression:

$$-0.5 * 9.8 * 2.0436 * 2.0436 + 25 * 2.0436 + 1.2$$

This method, however, requires us to type the long number 2.0436 three times. If would be easier if we could *store* that value, so we would only need to type it once and then we could refer to it. Fortunately, a computer contains many memory locations that can be used to store values. We need to create a *variable*. All we need to do is give the variable a name so we can find it again, and specify what type of value needs to be stored. We'll give our variable the name *time*, since it represents a quantity of time. You do not want to use your imaginative powers to come up with creative variable names; usually it is best to use a name that clearly describes the nature of the quantity the variable represents. The choice of clear variable names will go a long way toward making your Java programs easy for people to understand. (The computer, however, doesn't care what name you use for the variable; it will gladly compute the same result whether you call the variable *time* or *asparagus* or *r2d2c3po*. The only restriction is that you want to avoid using a variable name that also is a Java key word, such as **main, public,** or **static**. See Appendix A.)

Longer variable names are generally more descriptive. However, if you are typing the program remember that longer names are harder to type, so you don't want to get too carried away with long names. In this book we will generally choose longer, more descriptive names so it is easier for the reader to understand the program source code listings.

The number 2.0436 is an example of a *double precision number*, which is shortened in Java to **double**. Variables of type **double** represent *real number* values. You might recall from algebra that the real numbers include all whole numbers and fractions, as well as all decimal fractions with either a finite or infinite number of digits. Real numbers include all positive and negative values, and each real number corresponds to a point on a number line that extends to infinity in both directions. The measurement of a physical quantity such as distance, time, energy, and mass will be a real number. However, **double** values in Java cannot extend to positive and negative infinity, or contain an infinite number of digits, as can true real numbers. The maximum value for a **double** variable is about 1.8×10^{308}; the exact value is stored in a variable called **Double.MAX_VALUE**. (This variable is defined by the Java system, so you don't have to define it yourself.) The minimum positive **double** value is about 4.9×10^{-324}; the exact value is stored as **Double.MIN_VALUE**. (You might be wondering, "Do the real numbers include all possible numbers?" Actually not, since there is a type of number called a *complex number* that includes $\sqrt{-1}$.)

In order to create our variable *time*, we need this assignment statement:

double time=2.0436;

Note that there are three parts to the assignment statement: the variable type **double**; the variable name (time); and the value. Note the equal sign between the name and the value. Also note that time is not in boldface, since you can choose whatever name you like for the variable.

Now we can calculate the height of the ball with this statement:

System.out.println(-0.5*9.8*time*time+25*time+1.2);

Every time the computer reaches the variable name time, it will substitute the value 2.0436, so the result will be just the same as if the computer executed this statement:

System.out.println(-0.5*9.8*2.0436*2.0436+25*2.0436+1.2);

Here is the complete program:

```
class ballheight {
/*method*/ public static void main(String args[ ]) {
double time=2.0436;
System.out.println("time="+time+
"height="+(-0.5*9.8*time*time+25*time+1.2));
time=3.0436;
System.out.println("time="+time+
"height="+(-0.5*9.8*time*time+25*time+1.2));
} /*end main*/
} /*end ballheight*/
```

2.4 Assignment Statements

Note how the variable time is declared and then used in the expression to calculate the height, which is carefully labeled. We might need to use this program to find the height at more than one time, so we also have included two statements to find the height when time = 3.0436. Note that we can assign a new value to a variable by giving a new assignment statement. When the computer executes the statement

```
time=3.0436;
```

it will assign the new value 3.0436 to the variable time. The old value (2.0436) is lost and gone forever (that is, the computer has no memory of the old value). Every subsequent reference to the variable time in the program will use the value 3.0436. Since we have already declared the variable time to be of type **double**, we do not include the word **double** in the new assignment. If we did, the compiler would present an error message for us:

```
variable 'time' is already declared in this method
```

An error message such as this does not do any harm, but you do need to re-edit the source code to fix the error, then re-compile it, before you can run the program. In general, you only give the type of the variable when it is first used. This is called the *declaration* of that variable. You can also have a declaration separate from an assignment statement. For example, the statement **double** time; declares that time will be a variable of type **double**, but its value will be specified later.

Here is the output:

```
time=2.0436 height=31.826125296
time=3.0436 height=31.898845296
```

Interestingly enough, the ball is at about the same height at these two times. However, we might guess that it is on the way up the first time, and on the way down the second time. We'll check the height at time 2.5436 to see if this is the case.

We'd also like to make some other improvements to our program. The listing on page 12 is hard for a person to read, because it is full of numbers with no clear meaning. We can improve the readability by defining some more variables; each variable will have a comment explaining its meaning. Written in symbols, the height formula looks like this:

$$h = -0.5gt^2 + v_0t + h_0$$

In this formula, g represents a quantity from physics known as the acceleration of gravity, which has the value 9.8 meters per second squared, v_0 is the initial velocity of our ball (25 meters per second), and h_0 is the initial height (1.2 meters). Also, in this formula, we are using t to represent the time; in our program we will continue to use the complete word time. This is purely a stylistic choice; you can decide whether you prefer greater brevity or greater descriptiveness.

Another new feature we will use is the command

Math.pow(time,2)

This command will perform the exponent t^2. The result here is the same as our earlier expression time*time. If you are only raising a number to the second power, it is slightly more complicated to use the **Math.pow** form, but this form is much easier to use if you need to raise a number to a different power. The expression **pow** is short for "power." (For more on mathematical operations, see Chapter 12.)

Our program will calculate the height at four different times: 2.0436, 2.5436, 3.0436, and 4.0436. We could use the following four assignment statements: time=2.0436; time=2.5436; time=3.0436; and time=4.0436;. However, when we are adding 0.5 seconds to the number each time, it would be simpler to give an instruction causing the value to increase by 0.5 seconds, like this:

time=time+0.5;

If you are used to mathematical equations, you should instinctively recoil from this expression, since it obviously can't be a true equation. There is no way for time to be equal to time +0.5. However, it is important to realize that a Java assignment statement is not an equation, even though it uses an equal sign. We are not saying that the part to the left of the equal sign is equal to the part to the right of the equal sign. Instead, we are telling the computer, "Calculate the value of the expression on the right-hand side of the equal sign. Then, after you have calculated that value, assign it to the variable on the left-hand side." In this case it just happens that the expression on the right uses the old value of the variable that appears on the left side of the assignment statement.

Because it is so common to add a particular value to a variable, Java provides a shorter way of writing such an expression. We can write

time+=0.5;

This means exactly the same thing as the expression

time=time+0.5;

In general, the statement

variable_name+=value;

will mean the same as the statement

variable_name=variable_name+value;

It turns out that we will often wish to add 1 to a variable, so Java provides an even shorter way of doing that. Thus,

time++;

means the same as

time+=1;

which means the same as

time=time+1;

Here is the new version of the program:

```
class ballheight {
/*method*/ public static void main(String args[ ]) {
double g=9.8; /*acceleration of gravity, in meters per second squared*/
double v0=25; /*initial velocity, in meters per second*/
double h0=1.2; /*initial height, in meters*/
double time=2.0436;
        double h=-0.5*g*Math.pow(time,2)+v0*time+h0;
        System.out.println("time="+time+"␣␣height="+h);
time+=0.5;
        h=-0.5*g*Math.pow(time,2)+v0*time+h0;
        System.out.println("time="+time+"␣␣height="+h);
time+=0.5;
        h=-0.5*g*Math.pow(time,2)+v0*time+h0;
        System.out.println("time="+time+"␣␣height="+h);
time++; /*increase time by 1*/
        h=-0.5*g*Math.pow(time,2)+v0*time+h0;
        System.out.println("time="+time+"␣␣height="+h);
} /*end main*/
} /*end ballheight*/
```

(The ␣ represents a blank space.)

The use of the new variable names g, v0, h0, and h improves the clarity of the program.

Here's the output:

```
time=2.0436   height=31.826125295999997
time=2.5436   height=33.087485296
time=3.0436   height=31.898845296
time=4.0436   height=22.171565295999994
```

Our suspicion is confirmed: the ball is on its way up at 2.0436 seconds and is on its way back down at 3.0436 seconds.

Notice how indenting is used to indicate the different segments of the program listing. Indenting your program lines is optional, but it often can be used to make the program more readable.

After looking at the listing on page 15, you might suspect that we're not yet using the computer in the most effective way. We had to repeat nearly the same block of statements four times. If we wanted to show the height of the ball at twenty different times, we would need to repeat the same set of statements twenty times; that is, unless we could find a better way to do it . . . but we'll have to wait for Chapter 5 to see that.

Following are general forms for the statements we have used here.

• Assignment statement with declaration:

variable_type variable_name=expression;

- Assignment statement for a variable that has already been declared:

variable_name=expression;

In either case, the *expression* can be any expression that can be evaluated to have a value of the correct type. For example, the expression must evaluate to a **double** value if the variable is declared to be of type **double**. The *expression* might be a single number, such as 2.0436; or it might be an arithmetic expression involving numbers, such as $2 + 2$; or it might be an arithmetic expression involving variables, such as $x + 2$.

- Assignment statement to increase the variable by a specified value:

variable_name += value_to_add;

- Assignment statement to add 1 to a variable:

variable_name++;

The *variable name* must always be written on the left of the assignment statement. In algebra you can reverse the two sides of an equation when you want to, but you cannot do this with a computer assignment statement.

2.5   Rounding Numbers

Now we will take care of the problem of excessive decimal places. We need to add a new method to our program to round numbers to a specified number of decimal places. Our previous programs have had only one method (the **main** method); our new program will also have a method called r4, which will round a number to four decimal places. We will not go into more detail into how to use methods in your programs until Chapter 8, but since we have great need of the rounding method now we will include it here. At this point, all you need to do is copy the program; the details of the workings will become clear later.

```
class ballheight {

/*method*/ static double r4(double x) {
/*This method rounds a double value to four decimal places.*/
double z=((double)(Math.round(x*10000)))/10000;
return z;
} /*end method r4*/

/*method*/ public static void main(String args[ ]) {
double g=9.8; /*acceleration of gravity, in meters per second squared*/
double v0=25; /*initial velocity, in meters per second*/
double h0=1.2; /*initial height, in meters*/
double time=2.0436;
```

```
        double h=-0.5*g*Math.pow(time,2)+v0*time+h0;
        System.out.println("time="+r4(time)+"  height="+r4(h));
time+=0.5;
        h=-0.5*g*Math.pow(time,2)+v0*time+h0;
        System.out.println("time="+r4(time)+"  height="+r4(h));
time+=0.5;
        h=-0.5*g*Math.pow(time,2)+v0*time+h0;
        System.out.println("time="+r4(time)+"  height="+r4(h));
time++; /*increase time by 1*/
        h=-0.5*g*Math.pow(time,2)+v0*time+h0;
        System.out.println("time="+r4(time)+"  height="+r4(h));
} /*end main*/
} /*end ballheight*/
```

Notice how we have included the code for the r4 method along with the code for the **main** method; both methods are enclosed by the braces { and } that mark the beginning and end of the class ballheight. Also notice that the **System.out.println** lines now include the expressions r4(time) and r4(h), instead of plain time and h as they did before.

The output now looks much better:

```
time=2.0436   height=31.8261
time=2.5436   height=33.0875
time=3.0436   height=31.8988
time=4.0436   height=22.1716
```

2.6   Input from a Command Line Parameter

We might find still another reason to be dissatisfied with our baseball height program: it will show the height only for the values of time that are specified in the program. It would be helpful to have a program that would allow the user to enter a value for **time** when the program is being run. In our more advanced programs, we will see how the program can take keyboard input from a text field in a window. For now, we will look at a quick way for a program to accept input from a command line parameter.

We have executed our Java programs so far by typing a command line like this:

```
java ballheight
```

The command line can also include one or more values to use as input for the program. For example, if we want the program to determine the height 3.2 seconds after the ball is thrown, we could type this command line:

```
java ballheight 3.2
```

We now need to modify our program as follows:

```
class ballheight {

/*method*/ static double r4(double x) {
/*This method rounds a double value to four decimal places.*/
double z=((double) (Math.round(x*10000)))/10000;
return z;
} /*end method r2*/

/*method*/ public static void main(String args[ ]) {
double g=9.8; /*acceleration of gravity, in meters per second squared*/
double v0=25; /*initial velocity, in meters per second*/
double h0=1.2; /*initial height, in meters*/
double time=(Double.valueOf(args[0])).doubleValue();
        double h=-0.5*g*Math.pow(time,2)+v0*time+h0;
        System.out.println("time="+r4(time)+"␣height="+r4(h));
} /*end main*/
} /*end ballheight*/
```

command line input

We will execute the program with this command line:

```
java ballheight 3.2
```

This line of code will assign the command line parameter 3.2 to the variable time:

double time=(**Double.valueOf**(args[0])).**doubleValue**();

Now you know what the phrase "args" is for; we have included this in all of our **main** methods. The expression args[0] represents the first (in this case, only) command line parameter). (You might be wondering, "Why is the first parameter identified with a 0, instead of a 1?" This is the way it works for all arrays in Java; see Chapter 6.) The expression

(**Double.valueOf**(args[0])).**doubleValue**();

converts the characters that we type (3.2) into a value of type **double**. For more about this kind of conversion, see Chapter 7.

2.7   Character String (String) Variables

Variable names can also represent a string of letters or other characters. For example, suppose we would like to store the string "Hello. How are you?" We can declare a variable called s1 to represent this string with this assignment statement:

String s1="Hello. How are you?";

The characters that make up the string are enclosed in double quotes. (Java makes no distinction between opening and closing quotes, as do some word processors.)

We cannot perform arithmetic operations on string variables, but we can join them together with a plus sign, + (called concatenation). For example, here's a program that defines two strings, joins them together, and displays the result:

```
class stringexample {
/*method*/ public static void main(String args[ ]) {
String firstname="George";
String lastname="Washington";
String fullname=firstname+"␣"+lastname;
System.out.println(fullname);
} /*end main*/
} /*end stringexample*/
```

Here is the output:

```
George Washington
```

Note how we included a string consisting of one blank "␣" in the assignment statement for fullname so there would be a space between the first and last names. We'll see more about operations on strings in Chapter 7.

2.8   Integer (int) and Other Numerical Variables

If you know that a particular value will always be a whole number (or the negative of a whole number), you can declare it to be of type **int** (short for integer).

A variable of type **int** occupies 4 bytes (32 bits) in the computer's memory. This allows $2^{32} = 4,294,967,296$ different values to be represented. However, one of these bits is used as a sign bit to indicate whether the number is positive or negative. The other 31 bits represent the value of the number. The largest positive value that can be represented is $2^{31} - 1 = 2,147,483,647$. Recall that the largest number that can be represented with n decimal digits is $10^n - 1$ (for example, 999 is the largest number that can be represented by three decimal digits). The smallest negative number of type **int** is $-2^{31} = -2,147,483,648$. (Even though the computer stores numbers as binary numbers, you do not usually have to work with numbers in binary form.)

The arithmetic operations +, −, and * work the same way on integer variables as they do on **double** variables. However, division is different. Here is an example:

```
class divisionexamples {
/*method*/ public static void main(String args[ ]) {
System.out.println("double division: 60.0/7.0="+(60.0/7.0));
System.out.println("integer division: 60/7="+(60/7));
System.out.println("integer remainder: 60%7="+(60%7));
} /*end main*/
} /*end divisionexamples*/
```

Here is the output:

```
double division: 60.0/7.0=8.571428571428571
integer division: 60/7=8
integer remainder: 60%7=4
```

When the program comes to the expression 60.0/7.0, it will treat the two numbers as **double** values because of the ".0" they contain. The result will be a **double** value, which will be a decimal fraction with several digits past the decimal point.

When the program comes to the expression 60/7, however, it will treat the two values as integers. The result will be the integer 8, which is the number of times 7 goes into 60 while ignoring the remainder. If you need to determine the remainder, use the % (percent) symbol. So, **60%7** will be 4 (the remainder when 60 is divided by 7). You can also use the % symbol to see if one integer variable is divisible by another. The expression *a%b* will be zero if and only if a is divisible by b.

Java also allows you to create variables of type **byte**, which take up 1 byte = 8 bits and represent integer values from $-2^7 = -128$ to $2^7 - 1 = 127$. Another type is type **short**, which take up 2 bytes = 16 bits and represent integer values from $-2^{15} = -32,768$ to $2^{15} - 1 = 32,767$. We will not use these types much in this book, since it is less confusing to the programmer if you stick to type **int**. The only situations where you would need to use **byte** or **short** would be cases where you are very concerned about conserving computer memory.

There is another integer type: the **long** type, which occupies 8 bytes (64 bits), and can represent values from -2^{63} to $2^{63} - 1$ (about $\pm9.22 \times 10^{18}$). This type would be useful for numbers that are too big to fit in type **int**. However, when we come to problems that involve big numbers (such as the factorial calculations in Chapter 8), the **long** type is not big enough, so we have to use **double** variables.

Variables of type **double** also occupy 64 bits, but they can include fractional parts and they can also include numbers in exponential form. There is another numerical type called **float**, which is like **double** except that it only fills 32 bits of computer memory. Unless it is very important to conserve memory, it is better to use **double** instead of **float** because your calculations will be more accurate.

There are times when you need to convert one type of number into another type of number. In Java, the process of converting one object to another type of object is called *casting*. The statement

int x2=(int)(x1);

will convert a double value **x1** into an integer variable **x2**. (You might lose some information in the process, since any fractional part of **x1** will disappear.) The statement

double x4=(double)(x3);

will convert an integer value **x3** into a double value **x4**. In general, to cast a variable from one type to another, start by creating a regular assignment statement; then put the new type after the equal sign, surrounded by parentheses. And, for clarity, it helps to put parentheses around the expression that will be converted. The general form of a casting assignment statement is as follows:

target_variable=(target_type)(original expression)

In this statement, *target_variable* is a variable of type *target_type*. The *original_expression* must be some type of expression for which it makes sense to cast it into the *target_type*.

The variable types **double**, **int**, and the other numerical types discussed here are called *primitive* types. They are used as building blocks for objects. We will see that you can also create variables whose type can be an object that you have defined yourself.

Notes

Declaring Variables

If you try to use the variable time without declaring it, then the compiler will display an error message like this:

```
undefined variable: time
```

There are times when you see this error message that you might wish that the computer could just guess what the type of the variable should be, so it won't keep nagging you about the need to declare it. However, this requirement is there for your own protection. Suppose you are writing a long program, and make a typographical error by spelling the variable *timmy* instead of *time*. If the computer allowed you to use a variable without declaring it, then it would assume you meant to use a new variable called *timmy*. This would cause an error in your program, but it would be difficult to track down the cause of the error. However, the Java compiler won't let that happen; it will notice that *timmy* has not been declared and it will display an error message identifying the specific location where the undeclared variable appeared. That makes it much easier for you to find the problem and correct it.

Variable Declarations and Code Blocks

A variable in Java can only be used within the block in which it is declared. A block is any set of statements beginning with a left brace { and ending with the matching right brace }. This has not been much of an issue so far, because our programs have usually only had two blocks: the block for the class itself, and the main block. We have declared all of our variables inside the main block, which means that they cannot be used outside the main block. That doesn't really matter with the simple programs we have done so far, since there usually has not been any code outside of the main block. However, more complicated programs will have more than one method, so you need to be careful about where a variable is declared. This will be discussed more in Chapter 8.

Multiple Declarations

It is also possible to declare more than one variable with one statement. To do so, separate them by commas. For example, the statement

double x,y,z;

declares x, y, and z all to be variables of type **double**.

Subtracting, Multiplying, and Dividing

There also are operations for subtracting, multiplying, or dividing a particular value:

- x+=y means x=x+y
- x-=y means x=x-y
- x*=y means x=x*y
- x/=y means x=x/y

If you wish to subtract 1 from the variable x, then use the following command: x- -;.

Numerical Precision

Try this command:

System.out.println((1/7.0)+(1/7.0)+(1/7.0)+(1/7.0)+(1/7.0)+(1/7.0)+ (1/7.0));

The result should be exactly 1, but you will find that the number displayed is extremely close to, but not exactly equal to, 1. There will inevitably be some small inaccuracies when the computer performs certain numerical calculations involving **double** values. The problem is that it is often impossible to represent a double value exactly with a finite number of digits.

Special Characters

There are some characters that you cannot directly put in strings, such as the backspace key or a quotation mark. These characters are represented by special codes beginning with a backslash (\). Here is a list of these characters and their codes:

Code to use in strings	Meaning
\b	backspace
\t	horizontal tab
\n	line feed
\f	form feed
\r	carriage return
\"	double quote
\'	single quote
\\	backslash

EXERCISES

Write Java equivalents of these algebraic expressions.

1. $\frac{\frac{10}{4}}{\frac{16}{3}}$

2. $\frac{12}{\frac{3}{2}}$

3. $\frac{1}{1-x}$

4. $\frac{1}{1+x^2}$

5. $ax^2 + bx + c$

6. $(1 + w)^{(1/w)}$

7. $\frac{1}{\frac{1}{a} + \frac{1}{b}}$

8. $\frac{1}{1 + \left(\frac{x^2}{a}\right)}$

9. 6.02×10^{23}

10. $x^a y^{1-a}$

11. $(ax^p + (1-a)y^p)^{1/p}$

12. $\frac{rP(1+r)^{n-1}}{(1+r)^{n-1}-1}$

13. $4\pi r^2$

14. $\frac{4\pi r^3}{3}$

15. $16x^2 y^3$

For Exercises 16–35, is the expression a legal Java expression? If so, what will its value be? (Let a = 10, b = 6, *and* c = 4.)

16. 12+a

17. 6×c

18. 6*c

19. 6*4+5

20. (6*4)+5

21. 6*(4+5)

22. 10+(20*3

23. **Math.pow**(2,5)

24. **Math.pow**(4,3)

25. **Math.pow**(144,0.5)

26. **Math.pow**(-1,0.5)

27. 2*((3+5)-(2/4))

28. 14÷2

29. a/b/c

30. (a/b)/c

31. a/(b/c)

32. a/b*c

33. a/c*b

34. a/(b*c)

35. (a/b)*c

CHAPTER 3

APPLETS

3.1   Calculation Example Applet

Suppose we want the rest of the world to see the results of our calculations. To make our results available, we need to convert our program into a *Java applet*, and then publish it on the Internet/World Wide Web. One reason Java has quickly become so popular is because Java applets can be included on web pages, allowing people to add a variety of special effects to their web pages. The timing for this was perfect, since Java was released in 1995, the same year that the World Wide Web began to be widely used. Some people came to think of Java as if its only purpose was to add cute special effects to web pages. In reality, there are two kinds of Java programs: *applets*, which are usually included on web pages, and *applications*, which are stored on the disk of your own computer. The programs we have done so far have been applications.

To run an applet, all you need to do is connect to a web page that contains the applet. Your web browser will automatically start running the applet. There is another way to run an applet on your home computer: use a program called the *Appletviewer* (see page 27).

We will create an applet that shows the results for several of our example calculations. (In reality, there would be no point in putting a variety of unrelated calculations in one applet like this, but the purpose of the example is to show you how you could perform the calculations in an applet.)

```
import java.applet.*;
import java.awt.*;

public class calculationExamplesApplet extends Applet {

/*method*/ public void paint (Graphics g) {
g.drawString("2+2="+(2+2),10,10);
g.drawString("10-4="+(10-4),10,30);
```

```
g.drawString("16*3="+(16*3),10,50);
g.drawString("Batting Average="+(34.0/94.0),10,70);
g.drawString("Total Grocery Bill="+(34+50+35+66+34+37+41),10,90);
g.drawString("Average Grocery Bill="+
       ((34+50+35+66+34+37+41)/7.0),10,110);
g.drawString("Height of ball="+(-0.5*9.8*1.6*1.6+25*1.6+1.2),10,130);
} /*end paint*/
} /*end calculationExamplesApplet*/
```

Here are some notes about this program:

- Each applet includes the words **extends Applet** after the name of the program. Remember that the capitalization needs to be exactly as shown! The significance of the word "extends" will be discussed on page 118.

- The applet needs to read in some Java code that already comes with the language. To do this, it uses the **import** statement. An applet needs to import code from two code collections (called *packages*): **java.applet** and **java.awt**. The asterisk * in the import statement means to make all classes in that package available. The **applet** package, not surprisingly, contains code that is used by applets. The **awt** package includes code used by programs with Windows; "awt" stands for "abstract windows toolkit." For more about packages, see page 133.

- An applet does not have a **main** method, as does an application program. Instead, an applet will have a **paint** method, which is used to display output on the screen. In this simple applet, the **paint** method is the only method. Most applets will also contain a method called **init** that is automatically called when the applet is initialized.

- Instead of using **System.out.println** for the output, we are using g.**drawString**. Again, note the exact capitalization. Here "g" represents something called a *graphics object*. Every Java program that displays output in a window (rather than on a text screen, as our earlier programs did) must create a graphics object. You don't have to call it "g," but it is easier for you if you use standard names for objects you regularly use, so in this book we will always use the letter "g" to stand for the graphics object.

The g.**drawString** command is also slightly more complicated than **System.out.println** because in addition to specifying what you want the computer to display, you must specify where to put it. For example, the command

g.**drawString**("Batting Average="+(34.0/94.0),10,70);

means calculate 34.0/94.0, put the label "Batting Average" in front of that result, and then display that text 10 pixels from the left edge of the window and 70 pixels down from the top.

In general, the command

g.**drawString**(*string_expression*, *x_coordinate*, *y_coordinate*);

will display the *string expression* at the point given by the x and y coordinates. Both x and y are measured in pixels, where x is the distance from the left edge of the window, and y is the distance down from the top of the window. For more on screen coordinates, see page 151. The **drawString** command can also be used with an application that creates a graphics window (see page 147).

3.2   Applets and HTML

An applet must be contained in a file whose extension is .java and whose name is the same as the name of the program; in this case, the file is *calculationExamplesApplet.java*. The next step is to compile the program; this process is exactly the same as it was for an application program (see page 7). Go to the MS-DOS prompt and type this command:

```
javac calculationExamplesApplet.java
```

This command will create the file *calculationExamplesApplet.class*.

In order to run our applet, we need to create some HTML code. If you are interested in creating applets for web pages, then you probably already know a bit about HTML (HyperText Markup Language), which is the language in which web pages are written. If you don't know HTML, see Appendix B for an introduction to a few of the main features.

Here is an example of the HTML code for a web page containing an applet:

```
<HTML><HEAD><TITLE>Applet example</TITLE></HEAD>
<BODY>
<APPLET CODE="calculationExamplesApplet.class", HEIGHT=300,
    WIDTH=400>
a Java compatible browser is needed for this
</APPLET>
</BODY>
</HTML>
```

The expressions <HTML>, <HEAD>, <TITLE>, and <BODY> are all standard HTML tags that mark the beginning of certain features; each of these features is ended by the corresponding end tag: </HTML>, </HEAD>, </TITLE>, or </BODY>.

The <APPLET> tag was added to HTML with the introduction of Java to make it possible to include Java applets in web pages. In order to use this tag, you must specify three things:

- the name of the file containing the code for the applet; In our example, this is *calculationExamplesApplet.class*. Note how this name is enclosed in quotation marks and preceded by the word CODE.

- the height of the rectangle in which the applet will appear, measured in pixels

- the width of the applet's rectangle; In this example, we will use a rectangle of size 300 by 400. When you create a new applet, it is not crucial to determine the right values for height and width at first. You can make an initial guess and then adjust these figures later if you need to. Increase height and/or width if you don't see all of your applet on the screen; reduce them if the applet doesn't need as much space as you are giving it.

Notice how the CODE, HEIGHT, and WIDTH parameters all occur after the <APPLET symbol and before the > symbol that closes the applet tag. The next line contains the phrase

```
a Java compatible browser is needed for this
```

This phrase comes before the </APPLET> tag. If all web browsers implemented Java, you would not need this phrase. Although newer web browsers can be expected to handle Java applets, someone may visit your web site from anywhere in the world, and you have no guarantee what browser they might be using. An older browser will not understand the APPLET tag, but it will display whatever text comes before the </APPLET> tag. This allows you to give a brief message explaining why the browser is not displaying anything else.

In some cases, you may also include an alternate way of viewing your web site between the <APPLET> and </APPLET> tags. For example, you might have an elaborate, graphical interactive applet using Java, and then another simpler version using plain HTML providing similar information without the same quality of experience. You can put the plain version as the alternate to the Java version.

In the HTML code on page 26, we have not included anything other than our Java applet. However, you may include other features on the same web page that includes a Java applet; in fact, you can have more than one applet on the same web page.

Type the HTML code on page 26 with your text editor; give it the file name *calculationExamplesApplet.html*. (Note the html extension.)

Now we have two choices to view our applet. The quickest way is to use a program called the Appletviewer, provided with the JDK. Type this command at the MS-DOS prompt:

```
Appletviewer calculationExamplesApplet.html
```

(Note that the Appletviewer requires the HTML file, not the class file.) The applet will now appear in a window on your screen.

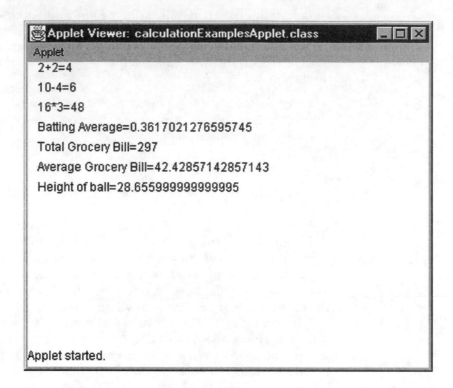

FIGURE 3–1

3.3   Publishing an Applet on the World Wide Web

The Appletviewer is a valuable tool that you will use often while testing your applets; however, it doesn't help you show your results to the rest of the world. In order to publish your applet on the web, you need to have an Internet service provider that allows you to publish material. Suppose that your Internet service provider is at *http://www.xyzisp.com*, and that your username is *myname*. You now need to copy the two files *calculationExamplesApplet.html* and *calculationExamplesApplet.class* from your home computer to the web server computer. You may do this with a program called FTP (File Transfer Protocol); you will need your service provider to give you specific information on how to do this. (If you have already published material on the web, then use the same procedure you have used before.) One technical note: the class file should be transferred as a binary file; the HTML file should be transferred as a text file. (Once you have copied these files, you may need to give a command to change the permission for these files.)

Now your applet is available for anyone on the world wide web to use; all they need to do is type in the URL (Uniform Resource Locater, or web address). In our example, the web address would be the following:

http://www.xyzisp.com/~myname/calculationExamplesApplet.html

If you have a home page, then you can create a link to the page with your applet with this HTML code:

```
<a href=http://www.xyzisp.com/~myname/
calculationExamplesApplet.html>
Click here to see the calculation applet</a>
```

Now, visitors will not need to type in the complete URL of the applet's page; instead, once they have reached your home page, they simply need to click on the link.

Another alternative would be to include the HTML code for your applet directly in your home page; then people will see the applet as soon as they point their browser to your home page.

3.4   Including Images in Applets

Applets can also display images that are available in *gif* or *jpg* format. You can obtain these images in several ways: with a scanner; with a digital camera; from clip-art collections; from web sites; or you can create your own with a drawing program. If you have worked with HTML before, you may already be familiar with including images on web pages.

Here is an applet that displays an image:

```
import java.applet.*;
import java.awt.*;
import java.awt.event.*;

public class image1 extends Applet {
/*This applet displays an image on the screen.*/
Image scene1;

/*method*/ public void init() {
setBackground(Color.white);
scene1=getImage(getCodeBase(), "scene1.gif");
} /*end init*/

/*method*/ public void paint(Graphics g) {
/*Draw the image scene1, with upper-left-hand corner 10 pixels from left
   edge of screen and 20 pixels down from top of screen:*/
g.drawImage(scene1, 10, 20, this);
} /*end paint*/
} /*end image1*/
```

The image file is named scene1.gif; it is in the same directory as the applet class file.

It is also possible to change the scale of the image as it is displayed. Here is a program that displays the same image with each dimension reduced by 1/3.

```
import java.applet.*;
import java.awt.*;
import java.awt.event.*;

public class image2 extends Applet {
Image scene1;
/*This applet displays the image scene1.gif with each dimension
   reduced by 1/3.*/
int iwidth; /*image width*/
```

```
int iheight; /*image height*/

/*method*/ public void init() {
setBackground(Color.white);
scene1=getImage(getCodeBase(), "scene1.gif");
} /*end init*/

/*method*/ public void paint(Graphics g) {
int xpos=10; int ypos=20;
iwidth=scene1.getWidth(this);
iheight=scene1.getHeight(this);
g.drawImage
        (scene1,xpos, ypos, iwidth/3, iheight/3, this);
} /*end paint*/

} /*end image2*/
```

If you arrange several images so they display one right after the other, you can create animation effects. See the book's web page at *http://www.spu.edu/~ddowning/cpjava.html*.

3.5   Adding Sound to an Applet

You can add sound effects to an applet, as long as you have the sound in the form of an audio file with extension au. Here is a program to demonstrate:

```
import java.applet.*;
import java.awt.*;

public class music extends Applet {
/*This applet plays sound from an au file.*/

/*method*/ public void init() {
setBackground(Color.white);
} /*end init*/

/*method*/ public void paint(Graphics g) {
g.drawString("Playing music", 10, 20);

/*This is the line that plays the music.*/
play(getCodeBase(),"test.au");

} /*end paint*/
} /*end music*/
```

3.6   Which to Use: Applications or Applets?

Here are some brief comments about the differences between Java applets and applications so you will know which is right for your particular project.

- If you intend for your program to be available on the World Wide Web, it must be an applet.

- If your program will run from the user's own hard drive, then it can be either an application (run with the "java" command from the command line) or an applet (viewed with the appletviewer, or a web browser pointed to a local file).

- If your program will use graphical user interface features such as Windows, it can be either an application or an applet, although an applet is slightly easier to create.

- Exception to the previous statement: If your program will use a menu, then it is easier to create it as an application (although menus can also be used with applets).

- If your program will read input from, or write output to, the user's hard drive, it needs to be an application. This is because applets are subject to tight security restrictions. Here's the problem: When you point your browser at a web page, any Java applet located on that page immediately begins to execute. Unfortunately, there are wicked programmers out there that like destructive tricks. What is to prevent someone from writing a Java applet that erases all of the files on your hard drive and then putting the applet on a web page where it will result in instant disaster for any user who browses that page? The answer is this: that can't happen because an applet cannot write (or erase) any data on your hard drive. You can sleep much easier at night knowing that this security restriction is in place. You might lose sleep over other computer security problems, but you don't need to worry about unsafe Java applets being downloaded from the web. For more information on Java security, see Sun's frequently asked question site: *http://java.sun.com/sfaq/*

For information on possible ways to get around the security restrictions, see the following site: *http://www.rstcorp.com/hostile-applets/index.html*

The security restrictions leave another nagging question: what good is a security restriction if it prevents you from doing something that you need to do? After all, one way to make a house more secure would be to build it with no doors or windows, but that would not be very functional. Does the file restriction on applets present the same kind of problem—a security measure so drastic that it prohibits necessary actions? This issue is still being debated. One solution is to allow an applet from a trusted source to have access to the local hard disk. How do you tell if an applet comes from a trusted source? First, you have to make sure that you truly know where it comes from; this can be verified with a *digital signature*. Second, you have to make sure that you do indeed trust the source from whence the applet came. In this book, we will not discuss the advanced security features needed to create trusted applets with digital signatures. All of our programs that use files will be written as applications, not applets.

You might wonder, "Why are applets prevented from reading from the local disk?" Answer: that also presents a security risk, because a malicious programmer could write an applet that spies on you by scanning your hard drive and e-mailing your secrets back to the author.

Applets are also prevented from connecting to an arbitrary web page; if they were allowed to do this, then malicious programmers could perform tricks at other web sites for which you could potentially receive the blame. An applet is allowed to connect back to the web page from whence it came. See the book's web page at

http//www.spu.edu/~ddowning/cpjava.html.

You might also be wondering, "How do I know that a Java application is safe? Since a Java application has access to my hard drive, can it erase everything there?" The answer is yes, so you do have to be careful. Here's the difference between applications and applets: An application will not start running on your computer without your knowledge. In the first place, an application will only get on your hard drive if you put it there. Be very careful when you load programs on your hard drive; make sure you trust their source. Second, an application will not start running until you give it a command to do so. By contrast, an applet begins executing whenever your browser is pointed to its web page; you have no advance knowledge that a program is going to run. That is why applets need to be under greater security restrictions. It is said that applets run in a "sandbox;" the idea is that a sandbox is a place where the applet can be safe (just as a real sandbox is a place where a child can play safely without breaking anything outside the sandbox).

All of the programs we include in Chapters 4 to 9 are Java applications, rather than applets. They all display their output on a text screen, rather than a window. You can convert them to applets fairly easily by converting the application's **main** method to an applet's **paint** method, as we did earlier in this chapter. Starting in Chapter 10, we will focus on programs that display their output in Windows, so both applets and applications will be discussed. If you have an applet that you would like to convert to an application, see page 147.

CHAPTER 4

IF

4.1 if/else Statements

Suppose we have the job of computing the payroll for a group of workers. We will need to read in the number of weekly hours for each worker, then multiply by the wage rate to determine the total pay. However, there is one complication: if a worker works more than 40 hours per week, then the hourly pay for the extra hours becomes 1.5 times the normal rate. Our program will need to use two different expressions for calculating the wage, and it will need to be able to test whether or not the hours are greater than 40 so it will know which expression to use.

Java provides an **if/else** statement that tells the computer to do one thing if the specified condition is true, and, otherwise, to do something else.

In our example, the statement we need looks like this:

```
if (hours<=maxhours) {pay=wage*hours;}
    else {pay=wage*maxhours+wage*otpremium*(hours-maxhours);}
```

In this case our condition is (hours<=maxhours). Here "<=" is a symbol for "less than or equal to." The condition is enclosed in parentheses, and the two action statements are enclosed in braces { }.

Here is the program:

```
class payroll {


public static void main(String args[ ]) {

double wage=12.20; /*wage per hour*/
double maxhours=40; /*maximum hours before overtime is paid*/
double otpremium=1.5; /*overtime premium pay rate*/
double pay; /*paycheck amount*/
```

```
double hours=(Double.valueOf(args[0])).doubleValue();
if (hours<=maxhours) {pay=wage*hours;}
     else {pay=wage*maxhours+wage*otpremium*(hours-maxhours);}
System.out.println("hours="+hours+"⎵⎵pay="+pay);
} /*end main*/
} /*end payroll*/
```

The input to this program is the number of hours; this comes from the command line parameter as on page 17. Notice how we define variables representing the different quantities we use; this will make it easier if we need to change these at a later date.

To execute the program for a worker with 36 hours, type this line at the command prompt:

```
java payroll 36
```

The following output is displayed:

```
java payroll 36
hours=36.0   pay=439.2
```

Here's an example with overtime hours:

```
java payroll 44
hours=44.0   pay=561.2
```

You might be thinking that there must be a better way to do the payroll, since this method requires you to restart the program for each worker, type the hours by hand, and then copy the results off the screen, since they are not saved anywhere. In Chapter 11, we will see how the use of files is a big help with a data processing job like this.

Notice how the braces { } surround both the **if** action and the **else** action. This means we can include more than one statement in these blocks. For example, suppose that we also wish to display a message that either gives the number of overtime hours worked, or else says "no overtime hours." Here is a revised version of the program:

```
class payroll {


public static void main(String args[ ]) {

double wage=12.20; /*wage per hour*/
double maxhours=40; /*maximum hours before overtime is paid*/
double otpremium=1.5; /*overtime premium pay rate*/
double pay; /*paycheck amount*/
double hours=(Double.valueOf(args[0])).doubleValue();

if (hours<=maxhours)
     {pay=wage*hours;
     System.out.println("No overtime wages paid");}
else {pay=wage*maxhours+wage*otpremium*(hours-maxhours);
     System.out.println("Overtime hours:"+(hours-maxhours));}
```

```
System.out.println("hours="+hours+"  pay="+pay);
} /*end main*/
} /*end payroll*/
```

Here are samples of the output for 36 and 44 hours:

```
java payroll 36
No overtime wages paid
hours=36.0  pay=439.2
java payroll 44
Overtime hours:4.0
hours=44.0  pay=561.2
```

We can also include another **if/else** statement inside either the **if** block or the **else** block. For example, suppose that we pay workers double the normal wage for each hour worked over 50 hours per week. Here is a program to do this:

```
class payroll {


public static void main(String args[ ]) {

double wage=12.20; /*wage per hour*/
double maxhours=40; /*maximum hours before overtime is paid*/
double maxhours2=50; /*maximum hours before double time is paid*/
double otpremium=1.5; /*overtime premium pay rate*/
double otpremium2=2; /*second overtime premium pay rate*/
double pay; /*paycheck amount*/
double hours=(Double.valueOf(args[0])).doubleValue();

if (hours<=maxhours)
     {pay=wage*hours;
     System.out.println("No overtime wages paid");}
else {if (hours<=maxhours2)
       {pay=wage*maxhours+wage*otpremium*(hours-maxhours);
        System.out.println("Overtime hours:"+(hours-maxhours));}
       else {pay=wage*maxhours
                +wage*otpremium*(maxhours2-maxhours)
                +wage*otpremium2*(hours-maxhours2);
        System.out.println("Double time hours:"+(hours-maxhours2));}
            }

System.out.println("hours="+hours+"  pay="+pay);
} /*end main*/
} /*end payroll*/
```

Notice how the **if** (hours<=maxhours2) block is inside the **else** block for the **if** (hours<=maxhours) condition.

4.2 Logical Conditions

Here is the general form of **if/else** statements:

if (*condition*) {*actions to take if condition is true*}
else {*actions to take if condition is false*}

The **else** clause is optional; if it is left out, then the computer will take no action if the condition is false. It will simply move on to the next statement.

Here are some examples of possible conditions we could use:

---

a==b   Does a equal b? Note that when we write a condition that tests for equality, we need to write two equal signs. This is so we don't confuse a condition that tests for equality with an assignment statement that sets the value of the left-hand variable equal to the expression on the right.

a!=b   Does a not equal b?

a>b   Is a greater than b?

a<b   Is a less than b?

a>=b   Is a greater than or equal to b?

a<=b   Is a less than or equal to b?

These are called *logical conditions*. Each of these conditions can be evaluated to be either true or false.

4.3 AND (&&), OR (||), NOT (!)

We can also combine conditions into more complicated conditions, using the logical phrases AND (represented by &&), OR (represented by ||), and NOT (represented by !). For example, suppose that we are concerned that we might make a typing mistake when entering the number of hours worked. We might accidentally type 400 when we meant 40; we know that cannot be right because we have a rule that no worker can work more than 65 hours per week. Also, we know that no worker can work a negative number of hours, so we will check for those two conditions before we perform any of the other payroll calculations. If the number of hours entered is invalid, then it will display a message.

Here is how we will write our condition:

if ((hours<0)||(hours>65))

Note that each individual condition (hours<0) and (hours>65) are enclosed in parentheses; the || between them represents OR. The entire condition is surrounded by another set of parentheses. Since this is an "OR" condition, the overall condition will be true if either one of the individual conditions (hours<40) or (hours>65) is true. In that case, we'll print the "invalid hours" message. If both of the individual conditions are false, then the overall condition is false, so we'll proceed to the **else** clause, which assumes that the hours entered was valid, and proceed to calculate the payroll accordingly. (This does not mean that the number of hours entered is necessarily correct; it only means that it passed our test for being within the valid range. We might still have made a mistake by entering 24 hours when it was supposed to be 42 hours. That kind of error cannot be caught unless you go back and check the original data.)

Here is the program:

```
class payroll {


public static void main(String args[ ]) {

double wage=12.20; /*wage per hour*/
double maxhours=40; /*maximum hours before overtime is paid*/
double maxhours2=50; /*maximum hours before double time is paid*/
double otpremium=1.5; /*overtime premium pay rate*/
double otpremium2=2; /*second overtime premium pay rate*/
double pay; /*paycheck amount*/
double hours=(Double.valueOf(args[0])).doubleValue();

if ((hours<0)||(hours>65)) /*Note: The vertical lines || mean "OR."*/
        {System.out.println("Invalid number of hours:"+hours);}
else {/*hours are valid*/
if (hours<=maxhours)
        {pay=wage*hours;
            System.out.println("No overtime wages paid");}
else {if (hours<=maxhours2)
        {pay=wage*maxhours+wage*otpremium*(hours-maxhours);
        System.out.println("Overtime hours:"+(hours-maxhours));}
else {pay=wage*maxhours+wage*otpremium*(maxhours2-maxhours)
                    +wage*otpremium2*(hours-maxhours2);
        System.out.println("Double time hours:"+(hours-maxhours2));}
        }

System.out.println("hours="+hours+"␣␣pay="+pay);
        } /*end hours are valid*/
} /*end main*/
} /*end payroll*/
```

Here is an example of NOT. Suppose we have a policy that we want all workers to work a standard 40 hours per week. We could add this statement:

```
if (hours!=40) {System.out.println("Non-standard hours worked");}
```

This condition can also be written with the NOT symbol ! in front of the condition:

```
if (!(hours=40))
{System.out.println("Non-standard hours worked");}
```

In general, the NOT symbol ! can be placed in front of any condition to reverse its meaning. For example,

if (!((hours<0)||(hours>65)))
{**System.out.println**("number of hours is valid");}

The conditions inside the innermost parentheses will be evaluated first. In this case, they are (hours<0) and (hours>65). If either of these is true, then the condition ((hours<0)||(hours>65)) will be true, which will make the condition (!((hours<0)||(hours>65))) false. When an expression contains many parentheses like this, be sure that you have a closing parenthesis for each opening parenthesis:

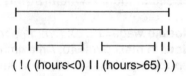

FIGURE 4–1   (! ((hours<0) I I (hours>65)))

If you look closely at the expression (!((hours<0)||(hours>65))), you might realize that it would be simpler to write it like this:

((hours>=0)&&(hours<=65))

In general,

NOT (*condition 1* OR *condition 2*)

is the same as

(NOT *condition 1*) AND (NOT *condition 2*)

4.4   The switch Statement: Choosing Between Several Alternatives

In our previous program, all workers received the same wage. Suppose, however, that we have four different classifications of workers (1, 2, 3, and 4), each with a different hourly wage rate (6.10, 8.70, 10.20, and 12.20, respectively). Now our program needs to read in the classification, as well as the number of hours, and determine the correct wage. This could be done with a series of **if** statements, like this:

if (jobclass==1) {wage=6.1;}
else if (jobclass==2) {wage=8.7;}
else if (jobclass==3) {wage=10.2;}
else if (jobclass==4) {wage=12.2;}

Another approach is to use the **switch** command, which allows us to examine the value of a variable and do one action if the variable has one specified value, another action if the variable has another value, and so on. Here's how this works for our example:

```
switch (jobclass) {
    case 1: wage=6.1; break;
    case 2: wage=8.7; break;
    case 3: wage=10.2; break;
    case 4: wage=12.2; break;
    default: wage=0; System.out.println("invalid job class:"+jobclass);
}
```

In this case, jobclass is the variable for the **switch** command. We will consider four specific values for jobclass; each of these values is preceded by the key word **case** and followed by a colon. Then we include the actions to be taken in that particular case. (There is only one statement in each case for this example, but there could be more statements for each case.) Finally, the key word **break** marks the end of that particular case, so we are ready to begin the next case. At the end of the specific cases we put the key word **default**; the statements following this word will be executed if jobclass does not have any of the specified values. In our case, that would mean that the job classification entered was invalid, so we will set the wage to zero and display an error message.

The job classification will be read in as the second command line parameter; that means it will be assigned to the string args[1]. We convert this string to an integer with this line:

```
int jobclass=Integer.parseInt(args[1]);
```

Here is the program:

```
class payroll {


public static void main(String args[ ]) {

double wage; /*wage per hour*/
double maxhours=40; /*maximum hours before overtime is paid*/
double maxhours2=50; /*maximum hours before double time is paid*/
double otpremium=1.5; /*overtime premium pay rate*/
double otpremium2=2; /*second overtime premium pay rate*/
double pay; /*paycheck amount*/
double hours=(Double.valueOf(args[0])).doubleValue();
int jobclass=Integer.parseInt(args[1]);

switch (jobclass) {
    case 1: wage=6.1; break;
    case 2: wage=8.7; break;
    case 3: wage=10.2; break;
    case 4: wage=12.2; break;
    default: wage=0; System.out.println("invalid job class:"+jobclass);
}


if ((hours<0)||(hours>65)) /*Note: the vertical lines || mean "OR."*/
    {System.out.println("Invalid number of hours:"+hours);}
```

```
else {/*hours are valid*/
if (hours<=maxhours)
        {pay=wage*hours;
      System.out.println("No overtime wages paid");}
else {if (hours<=maxhours2)
        {pay=wage*maxhours+wage*otpremium*(hours-maxhours);
System.out.println("Overtime hours:"+(hours-maxhours));}
else {pay=wage*maxhours+wage*otpremium*(maxhours2-maxhours)
        +wage*otpremium2*(hours-maxhours2);
      System.out.println("Double time hours:"+(hours-maxhours2));}
        }

System.out.println("hours="+hours+" wage="+wage+" pay="+pay);
      } /*end hours are valid*/
} /*end main*/
} /*end payroll*/
```

The job classification is read from the second command line argument; notice that it comes from **args[1]**, whereas the number of hours worked comes from the first command line argument, **args[0]**. To execute this program for a worker with 28 hours and job class 3, type this line at the command prompt:

```
java payroll 28 3
```

The output will indicate that the pay is 285.6.

Here is the general form of the **switch** command:

switch (*integer_expression*)
case *value1*: *actions taken if expression has value1*; **break**;
case *value2*: *actions taken if expression has value2*; **break**;
etc.
default: *actions taken if expression has any other values*;

4.5   Boolean Variables: true or false

There are times when it helps to store the value of a logical condition so it can be used later in the program. When we wanted to store the value of a number, we used a value of type **int** or **double**. In order to store the value of a logical condition, we need a new type of variable. This variable type is quite simple, since there are only two possible values: **true** and **false**. These variables are called **boolean** variables, in honor of George Boole, a nineteenth century mathematician who developed mathematical rules for logical statements. His work has found extensive application in the design of computers.

We'll write a program that determines whether or not a year is a leap year. This is slightly complicated, because a year divisible by 4 is a leap year, unless it is divisible by 100, in which case it's not, unless it also happens to be divisible by 400, in which case it is.

```
class leapyearcheck {
/*This program reads in a number representing a year
 and then determines if it is a leap year.*/

public static void main(String args[ ]) {

int year=Integer.parseInt(args[0]);
boolean isleapyear;

if (!((year%4)==0))
        /*The percent sign % represents modulus (remainder).*/
        /*The exclamation mark ! represents NOT.*/
{isleapyear=false;} /*It's not a leap year if it's not divisible by 4.*/
else {if (!((year%100)==0))
        {isleapyear=true;}
/*it is a leap year if it's divisible by 4 but not by 100*/
        else {if ((year%400)==0)
              {isleapyear=true;}
              else {isleapyear=false;}
              }
     }

if (isleapyear) {System.out.println(year+"␣is a leap year");}
else {System.out.println(year+"␣is not a leap year");}

} /*end main*/
} /*end leapyearcheck*/
```

The variable isleapyear is defined to be of type **boolean**. The **if/else** statements contain the conditions that determine if the year is a leap year or not.

Notes

The logical OR operator || can also be written with one vertical line, |. The effect on the program execution is almost the same. The difference is that when the computer evaluates the expression *condition1* || *condition2*, it will not bother to evaluate *condition2* if *condition1* is true, since the OR condition is automatically true when one of the conditions is true. This will save a very tiny bit of program execution time. By contrast, when the single vertical line is used, then the second condition will always be evaluated, even if the first condition is true. This might use a little extra execution time. However, using the single line form does make the program notation slightly more concise, which is an argument in favor of that form.

Likewise, the logical AND operation && can also be written with one ampersand, &. When the computer executes the comparison *condition1* && *condition2*, it will not check *condition2* if *condition1* is false. If the AND condition is written with only one ampersand, then both conditions will always be checked.

EXERCISES

1. Write a program that reads in a number and then calculates the square root of that number. In Java, the square root of x is written **Math.sqrt**(x). However, you cannot take the square root of a negative number. Have the computer display a warning message if a negative number is entered.

2. Write a program that reads in a temperature. If the temperature is less than 0 degrees, display the message "below zero;" if it is between 0 and 32, display "freezing;" if it is between 32 and 60, display "cold;" if it is between 60 and 80, display "pleasant;" if it is greater than 80, display "hot."

3. Look in a current IRS tax table and write a program that reads in the amount of taxable income and then determines the amount of the tax that is owed.

4. Write a program that reads in two integers and determines whether the first number is divisible by the second number. (Note: If a is divisible by b, then the remainder when a is divided by b ($a\%b$) is zero.)

5. Write a program that reads in three numbers and determines if they could possibly be the lengths of the three sides of a triangle. For this to be true, the sum of any two of the numbers must be greater than the third number.

6. Look at a chart describing the electromagnetic spectrum. Write a program that reads in a frequency and displays a message indicating what part of the spectrum contains this frequency. If the frequency is in the range of visible light, also indicate what color it represents.

7. Write a program that reads in the mass of a star (using units where the sun has a mass of 1) and then determines the fate of that star. If the mass is less than 1.4, it will become a white dwarf; if the mass is between 1.4 and 3, it will be a neutron star; if the mass is greater than 3, it will be a black hole.

8. Write a program that reads in the three dimensions of a piece of luggage and determines if the sum of the dimensions is less than a specified maximum value.

9. Write a program that reads in the weight of a letter and determines the amount of postage it requires.

CHAPTER 5

LOOPS

5.1   for Loop: Compound Interest

Imagine that we have just received $100 that we'll leave in the bank for ten years, where it will collect compound interest at the rate of five percent per year. We can write a program to calculate what our balance will be at the end of each year. We'll create a variable *balance* that will initially be 100. Each year we add to the balance our interest payment, which can be found by multiplying the variable *rate* times the balance:

$$balance = balance + rate * balance$$

Written in the shorter form of a Java statement, this is

```
balance+=rate*balance;
```

We could begin writing the program like this:

```
balance=100;
System.out.println("Year 0:"+balance);
balance+=rate*balance;
System.out.println("Year 1:"+balance);
balance+=rate*balance;
System.out.println("Year 2:"+balance);
balance+=rate*balance;
System.out.println("Year 3:"+balance);
```

You probably feel, however, that something doesn't seem quite right with writing the program this way. It is a lot of tedious, repetitive work to write the program in this fashion, since we keep repeating the same statements. Computers are supposed to spare us from boring work. At this point in the book, you may be wondering if this is really true, since for all of the programs we have done so far it has been more work to write a program than it would have been to solve the problem by hand. In fact, if you have a problem that only needs to be solved once, it might not be worthwhile to write a program to solve it. If, however, you have a problem that needs to be solved many times, then the value of the computer increases tremendously. The computer does not mind performing a repetitive task. What we need to do is find a way to set up the instructions for the computer so that we don't have to keep entering new instructions for each repetition.

The programming concept we need is called a *loop*, which provides a way for a computer to execute the same set of instructions repeatedly. Two kinds of loops are **for** loops and **while** loops. For our problem, a **for** loop will work, since this is a way to have a computer execute a set of statements a specified number of times.

We have two statements that need to be executed ten times each:

```
System.out.println("Year :"+balance);
balance+=rate*balance;
```

The second statement does not change at all when we put it in the loop. The first statement needs to be changed slightly, since the value of the year will be different for each pass through the loop. Therefore, instead of simply typing the year, we will include a reference to the variable **year**.

The **for** loop for our example looks like this:

```
for (int year=0; year<=10; year++) {
/*Here are the two action statements for this loop:*/
System.out.println("Year "+year+": "+balance);
balance+=rate*balance;
      } /*end for loop*/
```

The first word of a **for** loop is, not surprisingly, **for**. Following this, there are three statements enclosed in parentheses and separated by semicolons. The first statement declares and initializes a special variable called the *counter variable* for the loop; in our example, this is the statement "**year=0.**"

The second statement gives a *continuation condition*; that is, the loop will continue to be executed as long as the continuation condition is true. In our example, this is the statement "**year<=10.**" This means our loop will continue to be executed as long as the variable **year** is less than or equal to 10.

The third statement tells how to update the counter variable with each pass through the loop. In our case, this is the statement "**year++,**" since we will add one to the year each time. There is no semicolon after this third statement; instead, there is the right parenthesis that closes the **for** statement conditions. This is followed by the left brace { that marks the beginning of the **for** loop action statements. In our case, we have two action statements. As you should be able to guess by now, the end of the action statements is marked with a right brace }, and we will also include a comment to remind us that the right brace marks the end of the **for** loop.

When executing the loop, the computer will first set the counter variable **year** equal to zero, then it will execute the two action statements; then it will add one to the **year**, then execute the action statements again; and so on, until the **year** is no longer less than or equal to 10.

Here is the complete version of our program:

```
class compoundinterest {

/*method*/ static double r2(double x) {
/*This method rounds a double value to two decimal places.*/
double z=((double)(Math.round(x*100)))/100;
return z;
} /*end method r2*/

public static void main(String args[ ]) {

double balance=100.0;
double rate=0.05;
System.out.println("Bank balance with compound interest,
rate="+r2(rate));
System.out.println("Year Balance");

for (int year=0; year<=10; year++) {

System.out.println(year+"␣␣␣␣"+r2(balance));
balance+=rate*balance;
        } /*end for loop*/
} /*end main*/
} /*end compoundinterest*/
```

Alternatively, the balance could be calculated from this formula:

$$balance = (1 + rate)^{year}$$

In Java, the formula looks like this:

```
balance=Math.pow((1+rate),year);
```

The r2 method is included to round the results to two decimal places (see page 90).
Here is the output:

```
Bank balance with compound interest, rate=0.05
  Year    Balance
0     100.0
1     105.0
2     110.25
3     115.76
4     121.55
5     127.63
6     134.01
7     140.71
8     147.75
9     155.13
10     162.89
```

5.2   for Loop: General Form

Here is the general form of a **for** loop where the *counter_variable* starts at *initial_value*, then increases by 1 each time until it reaches *final_value*.

```
for (type counter_variable=initial_value;
counter_variable<=final_value;
counter_variable++) {
action statements for loop go here
} /*end for loop*/
```

Note carefully the location of parentheses, semicolons, and braces. Also note how the type of the *counter_variable* is declared in the **for** loop itself. It is not mandatory to declare the counter variable here; you can use a counter variable that is declared outside the loop. However, in general it is recommended that you declare the counter variable in the loop itself. That way, you are sure that you are not accidentally affecting some other variable that comes from outside the loop.

Here is another simple example of a **for** loop. Suppose you wish to add up all of the even numbers from 2 to 100, displaying the result each time you add a new number.

```
class addup {

public static void main(String args[ ]) {

int sum=0;

for (int x=2; x<=100; x+=2) {
sum+=x;
System.out.println(x+"␣␣␣"+sum);
} /*end loop*/
} /*end main*/
} /*end addup*/
```

The output from this program is too lengthy to show here, but you can see how the computer can easily perform lengthy calculations, as long as you know how to give the right instructions.

Note that the counter variable *x* increases by 2 with each pass through the loop (because the update action is *x+=2*).

Here is the general form of a **for** loop where the counter variable increases each time by a value *step_value*, which may be different from 1:

```
for (variable_type counter_variable=initial_value;
counter_variable<=final_value;
counter_variable+=step_value) {
action statements for loop go here
} /*end for loop*/
```

It is possible to create an even more general kind of **for** loop; this is discussed on page 53.

5.3   Dates

Whenever we write a program that involves different dates, it would help if the computer could label the dates. Although the actual process of calculating dates in a calendar is a bit complicated, Java does that automatically. Here is an example of a program that displays a list of consecutive dates before and after January 1, 2000:

```
import java.util.*;
import java.text.*;

class dates {
/*This program illustrates Java date calculation capabilities.*/
public static void main(String args[ ]) {
Calendar cal=new GregorianCalendar(1999,Calendar.DECEMBER,
21);
Format fmt=DateFormat.getDateInstance(DateFormat.FULL);
for (int i=1; i<=20; i++) {
        System.out.println(fmt.format(cal.getTime()));
        cal.add(Calendar.HOUR,24); /*advance to next day*/
} /*end for loop*/

Date now=new Date();
System.out.println("now:"+now);
} /*end main*/
} /*end dates*/
```

The statement

```
Calendar cal=new GregorianCalendar(1999,Calendar.DECEMBER,21);
```

creates a date representing December 21, 1999. (The reason it specifies the Gregorian calendar is because Java is so versatile it also can work with other calendars.)

The statement

```
Format fmt=DateFormat.getDateInstance(DateFormat.FULL);
```

determines the format to display the date. The FULL format includes day of week, month, day, and year. (You can also experiment with this program by trying other formats: SHORT, LONG, and MEDIUM.) Again, Java is flexible enough that you can adjust the format if your program will be used in other countries.

Our calendar program contains a **for** loop that is similar to the other loops in this chapter. The other new statement is this one:

```
cal.add(Calendar.HOUR,24); /*advance to next day*/
```

This statement adds 24 hours to the date; that is, it advances the date to the next day.

Finally, this example program also shows you how you can display the current date and time using Java.

5.4   Nested Loops

Now we'll do another example with compound interest. The problem with our earlier program is that it only works with an interest rate of 0.05 (5 percent). It would be helpful to create a table with several columns, where each column represents a different interest rate. We'll use a loop to determine the rates. We also need a loop for the years. This brings us to a very powerful programming tool: we can have loops inside of loops. (In this case the inner loop is *nested* inside the outer loop.)

Here is a sketch of what the two loops will look like:

```
for (int year=0; year<=10; year++) {
      for (rate=startrate; rate<=stoprate; rate+=steprate) {
         /*here are the action statements:*/
            balance=balance0*Math.pow((1+rate),year);
            System.out.print("␣␣␣"+r2(balance));
            } /*end inner loop (counter variable: rate)*/
      } /*end outer loop (counter variable: year)*/
```

The outer loop counts up the values of the year, corresponding to each row. The inner loop counts the values of the rate, which determine the values in each column.

Indenting often can be used to illustrate the structure of the nested loops; indent the inner loop more than the outer loop, which is indented more than the rest of the program.

We need to add a couple of refinements to the loops in the final program. We don't want the program to start a new line after each pass through the inner loop, since we want all the results for a particular year on the same line. Therefore, we will use **System.out.print** instead of **System.out.println** for this output. However, we need to make sure that the program does start a new line each time it has finished the inner loop; we can do this with a **System.out.println("␣")** statement after the end of the inner loop. Also, we need to put labels on the rows and columns, because otherwise the results are not very meaningful. We can put column labels on the top by including a separate loop before the two nested loops. The label for the rows can be included by putting a statement just before the beginning of the inner loop. Here is the program:

```
class compoundinterest2 {

/*This program prints a table of compound interest
  for different interest rates.*/

/*method*/ static double r2(double x) {
/*This method rounds a double value to two decimal places.*/
double z=((double)(Math.round(x*100)))/100;
return z;
} /*end method r2*/

public static void main(String args[ ]) {
```

```
double balance0=100.0;
double startrate=.03;
double stoprate=.11;
double steprate=.02; /*The amount rate is increased with
                              each pass through the loop.*/
double rate;
System.out.println("Bank balance with compound interest");

System.out.print("Year␣");
/*Put headings on each column.*/
for (rate=startrate; rate<=stoprate; rate+=steprate) {
            System.out.print("␣␣r="+r2(rate));}
/*The next statement is included so subsequent output
  will start on a new line.*/
System.out.println("␣");


/*Here is the start of the outer loop:*/
for (int year=0; year<=10; year++) {
/*Include the heading for each label:*/
        System.out.print("␣␣␣"+year);
          /*here is the start of the inner loop:*/
        for (rate=startrate; rate<=stoprate; rate+=steprate) {
                double balance=balance0*Math.pow((1+rate),year);
                System.out.print("␣␣␣"+r2(balance));
                } /*end inner loop (counter variable: rate)*/
/*The next statement is included so subsequent output
  will start on a new line.*/
System.out.println("␣");
} /*end outer loop (counter variable: year)*/
} /*end main*/
} /*end compoundinterest2*/
```

Note how we have defined three variables to govern the interest rate loop: startrate, stoprate, and steprate. If we want to change these, we only need to make the change at the beginning of the program where these values are defined. Then the rest of the program will automatically work with these new values.

Here is the output of the program:

```
Bank balance with compound interest
Year    r=0.03   r=0.05   r=0.07   r=0.09
   0    100.0    100.0    100.0    100.0
   1    103.0    105.0    107.0    109.0
   2    106.09   110.25   114.49   118.81
   3    109.27   115.76   122.5    129.5
   4    112.55   121.55   131.08   141.16
   5    115.93   127.63   140.26   153.86
   6    119.41   134.01   150.07   167.71
   7    122.99   140.71   160.58   182.8
   8    126.68   147.75   171.82   199.26
   9    130.48   155.13   183.85   217.19
  10    134.39   162.89   196.72   236.74
```

Unfortunately, the columns do not line up perfectly; see page 90 where we develop a method for improving the appearance of the output of numerical data.

We can also have three (or more) nested loops. Suppose we are tossing three dice, and we would like to see all of the $6^3 = 216$ possible outcomes. Here is a program to do this:

```
class threedice {
/*This program displays all possible results of tossing three dice.*/
public static void main(String args[ ]) {

for (int d1=1; d1<=6; d1++) {
for (int d2=1; d2<=6; d2++) {
for (int d3=1; d3<=6; d3++) {
System.out.print("␣␣␣"+d1+d2+d3);
} /*end d3 loop*/
System.out.println("␣"); /*next output will be on new line*/
} /*end d2 loop*/
System.out.println("␣"); /*insert blank line*/
} /*end d1 loop*/
} /*end main*/
} /*end threedice*/
```

If we had written the output statement this way:

```
System.out.print(d1+d2+d3);
```

the computer would have interpreted the + sign to mean addition, so it would have added the three numbers and displayed the result. However, this is not what we want in this case; we want the program to treat the three numbers as if they were strings, and then treat the plus sign as representing concatenation so it will display the three strings next to each other. To do this, we put a blank string at the start of the output expression, like this:

```
System.out.print("␣␣␣"+d1+d2+d3);
```

When the output expression starts with a string, all subsequent plus signs in that expression will be treated as representing concatenation, not addition (that is, unless you enclose the numbers in another set of parentheses, like this: **System.out.println("␣"+(d1+d2+d3));**).
Here is the output:

111	112	113	114	115	116
121	122	123	124	125	126
131	132	133	134	135	136
141	142	143	144	145	146
151	152	153	154	155	156
161	162	163	164	165	166

```
211    212    213    214    215    216
221    222    223    224    225    226
231    232    233    234    235    236
241    242    243    244    245    246
251    252    253    254    255    256
261    262    263    264    265    266

311    312    313    314    315    316
321    322    323    324    325    326
331    332    333    334    335    336
341    342    343    344    345    346
351    352    353    354    355    356
361    362    363    364    365    366

411    412    413    414    415    416
421    422    423    424    425    426
431    432    433    434    435    436
441    442    443    444    445    446
451    452    453    454    455    456
461    462    463    464    465    466

511    512    513    514    515    516
521    522    523    524    525    526
531    532    533    534    535    536
541    542    543    544    545    546
551    552    553    554    555    556
561    562    563    564    565    566

611    612    613    614    615    616
621    622    623    624    625    626
631    632    633    634    635    636
641    642    643    644    645    646
651    652    653    654    655    656
661    662    663    664    665    666
```

5.5   while Loops

Recall the example from page 11, in which a baseball was thrown straight up in the air. Its height at time t was given by this formula:

$$-0.5 \times 9.8 \times t^2 + 25t + 1.2$$

Now we will write a program that calculates the height of the baseball at several different times. In fact, we will calculate its height every half second from the time it is thrown until it is back on the ground. This sounds like a problem for a loop. We want the program to keep calculating the height as long as the baseball is still in the air, so the program needs to have this general form:

while (*baseball is still in air*) {*calculate height*}

Fortunately, Java provides a **while** loop. This allows you to state a condition and then some action statements; those statements will be executed repeatedly as long as the stated condition is true.

Here is the program:

```
class baseballheight {

/*method*/ static double r2(double x) {
/*This method rounds a double value to two decimal places.*/
double z=((double)(Math.round(x*100)))/100;
return z;
} /*end method r2*/

public static void main(String args[ ]) {

double time=0;
double height=-0.5*9.8*Math.pow(time,2)+25*time+1.2;

System.out.println("  time   height"); /*include label at top*/

while (height>=0) {
System.out.println("  "+r2(time)+"    "+r2(height));
time+=0.5; /*The time advances one-half second each step.*/
height=-0.5*9.8*Math.pow(time,2)+25*time+1.2;
      } /*end while loop*/
} /*end main*/
} /*end baseballheight*/
```

Note that the condition (height>=0 in our example) is enclosed by parentheses.

When writing a program with a **while** loop, it is imperative that somewhere in the middle of the loop there is a statement that will change some value that affects the condition. In our example, the statement "time+=0.5" advances the time with each pass through the loop; in turn, this will change the height each time. If we had left out the statement "time+=0.5," then the time would never change, no matter how many times we passed through the loop. As a result, the height would never change, so the condition (height>=0) would always be true, and the loop would run forever. (Actually, you would eventually realize what was going on and would interrupt the program. In Windows, press the control, alt, and delete keys simultaneously to call for a dialog box that will allow you to break out of the program.) In general, you want to avoid creating programs with endless loops.

Here is the output from our program:

```
time    height
0.0     1.2
0.5     12.48
1.0     21.3
1.5     27.68
2.0     31.6
2.5     33.07
```

```
3.0    32.1
3.5    28.67
4.0    22.8
4.5    14.47
5.0    3.7
```

Here is the general form of a **while** loop:

while (*condition*) {
action statements
} /*end while loop*/

The *condition* can be any logical expression that evaluates as true or false; see page 36 for a list.

Now we have seen how the ability to use loops greatly increases the power of our computer programs, because we can have the computer perform the tedious process of repeatedly executing the same set of instructions.

Notes

Here is the most general form for a **for** loop:

for (*initialization_action*;
continuation_condition;
update_action) {
action statements for loop go here
} /*end for loop*/

When the computer first reaches the loop, it will check the *continuation_condition*. If true, the *initialization_action* will be executed. Then, the computer will pass through the action statements for the first time. Then, the *update_action* will be executed. Next, the *continuation_condition* will be checked. This condition can be any one of the logical conditions described on page 36. If the condition is true, then the computer will repeat the action statements, then the update action, and so on. It will keep repeating that process until the continuation condition becomes false. This form allows a **for** loop to be very general; however, in this book we will use a **while** loop when we need this kind of a loop. We will only use a **for** loop when our loop contains a counter variable that increases a set amount with each pass through the loop.

EXERCISES

1. Write a program that displays a multiplication table, such as a continuation of the table below.

	1	2	3	4	5	6	7	8	9	10	11	12
1	1	2	3	4	5	6	7	8	9	10	11	12
2	2	4	6	8	10	12	14	16	18	20	22	24
3	3	6	9	12	15	18	21	24	27	30	33	36

2. Write a program that displays a table of winning percentages. The numbers along the top of the table will represent games played; the numbers along the left side of the table will represent games won. The numbers in the table represent the winning percentages, rounded to three decimal places.

3. Suppose a computer password consists of an eight-digit number. Write a program that generates all possible eight-digit numbers. Then experiment to see how long it takes for this program to execute as the password becomes longer.

4. The *factorial* of a positive integer n (represented by $n!$) is the product of all of the whole numbers from 1 up to that number:

$$n! = n \times (n-1) \times (n-2) \times \ldots \times 3 \times 2 \times 1$$

Write a program that reads in the value of n and calculates $n!$.

For Exercises 5–9, write a program that calculates the sum of the series. In each case, have the program display the result after each new term is added to the series.

5.
$$1 + 2 + 3 + 4 + 5 + 6 + 7 + 8 + 9 + 10 + \ldots$$

6.
$$1 + 4 + 9 + 16 + 25 + 36 + 49 + 64 + 81 + 100 + \ldots$$

7.
$$1 + \frac{1}{2} + \frac{1}{4} + \frac{1}{8} + \frac{1}{16} + \ldots$$

8.
$$4\left(1 - \frac{1}{3} + \frac{1}{5} - \frac{1}{7} + \frac{1}{9} - \frac{1}{11} + \ldots +\right)$$

This series will give you an approximate value for π. This method takes a long time to reach an accurate value. As you add each new term to this series, the result will alternate between being too large and being too small. You can improve the accuracy of the approximation by calculating the average of the current sum and the previous sum.

9.

$$2 + \frac{1}{2!} + \frac{1}{3!} + \frac{1}{4!} + \ldots$$

This series will give you an approximation for a special number called e (see Chapter 12).

10. The Tourist Trap Souvenir Manufacturing Firm is a monopolist. The following relationship exists between the price it charges (p) and the quantity (q) of output it can sell:

$$q = 100 - 0.5p$$

The cost (c) of making q souvenirs is given by the following relationship:

$$c = 0.5q^2 + 10$$

Write a program that calculates the firm's profits for each possible value of the price from $p = 0$ to $p = 200$. Have the program identify the price that leads to the maximum profits.

11. Suppose P is the amount you will borrow for a home loan, and r is the monthly interest rate (equal to 1/12 of the annual interest rate). The loan will last for $n = 360$ months. Have the program calculate the monthly payment amount C:

$$C = \frac{rP(1+r)^n}{(1+r)^n - 1}$$

(The Java expression **Math.pow**(x,n) calculates the exponent x^n.) Then, have the program calculate the table showing how the mortgage balance changes over time. Each month, you need to pay an interest payment equal to the interest rate times the previous pricipal balance. The rest of the payment is used to reduce the remaining principal, so each month the new principal balance becomes

$$P_{new} = P_{previous} - (C - rP_{previous})$$

You should see that the balance falls to very close to 0 after making the 360th payment. (The complete table will not fit on the screen, so after you read Chapter 11 you may wish to convert this program so that it writes its output to a file.)

12. Write a number-guessing program. The program code includes a secret number. The user makes a guess for the number, and the computer responds by indicating whether the guess is equal to, less than, or greater than the actual number. Keep repeating the process until the user has guessed the number.

13. Write a program that determines whether or not a number is a prime number.

14. Write a program that calculates the number of trailing zeros in a whole number. For example, 1050 has one trailing zero; 9,000,000 has six trailing zeros; and 307 has no trailing zeros.

15. Write a program that displays all of the prime factors of a number. For example, the prime factors of 12 are $2 \times 2 \times 3$; the prime factors of 60 are $2 \times 2 \times 3 \times 5$; and the prime factors of 39 are 3×13.

CHAPTER 6

ARRAYS

6.1 Arrays and Subscripts

Our next task is to prepare a report summarizing our budget. We have five spending categories, and we would like to know what fraction of spending occurred in each category. Assuming that the amounts spent on each category are 12, 15, 80, 40, and 30, respectively, we could approach the program like this:

```
spend1=12; spend2=15; spend3=80; spend4=40; spend5= 30;
total=spend1+spend2+spend3+spend4+spend5;
System.out.println("Category 1␣␣Spending:"+spend1+"␣␣Share:"
    +(spend1/total));
System.out.println("Category 2␣␣Spending:"+spend2+"␣␣Share:"
    +(spend2/total));
System.out.println("Category 3␣␣Spending:"+spend3+"␣␣Share:"
    +(spend3/total));
System.out.println("Category 4␣␣Spending:"+spend4+"␣␣Share:"
    +(spend4/total));
System.out.println("Category 5␣␣Spending:"+spend5+"␣␣Share:"
    +(spend5/total));
```

This approach, however, is too much work. For one thing, in a realistic problem you might have a hundred different categories, so there should be some way to avoid having to repeat the same set of instructions each time.

In the last chapter we saw how loops allow us to program repetitious tasks. However, a loop alone is not sufficient for this task, since we need to be able to identify each spending category separately. What we need is a way to use one name to stand for all of the spending categories, and then attach a number to identify each individual category. In math, identifying numbers are traditionally written as subscripts, like this:

$$\text{spend}_1, \text{spend}_2, \text{spend}_3, \text{spend}_4, \text{spend}_5$$

In Java, we will still call the identifying numbers subscripts, even though they are not written below the line. Instead, the subscripts are enclosed in square brackets:

spend[1], spend[2], spend[3], spend[4], spend[5]

This is called an *array*. An array is a way of storing many different items under the same name, with each individual identified by a subscript. Arrays are essential tools for programming computers to perform repetitive tasks, because a loop can be written to handle the processing of each element of the array.

In the example above, the elements of the array are all numbers. We will later see that the elements can be other types of objects as well.

As with all variables in Java, an array must be declared before it can be used. As with other variables, we may specify values for the array at the time it is declared, but we don't have to. Here is the declaration for the array **spend** when the values are specified:

double spend[ ] = {0,12,15,80,40,30};

We could also declare the array first without giving the values. In that case, we must specify the size of the array.

double spend[ ]=**new double**[6];

Then we could specify the individual values like this:

spend[0]=0; spend[1]=12; spend[2]=15;
spend[3]=80; spend[4]=40; spend[5]=30;

You have probably noticed one odd thing about our list of spending values: the subscripts start at 0. This is a feature of Java you need to know: arrays always start with subscript 0. That means that the maximum subscript (5, in our case) is always one less than the total number of elements in the array (6). There are many cases where having the subscripts start at 0 is more convenient than starting at 1, but there also are cases, as in our example, where it would be more convenient if the subscripts started at 1. One solution is to declare the array to have one more element than you actually need, and then ignore the 0 subscript. If this approach makes it easier for you to keep track of the subscripts, then it is probably worth it even though it does use slightly more computer memory.

Here is our program:

```
class budget1 {

/*method*/ static double r3(double x) {
/*This method rounds a double value to three decimal places.*/
double z=((double)(Math.round(x*1000)))/1000;
return z;
} /*end method r3*/
```

```
public static void main(String args[ ]) {

double spend[ ] = {0,12,15,80,40,30};
double total=0;

for (int category=1; category<=5; category++) {
total+=spend[category];}

for (int category=1; category<=5; category++) {
double share=spend[category]/total;
System.out.println("Category:␣"+category+"␣␣Spending:"+
      spend[category]+"␣␣Share:"+r3(share));
      } /*end for loop*/
} /*end main*/
} /*end budget1*/
```

Here is the output:

```
Category:  1  Spending:12.0  Share:0.068
Category:  2  Spending:15.0  Share:0.085
Category:  3  Spending:80.0  Share:0.452
Category:  4  Spending:40.0  Share:0.226
Category:  5  Spending:30.0  Share:0.169
```

In the last chapter, we prepared a program to display all of the possible results of tossing three dice (see page 50). We might also like to have a table showing the probabilities that the sum of the three numbers on the dice will equal a particular value. We will again use three nested loops. This time we will not display the three numbers; instead, we will add them up, and then add one to an array that counts the number of possibilities for each possible sum. Since the sum can range between 3 and 18, it would be nice if we could create an array with subscripts between 3 and 18. We can't do that, but we can create an array with subscripts that go from 0 to 18 with this declaration:

```
int numberofpossibilities[ ]=new int[19];
```

Note that we declare the size of the array as 19 because the subscripts run from 0 to 18.

Here's the program:

```
class threedice2 {
/*This program calculates the probabilities for
  all possible results of tossing three dice.*/

/*method*/ static double r3(double x) {
/*This method rounds a double value to three decimal places.*/
double z=((double)(Math.round(x*1000)))/1000;
return z;
} /*end method r3*/
```

```
public static void main(String args[ ]) {

int maxsubscript=18;
int numberofpossibilities[ ]=new int[maxsubscript+1];
/*The values in the array are automatically set to 0.*/

for (int d1=1; d1<=6; d1++) {
        for (int d2=1; d2<=6; d2++) {
                for (int d3=1; d3<=6; d3++) {
                        int sum=d1+d2+d3;
                                numberofpossibilities[sum]++;
                } /*end d3 loop*/
        } /*end d2 loop*/
    } /*end d1 loop*/

int totalpossibilities=6*6*6;
double totalprobability=0;

System.out.println("Sum  Possibilities  Probability");

for (int sum=3; sum<=maxsubscript; sum++) {
double probability=
((double)numberofpossibilities[sum])/totalpossibilities;

System.out.println(" "+sum+"          "+numberofpossibilities[sum]+
            " "+r3(probability));
totalprobability+=probability;
        } /*end sum loop*/
System.out.println("Total probability:  "+r3(totalprobability));
} /*end main*/
} /*end threedice2*/
```

Look again at this statement:

```
double probability=
((double)numberofpossibilities[sum])/totalpossibilities;
```

Notice that the statement has to make a cast to type **double** before performing the division (see note about casting on page 20).

Here is the output:

Sum	Possibilities	Probability
3	1	0.0050
4	3	0.014
5	6	0.028
6	10	0.046
7	15	0.069
8	21	0.097
9	25	0.116
10	27	0.125
11	27	0.125
12	25	0.116
13	21	0.097

```
14          15         0.069
15          10         0.046
16           6         0.028
17           3         0.014
18           1         0.0050
Total probability:    1.0
```

6.2   Arrays of Character Strings: Sorting

So far we have only looked at arrays of numbers. Arrays become an even more powerful tool when we use arrays of character strings or even other kinds of objects. For example, a common task is to alphabetize a list of names. We can store each name as a string, and then the entire list becomes an array of strings. For example, we will look at a list of names of the first sixteen presidents of the United States.

We can declare the list and assign its initial values in the same way we can for a list of numbers:

String presidentlist[ ]=
{"blank","Washington","Adams","Jefferson","Madison","Monroe",
"Adams","Jackson","Van Buren","Harrison","Tyler",
"Polk","Taylor","Fillmore","Pierce","Buchanan","Lincoln"};

(We insert a blank string at array position zero so that Washington will appear in position one. See page 58.)

There are many different methods to sort the items in an array. We will use a method called the *bubble sort* method. This is not the best method to use if you need to sort a very long list and you are worried about the actual amount of computer time that will be taken up by the sorting process. However, the bubble sort method does have one big advantage: a program to implement it is very short. Often you will be more concerned about the amount of time you have to spend writing the program than you are with the amount of time the computer will spend running the program, so that makes the bubble sort method very attractive.

Here is the way the bubble sort method works for a list of n names. First, look at the first two names in the list. If they are in order, leave them alone. If they're not in order, then swap those two names. Next, look at the second and third names in the list; again swap them if they're not in order. Keep repeating this process until you come to the last two names in the list. At this point, we are guaranteed that the last name alphabetically in the list will have been moved to the last position in the list. We have to repeat the process, but this time we only have to work on the first $n - 1$ names. After the second pass through the list, we are guaranteed that the last two names are in the right places. Then we repeat the process, working with only the first $n - 2$ names. Each pass becomes shorter and shorter; by the time we have completed the last pass, we are guaranteed that the list will be in order.

Figure 6–1 illustrates this process. We will sort a very short list of five names: Maine, Vermont, New Hampshire, Connecticut, Massachusetts. An "x" in the figure shows a stage where two items are swapped; two vertical lines indicate that the two items being compared were not swapped during that step. Maine and Vermont are in the correct order, so no swap is made. During the rest of the first pass, Vermont is repeatedly swapped with another state until it reaches its correct place at the end of the list. At the end of the second pass, New Hampshire has reached its correct position as the second to the last item. In the third pass Connecticut and Maine are swapped, and then the list is in order.

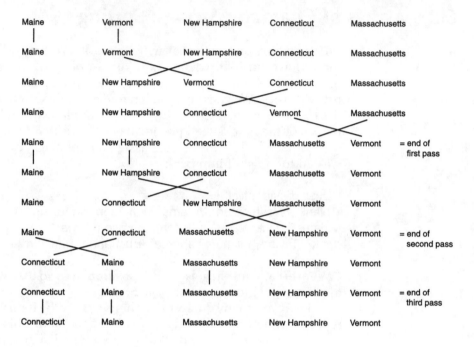

FIGURE 6–1

In order to implement the procedure, we need to be able to compare two strings to see which comes first in alphabetical order. If we have two strings **a** and **b**, this statement will create a boolean variable called **inorder** that will be true if string **a** comes before string **b** in alphabetical order:

boolean inorder=(a.**compareTo**(b)<=0);

If string **a** is the same as string **b**, then our variable **inorder** will also become true. This is fine for the bubble sort, since there is no need to swap the two strings if they are the same.

Here is the program:

```
class alphabetize {

/*This program uses the bubble sort method to
  sort an array of names.*/

public static void main(String args[ ]) {

String presidentlist[ ]=
{"blank","Washington","Adams","Jefferson","Madison","Monroe",
"Adams","Jackson","Van Buren","Harrison","Tyler",
```

"Polk","Taylor","Fillmore","Pierce","Buchanan","Lincoln"};

int n=presidentlist.**length**-1; /*number of names in list*/

```
for (int i=1; i<=n-1; i++) {
for (int j=1; j<=(n-i); j++) {
boolean inorder=(presidentlist[j].compareTo(presidentlist[j+1])<=0);
if (!inorder) { /*swap these two elements*/
          String temporarystring=presidentlist[j];
          presidentlist[j]=presidentlist[j+1];
          presidentlist[j+1]=temporarystring;
          } /*end if*/
} /*end j loop*/
} /*end i loop*/

/*Now, display the results:*/

for (int i=1; i<=n; i++) {
System.out.println(presidentlist[i]);
} /*end for loop*/
} /*end main*/
} /*end alphabetize*/
```

Note how the variable temporarystring is created to help in the process of swapping. Also note how the j loop is nested inside the i loop.

Here is the output:

```
Adams
Adams
Buchanan
Fillmore
Harrison
Jackson
Jefferson
Lincoln
Madison
Monroe
Pierce
Polk
Taylor
Tyler
Van Buren
Washington
```

6.3   Two-dimensional Arrays

Our previous budget program (page 58) only works for one time period. In reality, we will have budget data for several periods, and we might like to have a table showing the amount spent on each category per period, as well as the totals for each category and each period.

Here's our data:

	Books	Clothes	Food	Travel	Entert.
January	12.0	15.0	80.0	40.0	30.0
February	34.0	20.0	76.0	11.0	28.0
March	21.0	15.0	56.0	80.0	20.0
April	38.0	59.0	94.0	17.0	24.0

We can store a table of numbers as an array, but it must be a two-dimensional array. It takes two subscripts to identify each element. Traditionally, the first subscript identifies the row of the element, and the second subscript identifies the column. In our case, the rows represent months, and the columns represent categories.

As always, we must first declare an array before we can use it. Recall how we declared **spend** as a one-dimensional array:

double spend[ ]=**new double**[6];

We will now declare the array **spend** to be a two-dimensional array with 5 rows and 6 columns of double values:

double spend[ ][ ]=**new double**[5][6];

In order to make it a two-dimensional array, we need to include two pairs of empty brackets in the first part, and then we need to give the number of rows and columns in the second part (both surrounded by brackets). As always, the subscripts start at zero, so our declaration states that **spend** will have 5 rows, numbered 0 to 4, and 6 columns, numbered from 0 to 5.

Alternatively, we can declare the array by specifying the initial values, like this:

```
double spend[ ][ ] = {
            /*ignore first row*/ {0, 0, 0, 0, 0, 0},
            /*January:*/ {0,12,15,80,40,30},
            /*February:*/ {0,34,20,76,11,28},
            /*March:*/ {0,21,15,56,80,20},
            /*April:*/ {0,38,59,94,17,24}
                              };
```

As we did with a one-dimensional array, the values are surrounded by braces and separated by commas. However, we now need to put one set of braces around each row, and then another set of braces around the entire array. As before, we are putting values of 0 in column 0 and row 0 because we will not be using those positions. The comments in the above code segment are optional, but you can see how they help identify what the values mean.

Here's the program to display the table of data with labels, and calculate the totals for each row and column:

```
class budget2 {

/*method*/ static double r2(double x) {
/*This method rounds a double value to two decimal places.*/
double z=((double)(Math.round(x*100)))/100;
return z;
} /*end method r2*/

public static void main(String args[ ]) {

int maxrow=4;
int maxcol=5; /*col is short for column.*/

/*Initialize the data:*/
                    /*categories: 1 2 3 4 5*/
double spend[ ][ ] = {
/*row 0: ignore*/ {0, 0, 0, 0, 0, 0},
/*row 1:January:*/ {0,12,15,80,40,30},
/*row 2:February:*/ {0,34,20,76,11,28},
/*row 3:March:*/ {0,21,15,56,80,20},
/*row 4:April:*/ {0,38,59,94,17,24}
                                    };

double coltotal[ ]={0,0,0,0,0,0}; /*to hold column totals*/

+","April␣␣␣"};
+","Travel␣","␣Entert."};
String month[ ]={"␣","January␣","February", "March␣␣␣","April␣␣␣"};
String categ[ ]=
{"␣␣␣␣␣␣␣␣␣␣","Books␣␣␣","Clothes␣␣␣","Food␣␣␣","Travel␣","␣Entert."};

/*Display the labels at the top of each column:*/
for (int col=0; col<=maxcol; col++) {
        System.out.print(categ[col]);}
System.out.println("␣Total");


/*These two nested loops display the values and
  calculate the row and column totals.*/
for (int row=1; row<=maxrow; row++) {
        double rowtot=0; /*This must be set to 0 before
                          the inner loop begins.*/
        System.out.print(month[row]);
        for (int col=1; col<=maxcol; col++) {
            System.out.print("␣␣␣␣"+r2(spend[row][col]));
            rowtot+=spend[row][col];
            coltotal[col]+=spend[row][col];
            } /*end col loop*/
```

```
                System.out.println("␣␣␣"+r2(rowtot));
        } /*end row loop*/

/*Display the column totals below each column:*/
System.out.print("Total:␣␣");
double grandtotal=0;
for (int col=1; col<=maxcol; col++) {
        System.out.print("␣␣␣"+coltotal[col]);
            grandtotal+=coltotal[col];
        } /*end for loop*/
System.out.println("␣␣␣"+r2(grandtotal));

} /*end main*/
} /*end budget2*/
```

In this case the values are all integers, but they are declared to be of type **double** to make the program more general so that it can handle fractional dollar amounts. Notice how each reference to the array spend contains two subscripts, with the row subscript coming first.

Here is the output:

	Books	Clothes	Food	Travel	Entert.	Total
January	12.0	15.0	80.0	40.0	30.0	177.0
February	34.0	20.0	76.0	11.0	28.0	169.0
March	21.0	15.0	56.0	80.0	20.0	192.0
April	38.0	59.0	94.0	17.0	24.0	232.0
Total:	105.0	109.0	306.0	148.0	102.0	770.0

Although an interesting example, this budget program still leaves a lot to be desired. We do not yet have an easy way to format the numbers so they line up in even columns (this will come on page 96). We do not yet have a way to read input into our program; we don't want a program that only works for data that is part of the source code. For one thing, our program would need to be recompiled whenever you change the data in the source code. We will learn about input data that comes from files in Chapter 11, and we will learn about keyboard input in windows in Chapters 14 and 15. Finally, we might have a problem with the fact that the labels and the data are in separate arrays. If we later made a change to the program (such as adding a new category), we run the risk that the label array might not be updated in the same way as the data array, so the labels would no longer match the data they belong to. Therefore, instead of using multidimensional arrays, we will often find it to be better to use an array of objects, where each individual object also contains an array. This approach will allow us to include the labels in the same object as the data. See the book's web page (*http://www.spu.edu/~ddowning/cpjava.html*) for more about finance and budgeting programs.

6.4 Vectors

Arrays have two disadvantages: (1) when the array is full, the computer will suffer an "ArrayIndexOutofRange" error if you try to add another element to it; (2) all of the elements of an array must be of the same type. Sometimes it is helpful to create a **Vector**, which is similar to an array except it can grow as needed and can store objects of different types.

Here is an example of a command to create a new vector:

Vector vectorname=**new Vector**(100,20);

This vector will start with a capacity of 100 elements, and it will add 20 to the capacity whenever the capacity is full. The capacity of a vector is the maximum amount of space it currently has available; the size is the number of objects currently stored. The following command will eliminate the excess capacity (that is, make the capacity of the vector equal to its current size):

vectorname.**trimToSize**( );

To add an object to the end of the vector, use this command:

vectorname.**addElement**(objectname);

To insert an element at position 6, use this command:

vectorname.**insertElementAt**(objectname, 5);

(As with arrays, the numbering starts at zero, which is why you use a 5 to indicate the 6th position of the vector.)
To change the element at position 6, use this command:

vectorname.**setElementAt**(objectname, 5);

To retrieve the element at position 6, use this command:

vectorname.**elementAt**(5);

Using the command above, however, will return this object with the generic type **Object**; you most likely will need to cast it into the type you want. For example, this is the command to use if the vector holds integers:

int newintegervariablename=(**int**) vectorname.**elementAt**(5);

To find the current size of the vector, use this command:

vectorname.**size**();

Although their flexible size is an advantage, vectors do have a disadvantage: the computer takes more time to process them than it would if it were dealing with an equivalent array. In many cases you will be more concerned about execution speed than you are about memory size, so it would be more efficient for your program to use arrays instead of vectors. Just make sure you declare the size of the array to be larger than you would ever need it to be. (This assumes that you need to store objects of the same type; if you need to store objects of more than one type, you will have to use a vector.) For an example of a vector in action, see page 275.

Later, we will explore some other data structures related to arrays: a *hash table*, which allows objects to be stored along with labels that can be used to locate them quickly, and a *collection* (new in Java version 2), which has additional features for arranging and locating individual items (see the book's web page at *http://www.spu.edu/~ddowning/cpjava.html*).

EXERCISES

(Unless otherwise indicated, in these exercises we will ignore element 0. That means that if the exercise indicates that the subscripts run from 1 to n, you must declare the array as having n + 1 elements.)

1. Write a program that checks to see if a list of numbers is arranged in ascending order.

2. Write a program that displays the elements of a list in the opposite order.

3. If A is an array of n **double** values, write a program that calculates the average $\overline{A}$ and the standard deviation σ_A (sigma):

$$\overline{A} = \frac{A_1 + A_2 + A_3 + \ldots + A_n}{n}$$

$$\sigma_A = \sqrt{\frac{(A_1 - \overline{A})^2 + (A_2 - \overline{A})^2 + (A_3 - \overline{A})^2 + \ldots + (A_n - \overline{A})^2}{n}}$$

4. Assume that A and B are both arrays of n **double** values, representing paired observations of two quantities. For example, A_i might be the rainfall that fell on farm i, and B_i could be the crop output from farm i. Calculate the correlation between A and B from the formula

$$\text{correlation} = \frac{\overline{AB} - \overline{A} \times \overline{B}}{\sigma_A \sigma_B}$$

where σ_A and σ_B are defined in the previous exercise, and

$$\overline{AB} = \frac{A_1 B_1 + A_2 B_2 + A_3 B_3 + \ldots + A_n B_n}{n}$$

5. Let A represent an array of n **double** values, where A_i represents the amount of money you will earn i years in the future. Write a program that calculates the present value of this future income stream, using this formula:

$$\text{present value} =$$
$$A_0 + \frac{A_1}{1+r} + \frac{A_2}{(1+r)^2} + \frac{A_3}{(1+r)^3} + \frac{A_4}{(1+r)^4} + \ldots + \frac{A_n}{(1+r)^n}$$

6. Assume that H is a 162-element array consisting of the number of hits by a major league baseball player in each game during a season. Write a program that calculates the longest consecutive string of games during which the player has at least one hit during the game. (If the result is larger than 56, have the computer display a message indicating that Joe DiMaggio's record has been broken.)

7. Assume that M is a list of arbitrary integers. Write a program that counts how many times each of these numbers occurs in the list.

8. Assume that A is an array containing N positive integers. Write a program that tests to see whether A contains every integer from 1 to N.

9. Write a program that removes all the zeros from a list of numbers but leaves all nonzero elements of the list in the same order.

10. Assume that S is a 20-by-2 array. The first column contains the scores for your football team in the game with your archrival each year for 20 years; the second column contains the score for the other team. Write a program that determines how many times your team won the game, how many times the other team won, and how many times there were ties.

11. Write a program that determines if a particular number X is contained in an array A. If the list is not in order, you will have to search through the entire list to see if you find X. If the list is in order, you can use a binary search. Go to the middle of the list; if the value there is greater than X, then you know that X must be in the first half (if it is there at all). If the value in the middle of the list is less than X, then X could only be in the last half of the list. Once you know which half of the list might contain X, then repeat the process by checking the value in the middle of that half. Keep repeating the process until you either find X or find two adjacent values where one is greater than X and one is less than X.

12. Consider two ordered arrays, A and B, each with n numbers. Write a program that merges A and B to form a new array C that contains all the elements from A and B in numerical order.

13. Assume that A and B are two lists. You are guaranteed that no number appears more than once in list A or list B, but some numbers might be in both lists. Write a program that calculates how many items are contained in both A and B. Then write a program that counts how many items in total are contained in A and B, where items contained in both are only counted once.

14. Write a program that calculates the five term moving average for the elements in A. Store the moving averages in an array B. For $2 < I < (n - 2)$, the elements of B can be found from this formula:

$$B(I) = \frac{A(I - 2) + A(I - 1) + A(I) + A(I + 1) + A(I + 2)}{5}$$

CHAPTER 7

STRINGS

7.1 Operations on Strings

In order for our computer to deal with words, rather than just numbers, we need to be able to handle character strings. Fortunately, Java provides several different methods that can be used to perform manipulations of strings. There are several different kinds of things that you might like to do with strings:

- join two strings together (called concatenation); we have already seen how to do this with the plus sign + (see page 11)

- compare two strings to see which comes first in alphabetical order with the **compareTo** method (we did this on page 62)

- alphabetize an array of strings (we did this on page 62)

- find the length (the number of characters in the string)

- extract selected characters (called a substring) from the middle or ends of a string

- remove blanks (or other specified characters) from a string

- rearrange the order of the characters in the string

- determine whether one string occurs anywhere in another string, and if so, where it occurs (called the **indexOf** method)

- convert a string representing a number to its numerical value

- convert a numerical value to a string

- convert all the characters to upper case

- convert all the characters to lower case

- convert a character to its numerical value used by the computer for storing it (called its ASCII or unicode value)

- convert a unicode value to a character

• change all of one kind of character into another kind

If you only need to work with one character at a time, then you can declare a variable of type **char**. For example,

char x='*';

declares *x* to be a character variable representing an asterisk. Note that single quotation marks are used around a **char** variable, whereas double quotation marks are used around a **String** variable. Most of this chapter will focus on strings, since they are more versatile, but there will be a couple of examples where **char** variables will be useful.

7.2   Concatenation (+) and length

Here are examples of concatenation:

x="Walla";
y="Washington";
System.out.println(x+x+y);

result: `WallaWallaWashington`

System.out.println(x+"␣"+x+"␣"+y);

result: `Walla Walla Washington`

Here are some examples of finding the length of a string:

x="A";
x.**length()** is 1.

x="George";
x.**length()** is 6.

x="␣"; /*string consisting of one blank*/
x.**length()** is 1.

x=""; /*string consisting of no characters*/
x.**length()** is 0.

x=**null**;
x.**length()** generates an error message.

x="Hello.";
y=" How are you?";
(x+y).**length()** is 19 (blank spaces count).

Here is the general form for finding the length of a string:

yourstring.**length()**;

7.3   Substrings

We can find the character at a specific position in a string with the **charAt** method. For example, if x is "ABCDEFGH", then x.**charAt**(3) is the character 'D'. (As with arrays, the first character is treated as position 0.)

Sometimes we will need to extract characters from a specific location in the string. To do this, use the **substring** method. The two-argument version is the most general, because you specify the position of the first character to include (remembering that the first position is numbered 0), then give the first character position *not* to include.

For example, if x="George Washington", then x.**substring**(2,5) results in the string "org", because the characters are numbered like this:

G	e	o	r	g	e		W	a	s	h	i	n	g	t	o	n
0	1	2	3	4	5	6	7	8	9	10	11	12	13	14	15	16

Note that the difference between the two arguments of **substring** gives the number of characters taken (in this example, $5 - 2 = 3$).

Here are other examples using x="George Washington":

- x.**substring**(0,8) results in "George W".

- We can extract George's first name with x.**substring**(0,6), which results in "George".

- If we want to extract the last name, it is even easier because the **substring** function does not require us to give the second argument if we wish to take all of the characters to the end of the string. So, x.**substring**(7) results in "Washington" (that is, start at character position 7, which is W, and take all of the rest of the characters in the string).

Here are still more examples of finding substrings:

- x="Tutankhamen";

  x.**substring**(0,3) results in "Tut".

- x="ABCDEFGHIJK";

  — x.**substring**(3,3) results in nothing.

  — x.**substring**(3,4) results in "D".

  — x.**substring**(3,5) results in "DE".

  — x.**substring**(3,6) results in "DEF".

- x="Computer";

  x.**substring**(3,6) results in "put".

- x="OHIO";

  x.**substring**(1,3) results in "HI".

Sometimes we might need to shorten a string by cutting off all characters after a certain point. We can do that with this program:

```
class truncator {

static int maxlength=10;

public static void main(String args[ ]) {
String x=args[0];
if (x.length()>maxlength)
          {x=x.substring(0,maxlength);}
System.out.println(x);


} /*end main*/
} /*end truncator*/
```

Here are examples of the output:

```
java truncator ABCDEFGHIJKLMNOPQRSTUVWXYZ
ABCDEFGHIJ
java truncator ABCDE
ABCDE
```

7.4   Removing Blanks: trim

Often it is helpful to remove the leading and trailing blanks in a string. Suppose we have defined x as follows:

```
x="␣␣␣␣␣Welcome␣␣␣␣␣␣to␣␣␣␣our␣web␣␣␣page␣␣␣␣";
```

The method **x.trim()** will result in this:

```
"Welcome␣␣␣␣␣␣to␣␣␣␣our␣web␣␣␣page"
```

Note that the blank spaces in the middle are not touched; only the leading and trailing blanks are removed.

We might want to remove all of the blanks in the string; we can write a program to do that:

```
class blankremover {

public static void main(String args[ ]) {
String x=args[0];
String z="";
for (int i=0; i<=(x.length()-1); i++)
{if (!(x.charAt(i)==' ')) {z=z+x.charAt(i);}}
       /*Note: ! means "not."*/
System.out.println(z);
} /*end main*/
} /*end blankremover*/
```

Now if we execute this program with the command line

```
java␣blankremover␣"␣␣␣␣␣Welcome␣␣␣␣␣␣␣to␣␣␣our␣web␣␣␣page␣␣␣␣";
```

the result is:

```
"Welcometoourwebpage";
```

Sometimes we might truly want to remove all of the blanks, as we have done here. However, in this case what we really want is to remove only those blanks that are duplicate blanks. That is, if there is only one blank between two characters, we will leave it; if there is more than one, then we will leave one blank there, regardless of how many blanks the original string contains at that point.

```java
class duplicateblankremover {

public static void main(String args[ ]) {
String x=args[0];
x=x.trim(); /*Remove all leading and trailing blanks.*/
String z=""+x.charAt(0);
for (int i=1; i<=(x.length()-1); i++)
{if ( (!(x.charAt(i)==' ')) | (!(x.charAt(i-1)==' ')) )
            {z=z+x.charAt(i);}}
        /*note: ! means "not"; | means "or."*/
System.out.println(z);
} /*end main*/
} /*end duplicateblankremover*/
```

Now, the output from this revised program is what we want. If we enter the command line

```
java␣duplicateblankremover␣"␣␣␣␣␣Welcome␣␣␣␣␣␣to␣␣␣␣our␣web␣␣␣page␣␣␣␣";
```

we now get our desired result:

```
"Welcome␣to␣our␣web␣page";
```

7.5   Reversing Strings and Palindrome Testing

We can reverse the order of the characters in a string:

```java
class reverser {
/*This program reverses the order of the characters in a string.*/


public static void main(String args[ ]) {
String x=args[0];
int len = x.length()-1;
String z="";
for (int i=0; i<=len; i++)
        {z=z+x.charAt(len-i);}
System.out.println(z);
```

```
} /*end main*/
} /*end reverser*/
```

Here are examples of the output:

```
java reverser "ABCDEF"
FEDCBA
java reverser "1234567"
7654321
java reverser "EREHWON"
NOWHERE
java reverser "ABLE WAS I ERE I SAW ELBA"
ABLE WAS I ERE I SAW ELBA
```

The program doesn't seem to have worked in the last case, because the output is the same as the input. However, upon closer inspection, we see that this is a rare string that is a *palindrome*—that is, it reads the same either backward or forward. We can write a program that checks to see if its input string is a palindrome:

```
class palindromecheck {

public static void main(String args[ ]) {
String x=args[0];
int len = x.length ( ) -1;
boolean ispalindrome=true;
int i=0;
while (i<=len/2 && ispalindrome)
        {if (!(x.charAt(i)==x.charAt(len-i)))
        {ispalindrome=false;}
          i++;
        }
System.out.println("is this a palindrome? "+ispalindrome);
} /*end main*/
} /*end palindromecheck*/
```

Here are samples of the output:

```
java palindromecheck "ABC"
is this a palindrome? false
java palindromecheck "ABBA"
is this a palindrome? true
java palindromecheck "HANNAH"
is this a palindrome? true
java palindromecheck "ABLE WAS I ERE I SAW ELBA"
is this a palindrome? true
java palindromecheck "A MAN A PLAN A CANAL PANAMA"
is this a palindrome? false
java palindromecheck "AMANAPLANACANALPANAMA"
is this a palindrome? true
```

7.6   Finding Strings Within Strings: indexOf

Suppose our computer program reads in a name with the last name first, as in "Washington George". For example, names are often put in this form for alphabetizing. However, we now want to display the name with the first name first. In order to do this, we need a program that can read through the string and determine the location of the blank. Then, it can extract the first and last names using the **substring** function.

In order to find strings within other strings, we use the **indexOf** function. Here are some examples:

- x="ABCDEFGHIJKLMNOPQRSTUVWXYZ";

— x.**indexOf**("A") results in 0 (since the characters in the string are numbered starting with 0).

— x.**indexOf**("J") results in 9.

— x.**indexOf**("5") results in −1, since the character "5" never occurs in the string x.

— x.**indexOf**("Z") results in 25.

- x="ABCDEFGHIJKMNOPQRSTUVWXYZ";

x.**indexOf**("L") results in −1 (there is no L in that string).

- x="Puuanahulu"; /* a town on the island of Hawaii*/

x.**indexOf**("u") results in 1.

The **indexOf** function found only the first occurrence of "u" at position 1. However, sometimes we might want to find all occurrences of a particular string. In this case, there are four occurrences of "u", at positions 1, 2, 7, and 9.

P	u	u	a	n	a	h	u	l	u
0	1	2	3	4	5	6	7	8	9

Fortunately, there is another version of the **indexOf** method that takes two arguments. The second argument tells where in the main string to start looking for the search string. (If the second argument is left out, then the computer automatically starts at the beginning of the main string.)

For example, x.**indexOf**("u",4) will return 7, since that is the position of the first "u" after position 4.

Here is a program that will find all occurrences of the search string in the main string:

```
class findall {

    /*This program finds all occurrences of the string z
      within the string x.*/

public static void main(String args[ ]) {
String x="Puuanahulu";
String z="u";
```

```
System.out.println("finding all occurences of "+z+" in "+x);
int location = x.indexOf(z);
while (location>0) {
        System.out.println(location);
        location = x.indexOf(z,location+1);
} /*end while loop*/
} /*end main*/
} /*end findall*/
```

There also is a **lastIndexOf** method, which is the same as **indexOf** except that it returns the location of the last occurrence of the search string in the main string.

Now to return to our problem of converting "Washington George" into "George Washington". We can use the **indexOf** function to find the location of the first blank in the string; then the **substring** function will be used twice to extract the first and last name. (This will also work if a middle name or initial is included since everything after the first blank will be extracted and put before the last name.) Note that the **trim** function is used to make sure that there are no blanks at the beginning of the string, since that would confuse the whole process.

Here is the program:

```
class namereverser {
/*This program reads in a name with the last name first, followed
  by a blank, followed by the first and possibly a middle name.
  Then, it rearranges the name so the last name is last.*/

public static void main(String args[ ]) {
String x=args[0];
x=x.trim();
int L=x.indexOf(" ")+1;
String z=x.substring(L) + " "+ x.substring(0,(L-1));
System.out.println(z);
} /*end main*/
} /*end namereverser*/
```

Here is an example of the output:

```
java namereverser "Washington George"
George Washington
```

You may think that this program is not too helpful, since it only reads in one name. In practice, this program would be modified so that it reads in a list of names from a file (see Chapter 11).

7.7   Conversion Between Strings and Numbers

Consider these two statements:

```
int x1=1234;
String x2="1234";
```

If we try to display these two variables on the screen, the results will be exactly the same. However, in reality the computer treats them as very different. The integer variable x1 is stored as a binary representation of an integer (filling 4 bytes of memory). Since the variable is a number, you can add, multiply, subtract, divide, or perform other arithmetic operations on it. The string variable x2 is stored as a series of codes: one code for the character "1"; one for the character "2"; and so on. Each character requires two bytes, so overall this variable will require eight bytes (or 64 bits). If we use the plus sign + for a string, the result will be concatenation, not addition. There are times, however, when we need to convert a string into its equivalent numerical form, and vice versa. For example, our program may take input from a dialog box (see Chapter 14). This input is read in as a string; then we need to convert the string to a numerical value to process it. Here are the different methods to use:

- to convert integers to strings:

String *string_variable*=**String.valueOf**(*integer_variable*);

For example, entering the statements

int z=234;
String x=**String.valueOf**(z);

gives the result that x becomes "234".

- to convert strings to integers:

int *integer_variable*=**Integer.parseInt**(*string_variable*);

For example, entering the statements

String x= "234";
int z=**Integer.parseInt**(x);

gives the result that z becomes 234.

- to convert doubles to strings:

String *string_variable*=**String.valueOf**(*double_value*);

For example, entering the statements

double z=234.567;
String x=**String.valueOf**(z);

gives the result that x becomes "234.567".

• to convert strings to doubles:

double *double_variable*=
(**Double.valueOf**(*string_variable*)).**doubleValue();**

For example, entering the statements

String s="234.567";
double z=(**Double.valueOf**(s)).**doubleValue();**

gives the result that z becomes 234.567. (We already used this method on page 35.)

As always with Java, be sure to follow the exact capitalization pattern. You may wonder, "Why is it **Integer** instead of **int**, and why is it **Double** instead of **double**?" The answer to this mystery is on page 133.

7.8 Unicode Values and Encryption

Suppose we need to send a secret message. We can encrypt the message by changing each character to another character according to a rule that only the recipient knows. For example, we can convert each letter into the letter that is seven spaces after it in alphabetical order. If this shifting takes us past Z, then we will shift back to A. We can imagine the letters are all in a circle, as shown in Figure 7–1.

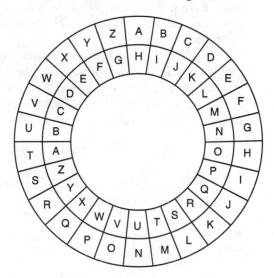

Outer ring: original letter
Inner ring: letter used in encryption

FIGURE 7–1

Although tedious for a person to do, this type of encryption and decryption is easy for a computer. In order to shift the letters, we need access to the numerical codes that the computer uses to store the letters. Traditionally, microcomputers have used a system called ASCII (short for American Standard Code for Information Interchange). The ASCII code assigns each letter (and other characters) a number from 0 to 255. This provides 256 different codes. The number 256 is significant because $2^8 = 256$. This means that each number from 0 to 255 can be stored as a binary number with eight binary digits, or *bits*. A group of 8 bits is called a *byte*. You are likely familiar with the term "byte" and its related terms: kilobyte ($= 2^{10} = 1024$, approximately one thousand bytes); megabyte ($= 2^{20} = 1,048,576$, approximately one million bytes); and gigabyte ($= 2^{30} = 1,073,741,824$, approximately one billion bytes). These units are used to measure the capacity of computer memories and disks.

There is, however, a problem with using ASCII codes: the world is very big, and not everybody uses the same characters. If you would like your program to be useful around the world, you need a way of representing other languages. Fortunately, the designers of Java intended that Java programs would be easy to internationalize. In order to do that, they had to be able to represent characters from languages all over the world. Therefore, Java uses a system of coding characters called *unicode*. This system uses 16 bits (2 bytes) for each character. This means that there are $2^{16} = 65,536$ different possible codes, more than enough to represent most languages. Unfortunately, just because Java is designed to support unicode does not mean you can use all of these characters in your programs. If your local system does not have these characters available, then you will not be able to display them on your screen (nor will World Wide Web users who access your applets, if they don't have the characters available on their systems).

In this book, we will stick with characters in the Latin alphabet used in English and other languages such as Spanish, French, German, Swedish, Italian, and Polish. (However, in many other languages you need accents, so special character codes are needed for accented characters.)

Fortunately, the unicode system is designed so that the codes for all characters in our alphabet are the same as their ASCII codes. (See the web site *http://www.unicode.org* for more about unicode values.)

In order to find the character connected to a particular unicode number, all we need to do is enter this statement:

char *character_variable*=(**char**) *integer_value*

This casts the integer value into the corresponding character value. For example, the statements

int k=65;
char c=(**char**) k;

will cause c to take the value 'A', since 'A' is the character with unicode (and ASCII code) equal to 65.

Here is a program that will display many of these characters, along with their unicode numbers:

class characterlist {

```
public static void main(String args[ ]) {

System.out.println("List of characters and unicodes");

for (int k=32; k<=126; k++) {
                char c=(char) k;
                String c0=k+":"+c+"␣␣␣␣";
                System.out.print(c0);
                if (((k+1)%8)==0) {System.out.println(" ");}
} /*end loop*/
} /*end main*/
} /*end characterlist*/
```

Here is the output:

```
32:       33:!      34:"      35:#      36:$      37:%      38:&      39:'
40:(      41:)      42:*      43:+      44:,      45:-      46:.      47:/
48:0      49:1      50:2      51:3      52:4      53:5      54:6      55:7
56:8      57:9      58::      59:;      60:<      61:=      62:>      63:?
64:@      65:A      66:B      67:C      68:D      69:E      70:F      71:G
72:H      73:I      74:J      75:K      76:L      77:M      78:N      79:O
80:P      81:Q      82:R      83:S      84:T      85:U      86:V      87:W
88:X      89:Y      90:Z      91:[      92:\      93:]      94:^      95:_
96:`      97:a      98:b      99:c      100:d     101:e     102:f     103:g
104:h     105:i     106:j     107:k     108:l     109:m     110:n     111:o
112:p     113:q     114:r     115:s     116:t     117:u     118:v     119:w
120:x     121:y     122:z     123:{     124:|     125:}     126:~
```

Here are some things to note:

• Characters with code numbers below 32 are often special characters. For example, character 8 is backspace; 10 is line feed; 13 is carriage return; 26 is end of file; and 27 is escape.

• Character 32 is a blank.

• Character 58 is a colon.

• Uppercase letters have codes from 65 (A) to 90 (Z).

• Lowercase letters have codes from 97 (a) to 122 (z).

• You can adjust this program on your own computer so that it will print characters with higher numbers; that way, you can see exactly what characters are available for your machine.

Now we return to our problem of encryption. Here's the program:

```
class encrypt1 {


public static void main(String args[ ]) {

short shiftkey=7; /*number of positions to shift each letter*/

String x1="TOPSECRETMESSAGEJAVAISFUN";
```

```
System.out.println("⎵original message:"+x1);
String x2="";

for (int i=0; i<=(x1.length()-1); i++) {
char c=x1.charAt(i);
short k=(short) c;
short k2=(short) (k+shiftkey);
if (k2>90) {k2=(short)(k2-26);}
        /*Note: 90 is the code for Z.*/
char c2=(char) k2;
        x2=x2+c2;

} /*end for loop*/

System.out.println("encrypted message:"+x2);

} /*end main*/
} /*end encrypt1*/
```

Here is the output:

```
original message:TOPSECRETMESSAGEJAVAISFUN
encrypted message:AVWZLJYLATLZZHNLQHCHPZMBU
```

Now we need a way to decrypt this message. We could write a new program that looks about the same as the original program, except that it subtracts 7 from the character's code, instead of adding as our encryption program does. However, you should be thinking, "We shouldn't have to go through all the work of rewriting a program that is almost the same. Isn't there a way of modifying that code so it works for both encryption and decryption?"

If you are thinking like that, then this is a good sign — it means you are beginning to think like a computer programmer looking for efficient ways to have the computer do work for you. We will see how this can be done in the next chapter (page 105, Exercise 6).

Another problem with this encryption program is that it would be very easy for spies to crack the code. All they would have to do would be to try all possible keys until they stumbled upon a message instead of random characters. The problem is that all letters were shifted by the same number (7); there are only 26 possibilities for the key in this case. A better approach to encryption would be to shift different letters differently, according to a longer key (see page 84, Exercise 6).

Another useful thing we can do with the unicodes for each character is to convert from uppercase to lowercase, or vice versa. Notice on page 81 how the code for each lowercase letter is always 32 more than the code for the corresponding uppercase letter. Therefore, to convert a lowercase letter to uppercase, all we need to do is find its code, subtract 32, and then convert back to a character. However, since this is a common problem, the designers of Java have already built in a command for doing this. The expression x2=x.**toUpperCase()** will cause *x2* to be a string that is the same as *x* except that all of the lowercase letters are changed to uppercase. If you need to go the other direction, the expression x2=x.**toLowerCase()** will cause *x2* to be a string that is the same as *x* except that all of the uppercase letters are changed to lowercase.

Characters that are not letters are not changed by **toUpperCase()** or **toLowerCase()**.

Here is an example program:

```
class string13 {

public static void main(String args[ ]) {

String x="abcdefghijklmnopqrstuvwxyz0123456789";
System.out.println("␣original:"+x);
String x2=x.toUpperCase();
System.out.println("uppercase:"+x2);
String x3=x2.toLowerCase();
System.out.println("lowercase:"+x3);
System.out.println("␣");
String x4="What's new? New York, New Jersey, New Mexico";
System.out.println("␣original:"+x4);
String x5=x4.toUpperCase();
System.out.println("uppercase:"+x5);
String x6=x4.toLowerCase();
System.out.println("lowercase:"+x6);

} /*end main*/
} /*end string13*/
```

Here is the output:

```
 original:abcdefghijklmnopqrstuvwxyz0123456789
uppercase:ABCDEFGHIJKLMNOPQRSTUVWXYZ0123456789
lowercase:abcdefghijklmnopqrstuvwxyz0123456789

 original:What's new? New York, New Jersey, New Mexico
uppercase:WHAT'S NEW? NEW YORK, NEW JERSEY, NEW MEXICO
lowercase:what's new? new york, new jersey, new mexico
```

That's all about strings for now.

Notes

Following are some other useful string methods:

- x.**equals**(y) will be true if x and y are two strings that are the same.

- x.**equalsIgnoreCase**(y) will be true if x and y have the same characters; it will treat 'a' and 'A', etc., as if they are the same.

- x.**endsWith**(y) will be true if the last characters in string x match string y.

- x.**startsWith**(y) will be true if the first characters in string x match string y.

EXERCISES

1. Write a program that reads in a string and a number n and then creates a string consisting of that original string repeated n times.

2. Write a program that reads in a number and creates a string consisting of a dollar sign followed by that number.

3. Write a program that reads in a sentence and then counts how many times each letter appears.

4. Write a program that reads in a sentence and checks to make sure that every q is followed by a u.

5. Write a program that reads in a sentence and checks to make sure that the rule "i before e except after c" is followed.

6. Write a program that encrypts a string according to a 5-letter key. For example, if the key is "CDEYZ", then the first letter of the original string will be shifted by 3; the second letter will be shifted by 4; the third by 5; the fourth by 25; and the fifth by 26. When you reach the sixth letter, start over again at the beginning of the key and shift the letter by 3. Keep repeating this process of cycling through the key until you have encrypted all of the letters of the string. In order to make your encryption more secure, you can also revise the program to use a longer key.

CHAPTER 8

METHODS

8.1   Methods for Common Tasks: Rounding Numbers

One common problem that we have faced so far is the need to round numbers to the appropriate number of decimal places before displaying them. We have already used methods for rounding numbers to a specified number of decimal places (see page 16). (The text class in Java also provides methods for formatting the appearance of numbers; see the web site at

http://www.javasoft.com/products/jdk/1.1/docs/api/java.text.DecimalFormat.html

for more information. These methods will be particularly helpful if you will be adapting your program to run in more than one country. However, the methods that we will develop in this chapter will be more convenient to use for our purposes.)

Instead of writing a new chunk of code whenever we change the number of decimal places to round to, it would help to prepare a general function that would allow us to specify the number of decimal places to use. This sounds like a function that we will be using a lot. You should by now have an aversion to repetitive work, so you should be thinking, "If we need to use the same code over again, there should be a way to enter it only once while still reusing it whenever we need it." In fact, this illustrates one key word that underlies the philosophy of Java: *reusability*.

We can create a block of code called a *method*, which can be called for whenever we need it.

We have already seen some methods. Each Java application has a method called **main**, which is executed when the application begins. Each Java applet usually has some special methods, such as the **paint** method. We have already used the *r2*, *r3*, and *r4* rounding methods.

Here is our first attempt at a program with a method to round numbers to a specified number of decimal places:

```
class numberformattest {

/*Here is the code defining the method called nf. The return type is
    double; it uses two parameters: a double value x and an integer value
    dp.*/

/*method*/ static double nf(double x, int dp) {
/*nf stands for number format; dp stands for decimal places.*/

double k=Math.pow(10,dp); /*calculate power*/
double z=((double)(Math.round(x*k)))/k;
return z;
} /*end nf method*/


public static void main(String args[ ]) {

double y=2.0/7.0;

for (int dp=1; dp<=6; dp++) {
        /*The method is called in the next line with the
          expression nf(y,dp).*/
        System.out.println("dp:"+dp+"⎵⎵⎵"+nf(y,dp));
} /*end for loop*/
} /*end main*/
} /*end numberformattest*/
```

We put the comment /*method*/ at the start of the method definition, but this is not necessary. Sometimes you specify modifiers for the method; in our case, there is only one modifier: **static**. The significance of this will be explained on page 124. A method must always specify the type of its return value; in our case, this is **double**. (If there is no value returned, then you write **void**.) After the return type you must give the method name. Our method is called nf, short for number format. After the method name you need to put the parameter list, enclosed by parentheses. The parameter list must specify the type and name of each parameter used by the method. In our case, we have two parameters: *x*, the number to be rounded, which is of type **double**; and *dp*, the number of decimal places, which is of type **int**. If the method needs no parameters, then you need to enclose an empty pair of parentheses () after the method name.

After the parameter list, you begin the action statements of the method. As you can probably guess by now, this block of code begins with a left brace { and ends with a right brace }. In this book, we will include a comment to mark the end of the method. If the method is to return a value, then before the end of the method you need to put the word **return**, followed by an expression representing the value to be returned (in this case, the variable z).

To use the method elsewhere in the program, you simply give the name of the method, followed by a list of values to use for the parameters (enclosed by parentheses and separated by commas). The values that the method will use are called the *arguments*. (An alternative terminology is to call the names used in the method definition the *formal parameters*, and the values given the method when it is executed the *actual parameters*.)

The **main** method in our program "calls" for the nf method, so we can say it is the calling method. In order to be executed, every method in an application program needs to be called by another method. (You may wonder about that last statement, because if this is true how would the **main** method ever be called? The answer is this: the **main** method is an exception; it will be called automatically when the program starts. Applets are slightly different, because they have some methods that are called automatically [**init** and **paint**, for example]. Also, we will later see how some methods can be called by events such as mouse clicks.) In our program, the method nf is called by the expression nf(*y,dp*), which is in the middle of the **System.out.println** statement in the **for** loop in the **main** method.

8.2 Method Parameters

The names used for the arguments when the method is called (nf(*y,dp*) in our example) may or may not be the same as the names used in the method declaration parameter list. For our example, the argument list in the declaration uses the names *x* and *dp*. The order is very important, because the computer will match up the arguments in order. In this case, the computer will take the value of *y* from the calling program and use this value whenever it runs into an *x* in the method's code. Likewise, it will take the value of *dp* in the calling program and use this value whenever it runs into the variable *dp* in the method's code.

The following diagram illustrates the process. The calling method calculates values for the variables *y* and *dp*. When it calls the function nf, it passes along these values of the arguments. When the nf method is executed, it will use the value 2.0/7.0 in place of *x* and the value 1 in the place of *dp*. Then it calculates the value of *z* and returns it to the calling method, which will then use that value in place of the original nf expression. In this case, all the calling method needs to do with the return value is display it using **System.out.println**. In other cases you may wish to assign the return value to another variable.

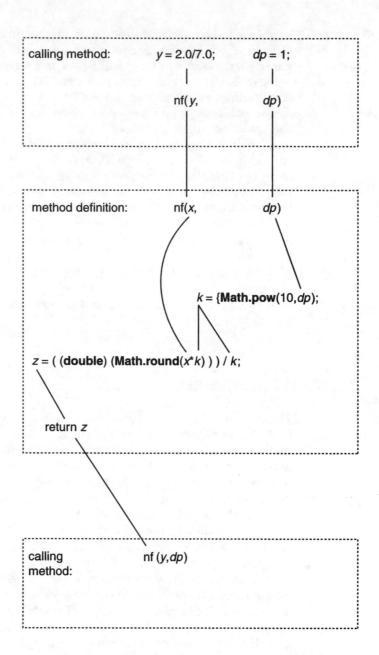

FIGURE 8–1

It is important that we have the ability to use a different name when the method is called. It would be terribly restrictive if we could only use our rounding method with a variable named *x* just because *x* was used in the method definition. We will want to use this method with lots of different variables; we obviously don't know in advance what are all the possible variables for which we would like to use our method.

On the other hand, it would be bad if there were some rule preventing us from using the same name in the calling method and the method definition. In our case, *dp* is a sensible abbreviation for decimal places in both methods.

Our rounding program (page 86) generates this output:

```
dp:1    0.3
dp:2    0.29
dp:3    0.286
dp:4    0.2857
dp:5    0.28571
dp:6    0.285714
```

The **main** method of this program doesn't do anything interesting; all it does is provide a way of showing how the nf method works. The **for** loop calls the nf function several times. Each time the first parameter is the fraction 2.0/7.0; the number of decimal places changes each time.

8.3   General Form: Method Declaration

Here is the general form for a method declaration:

/*method*/ *optional_modifiers return_type method_name*
(*parameter_list*) {
action_statements
return *expression_to_return*
} /*end *method_name**/

You may leave out the opening and closing comments; as always, the computer doesn't pay any attention to the comments.

The *optional_modifiers* can include the following words: **static** (see page 124), **public** (see page 96), **private** (see page 131), **protected** (see page 131), **final** (see page 131), or **abstract** (see page 120).

The *return_type* can be a Java type, such as **int**, **double**, or **String**, or it may be another type that you create. If the method will not return a value, then you must put the word **void**, and leave out the **return** statement.

The *parameter_list* consists of one or more items of the form *parameter_type parameter_name*. If there is more than one parameter, they are separated by commas. If there are no parameters, you need to include an empty pair of parentheses ().

If the method does return a value, then it must include a **return** statement (usually at the end), which gives an expression to return (which must be of the type listed as the *return_type*.)

Any variable declared within a method is *local* to that method; that is, it can only be used in that method. This also applies to the argument list. In our example, *x*, *dp*, *k*, and *z* are all local to the method nf. This means that we cannot use these variables outside the method; the computer won't recognize them. However, we can declare a separate variable with the same name outside the method. In our program, *dp* is declared both as a local variable inside the nf method and as a different variable inside the **for** loop of the **main** method. It is very fortunate that we can reuse a name in this way. When we start writing long programs later on, we may well want to use the same name for different things, which we can do as long as the names are declared in different blocks. Java treats every pair of braces { } as a block; any variable declared inside a pair of braces can only be used inside those braces. Another thing that can happen when writing long programs is that we might accidentally use the same name twice; again, it is fortunate that we can do that as long as the names are declared in different blocks.

8.4 Rounding Numbers: Improved Version

Our method from page 86 is not very satisfactory as a means of formatting numbers. There are two deficiencies. If we try to format a number such as 0.25 with three decimal places, the result will still be 0.25; instead, we would want it to be 0.250. Also, you might recall our problem with columns of numbers not lining up (see page 50, for example). In order to solve this problem, we need to be able to specify the number of characters that the number will take up (called the *field width*). We would also like our method to right justify all numbers. This means it might need to insert blanks in front of a number. Since these blanks are characters, not numeric digits, it means that the result of our method will be a **String**, rather than a number.

Here is our new version of the program:

```
class numberformat1 {

/*method*/ static String nf(double x, int fw, int dp) {
/*nf stands for number format; fw stands for field width; dp stands for
   decimal places; x is the number to be formatted.*/

double k=Math.pow(10,dp);
double z=((double)(Math.round(x*k)))/k;
String z2=String.valueOf(z);
int len=z2.length( );
int dploc=z2.indexOf(".");
if (dp>0) {
if (!((len-dploc-1)==dp)) {
String zerostring="000000000000000000000000000000000";
z2=z2+zerostring.substring(0,(dploc+dp+1-len));
        }
len=z2.length();
} /*end if dp>0*/
else {z2=z2.substring(0,dploc);
                 len=z2.length();}
if (len<fw) {
String blankstring="                                   ";
z2=blankstring.substring(0,(fw-len))+z2;
}


return z2;
} /*end nf method*/


public static void main(String args[ ]) {
```

```
double y=10.234;

for (int fw=5; fw<=8; fw++) {
System.out.println("␣");
for (int dp=0; dp<=3; dp++) {
System.out.println("dp:"+dp+"␣␣␣fw:"+fw+"␣␣␣<"+nf(y,fw,dp)+">");
        } /*end dp for loop*/
} /*end fw for loop*/
} /*end main*/
} /*end numberformat1*/
```

Note that our nf function now has three parameters: *x*, the **double** value to be rounded; *fw*, the field width; and *dp*, the number of decimal places.

Here is the result of this test:

```
dp:0    fw:5    <    10>
dp:1    fw:5    < 10.2>
dp:2    fw:5    <10.23>
dp:3    fw:5    <10.234>

dp:0    fw:6    <    10>
dp:1    fw:6    <  10.2>
dp:2    fw:6    < 10.23>
dp:3    fw:6    <10.234>

dp:0    fw:7    <     10>
dp:1    fw:7    <   10.2>
dp:2    fw:7    <  10.23>
dp:3    fw:7    < 10.234>

dp:0    fw:8    <      10>
dp:1    fw:8    <    10.2>
dp:2    fw:8    <   10.23>
dp:3    fw:8    <  10.234>
```

The < and > symbols are included only to show you exactly where each string starts and stops.

8.5 Inserting Commas and Other Strings

If we are dealing with big numbers, then it would be very helpful to be able to insert commas after every three digits. We can write a new method to do that. However, before we do that, you should begin thinking like this: "This method will require us to insert a string at a particular place in another string. This sounds like a common problem that we might use elsewhere, so let's create a method to do that."

Here is a simple program demonstrating our new insertstring method:

```
class insertexample {

/*method*/ static String insertstring(String x, String y,
int pos) {
/*This method inserts string y into string x starting at position pos.*/
String z=x.substring(0,pos)+y+x.substring(pos);
return z;
} /*end insertstring method*/


public static void main(String args[ ]) {
String x1="ABCDEFGHIJKLMNOP";
String x2="insert";
for (int i=1; i<=8; i++) {
String z= insertstring(x1,x2,i);
System.out.println(i+" "+z);
} /*end for loop*/
} /*end main*/
} /*end insertexample*/
```

Here is the output:

```
1   AinsertBCDEFGHIJKLMNOP
2   ABinsertCDEFGHIJKLMNOP
3   ABCinsertDEFGHIJKLMNOP
4   ABCDinsertEFGHIJKLMNOP
5   ABCDEinsertFGHIJKLMNOP
6   ABCDEFinsertGHIJKLMNOP
7   ABCDEFGinsertHIJKLMNOP
8   ABCDEFGHinsertIJKLMNOP
```

Now we can write our comma insertion method, which we will call cf, short for comma format. It will call both the nf method and the insertstring method.

```
class numberformat2 {

/*method*/ static String nf(double x, int fw, int dp) {
/*nf stands for number format; fw stands for field width; dp stands for
    decimal places.*/

double k=Math.pow(10,dp);
double z=((double)(Math.round(x*k)))/k;
String z2=String.valueOf(z); /*convert double to string*/
int len=z2.length();
int dploc=z2.indexOf(".");

if (dp>0) {
if (!((len-dploc-1)==dp)) {
String zerostring="000000000000000000000000000000000000";
z2=z2+zerostring.substring(0,(dploc+dp+1-len));
        }
len=z2.length();
} /*end if dp>0*/
```

```
else {z2=z2.substring(0,dploc);
                  len=z2.length();}
if (len<fw) {
String
blankstring="_____";/*****<<<*/
z2=blankstring.substring(0,(fw-len))+z2;
}
return z2;
} /*end nf method*/


/*method*/ static String insertstring(String x, String y,
int pos) {
/*This method inserts string y into string x starting at position pos.*/
String z=x.substring(0,pos)+y+x.substring(pos);
return z;
} /*end insertstring method*/


/*method*/ static String cf(double x, int fw, int dp) {
/*cf stands for comma format.*/
String z2=nf(x,fw,dp);
z2=" "+z2;
int dploc=z2.indexOf(".");
int commapos=dploc-3;
while (!(z2.charAt(commapos-1)==' ')) {
z2=insertstring(z2,",",commapos);
commapos-=3; /*Subtract 3 from previous value of commapos.*/
} /*end while*/
z2=z2.trim();
int len=z2.length();
if (len<fw) {
String blankstring="_____";
z2=blankstring.substring(0,(fw-len))+z2;
                         }
return z2;
} /*end comma format*/

public static void main(String args[ ]) {

double x=1;
for (int i=2; i<=8; i++) {
System.out.println("<"+cf(x,14,2)+">");
x=10*x+i;
        } /*end for loop*/
} /*end main*/
} /*end numberformat1*/
```

Here are the results:

```
<         1.00>
<        12.00>
<       123.00>
<     1,234.00>
<    12,345.00>
<   123,456.00>
```

< 1,234,567.00>

8.6 Making Methods Available in Public Classes

These methods seem like they will be so useful that we will want to have them available in other programs we do. One option would be to copy the source code into the other programs we write. However, in addition to being cumbersome, this plan has a serious flaw: what happens if we later decide to improve one of these methods? Then we would have to go back and change the source code of every program that includes it. There must be a better way. The key idea here is to think of programs as built up of components that can be reused. The way that reusable components work in Java will be discussed many times more in this book. For our purpose at the moment, we will collect our useful methods in a separate class. We will call this class cpj (an abbreviation for computer programming in Java).

Here is the source code for this class:

```
public class cpj {

/*This class contains methods that will be useful for other programs in this
    book. The abbreviation cpj is short for computer programming in Java.*/

/*method*/ public static String nf(double x,
        int fw, int dp) {
/*nf stands for number format; fw stands for field width;
    dp stands for decimal places.*/

double k=Math.pow(10,dp);
double z=((double)(Math.round(x*k)))/k;
String z2=String.valueOf(z);
int len=z2.length();
int dploc=z2.indexOf(".");
if (dp>0) {
if (!((len-dploc-1)==dp)) {
String zerostring="00000000000000000000000000000000000";
z2=z2+zerostring.substring(0,(dploc+dp+1-len));
        }
len=z2.length();
} /*end if dp>0*/
else {z2=z2.substring(0,dploc);
                len=z2.length();}
if (len<fw) {
String blankstring="�...................................................."; /*<<<*/
z2=blankstring.substring(0,(fw-len))+z2;
}
return z2;
} /*end nf method*/

/*method*/ public static String insertstring(String x, String y,
int pos) {
/*This method inserts string y into string x starting at position pos.*/
```

```
String z=x.substring(0,pos)+y+x.substring(pos);
return z;
} /*end insertstring method*/

/*method*/ static String cf(double x, int fw, int dp) {
/*cf stands for comma format.*/
/*fw stands for field width, dp stands for number of decimal places.*/
String z2=nf(x,fw,dp);
z2=" "+z2;
int dploc=z2.indexOf(".");
int commapos=dploc-3;
if (dploc<0) {commapos=(z2.length()-3);}
while (!(z2.charAt(commapos-1)==' ')) {
z2=insertstring(z2,",",commapos);
commapos-=3;
} /*end while*/
z2=z2.trim();
int len=z2.length();
if (len<fw) {
String blankstring="                                              ";
z2=blankstring.substring(0,(fw-len))+z2;
                               }
return z2;

} /*end comma format*/


/*method*/ public static String cf(int x, int fw) {
/*cf stands for comma format. This method works for integers.*/
/*fw stands for field width.*/
String z2=String.valueOf(x);
z2=" "+z2;
int commapos=(z2.length()-3);
while (!(z2.charAt(commapos-1)==' ')) {
z2=insertstring(z2,",",commapos);
commapos-=3;
} /*end while*/
z2=z2.trim();
int len=z2.length();
if (len<fw) {
String blankstring="                                              ";
z2=blankstring.substring(0,(fw-len))+z2;
                               }
return z2;

} /*end comma format*/

/*method*/ public static String dupblankrem(String x) {
/*Every place there are consecutive blanks, this method will convert
   those into a single blank.*/
x=x.trim(); /*Remove all leading and trailing blanks.*/
String z=""+x.charAt(0);
for (int i=1; i<=(x.length()-1); i++)
```

```
{if ( (!(x.charAt(i)==' ')) | (!(x.charAt(i-1)==' ')) )
          {z=z+x.charAt(i);}}
    /*Note: ! means "not"; | means "or".*/
return z;
} /*end dupblankrem*/

/*method*/ public static String replacestring
(String x, String a, String b) {
/*This method looks through the string x, finding all occurrences of the
    string a and changing them to b.*/
String x2=x;
String z="";
int alen=a.length();
int L=x2.indexOf(a);
while (L>=0) {
z+=x2.substring(0,L)+b;
x2=x2.substring(L+alen);
L=x2.indexOf(a);
} /*end while loop*/
z+=x2;
return z;
} /*end replacestring*/

/*method*/ public static String blanks(int n) {
/*This method returns a string of blanks of length n.*/
String
blankstring="ⓤⓤⓤⓤⓤⓤⓤⓤⓤⓤⓤⓤⓤⓤⓤⓤⓤⓤⓤⓤⓤⓤⓤⓤⓤⓤⓤⓤⓤⓤⓤⓤⓤⓤⓤⓤⓤⓤⓤⓤⓤⓤⓤⓤⓤⓤⓤⓤⓤ";
String z="";
if ((n>0)&(n<blankstring.length())) {z=blankstring.substring(0,n);}
return z;
} /*end blanks*/

} /*end cpj*/
```

One thing you may notice about this class is that it has no **main** method, so you should be thinking, "We can't run this program." That's right; if you compile this program to create cpj.class and then try java cpj, you will get an error message saying that the main method is not defined. However, that's not a problem, because we don't intend for this class to run on its own. Its only purpose is to contain methods available to other programs. Note that the word **public** now appears in front of the class name. This word means that this class is publicly available; that is, other classes can use the methods and data it contains. (To make it accessible, you can either copy the file cpj.class to the directory where your program is; or copy the file to the directory where the standard Java class files are; or include the class in a package and then import it (see page 133).

Any other program can use our nf method by writing it like this:

cpj.nf(x,fw,dp)

Note that the name of the class is given before the method name; they are separated by a period. We'll see how we can use this method in the next section.

8.7 Methods for Playing Cards: Factorial, Combinations, and Probabilities

We'll now turn to playing cards. We want to find out how many ways there are of shuffling a deck of 52 cards. There are 52 choices for the first card, but then there are only 51 choices left for the second card. We need to multiply these two numbers together to find that there are $52 * 51 = 2,652$ ways of choosing the first two cards in the deck. To find the total number of choices, we need to keep multiplying all of the numbers all the way down to 1. (After we have chosen the first 51 cards, there is only 1 choice left for the final card in the deck.) Therefore, the total number of ways of shuffling 52 cards is

$$52 \times 51 \times 50 \times 49 \times 48 \times \ldots \times 3 \times 2 \times 1$$

This works out to be a very big number, about 8.07×10^{67}. In general, if there are n cards in the deck, the number of ways of placing the cards in different orders is given by the product of all of the whole numbers from n down to 1. This quantity is important enough to be given a special name: it's called the *factorial* of n (symbolized by an exclamation mark):

$$n! = n \times (n-1) \times (n-2) \times (n-3) \times \ldots \times 3 \times 2 \times 1$$

We can write a method to calculate the factorial function. This is fairly simple, since all the method needs to do is loop from 1 to n and multiply all of the numbers.

```
class factorialcalc {

/*method*/ static double factorial(double n) {
double z=1;
for (double i=1; i<=n; i++) {z=z*i;}
return z;
} /*end factorial*/

public static void main(String args[ ]) {

for (double i=0; i<=20; i++) {
        System.out.println(i+"␣␣␣"+factorial(i));
        } /*end for loop*/
} /*end main*/
} /*end factorialcalc*/
```

Here is the output:

```
0.0    1.0
1.0    1.0
2.0    2.0
3.0    6.0
4.0    24.0
5.0    120.0
6.0    720.0
7.0    5040.0
```

```
8.0    40320.0
9.0    362880.0
10.0   3628800.0
11.0   3.99168E7
12.0   4.790016E8
13.0   6.2270208E9
14.0   8.71782912E10
15.0   1.307674368E12
16.0   2.0922789888E13
17.0   3.55687428096E14
18.0   6.402373705728E15
19.0   1.21645100408832E17
20.0   2.43290200817664E18
```

The numbers become so big that they are expressed in exponential notation. For example, 11! is represented as $3.99168E7$, which means 3.99168×10^7 (about 39,916,800).

The value of the factorial function is actually an integer, but we need to declare it as a **double** because the numbers become too big for the integer class (or even the long class).

Suppose we are dealt a hand of five cards. We would like to know how many possible hands there are. We can find this using the factorial function:

$$\text{number of 5-card hands from 52-card deck: } \frac{52!}{5!47!}$$

In general, the number of hands with j cards that can be dealt from a deck of n cards is given by the following formula:

$$\frac{n!}{j!(n-j)!} \text{ , represented by } \binom{n}{j}$$

This is called the number of *combinations* of n things taken j at a time.

Now you can see how valuable methods can be; since we have already written a factorial method, we can call it three times in a combinations method.

```
class cardcombinations2 {

/*method*/ static double factorial(double n) {
double z=1;
for (double i=1; i<=n; i++) {z=z*i;}
return z;
} /*end factorial*/

/*method*/ static double combinations(double n, double j) {
double z=factorial(n)/(factorial(j)*factorial(n-j));
return z;
} /*end combinations*/


public static void main(String args[ ]) {

System.out.println("Cards␣␣␣␣Number");
```

```
System.out.println("in hand of hands");
for (double i=0; i<=5; i++) {
System.out.println(cpj.cf(i,4,0)+cpj.cf(combinations(52,i),12,0));
} /*end for loop*/
} /*end main*/
} /*end cardcombinations2*/
```

Here is the output:

```
Cards    Number
in hand  of hands
   0            1
   1           52
   2        1,326
   3       22,100
   4      270,725
   5    2,598,960
```

The number of 5-card hands is over two and a half million (2,598,960).

Now, suppose you draw 10 cards at random from a deck of 52 cards, and you would like to know the probability that you will draw 4 hearts.

Here is the formula:

$$\frac{\dbinom{13}{4}\dbinom{39}{6}}{\dbinom{52}{10}}$$

In general, we can write the formula like this:

$$\frac{\dbinom{M_{\mathrm{pop}}}{m_{\mathrm{samp}}}\dbinom{N_{\mathrm{pop}} - M_{\mathrm{pop}}}{n_{\mathrm{samp}} - m_{\mathrm{samp}}}}{\dbinom{N_{\mathrm{pop}}}{n_{\mathrm{samp}}}}$$

In the formula, $N_{\mathrm{pop}} = 52$ is the number of cards in the entire hand (called the *population*); $M_{\mathrm{pop}} = 13$ is the number of hearts in the population; $n_{\mathrm{samp}} = 10$ is the number of cards in the hand (called the *sample*); and $m_{\mathrm{samp}} = 4$ is the number of hearts in the sample. This formula is called the *hypergeometric distribution*. It uses the combinations formula three times, so when we write a program to calculate it, we will call the **combinations** method. Once we've written the program, we may as well use it for all values of m_{samp} from 0 to 10, instead of just 4.

Here's the program:

```
class cardprobabilities {

/*method*/ static double factorial(double n) {
double z=1;
for (double i=1; i<=n; i++) {z=z*i;}
return z;
} /*end factorial*/
```

```
/*method*/ static double combinations(double n, double j) {
double z= factorial(n)/(factorial(j)*factorial(n-j));
return z;
} /*end combinations*/

/*method*/ static double hypergdist(
double npop, double nsamp, double mpop, double msamp) {
double z=
combinations(mpop,msamp)*
        combinations((npop-mpop),(nsamp-msamp))/
        combinations(npop,nsamp);
return z;


} /*end hypergdist*/


public static void main(String args[ ]) {
double totalprob=0;
System.out.println("⎵Hearts⎵⎵⎵Probability");
for (double i=0; i<=10; i++) {
double prob=hypergdist(52.0,10.0,13.0,i);
        totalprob+=prob;
System.out.println(cpj.nf(i,6,0)+cpj.nf(prob,12,5));
}
System.out.println("Total probability:"+cpj.nf(totalprob,12,5));
} /*end main*/
} /*end cardprobabilities*/
```

The **main** method calls the hypergdist method, which calls the combinations method, which calls the factorial method. You can see how the pattern of methods-calling-methods can become complicated. However, writing the program is not that complicated, because each method is reasonably simple, and the methods can be written independently. That means you don't have to think about how the hypergdist method or the number format method will work while you're writing the factorial method. It is much easier on you as a programmer when you have fewer things you need to think about at once.

Here is the output:

```
Hearts    Probability
    0       0.0402
    1       0.1741
    2       0.3033
    3       0.2781
    4       0.1475
    5       0.0468
    6       0.0089
    7       0.0010
    8       1.0E-4
    9       0.0000
   10       0.0000
Total probability:     1.0000
```

8.8   Recursion

Ten people are going on a trip and need to be divided up into roommate pairs. You would like to check all of the possible ways of forming roommates before you decide which way is best. The general question is this: How many different ways are there of dividing n people into roommate pairs (assuming that n is an even number)?

We can reason like this: There are $n - 1 = 9$ choices for your roommate. After your roommate has been chosen, you need to figure out how many ways there are of arranging the remaining $n - 2 = 8$ people into roommates. That problem sounds familiar: it is the same as our original problem, except with a smaller value of n. When we write a program to solve the original problem, we should be able to take advantage of the fact that it can be solved by referring to a simpler version of the same problem. Our rule to solve the problem goes like this:

$$\text{roommate}(n) = (n - 1) \times \text{roommate}(n - 2)$$

In this rule, roommate(n) is the number of ways of arranging n people into roommates.

Here is the way the procedure works for $n = 10$:

- roommate(10) = 9 × roommate(8)

- roommate(8) = 7 × roommate(6)

- roommate(6) = 5 × roommate(4)

- roommate(4) = 3 × roommate(2)

Of course, we cannot keep going like this forever. Fortunately, by the time we need to calculate roommate(2), we can use a simple rule:

$$\text{roommate}(2) = 1$$

This is because there is only one way to arrange two people into roommates. Therefore, our rule for calculating the number of roommate arrangements looks like this:

if $(n > 2)$ then roommate$(n) = (n - 1) *$ roommate$(n - 2)$
else roommate$(2) = 1$

Here is a program to perform the calculations:

```
class rcalc {

/*method*/ static double roommate(double n) {
/*This method calculates the number of ways of arranging n people
  into roommates.*/
if (n==2.0) {return 1;}
else {return (n-1)*roommate(n-2);}
/*In the previous line, the roommate method calls itself.*/
} /*end rcalc*/


public static void main(String args[ ]) {
```

```
for (double n=2; n<=40; n+=2) {
System.out.println("n="+n+"␣roommates="+roommate(n));
} /*end for loop*/
} /*end main*/
} /*end rcalc*/
```

The result for roommate(10) equals 945.

What makes the method roommate different from any method we have done so far is that it calls itself. When a method calls itself, it is called *recursion*. This is a general technique for solving a problem that can be broken down into smaller versions of the same problem. Whenever you use recursion, be sure that the method also provides a nonrecursive process for some cases. Otherwise, the method will keep calling itself forever and will never complete the calculation. (For our example, if $n = 2$, then the method does not use recursion; it simply returns the result that roommate(2) = 1.)

For another example, consider the factorial function (page 97). We could define the function like this: to find the factorial of a number n, multiply n by the factorial of $n - 1$. We could write a method like this:

```
/*method*/ double factorial(int n) {
return n*factorial(n-1);}
```

If we try to use this method to find the factorial of 4, this is what will happen:

1. To find factorial(4), the computer will calculate 4 * factorial(3). So, it calls the factorial method again to find factorial(3).

2. To find factorial(3), the computer will calculate 3 * factorial(2). So, it calls the factorial method again to find factorial(2).

3. To find factorial(2), the computer will calculate 2 * factorial(1). So, it calls the factorial method again to find factorial(1).

4. To find factorial(1), the computer will calculate 1 * factorial(0). So, it calls the factorial method again to find factorial(0), which is 1.

Here's an example of a program that calculates the factorial function by using recursion.

```
class factorialrecursion {

/*method*/ static double factorial(double n) {
/*This program calculates the factorial of n by using recursion.*/
if (n<=0) {return 1;}
            else {return n*factorial(n-1);}
} /*end factorial*/

public static void main(String args[ ]) {

for(double i=1; i<=10; i++) {
System.out.println(""+i+"␣␣␣"+factorial(i));
        } /*end for loop*/
```

```
} /*end main*/
} /*end factorialrecursion*/
```

Note: The fact that the program contains the line

if (n<=0) {**return** 1;}

does not mean that the factorial function is defined for negative values. However, if you wrote the line like this:

if (n==0) {**return** 1;}

the program runs the risk of being trapped in an infinite loop if a negative or fractional value is given as the input to the factorial method. One useful addition you could add to this method would be to have it display an error message if a negative or fractional value was entered as the input. In general, when you are designing programs that other people will use, you need to think about ways of protecting the program from inappropriate input.

Here is the output of the factorial program:

```
1.0    1.0
2.0    2.0
3.0    6.0
4.0    24.0
5.0    120.0
6.0    720.0
7.0    5040.0
8.0    40320.0
9.0    362880.0
10.0   3628800.0
```

We did not need recursion to solve the factorial problem, since we previously found a way to solve the problem with a loop. Although the factorial method that uses recursion contains more elegant, concise code than the **for** loop version, it does have the disadvantage of using more computer memory.

Here is another example. Suppose we will toss *numdice* dice, and we want to know the number of ways of rolling the dice such that the sum equals a particular value *dicesum*. If there is only one die, then there is only one way (provided that *dicesum* is between 1 and 6; otherwise, there are zero ways). For two or more dice, we can use this recursive rule:

The number of ways of rolling *dicesum* on *numdice* dice equals:

- number of ways of rolling 1 on first die and *dicesum* − 1 on remaining *numdice* − 1 dice

- plus number of ways of rolling 2 on first die and *dicesum* − 2 on remaining *numdice* − 1 dice

- plus number of ways of rolling 3 on first die and *dicesum* − 3 on remaining *numdice* − 1 dice

- plus number of ways of rolling 4 on first die and *dicesum* − 4 on remaining *numdice* − 1 dice

- plus number of ways of rolling 5 on first die and *dicesum* − 5 on remaining *numdice* − 1 dice

- plus number of ways of rolling 6 on first die and *dicesum* − 6 on remaining *numdice* − 1 dice

Here's a program that performs this calculation:

```
class dice {

/*method*/ static double dicecalc(double numdice, double dicesum) {
/*This method calculates the number of ways of rolling numdice dice
   such that the sum is equal to dicesum.*/

if (numdice==1) {
        if ((dicesum>=1) && (dicesum<=6)) {return 1.0;}
                else {return 0.0;}
} /*end if numdice==1*/

else {
double z=0;
for (double i=1; i<=6; i++) {
            z+=dicecalc(numdice-1, dicesum-i);
/*The previous line contains the recursion.*/
            }
        return z;
} /*end else*/
} /*end dicecalc*/


public static void main(String args[ ]) {
double numdice=5;
double totalways=0;
for (double dicesum=numdice; dicesum<=6*numdice; dicesum++) {
        double numways=dicecalc(numdice,dicesum);
        totalways+=numways;
        System.out.println(numdice+" dice, "+dicesum+" sum, "+
        numways+" ways");
} /*end for loop*/
System.out.println ("total ways:"+totalways);
} /*end main*/
} /*end dice*/
```

For example, there are 780 ways of rolling a sum of 18 if you toss 5 dice.

The basic rule for when to use recursion is that it is a good way to solve a problem if the problem naturally can be broken into other (often smaller) versions of the same problem. As another example of recursion, see page 217 for a program that draws a snowflake pattern.

We've now seen the building blocks that you use to program in Java. We've seen data types, such as integers, doubles, and strings, and we've seen the operations that act on them. We've seen how loops, arrays, and if statements can control the flow of execution of a program, and we've seen how methods make it possible to reuse blocks of code. Next, we will see how these pieces are put together to form the key elements of a Java program: *objects* and *classes*.

EXERCISES

1. Write a method $f(x)$ with this behavior: $f(x) = x$ if $x > 0$; otherwise $f(x) = 0$.

2. Write a method that reads in two numbers a and b and returns a string representing the value of a/b. If, however, b is zero, return the string "—".

3. Write a method that reads in a **double** value representing a time, measured as the number of hours since midnight, and then returns a string representing the time measured in the common way with hours and minutes, with "am" or "pm" attached.

4. Write a method that reads in the wheel revolution rate and wheel diameter for a car, and then calculates the speed of the car.

5. Look back through Chapter 7 and convert the programs discussed there into methods, where appropriate.

6. Convert the encryption program from the previous chapter's exercises into a method. Then, also allow the method to act as a decryption program. Add a second argument to the method that determines whether the method should encrypt or decrypt.

7. Write new versions of the combinations and hypergeometric distribution methods that are less elegant but more efficient. That is, instead of calling the factorial method, these new methods will take advantage of cancellation to reduce the number of calculations required.

CHAPTER 9

OBJECTS AND CLASSES

9.1 Including Values in a Boat Object

We're on a boat moving along a lake. We can identify points on the lake with an xy coordinate system, where x is the distance we have traveled east of the origin point and y is the distance we have traveled north of the origin point (see Figure 9–1).

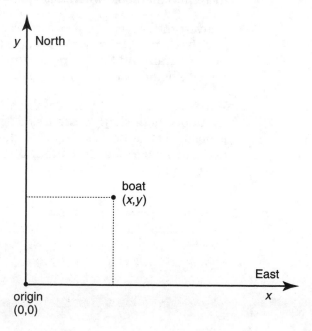

FIGURE 9–1

Assume that our lake is small enough that we can ignore the fact that the world is really round. (Later we will talk about navigating across an ocean, where you must take the curvature of the earth into account; see page 328.)

Our boat is traveling with a certain speed in a particular direction. To plot its course, we need to know its *velocity vector*, which consists of two numbers: v_x, the velocity in the x direction (east), and v_y, the velocity in the y direction (north) (see Figure 9–2).

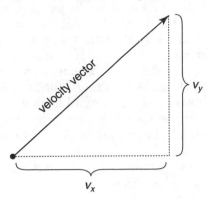

FIGURE 9–2

In order to describe the position and velocity of our boat, we need four numbers: x, y, v_x, and v_y. We could create four variables with these names, but there is a complication. Ours is not the only boat on the lake. We also need to keep track of the position and velocity of other boats on the lake, so we will need variables for those as well. We could possibly give each boat a number (1, 2, 3, etc.) and then create variables like this: x_1, x_2, y_1, y_2, v_{x1}, v_{x2}, v_{y1}, v_{y2}. However, this isn't the best approach, because we end up with a lot of different variables and we don't have a way to make sure that the variables belonging to a particular boat stay together.

What would be better would be to group all variables associated with a particular boat together. To do this, we'll create an *object* that represents a boat. Our boat object will have four attributes, which will all be values of type **double**: x, y, v_x, and v_y. When we create any object, there are two general steps:

1. Prepare a general description of what is included in an object of that type. This general description is called a **class**. The code for the class will describe the features that must be included in an object of that particular class. (We have already seen the word **class**, since all of our Java programs are examples of classes. This means that every Java program is actually the description of an object.)

2. Create a particular example of that class. When this happens, we are said to *instantiate* the object, and the object created is an *instance* of that class. For our example, we will instantiate an object of our boat class by specifying the values of x, y, v_x, and v_y for that particular boat.

Here is the general description of our class:

```
class boatclass {
double x=0; double y=0;
double vx=0; double vy=0;
} /*end boatclass*/
```

In this case the class description is very simple, since all it needs to do is say that a boat object has four variables, all of type **double**.

Each instance of the class (that is, each particular boat) is expected to provide its own values for these four variables, but the class description will set them all to the temporary default value of zero.

Each Java class description has the word **class** at or near its beginning. The only items that come before the word **class** are **import** statements (see page 133) or modifiers such as **public** (see page 132). Following the word **class** is the name of the class; in our case, the name is boatclass. We will sometimes include the word "class" at the end of our class names to remind us that it is the name of the class (so we won't confuse the class name with the names of the objects created of that class). As you might guess, the class description is contained within braces { }. In this case, the class description is very simple because it only contains the declarations of the four variables that are part of that class. (Later we'll see other items that can be included in class definitions.)

Now that we've prepared the description of the class, we're ready to write a program that uses it. Our first program will have only one boat; we'll call it boat1. Its initial position is ($x = 1.6, y = 0.3$); its initial velocity is ($v_x = 6.1, v_y = 10.4$).

Recall that we declare a variable to be a number by giving its type followed by its name (for example, **double** x). We do a similar thing when we declare a new object; we give the class name (since that determines the type of the object), and then the name of the object. In this case, we would write

boatclass boat1;

to declare *boat1* to be a new instance of *boatclass*. Before we can use an object, we also have to create a space for it in the computer's memory; we do this with the **new** command. For convenience, we are allowed to combine the **new** command and the declaration on the same line, so it will look like this:

boatclass boat1=**new** boatclass();

Now that our object has been instantiated, we can use the variables it contains in our program by giving the object name (boat1), followed by a period, followed by the variable name (for example, x). Therefore, boat1.x refers to the variable x for boat1, and boat1.vy refers to the variable vy for boat1. We can either assign values to these variables, or use their values in expressions. (In some cases, you will want to restrict access to the variables within a class; see page 131.)

Our first program using the boat object will be fairly simple; it will use a **while** loop to advance the time and then recalculate the position of the boat at each time. During each repetition of the loop, the variable time will increase by an amount deltatime. (Note: The Greek uppercase letter delta, Δ, is often used in mathematics to represent the change in a quantity; that is why we are referring to the change in time as *deltatime*.)

Here is the program:

```
class boatprogram {

static boatclass boat1=new boatclass();

public static void main(String args[ ]) {

boat1.x=1.6;
boat1.y=0.3;
boat1.vx=6.1;
boat1.vy=10.4;

double time=0;
double deltatime=0.2;

System.out.println("   Time       x       y");

while (time<2) {
        boat1.x+=deltatime*boat1.vx;
        boat1.y+=deltatime*boat1.vy;
        time+=deltatime;
        System.out.println(cpj.nf(time,7,2)+cpj.nf(boat1.x,7,2)+cpj.nf
            (boat1.y,7,2));
        } /*end while*/
} /*end main*/
} /*end boatprogram*/

class boatclass {
double x=0; double y=0;
double vx=0; double vy=0;


} /*end boatclass*/
```

The class description for boatclass is included in the same file as the rest of the program (which must have the name boatprogram.java, since that is the name of the class with the **main** method). Our class could also have been declared as a **public** class, in which case it would be in a file by itself with the name boatclass.java. In either case, the compiler creates two files: boatprogram.class and boatclass.class. Both of these class files must be present for the program to run. (A third option is to create an *inner class*; see page 131.)

We can run the program by typing "java boatprogram". Here's the output:

```
Time       x       y
0.20    2.82    2.38
0.40    4.04    4.46
0.60    5.26    6.54
0.80    6.48    8.62
1.00    7.70   10.70
1.20    8.92   12.78
1.40   10.14   14.86
```

```
1.60   11.36   16.94
1.80   12.58   19.02
2.00   13.80   21.10
2.20   15.02   23.18
```

9.2   Including Methods in a Class

In our previous program (page 109), we have to write the code that moves the boat (that is, calculates its new position) in the main part of the program. That brings up a thought: Wouldn't it be nice if our boats were smart enough to move themselves? That is, it would help if the code to calculate the position of the boat were in the boat class itself. This would make our job as programmers easier, because the code that acts on the data would be close to the data itself. In fact, this is a key concept of object-oriented programming: an object can contain methods as well as data.

We'll add a method to our boat class that advances the position of the boat by a certain amount of time, which is given to the method as a parameter. The class now looks like this:

```
class boatclass {
double x=0; double y=0;
double vx=0; double vy=0;

/*method*/ void moveboat(double deltatime) {
x+=vx*deltatime;
y+=vy*deltatime;
} /*end moveboat*/
} /*end boatclass*/
```

Notice how the definition of the method moveboat is included within the body of the code for the class boatclass, along with the declarations of the variables for that class. The method declares its parameter (deltatime) in the same manner as the methods we have previously seen.

To use this method in our program, we need to identify it with the notation boat1.moveboat(deltatime). Note how the characters "boat1." precede the name of the method, just as they do when a variable is being referenced in an expression such as boat1.x.

Here is the new version of the program:

```
class boatprogram {

static boatclass boat1=new boatclass();

public static void main(String args[ ]) {

boat1.x=1.6;
boat1.y=0.3;
boat1.vx=6.1;
```

```
boat1.vy=10.4;

double time=0;
double deltatime=0.2;

System.out.println("   Time      x      y");

while (time<2) {
        boat1.moveboat(deltatime);
        time+=deltatime;
        System.out.println(cpj.nf(time,7,2)+cpj.nf
            (boat1.x,7,2)+cpj.nf
        (boat1.y,7,2));
        } /*end while*/
} /*end main*/
} /*end boatprogram*/


class boatclass {
double x=0; double y=0;
double vx=0; double vy=0;

/*method*/ void moveboat(double deltatime) {
x+=vx*deltatime;
y+=vy*deltatime;
} /*end moveboat*/
} /*end boatclass*/
```

The output from this program is exactly the same as from the previous program (page 109).

9.3   Multiple Objects (Instances) of a Class

We need to make sure we do not crash into any other boats. Now we will begin to see the power of object-oriented programming. In order to create a new boat, we merely need to instantiate a new variable of type boatclass; we don't need to make any change to the class description for boatclass. However, it will be interesting to add another method to boatclass. This will calculate the distance between our boat and the other boat. The other boat is passed to the method as the argument. The distance is found from the following formula, which comes from the Pythagorean theorem (see Figure 9–3):

$$\sqrt{(x_1 - x_2)^2 + (y_1 - y_2)^2}$$

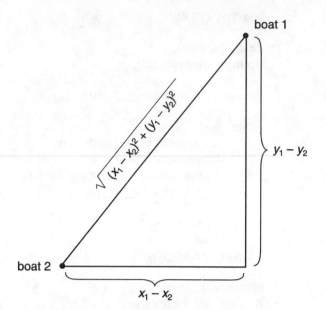

$$\sqrt{(x_1 - x_2)^2 + (y_1 - y_2)^2}$$

boat 1

$y_1 - y_2$

boat 2

$x_1 - x_2$

FIGURE 9–3

Here is the program:

```
class boatprogram {

static boatclass boat1=new boatclass();
static boatclass boat2=new boatclass();

public static void main(String args[ ]){

boat1.x=1.6;
boat1.y=0.3;
boat1.vx=6.1;
boat1.vy=10.4;

boat2.x=30.5;
boat2.y=46.8;
boat2.vx=-5.2;
boat2.vy=-1.4;

double time=0;
double deltatime=0.4;

System.out.println("   Time     x1      y1      x2      y2  distance");

while (time<4) {
        boat1.moveboat(deltatime);
        boat2.moveboat(deltatime);
        time+=deltatime;
        System.out.println(cpj.nf(time,7,2)+cpj.nf(boat1.x,7,2)+cpj.nf
          (boat1.y,7,2)+ cpj.nf(boat2.x,7,2)+cpj.nf(boat2.y,7,2)+
          cpj.nf(boat1.distance(boat2),7,2));
        } /*end while*/
} /*end main*/
```

```
} /*end boatprogram*/

class boatclass {
double x=0; double y=0;
double vx=0; double vy=0;

/*method*/ void moveboat(double deltatime) {
x+=vx*deltatime;
y+=vy*deltatime;
} /*end moveboat*/

/*method*/ double distance(boatclass otherboat) {
/*This method calculates the distance to the other boat given as the
  argument.*/
double z=
Math.sqrt(Math.pow((x-otherboat.x),2)+Math.pow((y-otherboat.y),2));
return z;
} /*end distance method*/

} /*end boatclass*/
```

Our moveboat method is declared **void**, because it does not return a value. The distance method returns a value of type **double**.

Here is the output:

```
Time    x1      y1      x2      y2    distance
0.40    4.04    4.46    28.42   46.24   48.37
0.80    6.48    8.62    26.34   45.68   42.05
1.20    8.92   12.78    24.26   45.12   35.79
1.60   11.36   16.94    22.18   44.56   29.66
2.00   13.80   21.10    20.10   44.00   23.75
2.40   16.24   25.26    18.02   43.44   18.27
2.80   18.68   29.42    15.94   42.88   13.74
3.20   21.12   33.58    13.86   42.32   11.36
3.60   23.56   37.74    11.78   41.76   12.45
4.00   26.00   41.90     9.70   41.20   16.32
4.40   28.44   46.06     7.62   40.64   21.51
```

You might be thinking, "It would be nice if the program could display a graph showing the movement of the boats." That will have to wait for the next chapter.

9.4 Constructors

We will often need to create new objects in Java, so it will help to be able to create a method that will be executed whenever we are instantiating a new object. These methods are called *constructor* methods. Each class may have one or more constructor methods. (If there is more than one, then there must be a difference in the number or types of their parameters.) A constructor method always has the same name as the class to which it belongs, and it is always declared with the **public** modifier.

In our case, the constructor method will be called boatclass. The only thing it will do is assign the values for x, y, v_x, and v_y; these values will be passed to the method as arguments. We could write the constructor method like this:

```
/*constructor method*/ public boatclass(
double x1, double y1, double vx1, double vy1) {
x=x1;
y=y1;
vx=vx1;
vy=vy1;
} /*end constructor method*/
```

The constructor method is declared to have four parameters: x1, y1, vx1, and vy1. All the body of the method does is assign these values to the corresponding values for boatclass (x, y, vx, and vy). However, it would be simpler if we didn't have to think of new names for the parameters. We could try this:

```
/*constructor method—wrong way*/ public boatclass(
double x, double y, double vx, double vy) {
x=x;
y=y;
vx=vx;
vy=vy;
} /*end constructor method*/
```

This, however, isn't going to work. Since the variable x is declared as a parameter for this method, it will be local to this method. Therefore, in the assignment statements, both x's refer to the local variable, not the variable x for the object itself. To get around that, we need to identify the name of the object. For example, if we were instantiating the object boat1, we could use this statement:

```
boat1.x=x;
```

That approach isn't going to work either, since the constructor method could be used for many different boatclass objects that won't all be called boat1. We need a symbol that we can put in a method that says "refer to this particular object (instance) for which this method applies." Java provides a keyword to do that: **this**. The expression "**this**.x", when it appears in a method in a class description, means "determine the value of the variable x from the object that is calling this method."

Here is what our constructor method looks like, using **this**:

```
/*constructor method*/ public boatclass(
double x, double y, double vx, double vy) {
this.x=x; this.y=y;
this.vx=vx; this.vy=vy;
} /*end constructor method*/
```

We call the constructor method when we want to instantiate a new object of the class boatclass. As with any method call, we put the arguments in parentheses, separated by commas, following the name of the method. One difference is that we always include the word **new** when we are calling a constructor, and then the result of the method is assigned to a variable of this class. Here's an example:

```
boatclass boat0=new boatclass(1.6, 0.3, 6.1, 10.4);
```

The order of the values given here must match the order given in the parameter list, just the same as with any other method call. The computer will execute the boatclass constructor method, using $x = 1.6$, $y = 0.3$, $vx = 6.1$, and $vy = 10.4$.

The next section shows examples of programs using constructors.

9.5 Arrays of Objects

We'll now prepare a program with four different boats. We could call them boat1, boat2, boat3, and boat4, but that should not sound quite right to you. It would be too much work if each boat is its own variable. Some memories from Chapter 6 should come back to you now: we solved this type of problem by creating an array. Fortunately, Java allows us to create arrays of any object class, just as we can create arrays of **double** and **String**.

Here is the program:

```
class boatprogram {

/*This program calculates the distance from
   each boat to every other boat for a group
   of four boats.*/

static int numboats=4;

/*declare boat[ ] as an array:*/
static boatclass boat[ ]=new boatclass[numboats+1];
        /*The array boat[ ] will have subscripts 0,1,2,3,4.*/

public static void main(String args[ ]) {

/*Now, call the constructor method for each of the boats.*/

boatclass boat0=new boatclass(1.6, 0.3, 6.1, 10.4);
boat[1]=boat0;
```

```
boat0=new boatclass(30.5, 46.8, -5.2, -1.4);
boat[2]=boat0;
boat0=new boatclass(15.8, 20.4, 7.2, -4.9);
boat[3]=boat0;
boat0=new boatclass(7.4, 14.8, 0.2, 8.6);
boat[4]=boat0;

double time=0;
double deltatime=0.4;

while (time<0.8) {
System.out.println ("Time:␣"+cpj.nf(time,7,2));

for (int i=1; i<=numboats; i++) {
for (int j=(i+1); j<=numboats; j++) {
System.out.println ("␣␣␣distance␣"+i+","+j+":
      "+cpj.nf(boat[i].distance(boat[j]),8,2));
} /*end j loop*/
} /*end i loop*/

      time+=deltatime;

for (int i=1; i<=numboats; i++) {
boat[i].moveboat(deltatime);}

      } /*end while*/
} /*end main*/
} /*end boatprogram*/

class boatclass {
double x=0; double y=0;
double vx=0; double vy=0;

/*constructor method*/ public boatclass(
double x, double y, double vx, double vy) {
this.x=x; this.y=y;
this.vx=vx; this.vy=vy;
} /*end constructor method*/

/*method*/ void moveboat(double deltatime) {
x+=vx*deltatime;
y+=vy*deltatime;
} /*end moveboat*/

/*method*/ double distance(boatclass otherboat) {
/*This method calculates the distance to the other boat given as the
  argument.*/
double z=
Math.sqrt(Math.pow((x-otherboat.x),2)+Math.pow((y-otherboat.y),2));
return z;
} /*end distance method*/

} /*end boatclass*/
```

We're ignoring element 0; sometimes this is the best way to avoid confusion.

Instead of displaying the location of each boat, the program is arranged so that it displays the distance between each pair of boats. Here's the output:

```
Time:     0.00
    distance 1,2:     54.75
    distance 1,3:     24.61
    distance 1,4:     15.62
    distance 2,3:     30.22
    distance 2,4:     39.47
    distance 3,4:     10.10
Time:     0.40
    distance 1,2:     48.37
    distance 1,3:     20.24
    distance 1,4:     14.20
    distance 2,3:     29.46
    distance 2,4:     34.96
    distance 3,4:     11.20
```

9.6 Inheritance: Creating a Class by Extending Another Class

So far, we have treated all boats the same. However, there are two kinds of boats on our lake: sailboats and motorboats. It would help if our program could treat them differently. For example, with sailboats it would be helpful to keep track of three variables: the height of the mast, the direction of the sail, and a boolean value indicating whether or not the sail was furled. With motorboats, we will keep track of the fuel tank size and the amount of fuel remaining.

We could create a sailboat class and a motorboat class that would include the variables listed above. Then we could add each of the variables and data from our boat class, since all of those apply to our new kind of boat.

"Wait a minute," you complain. "We should not have to duplicate all of the code that we wrote for the boat class for each of these other two classes. There must be some way to reuse it. . . ."

Here's the key idea: both sailboats and motorboats are specific types of boats. Therefore, every attribute that applies to a boat should also apply to one of these objects. But, each type of boat also has additional attributes that apply only to that kind of boat, not to boats in general. Mathematically, we say that sailboats and motorboats are *subsets* of the set of boats. Another way to say the same thing is that the set of boats is the *superset* for the set of sailboats and the set of motorboats. This can be represented on a diagram called a Venn diagram (see Figure 9–4).

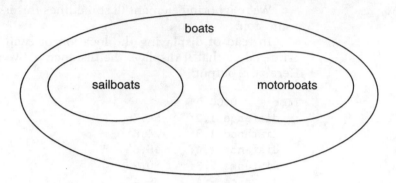

FIGURE 9–4

In object-oriented programming, we say that sailboats and motor-boats *inherit* all of the features of boats. In Java, when we want one class to inherit all of the features of another class, we use the keyword **extends**, like this:

class sailboatclass **extends** boatclass {

This statement declares that sailboatclass is a *subclass* of boatclass. Another way to say the same thing is that boatclass is the *superclass* for sailboatclass. In Java, a class may have any number of subclasses, but it can have only one superclass (that is, it can only extend, or inherit from, one other class).

You might recognize the word **extends**; we used it on page 25 in the command:

class calculationExamplesApplet **extends** Applet {

We now know what this means. **Applet** is the name of a class that includes features shared by all Java applets. Fortunately, this class comes with the Java language, so you don't need to create it yourself. When you write your own applet, you will extend the class **Applet**, which means that your applet will inherit all of the features of the standard applet, such as the ability to appear in a window. This saves you a huge amount of work, since you don't have to rewrite all of those features yourself whenever you write a new applet.

A sailboat will inherit all of the variables from the boat class (x, y, vx, vy) plus the methods of that class (moveboat, distance, and the constructor). The sailboat class definition will define three new variables: mastheight, sailsfurled, and saildirection.

9.7   Constructors for Subclasses That Call the Superclass Constructor

We will also add a constructor for the sailboat class. The constructor will take seven parameters, representing the seven variables listed in the previous paragraph. We could write the constructor with these statements:

```
this.x=x; this.y=y;
this.vx=vx; this.vy=vy;

this.mastheight=mastheight;
this.sailsfurled=sailsfurled;
this.saildirection=saildirection;
```

Writing these statements, however, involves one thing we are developing a strong aversion to: duplicate work. The statements defining (x, y, vx, vy) are also included in the constructor method for *boatclass*. Since sailboatclass inherits everything from boatclass, it inherits these statements in the constructor method as well. All we need to do is figure out a way to call them. Fortunately, Java provides a general way to call a method from the superclass of your class: use the word **super**. To call the boatclass constructor from within sailboatclass, use this command:

```
super(x,y,vx,vy);
```

Here's the complete definition of sailboatclass:

```
class sailboatclass extends boatclass {

private int mastheight=0;
boolean sailsfurled=false;
double saildirection=0;

/*constructor method*/ public sailboatclass(
double x, double y, double vx, double vy,
int mastheight, boolean sailsfurled,
double saildirection) {
super(x,y,vx,vy);
this.mastheight=mastheight;
this.sailsfurled=sailsfurled;
this.saildirection=saildirection;
} /*end constructor method*/

} /*end sailboatclass*/
```

The definition of motorboatclass is similar (see the program starting on page 121).

9.8   Abstract Classes: No Objects Allowed

Now we have a decision to make: what to do with our original boat-class. If we are sure that the only boats on the lake are sailboats and motorboats, we want to make sure that every boat object our program creates is one of those. We will not want any objects to be declared of boatclass. Therefore, we will add the word **abstract** in front of the class definition for boatclass:

abstract class boatclass {

This command declares that boatclass is an **abstract** class, which means that you cannot instantiate any objects of that class. Obviously, an **abstract** class is worthless unless there are other non-abstract classes that inherit from it. In our case, we can instantiate objects of sailboatclass and motorboatclass. In general, create an **abstract** class when you will have a group of classes that will all have some features in common. Put the common features in the **abstract** class, and then have the other classes inherit from it. This works as long as you are sure that all of the objects you need will fit in one of the subclasses of the **abstract** superclass. Otherwise, don't declare the superclass to be abstract, and you can create objects of that class.

You can also declare a method to be abstract. That means you do not give the body of the method in the current class; instead, the body of the method will be given a subclass that inherits from the class with the abstract method. If a class has one or more abstract methods, then it must be an abstract class. Here is an example of an abstract class **test** that defines an abstract method **xmethod**:

```
abstract class test {
abstract void xmethod();
} /*end test*/
```

9.9   Polymorphism

We are still very concerned about avoiding the other boats, so we will add a new variable to boatclass called nearestboat. You might become very concerned when you realize that we need to declare the class for the object nearestboat. Which class to use? We can't use sailboatclass, because the nearest boat to us might be a motorboat, and vice versa. It is clear that the object nearestboat needs to be declared as part of a class that allows for both sailboats and motorboats, which means it must be of class boatclass. "Wait a minute!" you object. "We have just decided that boatclass will be an **abstract** class, so you cannot instantiate any objects of that class." That is quite true. However, even though we cannot *instantiate* an object of the **abstract** class boatclass, we can *declare* an object to be of that class. "But it needs to be instantiated as something!" you correctly point out. Indeed, nearestboat will either be a member of sailboatclass or motorboatclass. You have one final question: "How can it be a member of sailboatclass or motorboatclass if it is declared to be of type boatclass?"

Now we come to a crucial feature that provides some of the magic of object-oriented programming. An object that is declared to be of a particular class can be assigned values not just from that class, but also from any of its subclasses. Therefore, any object declared to be of type boatclass can be assigned to be an object of type sailboatclass or motorboatclass. (In fact, it must be assigned to be one of these classes, since boatclass itself is an **abstract** class.) It will probably take a while for you to fully realize why this is such a powerful feature, but here is part of the explanation. When you write a program, you are sitting in your home or office. You will try to anticipate how the program will work when it is actually run, but you can't foresee everything. In our case, you have no way to know while you are writing the program whether at any particular time the nearest boat to your boat will be a sailboat or a motorboat. Your code would be much more complicated if you had to fill it with statements of the form "if the nearest boat is a motorboat, do this; if it is a sailboat, do something else." With object-oriented programming, the job is much easier because all of the features that are common to all boats (such as the distance from our boat) are incorporated into the boatclass, which is shared by motorboatclass and sailboatclass automatically. You don't need any special code to allow the program to handle the nearest boat being a sailboat any differently than if the nearest boat were a motorboat. This concept is called *polymorphism*.

Here is the boat program that identifies the nearest boat:

```
class boatprogram {

static Int numboats=4;

static boatclass boat[ ]=new boatclass[numboats+1];

public static void main(String args[ ]) {

boatclass boat0=new sailboatclass(1.6,0.3,6.1,10.4,35,false,65);
boat[1]=boat0;
boat0=new motorboatclass(30.5,46.8,-5.2,-1.4,18,25);
boat[2]=boat0;
boat0=new sailboatclass(15.8,20.4,7.2,-4.9,30,true,120);
boat[3]=boat0;
boat0=new motorboatclass(7.4,14.8,0.2,8.6,12,16);
boat[4]=boat0;

double time=0;
double deltatime=2.0;


while (time<=4.0) {
System.out.println ("Time:_"+cpj.nf(time,7,2));

for (int i=1; i<=numboats; i++) {
double nearestdistance=Double.MAX_VALUE;
for (int j=1; j<=numboats; j++) {
if (i!=j) { /*Check only if i does not equal j.*/
```

```
            if (boat[i].distance(boat[j])<nearestdistance) {
                    nearestdistance=boat[i].distance(boat[j]);
                    boat[i].nearestboat=boat[j];
                } /*end if*/
            } /*end if i!=j*/
        } /*end j loop*/

        System.out.println("Boat␣"+i+"␣is at␣"+boat[i].positionstring());
        System.out.println("␣␣␣␣nearest boat is at␣"
                +boat[i].nearestboat.positionstring());
        System.out.print("␣␣␣␣distance:"+cpj.nf(boat[i].nearestdistance(),7,2));
        String nearestboattype="";
        if (boat[i].nearestboat instanceof sailboatclass)
                {nearestboattype="sailboat";}
        if (boat[i].nearestboat instanceof motorboatclass)
                {nearestboattype="motorboat";}
        System.out.println("␣␣␣type="+nearestboattype);
    } /*end i loop*/

        time+=deltatime;
    for (int i=1; i<=numboats; i++) {
        boat[i].moveboat(deltatime);}

        } /*end while*/
    } /*end main*/
} /*end boatprogram*/

abstract class boatclass {
double x=0; double y=0;
double vx=0; double vy=0;

boatclass nearestboat;

/*constructor method*/ public boatclass(
double x, double y, double vx, double vy) {
this.x=x; this.y=y;
this.vx=vx; this.vy=vy;
} /*end constructor method*/


/*method*/ void moveboat(double deltatime) {
x+=vx*deltatime;
y+=vy*deltatime;
} /*end moveboat*/

/*method*/ double distance(boatclass otherboat) {
/*This method calculates the distance to the other boat given as the
  argument.*/
double z=Math.sqrt(Math.pow((x-otherboat.x),2)+
        Math.pow((y-otherboat.y),2));
return z;
} /*end distance method*/
```

```
/*method*/ double nearestdistance() {
return distance(nearestboat);
} /*end nearestdistance*/

/*method*/ String positionstring() {
return(" x="+cpj.nf(x,7,2)+" y="+cpj.nf(y,7,2));
} /*end positionstring*/

} /*end boatclass*/


class sailboatclass extends boatclass {

private int mastheight=0;
boolean sailsfurled=false;
double saildirection=0;

/*constructor method*/ public sailboatclass(
double x, double y, double vx, double vy,
int mastheight, boolean sailsfurled,
double saildirection) {
super(x,y,vx,vy);
this.mastheight=mastheight;
this.sailsfurled=sailsfurled;
this.saildirection=saildirection;
} /*end constructor method*/

} /*end sailboatclass*/


class motorboatclass extends boatclass {
double fuellevel=0;
private double fueltanksize=0;

/*constructor method*/ public motorboatclass(
double x, double y, double vx, double vy,
double fuellevel, double fueltanksize) {
super(x,y,vx,vy);
this.fuellevel=fuellevel;
this.fueltanksize=fueltanksize;
} /*end constructor method*/

} /*end motorboatclass*/
```

For each of the four boats, this program determines which boat is nearest and prints a message about it. We find out which is the actual type of nearestboat with **instanceof**. Here's the output:

```
Time:    0.00
Boat 1 is at  x=   1.60  y=   0.30
     nearest boat is at  x=   7.40  y=  14.80
     distance:  15.62   type=motorboat
Boat 2 is at  x=  30.50  y=  46.80
     nearest boat is at  x=  15.80  y=  20.40
```

```
                    distance:   30.22    type=sailboat
        Boat 3 is at   x=   15.80   y=   20.40
            nearest boat is at   x=    7.40   y=   14.80
            distance:   10.10    type=motorboat
        Boat 4 is at   x=    7.40   y=   14.80
            nearest boat is at   x=   15.80   y=   20.40
            distance:   10.10    type=sailboat
        Time:     2.00
        Boat 1 is at   x=   13.80   y=   21.10
            nearest boat is at   x=    7.80   y=   32.00
            distance:   12.44    type=motorboat
        Boat 2 is at   x=   20.10   y=   44.00
            nearest boat is at   x=    7.80   y=   32.00
            distance:   17.18    type=motorboat
        Boat 3 is at   x=   30.20   y=   10.60
            nearest boat is at   x=   13.80   y=   21.10
            distance:   19.47    type=sailboat
        Boat 4 is at   x=    7.80   y=   32.00
            nearest boat is at   x=   13.80   y=   21.10
            distance:   12.44    type=sailboat
        Time:     4.00
        Boat 1 is at   x=   26.00   y=   41.90
            nearest boat is at   x=    9.70   y=   41.20
            distance:   16.32    type=motorboat
        Boat 2 is at   x=    9.70   y=   41.20
            nearest boat is at   x=    8.20   y=   49.20
            distance:    8.14    type=motorboat
        Boat 3 is at   x=   44.60   y=    0.80
            nearest boat is at   x=   26.00   y=   41.90
            distance:   45.11    type=sailboat
        Boat 4 is at   x=    8.20   y=   49.20
            nearest boat is at   x=    9.70   y=   41.20
            distance:    8.14    type=motorboat
```

9.10   Static Variables and Methods

There is so much traffic on our lake that a speed limit is instituted. We will add a new variable to boatclass to represent the speed limit. However, since this variable will be the same for all of the boats, it seems wasteful if we would have to assign it separately to each of the boat objects. When we want a variable to be the same for all objects of a class, then we declare it with the modifier **static**. Therefore, we'll add this line to boatclass:

static double speedlimit=20;

Now all objects of the class *boatclass* can access the value of the speed limit. A *static* variable can be accessed either by giving the name of an object, like this:

System.out.println (boat1.speedlimit);

or by giving the name of the class itself:

System.out.println (boatclass.speedlimit);

Because they can be accessed by giving a class name, rather than an object name, this leads to another important property of static variables: they can be accessed even if you have not created an instance of that class. Since a static variable belongs to the class, it is automatically created when the class is compiled, whether or not any objects of that class are actually created.

We can also create static methods that can be called by referring to the class name, rather than an object name. For example, we can create a method showlakename that displays the name of our lake (which is the same for all of our boats).

Following is a program illustrating static variables and methods. (We've removed some of the features of our previous boat programs so that there will be less clutter as we illustrate the concepts we're looking at now.)

```
class boatprogram {

static boatclass boat1=new boatclass();
static boatclass boat2=new boatclass();

public static void main(String args[ ]) {

boat1.x=1.6;
boat1.y=0.3;
boat1.vx=6.1;
boat1.vy=10.4;


boat2.x=30.5;
boat2.y=46.8;
boat2.vx=-5.2;
boat2.vy=-1.4;

        System.out.println("speed limit:"+boatclass.speedlimit);
        System.out.println("speed limit (boat 1):"+boat1.speedlimit);
        System.out.println("speed limit (boat 2):"+boat2.speedlimit);
          boatclass.speedlimit=30;
        System.out.println("speed limit:"+boatclass.speedlimit);
        System.out.println("speed limit (boat 1):"+boat1.speedlimit);
        System.out.println("speed limit (boat 2):"+boat2.speedlimit);
          boat1.speedlimit=25;
        System.out.println("speed limit:"+boatclass.speedlimit);
        System.out.println("speed limit (boat 1):"+boat1.speedlimit);
        System.out.println("speed limit (boat 2):"+boat2.speedlimit);
          boatclass.showlakename();

} /*end main*/
} /*end boatprogram*/

class boatclass {
```

```
double x=0; double y=0;
double vx=0; double vy=0;

static double speedlimit=20;

static void showlakename() {
System.out.println("Lake Clearwater");
} /*end get lake name*/

} /*end boatclass*/
```

Here is the output:

```
speed limit:20.0
speed limit (boat 1):20.0
speed limit (boat 2):20.0
speed limit:30.0
speed limit (boat 1):30.0
speed limit (boat 2):30.0
speed limit:25.0
speed limit (boat 1):25.0
speed limit (boat 2):25.0
Lake Clearwater
```

When the speed limit is changed from 20 to 30 with the command

boatclass.speedlimit=30;

this changes the value of the speed limit for all of the boats. If we try to change the speedlimit just for boat1 with the command

boat1.speedlimit=25;

the speed limit also changes for all boats as well. Since speedlimit is a static variable, you cannot change its value for one boat object without changing it for all of them.

9.11   Overriding Methods

When one class extends another class, then the subclass may have one or more methods with the same name as in the superclass. In that case the subclass methods will override the superclass methods if you call them with a subclass object.

In the next version of our boat program, we'll add two static variables to boatclass: windvx and windvy, representing the wind speed in the x and y directions, respectively. (The wind is assumed to be the same for all boats on the lake.) In this version, sailboats will have their own *moveboat* method, which simply moves them in the direction of the wind. (In reality, sailboats can adjust the angle of their sails when they need to move in a different direction, but we'll leave out that complication here.)

```
class boatprogram {

static int numboats=4;

static boatclass boat[ ]=new boatclass[numboats+1];

public static void main(String args[ ]) {

boatclass.windvx=4.2;
boatclass.windvy=3.8;


boatclass boat0=new sailboatclass(1.6,0.3,6.1,10.4,35,false,65);
boat[1]=boat0;
boat0=new motorboatclass(30.5,46.8,-5.2,-1.4,18,25);
boat[2]=boat0;
boat0=new sailboatclass(15.8,20.4,7.2,-4.9,30,true,120);
boat[3]=boat0;
boat0=new motorboatclass(7.4,14.8,0.2,8.6,12,16);
boat[4]=boat0;

double time=0;
double deltatime=2.0;


while (time<=4.0) {
System.out.println ("Time:␣"+cpj.nf(time,7,2));

for (int i=1; i<=numboats; i++) {

System.out.println("Boat␣"+i+"␣is at␣"+boat[i].positionstring());
} /*end i loop*/

        time+=deltatime;
for (int i=1; i<=numboats; i++) {
        boat[i].moveboat(deltatime);}

        } /*end while*/
} /*end main*/
} /*end boatprogram*/

abstract class boatclass {
double x=0; double y=0;
double vx=0; double vy=0;

boatclass nearestboat;

static double windvx=0;
static double windvy=0;

/*constructor method*/ public boatclass(
double x, double y, double vx, double vy) {
this.x=x; this.y=y;
```

```
this.vx=vx; this.vy=vy;
} /*end constructor method*/


/*method*/ void moveboat(double deltatime) {
x+=vx*deltatime;
y+=vy*deltatime;
} /*end moveboat*/

/*method*/ String positionstring() {
return(" x="+cpj.nf(x,7,2)+" y="+cpj.nf(y,7,2));
} /*end positionstring*/


} /*end boatclass*/


class sailboatclass extends boatclass {

private int mastheight=0;
boolean sailsfurled=false;
double saildirection=0;

/*constructor method*/ public sailboatclass(
double x, double y, double vx, double vy,
int mastheight, boolean sailsfurled,
double saildirection) {
super(x,y,vx,vy);
this.mastheight=mastheight;
this.sailsfurled=sailsfurled;
this.saildirection=saildirection;
} /*end constructor method*/

/*method*/ void moveboat(double deltatime) {
/*The moveboat method in the sailboatclass will override the
   moveboat method in the superclass (boatclass).*/
        x=x+boatclass.windvx*deltatime;
        y=y+boatclass.windvy*deltatime;
} /*end moveboat*/


} /*end sailboatclass*/


class motorboatclass extends boatclass {
double fuellevel=0;
private double fueltanksize=0;

/*constructor method*/ public motorboatclass(
double x, double y, double vx, double vy,
double fuellevel, double fueltanksize) {
super(x,y,vx,vy);
this.fuellevel=fuellevel;
this.fueltanksize=fueltanksize;
```

} /*end constructor method*/

} /*end motorboatclass*/

Here is the output:

```
Time:     0.00
Boat 1 is at  x=    1.60  y=    0.30
Boat 2 is at  x=   30.50  y=   46.80
Boat 3 is at  x=   15.80  y=   20.40
Boat 4 is at  x=    7.40  y=   14.80
Time:     2.00
Boat 1 is at  x=   10.00  y=    7.90
Boat 2 is at  x=   20.10  y=   44.00
Boat 3 is at  x=   24.20  y=   28.00
Boat 4 is at  x=    7.80  y=   32.00
Time:     4.00
Boat 1 is at  x=   18.40  y=   15.50
Boat 2 is at  x=    9.70  y=   41.20
Boat 3 is at  x=   32.60  y=   35.60
Boat 4 is at  x=    8.20  y=   49.20
```

Now that we've learned about objects, we'll see how the ability to design a program as a collection of objects greatly increases our power to solve programming problems.

Notes

The Object Class

All objects are members of a special class called **Object**, which represents the most general type of object. All other classes are subclasses of this class.

Null Objects

Any object can be assigned to a special value called **null**, representing nothing. For example, if boat1 is temporarily not relevant, use this assignment statement:

boat1=**null**;

Then you can check to make sure that it is not null before taking action with this comparison:

if (boat1!=**null**)

Memory

You might worry that the computer will run out of memory if every object needs to store a copy of all of the information for a class. Fortunately, each object only needs to store those variables that are unique to that object. All of the methods for a class, plus the static variables for that class, are stored only once for the class, not once for each object.

Object Assignment Statements

You can use an assignment statement that assigns one object to another, but this does not work the same as it does for primitive types like **int** and **double**. Here's an example:

```
class boatprogram {

public static void main(String args[ ]) {

/*This program demonstrates the difference between assignment
  statements involving objects and assignment statements
  involving primitive types.*/

boatclass boat1=new boatclass();
boat1.x=1.6;
boatclass boat2=boat1;
/*The object boat2 is a reference to the object boat1, so any change
  to boat1 will also be reflected in boat2.*/
System.out.println("boat1.x="+boat1.x+"␣␣␣boat2.x="+boat2.x);
boat1.x=2.8;
System.out.println("boat1.x="+boat1.x+"␣␣␣boat2.x="+boat2.x);
boat2.x=3.9;
System.out.println("boat1.x="+boat1.x+"␣␣␣boat2.x="+boat2.x);
/*Here is an example with two integer variables. b2 is assigned
  the same value as b1, but the value of b2 will not
  change when the value of b1 is changed.*/
int b1=16;
int b2=b1;
System.out.println("b1="+b1+"␣␣␣b2="+b2);
b1=28;
System.out.println("b1="+b1+"␣␣␣b2="+b2);
b2=36;
System.out.println("b1="+b1+"␣␣␣b2="+b2);
} /*end main*/
} /*end boatprogram*/

class boatclass {
double x=0; double y=0;
double vx=0; double vy=0;
} /*end boatclass*/
```

This program generates the following output:

```
boat1.x=1.6    boat2.x=1.6
boat1.x=2.8    boat2.x=2.8
boat1.x=3.9    boat2.x=3.9
b1=16    b2=16
b1=28    b2=16
b1=28    b2=36
```

When the object **boat2** is assigned to be equal to **boat1**, the computer does not duplicate **boat1**. Instead, it turns **boat2** into a memory reference to the location where **boat1** is stored. Here's the significance:

if you subsequently change a value for the boat1 object, then it will also change any reference to that value in the boat2 object. In the example, changing boat1.x to 2.8 also causes the value of boat2.x to change. If you change the value of boat2.x, it also changes the value of boat1.x.

By contrast, when the integer variable b2 is assigned to be equal to the integer variable b1, a copy of the value stored in b1 is made and this copy is assigned to b2. This means that if you subsequently change the value of b1, it will *not* change the value of b2; or, if you change the value of b2, it will not change the value of b1.

What if you really want to copy all of the values in the object boat1 to the object boat2, but then have the two objects live independent lives after that? Define a new constructor for boatclass that takes another object of boatclass as its parameter. Then, the constructor assigns all of the values from the parameter object to the new object being created.

final Variables, Methods, and Classes

What if you know that a variable or method is perfect the way it is—in particular, you don't want to run the risk that any subclass of your class will redefine that variable or method and thus override the original version. To prevent this from happening, declare the variable or method to be **final**. For example, **final int** variable_name, or **final void** method_name. A final variable or method cannot be overriden in any subclass; the compiler will display an error if any subclass tries to do so.

If a class is declared as **final**, then it is not possible to create any subclasses that inherit from that class.

Inner Classes

It is also possible to create one class that is inside of another class (Java version 1.1 and after). Such a class is called an *inner class*. This is useful sometimes when the inner class will not ever be needed outside of the class where it is defined. We'll often use inner classes called listener classes to respond to events (see Chapter 13).

Access Control

You can control whether or not a variable or method can be accessed elsewhere with these modifiers (in order from most restrictive to least restrictive):

- **private**: A method or variable declared **private** is accessible only in the class in which it is declared.

- no access modifier: Methods or variables with no explicit access modifier are accessible to code in the same package as the class in which it is declared.

- **protected**: A method or variable declared **protected** is accessible to code in the same package and code in subclasses.

- **public**: methods or variables declared **public** are available anywhere their class is accessible.

You can also add the previous modifiers to a class to determine if it will be accessible elsewhere. For example, a class declared as **public** is accessible to other classes. If you create a public class called myclass, then it must be declared in a source file named myclass.**java**.

If you're writing some classes that will be used as part of a larger program with other parts written by other people, you can see how it would be advantageous to declare some of your variables **private** so you can be sure that nobody else accidentally affects their value. Even if you are designing the entire program yourself, there are advantages to declaring variables and methods **private**, because then you are protected from rogue code that you might accidentally write yourself that would tamper with variables in another class.

But what if the values of your variables are needed in other classes? If they're declared **private**, other classes will not be able to read those values. The solution is to have a public method that can read the value of the variable. Such a public method usually begins with the word get. For example, here is how you could make the variable Time accessible outside its class:

```java
class exampleclass {

private double Time=0;

/*method*/ public double getTime() {
return Time;
} /*end getTime*/

} /*end exampleclass*/
```

Now another class can include statements like this:

```java
exampleclass object1=new exampleclass();
double Time1=object1.getTime();
```

These statements will make the variable Time1 equal to the value of the variable Time in the object object1. In a real example, the class with the private variable Time would include some calculations that would determine what that value would be. The previous code effectively makes the variable Time into a read-only variable, since other classes can read its value but none of them can change it.

What if you do want other classes to be able to change the value of a private variable? You can create a **public** method to do that. The name of this kind of method traditionally begins with set. Here's an expanded version of our example class:

```java
class exampleclass {

private double Time=0;

/*method*/ public double getTime() {
return Time;
```

```
} /*end getTime*/

/*method*/public void setTime(double x) {
Time=x;
} /*end setTime*/

} /*end exampleclass*/
```

Now another class can change the value of Time with a statement like this:

```
object1.setTime(2.4);
System.out.println(""+object1.getTime());
```

The result of these statements will cause the value 2.4 to be displayed.

Since the other class now has both read and write access to the variable Time, you might wonder what the point is of making it private and including the setTime and getTime methods. The advantage of this approach becomes clearer if you start adding other code to the setTime method. For example, you might include checks for invalid values, or any other code that would be helpful to execute whenever the value of that variable is changed. This approach guarantees you that the value of the **private** variable cannot be changed by any other class without executing whatever code you put in the set method. This makes your code more robust and more secure, and it promotes greater reusability because all of the code for setting the value of the **private** variable is in one place.

Wrapper Classes

Because Java is built around objects, you might think that every variable in Java is an object. Actually this is not true, since the primitive types **int** and **double** are not objects. It is more efficient for the computer to store them differently from the way it stores objects. Sometimes, however, we need to call methods that work for numerical types. Therefore, Java provides an **Integer** class and a **Double** class. These classes store numerical values, but they also include methods and can be treated as objects. These classes are called **wrapper** classes because they "wrap" a class definition around a primitive type. Note that the conversion methods discussed on page 77 make use of these wrapper methods.

Packages

A **package** is a group of classes that are available to be used by other classes. In order to make these classes available in your program, use the **import** command. We have already used this command to import some of the packages provided with the standard Java class libraries. For example,

import java.applet.*;

means to import all of the classes in the package **java.applet**, and the command

import java.awt.*;

means to import all of the classes in the package **java.awt**. Note that package names may have periods in them. (You can also import a single class from a package by giving the name of the class instead of an asterisk after the package name.)

If you want some of your classes to be part of a package, include the statement **package** *yourpackagename* at the front of all of the class files that will go in the package. These files need to be located in a directory whose name matches the name of the package.

One advantage of packages is that it is possible for two classes to have the same name as long as they are in different packages. Appendix A gives some information on standard Java packages that you will frequently use in your programs.

Interfaces

An *interface* is similar to a class in that it defines variables and methods. However, instead of giving code for methods, it only gives the name and argument signature of the method. If a class will use those methods, then it includes the line **implements** *interfacename* after its class definition. There are several examples of programs that implement interfaces in Chapters 13, 14 and 15. Note that a class **extends** another class when it inherits from that class, but it **implements** an interface when it will use the methods of that interface. It is possible to implement more than one interface (which is different from inheritance, where it is not possible to extend more than one class). Once your class implements a particular interface, then your class needs to define methods for all of the method names that are given in that interface. In this book we will not present any examples where we will create our own interfaces, but we will often use some standard interfaces provided with Java:

Interface name	Uses
ActionListener	use if the class will respond to items such as buttons and menu items
KeyListener	use if the class will respond to keyboard events
MouseListener	use if the class will respond to mouse events
Runnable	use for threads
Serializable	use for a class that will be written to a file

EXERCISES

1. Write a class representing a person's name. The class will have three string variables, representing first, last, and middle names. Write methods to do the following: (a) return a string with the last name followed by the first name; (b) return a string with the first name first; (c) repeat (a) and (b) with the middle name; (d) repeat (a) and (b) using the middle initial instead of the middle name; (e) return a string giving only the last name and first initial; (f) return a string giving all three initials.

2. Write a class representing a length measurement. The class has one **double** variable, representing the length in meters. However, provide a constructor that allows the user to specify the units when reading in a value. For example, the user could enter a measurement in feet. This constructor will need to change the units to meters in order to store the value in the class's **double** variable. Finally, add a method that returns the value of the measurement in a unit that is specified by one of the arguments to the method.

3. Add methods to the class in the previous exercise that return strings including units (for example, return the string "100 cm" if the length object represents a length of one meter).

4. Write a class representing units of time, similar to the class in the previous two exercises.

5. Write a class representing units of speed. This class has one constructor, that takes two arguments: an object of class length and an object of class time. Then the class has several methods that give the speed in different units, for example, a miles per hour method or a meters per second method.

6. Create a set of classes representing different mammals. Start with a class mammal, which has subclasses prototheria and theria. The subclass theria has subclasses marsupials and placentals. There are 18 subclasses of placentals, representing different orders such as artiodactyls (such as cattle and pigs), carnivores (such as dogs and cats), perissodactyls (such as horses), rodents, cetaceans (whales), and primates. Then create classes representing specific animals that extend these classes. Each class has a showcharacteristics method, which displays characteristics for that animal, and also calls the showcharacteristics method for its superclass. For example, the showcharacteristics method for the mammal class includes the characteristic that mammals provide milk for their young, so all other classes that extend from this class will have this characteristic automatically.

CHAPTER 10

GRAPHICS

10.1 Java Commands for Drawing and Filling Shapes

The old saying goes "A picture is worth a thousand words." Computers become much more powerful when they display data visually. Fortunately, Java provides a rich array of graphical tools.

A computer screen is divided up into rows and columns of pixels (short for picture elements). Each pixel can be set to a different color; this gives us great flexibility in drawing pictures on the screen. Because the pixels are so small, our eyes can be tricked into thinking they are seeing continuous smooth images when in reality they are looking at an array of colored dots. (In this chapter, we will talk about drawing on the screen, but in reality we will be drawing on a window. You can move or resize that window just the same as you can with any other window).

In order to be able to draw pictures on the screen, we need to be able to identify which pixel is which. We can identify pixels with a coordinate system, where each pixel is identified with two numbers: the number of pixels from the left edge of the window, and the number of pixels down from the top of the window (see Figure 10–1. This is similar to the xy Cartesian coordinate system commonly used in math, except that you can see one important difference: the pixel y coordinates are zero at the top and become larger as you go down (the opposite of the Cartesian coordinates traditionally used in math).

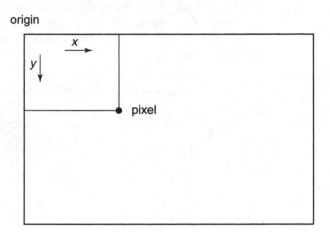

FIGURE 10–1

Now let's figure out the kinds of tools we need to draw pixel pictures. We should be able to:

- draw a line between two pixels

- draw a rectangle

- draw a rectangle and fill it with a specified color

- draw a circle, or part of a circle

- draw an oval

- draw or fill a polygon with an arbitrary number of sides

- draw text on the screen at a particular location

Following is a list of some basic Java graphics methods. All of these methods come from the **Graphics** class. To use them you must refer to an object of this class (which we will always call g).

- g.**drawLine**(x_1, y_1, x_2, y_2)

This method draws a line from the point with pixel coordinates (x_1, y_1) to the point with pixel coordinates (x_2, y_2).

- g.**drawRect**(*left_corner_x_coordinate*, *upper_corner_y_coordinate*, *width*, *height*)

This method draws a rectangle. The first two arguments give the pixel coordinates of the upper-left-hand corner of the rectangle; the last two coordinates give the width and height of the rectangle.

- g.**fillRect**(*left_corner_x_coordinate*, *upper_corner_y_coordinate*, *width*, *height*)

This method is the same as **drawRect**, except that the entire interior of the rectangle is filled with the color you have set with g.**setColor** (see page 149).

- g.**drawOval**(*left_corner_x_coordinate*, *upper_corner_y_coordinate*, *width*, *height*)

The arguments of **drawOval** are the same as for **drawRect**. Imagine that the computer draws a rectangle first, and then it draws an oval that fits inside the rectangle, just touching each of the four sides of the rectangle (see Figure 10–2). (In reality, the rectangle itself is invisible.) If the height and width of the rectangle are the same, then **drawOval** will draw a circle.

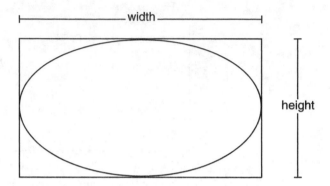

FIGURE 10–2

- g.**fillOval**(*left_corner_x_coordinate*, *upper_corner_y_coordinate*, *width*, *height*)

The method **fillOval** is exactly the same as **drawOval**, except that the interior of the oval is filled in with the color determined by **setColor** (see page 149).

- g.**drawArc**(*left_corner_x_coordinate*, *upper_corner_y_coordinate*, *width*, *height*, *starting_point_in degrees*, *size of arc in degrees*)

The **drawArc** method draws part of a circle or oval. The first four arguments are the same as for **drawOval**. You also need two more arguments: where to start the arc, and how much of the arc to draw. Both of these are measured in degrees. If you put (0,360) for these two arguments, the complete oval will be drawn. Figure 10–3 shows how the starting point is measured. The 0 degree mark points to the right; 90 degrees is straight up; 180 degrees is to the left; 270 degrees is straight down. (If you are familiar with trigonometry, you should recognize this as being a standard way of measuring angles.)

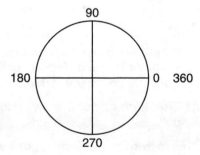

FIGURE 10–3

- g.**fillArc**(*left_corner_x_coordinate*, *upper_corner_y_coordinate*, *width*, *height*, *starting_point_in degrees*, *size of arc in degrees*)

The method **fillArc** is the same as **drawArc**, except it fills in a sector of a circle that is bounded by the given arc and two straight lines that connect to the center of the circle or oval. The area filled in by **fillArc** is shaped like a piece of pie.

- You can also draw or fill a polygon by giving the coordinates of all of the vertices. The first step is to create an object of class **Polygon**, with a statement like this:

Polygon *polygon_name* =
new Polygon(*x_array*, *y_array*, *numpoints*);

Here, *x_array* is the array of x coordinates of the vertices, *y_array* is the array of y coordinates of the vertices, and *numpoints* is the number of vertices. (In versions of Java before 1.1, the last vertex needed to be the same as the first vertex in order for the polygon to be connected. Later versions automatically connect the last vertex given to the first vertex).

Now you can draw the outline of the polygon with this statement.

g.**drawPolygon**(*polygon_name*);

You can fill the polygon with this statement:

g.**fillPolygon**(*polygon_name*);

Here are five reminders that apply to all the graphics commands:

1. All distances are measured in pixels.

2. Horizontal (x) coordinates are given before vertical (y) coordinates, as is traditional in mathematics.

3. Vertical (y) coordinates are measured down (the opposite of traditional mathematics).

4. As always with Java, you must follow the exact capitalization pattern.

5. For each of the above commands, the color will be determined by the **setColor** command (see page 149).

Although one important goal of Java is to be platform independent, there is no way around the fact that different computer monitors vary in terms of their resolution. This means that graphical drawings will look different on different monitors.

10.2   Smiling Face Applet

Now let's try an example. Following is a program that draws a coordinate grid on the screen (with labels for the screen coordinates). This will be very helpful for us later on when we draw specific patterns on the screen.

```
import java.applet.*;
import java.awt.*;

public class graphgrid extends Applet {

public void init() {
setBackground(Color.white);
} /*end init*/

void drawgrid(Graphics g) {
for (int i=0; i<=800; i+=50) {
for (int j=10; j<=40; j+=10) {
g.setColor(Color.cyan);
g.drawLine((i+j),0,(i+j),800);
g.drawLine(0,(i+j),800,(i+j));
} /*end j loop*/
g.setColor(Color.blue);
g.drawLine(0,i,800,i);
g.drawLine(i,0,i,800);
g.drawString(""+i,0,i);
g.drawString(""+i,i,10);
} /*end i loop*/
} /*end drawgrid*/


public void paint(Graphics g) {

drawgrid(g);

} /*end paint*/


} /*end class graphgrid*/
```

Since this program is an applet, we need to create an HTML file and then view it with a web browser or the appletviewer (see page 26). Here's what the screen looks like when we view this applet:

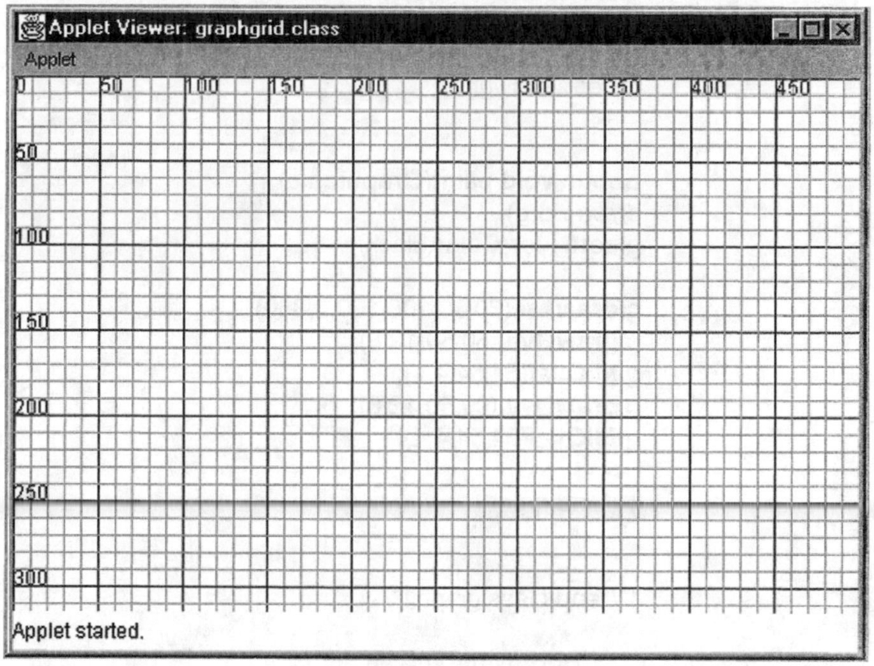

FIGURE 10–4

Now let's draw an example with two solid circles, each inside an oval, with both ovals inside a larger circle. The outer circle will be drawn with this statement:

g.drawArc(20,30,100,100,0,360);

The circle's left side will be 20 pixels from the left edge of the screen; the top of the circle will be 30 pixels down from the top of the screen; the diameter of the circle will be 100 pixels; and we'll draw the complete arc from 0 degrees to 360 degrees.

```
import java.applet.*;
import java.awt.*;

public class graph1 extends Applet {

public void init() {
setBackground(Color.white);
} /*end init*/

void drawgrid(Graphics g) {
for (int i=0; i<=800; i+=50) {
for (int j=10; j<=40; j+=10) {
g.setColor(Color.lightGray);
g.drawLine((i+j),0,(i+j),800);
g.drawLine(0,(i+j),800,(i+j));
} /*end j loop*/
g.setColor(Color.blue);
g.drawLine(0,i,800,i);
g.drawLine(i,0,i,800);
```

```
g.drawString(""+i,0,i);
g.drawString(""+i,i,10);
} /*end i loop*/
} /*end drawgrid*/


public void paint(Graphics g) {
drawgrid(g);
g.setColor(Color.black);

g.drawArc(20,30,100,100,0,360);
g.drawOval(50,50,12,8);
g.fillOval(54,54,4,4);
g.drawOval(90,50,12,8);
g.fillOval(94,54,4,4);

} /*end paint*/


} /*end class graph1*/
```

Here is the screen:

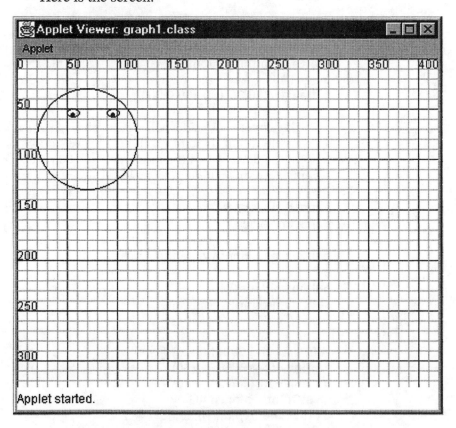

FIGURE 10–5

It looks like we have drawn part of a face. Here's an applet that draws some more features of the face; it also illustrates filling an arc and filling a triangle.

```java
import java.applet.*;
import java.awt.*;

public class graph1b extends Applet {

public void init() {
setBackground(Color.white);
} /*end init*/

void drawgrid(Graphics g) {
for (int i=0; i<=800; i+=50) {
for (int j=10; j<=40; j+=10) {
g.setColor(Color.lightGray);
g.drawLine((i+j),0,(i+j),800);
g.drawLine(0,(i+j),800,(i+j));
} /*end j loop*/
g.setColor(Color.blue);
g.drawLine(0,i,800,i);
g.drawLine(i,0,i,800);
g.drawString(""+i,0,i);
g.drawString(""+i,i,10);
} /*end i loop*/
} /*end drawgrid*/


public void paint(Graphics g) {
drawgrid(g);
g.setColor(Color.black);

g.drawArc(20,30,100,100,0,360); /*face*/
g.drawOval(50,50,12,8); /*left eye*/
g.fillOval(54,54,4,4); /*left pupil*/
g.drawOval(90,50,12,8); /*right eye*/
g.fillOval(94,54,4,4); /*right pupil*/
g.drawLine(70,80,65,90); /*nose*/
g.drawLine(65,90,70,90); /*nose*/
g.drawArc(20,20,100,100,240,60); /*mouth*/
g.drawRect(15,35,120,5); /*hat brim*/
g.fillRect(40,10,60,30); /*hat*/
g.fillArc(10,200,50,50,0,90); /*example of fillArc*/
int x[ ]={100,130,160};
int y[ ]={200,150,200};
int numpoints=x.length;
Polygon triangle1=new Polygon(x,y,numpoints);
g.fillPolygon(triangle1);


} /*end paint*/


} /*end class graph1b*/
```

Here is the screen view:

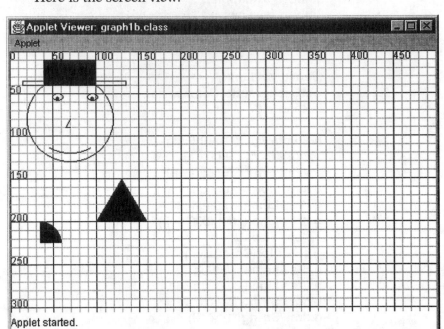

FIGURE 10–6

When you draw objects on the screen, the order does matter, since an object drawn later might cover up an object that was drawn earlier. In this case, the hat covers up the grid that was drawn before it.

Once we've completed the figure, then we can remove the grid. Here's the final version of the smiling face:

```
import java.applet.*;
import java.awt.*;

public class graph1c extends Applet {

public void init() {
setBackground(Color.white);
} /*end init*/

public void paint(Graphics g) {
g.setColor(Color.black);

g.drawArc(20,30,100,100,0,360); /*face*/
g.drawOval(50,50,12,8); /*left eye*/
g.fillOval(54,54,4,4); /*left pupil*/
g.drawOval(90,50,12,8); /*right eye*/
g.fillOval(94,54,4,4); /*right pupil*/
g.drawLine(70,80,65,90); /*nose*/
g.drawLine(65,90,70,90); /*nose*/
g.drawArc(20,20,100,100,240,60); /*mouth*/
g.drawRect(15,35,120,5); /*hat brim*/
g.fillRect(40,10,60,30); /*hat*/

} /*end paint*/

} /*end class graph1c*/
```

FIGURE 10–7

10.3 Converting a Java Applet to a Windows-based Java Application

We can also draw the same graphics figure in an application, instead of in an applet. All of our previous applications displayed their output in a plain text window. In Windows, you see a plain text window when you go to the MS-DOS prompt. Plain text windows are convenient for some purposes because they are easy to use, but they lack the normal behavior you expect in a window, such as the ability to show graphics. Now for the first time we will see how a Java application can display output in a window. It is slightly more complicated for a Java application to do this than it is for an applet. The reason, as you might guess, is that the applet inherits much of the capabilities that it needs from its superclass **Applet**. When you create an application, you need to code a few more steps explicitly. (For more on the difference between applets and applications, see page 31.) Here is the program; some explanatory notes will follow.

```
import java.awt.*;
import java.awt.event.*;

public class graph2 extends Frame {

static graph2 graph2frame;
```

```java
/*constructor method*/
public graph2(String title) {
super(title);
} /*end constructor*/

public void init() {
setBackground(Color.white);
} /*end init*/



public void paint(Graphics g) {
g.setColor(Color.black);

g.drawArc(20,30,100,100,0,360); /*face*/
g.drawOval(50,50,12,8); /*left eye*/
g.fillOval(54,54,4,4); /*left pupil*/
g.drawOval(90,50,12,8); /*right eye*/
g.fillOval(94,54,4,4); /*right pupil*/
g.drawLine(70,80,65,90); /*nose*/
g.drawLine(65,90,70,90); /*nose*/
g.drawArc(20,20,100,100,240,60); /*mouth*/
g.drawRect(15,35,120,5); /*hat brim*/
g.fillRect(40,10,60,30); /*hat*/
} /*end paint*/

/*to close the window:*/
static class winlis extends WindowAdapter {
public void windowClosing(WindowEvent e) {
System.exit(0);
} /*end windowClosing*/
} /*end winlis*/



public static void main(String args[ ]) {

graph2frame=new graph2("Graphics Example Application");
graph2frame.setBounds(10,10,400,300);
graph2frame.addWindowListener(new winlis());
graph2frame.init();
graph2frame.setVisible(true);

} /*end main*/

} /*end class graph2*/
```

For the result, see Figure 10–8. The screen is the same as the applet drawing on page 144, except that the label of the window is different.

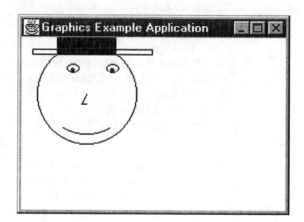

FIGURE 10–8

These are the steps to convert an applet to an application that will display in a window:

1. Instead of extending class **Applet**, our application program (called graph2 in this case) will extend a class called **Frame**. This class provides much of the basic functionality needed by a window.

2. You need to declare a variable that belongs to your program's class (that is, the class named at the start of your program, which is graph2 in our example). In our example, this variable is named graph2frame.

3. We need a constructor for our program's class. The simplest constructor takes only one argument: a string representing the title of the window. You might be thinking, "It will be a lot of work to write the code that makes sure that the window always displays its title bar." But then you realize—it doesn't matter whether that's a lot of work or not. The important thing is that somebody else has written that code and all we need to do is reuse it. Therefore, all that the constructor method for our class graph2 needs to do is call the constructor method of its superclass **Frame**. We've seen how we can do that with the **super** command (see page 119). Here's all the code we need for the constructor:

```
/*constructor method*/
public graph2(String title) {
super(title);
} /*end constructor*/
```

As always, the name of the constructor method matches the name of the class (graph2 in our example).

4. The **init** and **paint** methods can be copied directly from our applet with (almost) no change. However, there is one difference: these methods will no longer be called automatically, as they are with an applet. We need to add a command in the **main** method to call the **init** method explicitly. The command graph2frame.**setVisible(true);** in the **main** method will cause the **paint** method to be called.

5. You may have noticed one new block of code has been added:

```
/*to close the window:*/
static class winlis extends WindowAdapter {
public void windowClosing(WindowEvent e) {
System.exit(0);
} /*end windowClosing*/
} /*end WindowAdapter*/
```

This code defines an *inner class* (called that because it is defined inside the class graph2). The name ends in "lis" because it is a listener class. It is included so that you can close the window (and thereby end the program) in the normal manner (for example, in Windows 95/98/NT by clicking on the "X" in the upper-right-hand corner). This is an example of processing an event, such as a mouse click; more details on events will be in Chapters 13 to 15. Our example program does not need to respond to any other events, but in order to be a well-behaved window it needs to be able to respond to the window closing event.

6. Since our program is an application, rather than an applet, it must include a **main** method. Our main method has five lines:

```
public static void main(String args[ ]) {
graph2frame=new graph2("Graphics Example Application");
graph2frame.setBounds(10,10,400,300);
graph2frame.addWindowListener(new winlis());
graph2frame.init();
graph2frame.setVisible(true);
} /*end main*/
```

The first line instantiates our variable graph2frame (which already has been declared to belong to the class graph2). The string "Graphics Example Application", which is the title of the window, is used as the argument for the constructor.

The second line determines the size and shape of the window with the **setBounds** method. This method comes from the class **Frame**, so it can be used by graph2frame, which is a member of graph2 that inherits from **Frame**. The arguments of **setBounds** are the same as for **drawRect** (see page 137). The first two arguments give the x and y coordinates of the upper-left-hand corner of the window; the next two arguments give the width and height of the window. (All measurements are in pixels.)

The third line is needed so that the program can respond to the window closing event.

The fourth line calls our **init** method. In an applet, the **init** method is called automatically, but in an application only the **main** method is called automatically, so it must explicitly call the **init** method.

Finally, the command graph2frame.**setVisible(true)**; causes the window with our program to appear on the screen. It will call the **paint** method.

If you need to convert a Windows-based Java application to an applet, scc page 251.

10.4 Colors

There are several standard colors that are predefined in Java. Here is an applet that will draw bars on the screen showing the standard colors:

```
import java.applet.*;
import java.awt.*;

public class graph3 extends Applet {

int barheight=45;
int barwidth=600;

public void init() {
setBackground(Color.lightGray);
} /*end init*/

void fillrect2(Graphics g, String colorlabel,
Color barcolor, int barnumber) {
g.setColor(barcolor);
g.fillRect(0,(barnumber-1)*barheight,barwidth,barheight);
g.setColor(Color.black);
g.drawString(colorlabel,20,(barnumber*barheight-5));
} /*end fillrect2*/

public void paint(Graphics g) {
fillrect2(g,"red",Color.red,1);
fillrect2(g,"orange",Color.orange,2);
fillrect2(g,"yellow",Color.yellow,3);
fillrect2(g,"pink",Color.pink,4);
fillrect2(g,"magenta",Color.magenta,5);
fillrect2(g,"blue",Color.blue,6);
fillrect2(g,"cyan",Color.cyan,7);
fillrect2(g,"green",Color.green,8);
} /*end paint*/
} /*end class graph1*/
```

The class **Color** comes with Java; you need to import the **awt** package to include it in your programs. A color object is a specific instance of this class, which defines a particular color. The standard color names are variables in this class, so you can access them by typing an expression like **Color**.red. Notice how the **setColor** command is used. In addition to the eight colors shown in the above applet, you can also use these standard colors: black, white, lightGray, and darkGray.

The output from this applet is not reproduced in the book; instead, you will have to run it on your monitor to see what the colors look like there. Unfortunately, different monitors produce colors differently.

You might think that the standard colors do not provide you with the full range needed to fully express the uniqueness of your program. If so, you can create your own custom colors. All you need to do is understand how colors are stored. Each color is represented as 24 bits in the computer memory. Those bits are divided up into three bytes; one for red, one for green, and one for blue. Since a byte is eight bits, there are $2^8 = 256$ different levels of each color available. (Altogether, there are $2^{24} = 16,777,216$ different colors that can be represented in Java; unfortunately, in reality you are limited by the actual colors your monitor can reproduce.) Each color can be represented by giving three numbers, each from 0 to 255, representing the red, green, and blue levels. For example, (255,0,0) represents red (maximum intensity); (0,255,0) represents green, and (0,0,255) represents blue. If you leave two of the numbers at zero, and then choose a value for the third color, you can adjust the intensity of the color. However, if you adjust down to (0,0,0), then the color will be black. In order to create other colors, you need to mix two or three colors together. If you mix all three colors at highest intensity (255,255,255), then you get white. If your three colors all have equal intensity, then the result will be a shade of gray that will vary between white (255,255,255) and black (0,0,0) depending on the numbers you choose. Mixing red and green produces yellow; mixing red and blue gives magenta; and mixing green and blue gives cyan. Orange can be formed by mixing red and green, with red having a higher intensity than green.

In order to create your own color, you can create an object c of class **Color** with this command:

Color c=**new Color**(*red_level*, *green_level*, *blue_level*);

In the command, red_level, green_level, and blue_level are all integers between 0 and 255. We will usually call a color object c unless another obvious name suggests itself.

Following is an applet that lets you see different shades of red; it is designed so you can adjust it to see different shades of other colors. We have already written a method to display a colored rectangle on the screen with a string for a label (see page 149). We can reuse that method by having our new class graph4 extend our old class graph3.

```java
import java.awt.*;

public class graph4 extends graph3 {

public void paint(Graphics g) {

int numbars=8;
        /*Adjust these three variables to change the color of the top bar:*/
int redlevel=255;
int greenlevel=0;
int bluelevel=0;
        /*Adjust these three variables to see how the colors change
        for the subsequent bars:*/
```

```
int redstep=30;
int greenstep=0;
int bluestep=0;


for (int i=1; i<=numbars; i++) {
Color c=new Color(redlevel,greenlevel,bluelevel);
fillrect2(g,"("+redlevel+","+greenlevel+","+bluelevel+")",c,i);
redlevel-=redstep;
greenlevel-=greenstep;
bluelevel-=bluestep;
} /*end for loop*/
} /*end paint*/


} /*end class graph4*/
```

Because graph3 inherits from **Applet**, and graph4 inherits from graph3, it means that graph4 inherits everything in **Applet**.

10.5 Mathematical Curves

Graphs can be used to visualize mathematical curves as well as data. Next we'll turn to developing a general way of plotting a graph of a curve when we have a y as a function of x. Later we'll look at time series line graphs and xy scatter graphs. (We'll also create a pie chart on page 197.)

One complication we face in drawing graphs is that the pixel coordinate system we have used so far is unlikely to match the mathematical coordinate system that is most convenient for the problem we're working on. Let's figure out a way to convert any generalized coordinate system to pixel coordinates. Keeping in mind our mantra—reusability— we know that we want to write a class to perform this conversion once, and then make the same code available for all of our problems that need to do this.

Let x and y be the mathematical coordinates of a point, and let x_s and y_s be the screen coordinates (measured in pixels) of the same point. In order to do the conversion, we need to know the following:

- the mathematical coordinates of the center of the screen (call these x_c and y_c

- the width and height of the screen window (call these s_w and s_h). These can be obtained from the methods **getSize().width** and **get-Size().height**.

- the x and y axis scaling factors, which determine the mathematical width and height of the screen (call these x_{scale} and y_{scale}).

For example, suppose our window is $s_w = 800$ pixels wide and $s_h = 600$ pixels high. We would like to set up mathematical coordinates whose x values run from -5 to 11 and whose y values run from -2 to 10. This means that the center of the screen has mathematical coordinates $x_c = (-5 + 11)/2 = 3, y_c = (-2 + 10)/2 = 4$; the mathematical width of the screen is $x_{scale} = 11 - (-5) = 16$; and the mathematical height of the screen is $y_{scale} = 10 - (-2) = 12$ (see Figure 10–9). In the figure, the screen coordinate scale is given outside the box; the mathematical coordinate scale is given inside the box. The solid line shows the x and y axes for the mathematical coordinate system; the dotted lines pass through the center of the screen.

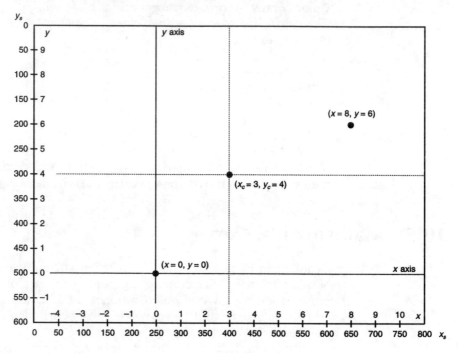

FIGURE 10–9

Suppose we need to find the screen coordinates of the point ($x = 8, y = 6$). First, find the mathematical distance from the center of the screen to this point:

$$x_{distance} = x - x_c = 8 - 3 = 5$$

$$y_{distance} = y - y_c = 6 - 4 = 2$$

Second, convert this distance into a screen distance by multiplying the x value by s_w/x_{scale} and the y value by s_h/y_{scale}:

$$x_{distance(screen\ coordinates)} = (x - x_c)\left(\frac{s_w}{x_{scale}}\right) = 5 \times \frac{800}{16} = 250$$

$$y_{distance(screen\ coordinates)} = (y - y_c)\left(\frac{s_h}{y_{scale}}\right) = 2 \times \frac{600}{12} = 100$$

The above coordinates give the distance from the center of the screen; to convert to the actual screen coordinates we need to add $s_w/2$ to the x coordinate and subtract the y coordinate from $s_h/2$ (recall that screen coordinates in the y direction are measured down):

$$x_s = \frac{s_w}{2} + (x - x_c)\left(\frac{s_w}{x_{scale}}\right)$$

$$y_s = \frac{s_h}{2} - (y - y_c)\left(\frac{s_h}{y_{scale}}\right)$$

For our example, $x_s = 800/2 + (8 - 3)(800/16) = 650$, and $y_s = 600/2 - (6 - 4)(600/12) = 200$. If $x = x_c$ and $y = y_c$, then the formula tells us that the screen coordinates are $(s_w/2, s_h/2)$, which is the center of the screen.

Sometimes we will also need to make the reverse transformation:

$$x = \left(x_s - \frac{s_w}{2}\right)\left(\frac{x_{scale}}{s_w}\right) + x_c$$

$$y = \left(\frac{s_h}{2} - y_s\right)\left(\frac{y_{scale}}{s_h}\right) + y_c$$

We'll create a class called cpjxy, for *Computer Programming in Java xy coordinate system*. It will need to have variables describing screen height and width, x_{center} and y_{center}, and some variables setting colors. It will have methods for converting screen coordinates (x_s, y_s) to mathematical coordinates (x, y), and vice versa. (The mathematical coordinates are **double** values, because they can include fractional values; the screen coordinates are **int** values because the pixels are represented by whole number values.) The power of this approach is that it reduces the amount of things we need to think about when we write future programs. We won't need to think about the screen coordinates any more; we can think of everything in mathematical coordinates and then let the cpjxy class take care of the conversion details.

Here is a list of the methods in the class:

- xs(x): returns the integer screen coordinate *xs* associated with a **double** mathematical coordinate *x*

- ys(y): returns the integer screen coordinate *ys* associated with a **double** mathematical coordinate *y*

- x(xs): returns the **double** mathematical coordinate *x* associated with an integer screen coordinate *xs*

- y(ys): returns the **double** mathematical coordinate *y* associated with an integer screen coordinate *ys*

- xs2(x): returns the integer screen distance (horizontal dimension) corresponding to a mathematical distance *x*

- ys2(y): returns the integer screen distance (vertical dimension) corresponding to a mathematical distance *y*

- dline(x1, y1, x2, y2, g, c): draws a line on the screen from the point with mathematical coordinates (x1,y1) to (x2,y2), of the color specified by c; g is a graphics object.

- dstring(*textstring*, x, y, g, c): draws the string *textstring* on the screen at the mathematical coordinates (x,y), of the color c; g is a graphics object.

- dcircle(r,x,y,g,c): draws a circle on the screen with radius *r* and center at (x,y), of color c; g is a graphics object.

- drawaxes(g): draws x and y axes with the origin at $(x = 0, y = 0)$; g is a graphics object.

- drawaxes(g,xaxisvalue,yaxisvalue): draws x and y axes that pass through the point (x=xaxisvalue, y=yaxisvalue); g is a graphics object.

- drawaxes(g,xaxisvalue,yaxisvalue,xaxisscalefactor,yaxisscalefactor): draws x and y axes that pass through the point $(x = $ xaxisvalue, $y = $ yaxisvalue); g is a graphics object. The numbers displayed on the x and y axis can be adjusted; for example, if xaxisscalefactor is 6, the scale labels on the x axis will read 1, 2, 3, 4, instead of 1,000,000, 2,000,000, 3,000,000, and 4,000,000. Also, a label will appear on the axes indicating that the units are expressed in millions (10^6).

Following is the source code for the class. You might find it interesting to see how the class is constructed, but even if you are not interested in looking at the details, rest assured you can still use the methods from this class in your programs.

```
import java.awt.*;

public class cpjxy {

static int sw=640; /*screen width (pixels)*/
static int sh=360; /*screen height (pixels)*/
static int lm=1; /*left margin, in pixels*/
static int tm=1; /*top margin, in pixels*/

static double xc=0; /*mathematical x coordinate of center of screen*/
static double yc=0; /*mathematical y coordinate of center of screen*/
static double xscale=100; /*width of screen, mathematical units*/
static double yscale=100; /*height of screen, mathematical units*/
static Color axiscolor=Color.blue;
static Color gridcolor=Color.lightGray;
static double xaxisgridstep=10;
static double yaxisgridstep=10;
static double xgridstartvalue=0;
static double ygridstartvalue=0;

static int gridxdp=0; /*xaxis grid label decimal places*/
static int gridydp=0; /*yaxis grid label decimal places*/
static int gridxfw=4; /*xaxis grid label field width*/
static int gridyfw=4; /*yaxis grid label field width*/


/*The next two methods convert mathematical coordinates (x and y)
  to screen coordinates (xs and ys).*/

/*method*/ static int xs(double x) {
return lm+sw/2+(int)((x-xc)*(sw/xscale));
} /*end xs*/

/*method*/ static int ys(double y) {
return sh/2-(int)((y-yc)*(sh/yscale))+tm;
} /*end ys*/
```

```
/*The next two methods convert screen coordinates (xs and ys)
  to mathematical coordinates (x and y).*/

/*method*/ static double x(int xs) {
return (xs-lm-sw/2)*(xscale/sw)+xc;
} /*end x*/

/*method*/ static double y(int ys) {
return (sh/2-ys+tm)*(yscale/sh)+yc;
} /*end y*/

/*method*/ static void dline(
/*Draw a line on the screen between the specified points, expressed
  in mathematical coordinates, of the specified color.*/
double x1, double y1, double x2, double y2,
Graphics g, Color c) {
g.setColor(c);
g.drawLine(xs(x1),ys(y1),xs(x2),ys(y2));
} /*end dline*/

/*method*/ static void dstring(
/*Draw a string on the screen at the specified location, given
  in mathematical coordinates, of the specified color.*/
String textstring, double x, double y,
Graphics g, Color c) {
g.setColor(c);
g.drawString(textstring,xs(x),ys(y));
} /*end dstring*/

/*The next two methods convert mathematical distances to
  screen distances.*/

/*method*/ static int xs2(double x) {
return (int)(x*sw/xscale);}

/*method*/ static int ys2(double y) {
return (int)(y*sh/yscale);}


/*method*/ static void dcircle(double r, double xc,
double yc, Graphics g, Color c) {
/*Note: xscale and yscale must be equal for this to draw a circle.*/
g.setColor(c);
g.drawOval(xs(xc-r),ys(yc+r),xs2(2*r),ys2(2*r));
} /*end dcircle*/


/*method*/ static void drawaxes(Graphics g) {
/*If no x and y axis values are specified, this method draws the
  axes at x = 0 and y = 0; if no axis scaling factors
  are specified, they are both set to 0, which means
  10 to the 0 power = 1.*/
```

```
drawaxes(g,0,0,0,0);
} /*end drawaxes*/
```

```
/*method*/ static void drawaxes(
Graphics g, double xaxisvalue, double yaxisvalue) {
/*This method specifies x and y axis values, but not the axis
  scaling factors, so the axis scaling factors are set
  to 0, which means 10 to the 0 power = 1.*/
drawaxes(g,xaxisvalue,yaxisvalue,0,0);
} /*end drawaxes*/
```

```
/*method*/ static void drawaxes(
Graphics g, double xaxisvalue, double yaxisvalue,
double xaxisscalefactor, double yaxisscalefactor) {
double xfactor=1; String xaxisstring="";
double yfactor=1; String yaxisstring="";
if (xaxisscalefactor!=0) {xfactor=Math.pow(10,xaxisscalefactor);
                                 xaxisstring="10E"+xaxisscalefactor;
                                 }
if (yaxisscalefactor!=0) {yfactor=Math.pow(10,yaxisscalefactor);
                                 yaxisstring="10E"+yaxisscalefactor;
                                 }

       /*If the origin (0,0) is on the screen, then xgridstartvalue
          and ygridstartvalue will both be 0.
          If the origin is not on the screen, then the following lines
          adjust these values so they are on the screen.*/
while (xgridstartvalue<(xc-xscale/2))
          {xgridstartvalue+=xaxisgridstep;}
while (xgridstartvalue>(xc+xscale/2))
          {xgridstartvalue-=xaxisgridstep;}
while (ygridstartvalue<(yc-yscale/2))
          {ygridstartvalue+=yaxisgridstep;}
while (ygridstartvalue>(yc+yscale/2))
          {ygridstartvalue-=yaxisgridstep;}


       /*Draw grid lines:*/
double xgrid=xgridstartvalue+xaxisgridstep;
double ygrid=ygridstartvalue+yaxisgridstep;

int numberofxgridlines=(int)(xscale/xaxisgridstep);
int numberofygridlines=(int)(yscale/yaxisgridstep);
int maxsteps=numberofxgridlines;
if (numberofygridlines>maxsteps) {maxsteps=numberofygridlines;}
```

```
        /*The program labels the scale along the x and y axes; it also
          adds a second set of labels if the x and y axes are off the screen.*/
boolean addsecondxgridlabels=false;
boolean addsecondygridlabels=false;
if (Math.abs(yaxisvalue-yc)>yscale/2) {addsecondxgridlabels=true;}
if (Math.abs(xaxisvalue-xc)>xscale/2) {addsecondygridlabels=true;}

for (int i=1; i<=maxsteps; i++) {

/*yaxisvalue is the y coordinate of where you draw the */
/*x axis, which is 0 when you draw the axes through the origin.*/
dline(xgrid,y(tm),xgrid,y(sh+tm),g,gridcolor);
/*Put labels along the positive x axis:*/
dstring(cpj.nf(xgrid/xfactor,gridxfw,gridxdp),xgrid,yaxisvalue,g,axiscolor);
if (addsecondxgridlabels) {
dstring(cpj.nf(xgrid/xfactor,gridxfw,gridxdp),xgrid,yc,g,axiscolor);}
dline(-xgrid,y(tm),-xgrid,y(sh+tm),g,gridcolor);
/*Put labels along the negative x axis:*/
dstring(cpj.nf(-xgrid/xfactor,gridxfw,gridxdp),-xgrid,yaxisvalue,g,axiscolor);
if (addsecondxgridlabels) {
dstring(cpj.nf(xgrid/xfactor,gridxfw,gridxdp),-xgrid,yc,g,axiscolor);}


/*xaxisvalue is the x coordinate of where you draw the */
/*y axis, which is 0 when you draw the axes through the origin.*/
dline(x(lm),ygrid,x(sw+lm),ygrid,g,gridcolor);
/*Put labels along the positive y axis*/
dstring(cpj.nf(ygrid/yfactor,gridyfw,gridydp),xaxisvalue,ygrid,g,axiscolor);
if (addsecondygridlabels) {
dstring(cpj.nf(xgrid/xfactor,gridxfw,gridxdp),xc,ygrid,g,axiscolor);}

dline(x(lm),-ygrid,x(sw+lm),-ygrid,g,gridcolor);
/*Put labels along the negative y axis*/
dstring(cpj.nf(-ygrid/yfactor,gridyfw,gridydp),xaxisvalue,-
ygrid,g,axiscolor);
if (addsecondygridlabels) {
dstring(cpj.nf(xgrid/xfactor,gridxfw,gridxdp),xc,-ygrid,g,axiscolor);}

xgrid+=xaxisgridstep;
ygrid+=yaxisgridstep;

} /*end for loop*/

/*Draw x and y axes:*/
dline(x(0),yaxisvalue,x(sw),yaxisvalue,g,axiscolor); /*x axis*/
dline(xaxisvalue,y(tm),xaxisvalue,y(sh+tm),g,axiscolor); /*y axis*/
dstring(xaxisstring,x(sw)-5,y(sh+tm),g,axiscolor);
dstring(yaxisstring,xaxisvalue+x(5),y(tm-10),g,axiscolor);


} /*end drawaxes*/


} /*end class cpjxy*/
```

We've defined a method dline, which is like **drawLine** except that it takes mathematical coordinates, rather than screen coordinates, and it also takes the color of the line as one of the arguments. (With **drawLine**, you have to specify the color with a separate **setColor** command before you call **drawLine**.) Likewise, the dstring function is like **drawString**, except that it takes mathematical coordinates, rather than screen coordinates, and it also takes the color as one of the arguments.

The most complicated part of the cpjxy class are the methods for drawing and labeling axes; these have been set up to be very general, which will be helpful later on.

We can use this class in many other programs that use graphics. Here's our first example: we want to draw a graph of the curve $y = x^2/5$.

```
import java.applet.*;
import java.awt.*;

public class curvegraph extends Applet {

public void init() {
setBackground(Color.white);
cpjxy.xscale=25; /*width of screen, mathematical units*/
cpjxy.yscale=50; /*height of screen, mathematical units*/
cpjxy.yc=20; /*y coordinate of center of screen*/
                /*x coordinate of center of screen will stay at 0*/
} /*end init*/

/*The following method is the method you need to change to display
  different curves.*/
/*method*/ double y (double x) {
return (x*x/5);
} /*end y*/

public void paint(Graphics g) {
double oldx1=0; double oldy1=0;

cpjxy.drawaxes(g);

/*xs is in screen coordinates; x1 and y1 are mathematical coordinates.*/

for (int xs=1; xs<=cpjxy.sw; xs++) {
double x1=cpjxy.x(xs);
double y1=y(x1);

if (xs>1) {cpjxy.dline(oldx1,oldy1,x1,y1,g,Color.black);}
oldx1=x1;
oldy1=y1;
} /*end for loop*/

} /*end paint*/

} /*end class curvegraph*/
```

The **init** method defines values for xscale, yscale, and yc, overriding the values defined in the cpjxy class. The other variables, such as sh and sw, are not overridden, so they will still have the same values defined in that class. (When using this program, you will often redefine xscale and yscale; but you should leave sh and sw the same as long as you are using the same monitor.)

Here is our graph on the screen:

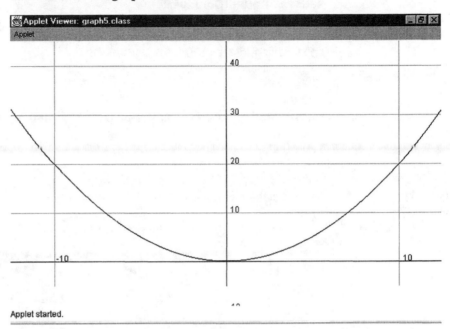

FIGURE 10–10

The **paint** method contains a loop, where xs (measured in screen coordinates) advances from the left edge to the right edge of the screen. The statement x1=cpjxy.x(xs) converts this value to mathematical coordinates; then $y_1 = y(x_1)$ calculates the corresponding value of y; then the dline method draws part of the curve. (It actually draws lines connecting two adjacent points, but since these points are only one pixel apart it creates the appearance of being a smooth curve, unless you magnify the pixels.) In order to print the graph in the book, we have used a black curve on a white background. You can experiment with different colors.

Our next problem is to draw a graph of a more complicated curve, the fourth-degree polynomial

$$y = x^4 - 4x^3 - 101x^2 + 444x + 540$$

How much work do you think it will be to write this program? The answer is: very little, because we've already done almost all of the work. Remember the key word: reusability. We'll create a new program class curvegraph2 that extends curvegraph, so that it takes advantage of all the work we did there. All we need to do is override the function y to represent our new curve, and then change the values of some of the scaling parameters.

```java
import java.applet.*;

import java.awt.*;

public class curvegraph2 extends curvegraph {

public void init() {
setBackground(Color.white);
cpjxy.xscale=30;
cpjxy.yscale=10000;
cpjxy.yaxisgridstep=500;
} /*end init*/

/*method*/ double y (double x) {
return (Math.pow(x,4)-4*Math.pow(x,3)-101*Math.pow(x,2)+
    444*x+540);
} /*end y*/


} /*end class curvegraph2*/
```

Here is the graph on the screen:

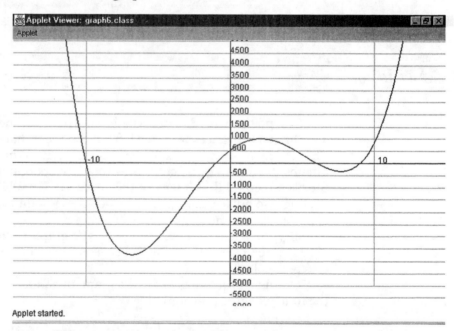

FIGURE 10–11   Applet started.

This curve is interesting because it changes direction three times, and crosses the x axis in four places ($x = -10, x = -1, x = 6$, and $x = 9$).

Making graphs of any curve is now very easy: write a new function for y, adjust the scaling parameters, and have your program extend the class *curvegraph*. "It's still not easy enough," you might say, "We should be able to adjust the scale of the graph while we are looking at it, instead of going back to the text editor to change the source file and then recompiling." We will learn how to do that later (see page 259).

You might also wonder, "What if your program asks the computer to plot a point that is not on the screen?" Fortunately, there is no harm done. The computer simply ignores that request and keeps working until it comes to some points that it can plot.

10.6   JAR Files

In our previous program, the computer needed access to two class files, curvegraph.class and curvegraph2.class. If someone connects to the web to view our applet, it will be inefficient because their browser will need to make two connections to the server so it can retrieve both class files. Also, since download time is very precious, you probably think it would help if the files could be compressed during the download process. Fortunately, Java 1.1 provides JARs. An ordinary jar allows you to store things; a JAR (Java Archive File) allows you to combine Java class files and other files into a single archived file that is compressed and downloaded as a unit.

To create our JAR file, use this command:

```
jar cf curve.jar curvegraph.class curvegraph2.class
```

Reading from left to right, "jar" is the name of the command; "cf" basically stands for "create file;" "curve.jar" is the name of the JAR file that will be created; and curvegraph.class and curvegraph2.class are the two class files that will be included in the JAR. If you have more than two files to include, you can also use file wildcard expressions (for example, a*.class will include all files beginning with "a" in the current directory). You can also include other files used by an applet, such as image files or sound files.

In order to post the JAR file on the web, create this HTML code:

```
<html>
<head><title>curve graph</title></head>
<body>
<APPLET CODE="curvegraph2.class" ARCHIVE="curve.jar"
width=500 height=300>
a java compatible browser is needed for this
</applet>
</body>
</html>
```

The CODE parameter of the APPLET tag gives the name of the class file that will be executed, as before. There is now one additional parameter, the ARCHIVE parameter, which gives the name of the JAR file.

If you study Java further you will also learn how JAR files provide additional features such as the ability to attach a digital signature and to check to make sure that the original files have not been tampered with.

10.7 Time Series Line Graph

Another useful graph is a graph that shows how a variable changes over time. The horizontal axis will indicate time; the vertical axis will indicate the value of the variable. We can use much of the same code we have already developed.

We'll do a sample with 10 data points, which we'll enter into an array a.

```java
import java.applet.*;
import java.awt.*;

public class tsgr1 extends Applet {

int numpoints=10;
double a[ ]=new double[numpoints+1];

public void setvals() {

a[1]=40.0; a[2]=55.0; a[3]=60.0; a[4]=72.0; a[5]=84.0;
a[6]=70.0; a[7]=60.0; a[8]=40.0; a[9]=30.0; a[10]=28.0;

numpoints=10;

cpjxy.yscale=100;
cpjxy.xscale=12;
cpjxy.yaxisgridstep=20;
cpjxy.xaxisgridstep=2;
cpjxy.xc=5;
cpjxy.yc=40;
} /*end setvals*/

public void init() {

setvals();
setBackground(Color.white);
cpjxy.lm=10; /*left margin*/
cpjxy.tm=10; /*top margin*/
            /*xc and yc are the mathematical
               coordinates of the center of the screen.*/


} /*end init*/

public void paint(Graphics g) {
cpjxy.drawaxes(g);

/*set initial value of x:*/
double xvalue=1;

for (int i=1; i<=(numpoints-1); i++) {
        cpjxy.dline (xvalue,a[i],(xvalue+1),a[i+1],g,Color.black);
        xvalue++;
```

```
} /*end for loop*/

} /*end paint*/

} /*end class tsgr1*/
```

Note that the program allows for the grid step to be different from the distance between values. However, we want a program that is more versatile, since we don't want the horizontal axis values always to start at 1.

Here is a revised version of the time series graph program:

```
import java.applet.*;
import java.awt.*;

public class tsgr2 extends Applet {

int numpoints=100;
double a[ ]=new double[numpoints]; /*assume 100 maximum data
points*/
double deltax=1.0;
double xaxisscalefactor=0; /*used for determining how numbers on*/
double yaxisscalefactor=0; /*axes will appear*/
double datastartvalue=0;

public void setvals() {

a[1]=40.0; a[2]=55.0; a[3]=60.0; a[4]=72.0; a[5]=84.0;
a[6]=70.0; a[7]=60.0; a[8]=40.0; a[9]=30.0; a[10]=28.0;

numpoints=10;

cpjxy.yscale=100;
cpjxy.xscale=12;
cpjxy.yaxisgridstep=20;
cpjxy.xaxisgridstep=2;
datastartvalue= 1990; /*1990 is the first year for our data.*/
} /*end setvals*/

public void init() {

setvals();
setBackground(Color.white);
cpjxy.lm=10; /*left margin*/
cpjxy.tm=10; /*top margin*/
cpjxy.xgridstartvalue=datastartvalue-deltax;
cpjxy.xc=cpjxy.xscale/2+cpjxy.xgridstartvalue;
cpjxy.yc=cpjxy.yscale/2;
                /*xc and yc are the mathematical
                    coordinates of the center of the screen.*/


} /*end init*/
```

```
public void paint(Graphics g) {
cpjxy.drawaxes(g,cpjxy.xgridstartvalue,0,xaxisscalefactor,yaxisscalefactor);

/*Set initial value of x:*/
double xvalue=datastartvalue;

for (int i=1; i<=(numpoints-1); i++) {
        cpjxy.dline(xvalue,a[i],(xvalue+deltax),a[i+1],g,Color.black);
        xvalue+=deltax;
} /*end for loop*/

} /*end paint*/

} /*end class tsgr2*/
```

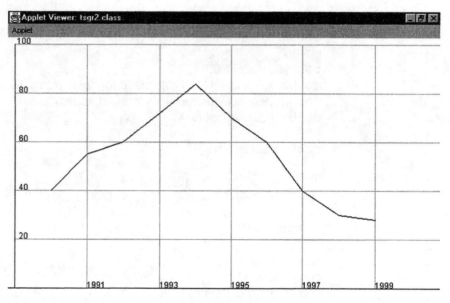

FIGURE 10–12   Applet started.

Following is an example with real data, showing how the population of the U.S. has grown. All we need to do is extend the **tsgr2** class, and override the **setvalues** method.

```
import java.applet.*;
import java.awt.*;

public class popgr extends tsgr2 {


public void setvals() {
a[1]=76212168; /*1900*/
a[2]=92228496; /*1910*/
a[3]=106021537; /*1920*/
a[4]=123202624; /*1930*/
```

```
a[5]=132164569; /*1940*/
a[6]=151325798; /*1950*/
a[7]=179323175; /*1960*/
a[8]=203302031; /*1970*/
a[9]=226542203; /*1980*/
a[10]=248718301; /*1990*/
numpoints=10;
deltax=10;
datastartvalue=1900; /*1900 is the first year for our data.*/

cpjxy.yscale=250000000; /*250,000,000*/
cpjxy.xscale=120; /*The width of the screen will be 120 years.*/
cpjxy.yaxisgridstep=25000000; /*25,000,000*/
cpjxy.xaxisgridstep=20; /*Draw a grid line every 20 years.*/

yaxisscalefactor=6; /*Show the y axis numbers divided by a factor
                      of 10 to the 0th power, or one million.*/
} /*end setvals*/


} /*end class popgr*/
```

Here is the graph:

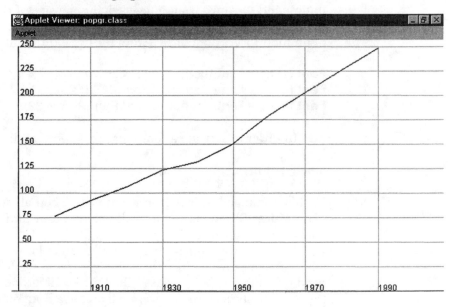

FIGURE 10–13

10.8   Fonts

As we're designing special graphical effects for our Java programs, most likely we will want more flexibility in the display of text. Fortunately, we have several options for adjusting the style and size of the fonts used for our text.

First, we need to know what fonts we have available. The following commands will display a list of fonts available on your system:

String fontslist=**this.getToolkit().getFontList**();

for (int i=0; i<=fontslist.**length**-1; i++) {
System.out.println("␣"+i+"␣␣"+fontslist[i]);
                                                                } /*end for loop*/

You should expect at least three standard fonts: a font with serifs, such as Times Roman; a sans-serif font, such as Helvetica, and a monospaced (not proportionally spaced) font, such as Courier.

To use a font, we need to create an object of the **Font** class. The constructor we'll use takes three arguments: the first is a string describing the font; the second describes the style of the font (plain, bold, or italic); and the third is an integer giving the size of the font, measured in points. (A point is a unit of measurement in typesetting equal to 1/72 of an inch.) Here are constructors for three different font objects:

Font f1=**new Font("serif",Font.ITALIC**,16);
Font f2=**new Font("sanserif",Font.BOLD**,24);
Font f3=**new Font("monospaced",Font.PLAIN**,32);

In order to activate a font f, use this command:

g.**setFont**(f);

In this command, **g** is a graphics object. Then all subsequent output from a **drawString** command will use this font until another **setFont** command is called.

There also are times when we will need to know the size of a string when it is displayed. Since the size depends on the font being used, we need information from a class called the **FontMetrics** class. For each of the three fonts declared above, we'll create a **FontMetrics** object, using the **getFontMetrics** method, whose argument is a font:

FontMetrics fm1=**getFontMetrics**(f1);
FontMetrics fm2=**getFontMetrics**(f2);
FontMetrics fm3=**getFontMetrics**(f3);

These statements mean that fm1 will be the **FontMetrics** object that applies to font f1, while fm2 applies to f2, and so on. Once we have a **FontMetrics** object fm, we can find the width of a string **s** with fm.**getWidth**(s); we can find the total height of the font with fm.**getHeight**(); and we can find the descent (that is, the distance that the letters g, j, p, q, and y extend below the baseline of the font) with fm.**getDescent**(). (All measurements are in pixels.) We need all three of the above items to determine the exact amount of space occupied by a particular string. To illustrate these concepts, a program follows that first displays the list of available fonts, and then writes three strings to the screens with different fonts. For each of these strings, the program draws a rectangle that surrounds the string exactly.

```java
import java.applet.*;
import java.awt.*;
import java.awt.event.*;

public class font1 extends Applet {

String[ ] fontslist;
Font f1; FontMetrics fm1;
Font f2; FontMetrics fm2;
Font f3; FontMetrics fm3;

/*method*/ public void init() {
setBackground(Color.white);

fontslist=this.getToolkit().getFontList();

for (int i=0; i<=fontslist.length-1; i++) {
System.out.println("␣"+i+"␣␣"+fontslist[i]);
                                    } /*end for loop*/
f1=new Font("serif",Font.ITALIC,16);
f2=new Font("sanserif",Font.BOLD,24);
f3=new Font("monospaced",Font.PLAIN,32);

fm1=getFontMetrics(f1);
fm2=getFontMetrics(f2);
fm3=getFontMetrics(f3);

} /*end init*/

/*method*/ void showfont
(String s, Font f, FontMetrics fm, int yloc, Graphics g) {
g.setColor(Color.black);
g.setFont(f);
g.drawString(s,10,yloc);
int swidth=fm.stringWidth(s);
int sheight=fm.getHeight();
int sdescent=fm.getDescent();
g.setColor(Color.blue);
g.drawRect(10, yloc-sheight+sdescent, swidth, sheight);
} /*end showfont*/

/*method*/ public void paint(Graphics g) {
showfont("serif italic 16 point",f1,fm1,30,g);
showfont("sanserif bold 24 point",f2,fm2,100,g);
showfont("monospaced 32 point",f3,fm3,200,g);
} /*end paint*/

} /*end font1*/
```

Here is the screen showing the results:

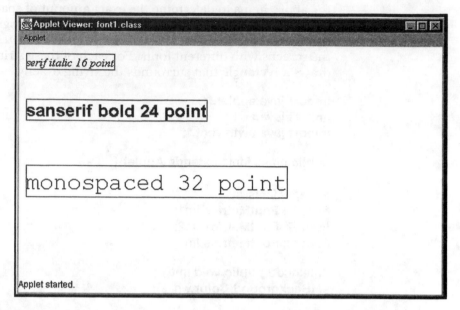

FIGURE 10–14

10.9   Including a Graphing Method in Our Boat Class

We'll do one more program in this chapter. You recall that we developed a boat object in the last chapter. Now, we can add a method to the boat class that plots the course of the boat on the screen. Following is the program (converted to an applet). Notice that we have added some variables to the boatclass: color; oldx; and oldy.

```
import java.applet.*;
import java.awt.*;

public class boatprogram2 extends Applet {

static int numboats=4;

static boatclass boat[ ]=new boatclass[numboats+1];

double time=0;
double deltatime=0.4;

public void init () {

setBackground(Color.lightGray);
boatclass boat0=new boatclass(1.6, 0.3, 6.1, 10.4, Color.red);
boat[1]=boat0;
boat0=new boatclass(30.5, 46.8, -5.2, -1.4, Color.blue);
boat[2]=boat0;
boat0=new boatclass(15.8, 20.4, 7.2, -4.9, Color.green);
boat[3]=boat0;
boat0=new boatclass(7.4, 14.8, 0.2, 8.6, Color.magenta);
boat[4]=boat0;
```

```
cpjxy.xscale=200;
cpjxy.yscale=200;
cpjxy.xc=50;
cpjxy.yc=50;
cpjxy.xaxisgridstep=20;
cpjxy.yaxisgridstep=20;

} /*end init*/


public void paint(Graphics g) {

cpjxy.drawaxes(g);

while (time<5) {

for (int i=1; i<=numboats; i++) {
boat[i].moveboat(deltatime);
boat[i].plotcourse(g);
/*The next lines introduce a time delay of 1 second (1000 milliseconds).*/
try {
Thread.currentThread().sleep(1000);
} catch (InterruptedException ex) { }
} /*end i loop*/

      time+=deltatime;
       } /*end while*/
} /*end paint*/

} /*end boatprogram2*/

class boatclass {
double x=0; double y=0;
double vx=0; double vy=0;
double oldx=0; double oldy=0;

Color boatcolor=Color.black;

/*constructor method*/ public boatclass(
double x, double y, double vx, double vy,
Color c) {
this.x=x; this.y=y;
this.vx=vx; this.vy=vy;
this.boatcolor=c;
} /*end constructor method*/

/*method*/ void moveboat(double deltatime) {
oldx=x;
oldy=y;
x+=vx*deltatime;
y+=vy*deltatime;
} /*end moveboat*/
```

```
/*method*/ void plotcourse(Graphics g) {
cpjxy.dline(oldx,oldy,x,y,g,boatcolor);
} /*end plotcourse*/

} /*end boatclass*/
```

EXERCISES

For Exercises 1–17, write a program that draws the figure on the screen.

1. checkerboard

2. dartboard

3. analog clock (that is, a clock with hands that move around a circular dial)

4. phases of the moon

5. spiral

6. Valentine's day heart

7. five-pointed star

8. hourglass

9. football

10. football field

11. baseball diamond

12. profile of a car

13. ellipse

14. eye

15. cube (Create a perspective drawing that makes the cube look three-dimensional.)

16. donut

17. comet with a long tail

18. Write a method that draws a triangle on the screen. Have the method take six arguments, representing the coordinates of the three vertices of the triangle. Then write similar methods for other polygons, such as quadrilaterals, pentagons, and hexagons.

19. Write a program that draws an xy (scatter) graph, which shows the relationship between two variables when you have n pairs of observations for the variables.

20. Write a program that draws a bar graph, where the height of each bar represents the relative sizes of the data items.

21. Convert the bar graph program from the previous exercise into a three-dimensional bar graph program.

22. Write a dynamic pie chart program that adds one slice to the pie chart each time the mouse is clicked.

CHAPTER 11

FILES

11.1   Input and Output from Text Files

So far, the only output we have generated in our programs has been sent to the screen. For many purposes, screen output is too ephemeral; as soon as the screen changes, the output is lost forever. What we need is a way of storing output. We can do that (at least with text output) by writing it to a file.

Also, our programs so far have taken input from the keyboard. We will also want to be able to take input that we have previously stored, or that has been generated by other programs. To do that, we need to take input from files.

We will first work with text files, and then later look at files of objects. Text files themselves are very versatile and let us work with many kinds of data. We can work with anything that can be represented as a text file. . . which includes Java source code files. Take a moment to realize how this will significantly increase our power: we can write programs that generate other programs. Programs are designed to reduce the tedious work we need to do, so we will eventually see how we can reduce the amount of work required for writing programs. Any programming construct that follows a regular pattern can be generated this way.

11.2   Generating the HTML File for an Applet

Here is one useful task we can do right away. Each time we have created a new applet, we have had to generate a block of HTML code that looks like this (see page 26):

```
<html>
<head><title>file1</title></head>
<body>
<APPLET CODE="file1.class" width=720 height=480>
a java compatible browser is needed for this
</applet>
```

```
</body>
</html>
```

Wouldn't it be nice if we could automatically generate this code? These are the general steps we need to take to write output to a text file:

- Import the package **java.io.***

- Instantiate an object of class **DataOutput**, which is linked to a **FileOutputStream**.

- Use the command **writeBytes** to send string output to this file.

- Check for errors in case the program cannot create the requested file.

Here is the program:

```
import java.io.*;

public class file1a {

public static void main(String arg[ ]) {

try{
DataOutput f1 =
    new DataOutputStream(new FileOutputStream("example.htm"));

f1.writeBytes("<html>"+"\r\n");
f1.writeBytes("<head><title>file1</title></head>"+"\r\n");
f1.writeBytes("<body>"+"\r\n");
f1.writeBytes("<APPLET CODE="example.class" width=720
height=480>"+"\r\n");
f1.writeBytes("a java compatible browser is needed for this"+"\r\n");
f1.writeBytes("</applet>"+"\r\n");
f1.writeBytes("</body>"+"\r\n");
f1.writeBytes("</html>"+"\r\n");

} catch (Exception ex) {String err = ex.toString();
                                    System.out.println(err);}

} /*end main*/

} /*end class file1a*/
```

The statement

```
DataOutput f1 =
    new DataOutputStream(new FileOutputStream("example.htm"));
```

creates an object f1 that will write to a file called "example.htm". We can use the **writeBytes** method to write a string to that file; for example, the command

```
f1.writeBytes("<html>");
```

will write the string <html> to the file. However, after we write a string, then we need to include a marker to tell the computer to write the next string on a new line. Otherwise, there would be a jumble like this:

```
<html><head><title>file1</title></head><body><APPLET CODE="fi
```

The string "\r\n" stands for carriage return and line feed (see page 22). Therefore, we include it at the end of each string when we want the following string to appear on a new line.

There is one other complication with writing characters to the file. We want to write these characters for our specific example:

```
<APPLET CODE="example.class" width=720 height=480>
```

However, we have a problem if we write it like this:

```
f1.writeBytes("<APPLET CODE="example.class" width=720
      height=480>");
```

The problem is that the " character is used to mark the end of the string, so we cannot use it in the middle of the string. The solution is to precede it by the backslash character \ (see page 22).

```
f1.writeBytes("<APPLET CODE=\"example.class\"
      width=720 height=480>");
```

Another new feature of our program is that we have enclosed most of the **main** method in a block beginning with **try**. A **try** block is used in Java when you have a block of code that might cause a particular exception (error). Following the **try** block is a **catch** block, which contains some code to execute if an exception occurs. In our program, the code in the **catch** block only causes an error message to be displayed. If you try to compile the program without the **try** and **catch** blocks, this error message will appear:

```
Exception java.io.IOException must be caught, or it must be
declared in the throws clause of this method
```

Any operation involving writing to a file has the potential for causing an IOException (if, for example, the file name given in the program is invalid, or the disk is full or write-protected). Therefore, the Java compiler tells you, "I'm not going to let you compile a program involving files unless I have specific instructions about what to do if there is a problem."

There is one other complication: the programs in this chapter that write data to files only work with applications, not applets. The reason is that an applet can be put on a web page, which means it will be automatically executed whenever a browser comes to that page. If an applet could read and write files to your hard disk, then a malicious programmer could write an applet that could trash your hard disk. The programmer could put the applet on the web, and then wait for unwary browsers to fall into the trap. The applet code would start executing before you knew it, and your disk could be trashed. Therefore, Java was created with a very strong security restriction preventing applets from doing that. You might be asking, "Isn't there a danger that a malicious programmer could write a Java application that would trash your disk?" The answer is yes, but you are much better protected from applications because you have much more control over running them. To run an application, you need to have it loaded on your disk first, and then make a specific command to run it. You still should be careful; so if a mysterious stranger hands you a disk with a Java application and asks you to run it on your computer, you should say no. Normally an application program will come from some source that you trust.

11.3   Writing to a File Named by the User

Our previous program is rather limited, because it only creates files with the name "example.htm". We can write a new version of the program that will allow us to specify the name of the file that will be created. We will assume that you wish to use the same name for the htm file that you use for the class file that is included in the applet tag.

```java
import java.io.*;

public class file1 {


public static void main(String arg[ ]) {
String filename=arg[0];

try{
DataOutput f1 = new DataOutputStream (new
        FileOutputStream(filename+".HTM"));

f1.writeBytes("<html>"+"\r\n");
f1.writeBytes("<head><title>file1</title></head>"+"\r\n");
f1.writeBytes("<body>"+"\r\n");
f1.writeBytes("<APPLET CODE=""+filename+".class" width=720
        height=480>"+"\r\n");
f1.writeBytes("a java compatible browser is needed for this"+"\r\n");
f1.writeBytes("</applet>"+"\r\n");
f1.writeBytes("</body>"+"\r\n");
f1.writeBytes("</html>"+"\r\n");

} catch (Exception ex) {String err = ex.toString();
                                System.out.println(err);}

} /*end main*/

} /*end class file1*/
```

This program will take the file name that it will write to from the command line. For example, type the command line

```
java file1 example
```

if you want to create the file for an applet called *example*.

Notes:

- In Windows, file names are not case sensitive; however, you should be consistent with capitalization of file names because strings representing file names in Java are case sensitive.

- If you would like to generalize the program, have it read in the values for height and width.

- This program uses the file extension ".htm" in case you would ever need to copy the file to a system that is limited to short file names. If you are sure you will always work on a system allowing long file names, you can change the extension to ".html".

11.4   Reading from a Text File

Our next task is to write a program that reads in a text file and displays it on the screen.

```
import java.io.*;

public class file2 {
public static void main(String arg[ ]) {
    /*This program reads in a text file whose name is given in the
      command line argument, and it displays the text on the screen.*/

String fn=arg[0]; /*fn is short for file name.*/
try{
DataInput f1 = new DataInputStream(new FileInputStream(fn));
String textline;
textline=f1.readLine();
while (textline!=null) {
        System.out.println(textline);
        textline=f1.readLine();
            } /*end while*/
} catch (Exception ex) {String err = ex.toString();
                                        System.out.println(err);}

} /*end main*/
} /*end class file2*/
```

From now on, we will use fn as an abbreviation for file name. With this program, we will need to give the complete file name (including extension) in the command line. For example, use the command line

```
java file2 example.htm
```

to display the file *example.htm*.

Note that our program creates a **DataInput** object f1, instead of a **DataOutput** object as we did in the programs earlier in the chapter. When reading from a file, we need a **while** loop, since we will usually not know in advance how many lines the file will contain. The **readLine** method will read one line of the file. The **while** loop will continue executing until the line read in is **null**, which will happen at the end of the file.

11.5   Copying from One File to Another

Another common task is to copy one file to another file. Here is the program:

```java
import java.io.*;

class filecopy {
/*This program copies one text file to another.*/
/*The file names are read as command line arguments.*/

public static void main(String arg[ ]) {
String f1n=arg[0]; /*name of file to read from*/
String f2n=arg[1]; /*name of file to write to*/

try{
DataInput f1 = new DataInputStream(new FileInputStream(f1n));
DataOutput f2 = new DataOutputStream(new
          FileOutputStream(f2n));

String x=f1.readLine();
while (x!= null) {
          f2.writeBytes(x+"\r\n");
          x=f1.readLine();
} /*end while*/
} catch (Exception ex) {String err = ex.toString();
                                    System.out.println(err);}

} /*end main*/
} /*end class filecopy*/
```

The pieces we see here are the same as we saw in the program to write to a file (page 175) and the program to read from a file (page 176), but now they're combined into one program.

The input file is the first command line argument and the output file is the second command line argument. So, for example, use the command line

```
java filecopy test1.doc test2.doc
```

to copy the file *test1.doc* to the file *test2.doc*.

We will commonly use these variable names:

- f1: the name of the data input stream in our Java program

- f1n: the string variable representing the name of the input file used by the operating system

- f2: the name of the data output stream in our Java program

- f2n: the string variable representing the name of the output file used by the operating system

11.6   Copying Selected Lines of One File to Another File

Sometimes we will want to copy the contents of one file to another, but also make some changes along the way. Once we have our own program, we can make whatever changes we wish in the way it processes the strings before it writes them to the output file.

For example, suppose we wish to copy only those lines that contain "*". The other lines in the input file will be ignored. We'll want to write our program as generally as possible so it is easy to reuse it for a variety of different problems. First, we'll write a class containing the code for reading the input file and writing the output file:

```
import java.io.*;

public class procfile {

/*method*/ static void processfile
(String f1n, String f2n, processstringclass ps) {
/*f1n=name of file to read from*/
/*f2n=name of file to write to*/

try{
DataInput f1 = new DataInputStream(new FileInputStream(f1n));
DataOutput f2 = new DataOutputStream(new
        FileOutputStream(f2n));

boolean writeok=true;
ps.x=f1.readLine();
while (ps.x!=null) {
        System.out.println("reading line:"+ps.x);
          writeok=ps.processstring(writeok);
        if (writeok) {f2.writeBytes(ps.z+"\r\n");
                                System.out.println(" writing line:"+ps.z);}
            ps.x=f1.readLine();
            } /*end while*/
} catch (Exception ex) {String err = ex.toString();
                                System.out.println(err);}

} /*end processfile*/

} /*end class procfile*/
```

This class contains only one method, processfile. It calls the method processstring from an object ps. This method returns a **boolean** value writeok that will be true if we should write this line and false otherwise. In addition, processstring takes the line x from the input file and converts it to a line z that is written to the output file. This means that we can write the method processstring to perform whatever task we wish to each line of the file.

To make things as general as possible, we'll define an abstract class processstringclass:

```
abstract class processstringclass {
```

```
String x; String z;
abstract boolean processstring
(boolean previouswriteok);
} /*end processstringclass*/
```

When we face an actual problem, we will extend processstringclass by defining the method processstring to do what we want. For example, suppose we would like to create a new file where we copy every line from the original file containing an asterisk, but no other lines. We'll create a class processstring1 that defines the processstring method like this:

```
class processstring1 extends processstringclass {

boolean processstring(boolean previouswriteok) {
boolean result=false;
int L=x.indexOf("*");
if (L>=0) {result=true;
                          z=x;}
return result;
} /*end processstring*/

} /*end processstring1*/
```

This method checks to see if the input string x contains an asterisk. If it does, it returns the value **true**; otherwise, it returns **false** (meaning that line will not be written to the output file). Since we do not want to make any change in the output string in this problem, the method includes the assignment statement z=x;. The method also contains a third parameter, previouswriteok, which we are ignoring for now. We'll use that parameter on page 180.

We need one more class: the one containing the **main** method that will actually execute our program. Since we've already done most of the work, it will be easy to write this class:

```
import java.io.*;

public class filerw {

public static void main(String arg[ ]) {
String f1n=arg[0]; /*input file*/
String f2n=arg[1]; /*output file*/

processstring1 ps1=new processstring1();
procfile.processfile(f1n,f2n,ps1);

} /*end main*/

} /*end class filerw*/
```

If we type the command line

```
java filerw test1.doc test2.doc
```

the computer will read through each line of *test1.doc* and copy the lines containing asterisks to *test2.doc*.

Now we'll see how quickly we can write additional programs to process files. Suppose we want to change all of the letters in a file to uppercase. We only need to change one class, processstring1, as follows:

```
class processstring1 extends processstringclass {

boolean processstring(boolean previouswriteok) {
z=x.toUpperCase();
return true;
} /*end processstring*/

} /*end processstring1*/
```

Now the command line

```
java filerw test1.doc test2.doc
```

will cause file *test2.doc* to be the same as *test1.doc*, except that all of the lowercase letters will be uppercase. (There is one other approach we could have followed. If we had wanted to keep our original processstring1 class [page 179] intact, we could have defined our new code to be a new class [say, processstring2] that would also extend processstring. Then we would have to change the filerw class to reflect the change from processstring1 to processstring2.)

Now we can write a program to replace all occurences of one string in a file with another string. We'll use the method replacestring, which is in the class cpj.

```
class processstring1 extends processstringclass {

 boolean processstring(boolean previouswriteok) {
z=cpj.replacestring(x,"1999","2000");
return true;
} /*end processstring*/

} /*end processstring1*/
```

This method will cause every occurrence of the string "1999" to change to the string "2000" (which could be useful if you had a document whose year needed to be updated for the new year).

Or, suppose we wish to delete blocks of lines from a file. We'll mark the beginning of a block of lines to delete with <DELETE>, and mark the end of the block with </DELETE>.

```
class processstring1 extends processstringclass {

boolean processstring(boolean previouswriteok) {
z=x;
boolean result=previouswriteok;
if (x.indexOf("<DELETE>")>=0) {result=false;}
if (x.indexOf("</DELETE>")>=0)
          {result=true;
```

```
z="";}
```

return result;
} /*end processstring*/

} /*end processstring1*/

In summary, you need these classes to operate our file processing system: procfile.class, processstringclass.class, processstring1.class, and filerw.class. Change the file processstring1.class depending on how you want to process the file. After recompiling the processstring1.class, you can execute the file processing with the command line

```
java filerw file1.doc file2.doc
```

where `file1.doc` is the input file and `file2.doc` is the output file.

In fact, many of the string programs we wrote in Chapter 7 can be converted to file programs; they will be much more useful when they can operate on all of the contents of a file.

11.7   Alphabetizing the Lines in a File

We have already written a program to alphabetize an array of strings (see page 62). It would be much more useful to be able to alphabetize the lines in a text file. We have already seen all of the tools we need for this job; all we need to do is put them together.

import java.io.*;

class filealph {
/*This program reads in the lines of a text file and generates
  an output file that is in alphabetical order. The input
  and output files are specified in the command line.*/

public static void main(String arg[ ]) {

String textlines[ ] = **new String**[100]; /*maximum 100 lines*/
int n=0; /*number of lines read in*/

String f1n=arg[0]; /*name of file to read from*/
String f2n=arg[1]; /*name of file to write to*/

try{
DataInput f1 = **new DataInputStream(new FileInputStream**(f1n));
DataOutput f2 = **new DataOutputStream(new FileOutputStream**(f2n));

/*Read in text lines:*/
n=0;
String x=f1.**readLine**();
while (x!=**null**) {
        n++;
```
```

```
                textlines[n]=x;
                x=f1.readLine();
} /*end while*/

/*The next four lines check for a line consisting only of an end of file
    character (code 26); the value of n is reduced by one if the
    last line is only an end of file character.*/
String z=textlines[n];
char c=z.charAt(0);
short k=(short)c;
if (k==26) {n- -;};

/*bubble sort procedure:*/
for (int i=1; i<=n; i++) {
for (int j=1; j<=(n-i); j++) {
boolean inorder=(textlines[j].compareTo(textlines[j+1])<=0);
if (!inorder) { /*Swap these two elements.*/
                String temporarystring=textlines[j];
                textlines[j]=textlines[j+1];
                textlines[j+1]=temporarystring;
                } /*end if*/
} /*end j loop*/
} /*end i loop*/

/*write to output file:*/
for (int i=1; i<=n; i++) {
        f2.writeBytes(textlines[i]+"\r\n");
        } /*end for loop*/

} catch (Exception ex) {String err = ex.toString();
                                            System.out.println(err);}

} /*end main*/
} /*end class filealph*/
```

This program reads all of the lines from the input file into an array before it starts to alphabetize them. This approach does not work well if you have a very large file because it takes up a large amount of computer memory. Also, if you have a very large number of lines to sort, the bubble sort method is fairly slow. However, if you have a relatively small file that needs to be alphabetized, the program above is about the easiest way to do it.

11.8 Files of Objects

Reading and writing text files is tremendously helpful, but at this point you should be thinking, "Since Java is object-oriented, what we really need are files of objects. Since we define objects in Java programs, we should be able to save those objects to a file and then have them be read back." As you might expect, this capability is built into Java.

We'll write a program that writes our boat objects to a file, and then another program that reads them back in. When an object is written to a file, it is said to be *serialized*. In order to do this, the class file must contain the words **implements Serializable** in the heading line. (**Serializable** is an interface; see page 134.) Also, the class must be declared to be a public class, which means it must be in its own file.

Here is the file *boatcl.java*:

```
import java.io.*;

import java.awt.*;


public class boatcl implements Serializable {
double x=0; double y=0;
double vx=0; double vy=0;
double oldx=0; double oldy=0;

Color boatcolor=Color.black;

/*constructor method*/ public boatcl(
double x, double y, double vx, double vy,
Color c) {
this.x=x; this.y=y;
this.vx=vx; this.vy=vy;
this.boatcolor=c;
} /*end constructor method*/


/*method*/ void moveboat(double deltatime) {
oldx=x;
oldy=y;
x+=vx*deltatime;
y+=vy*deltatime;
} /*end moveboat*/

/*method*/ double distance(boatcl otherboat) {
/*This method calculates the distance to the other boat given as the
  argument.*/
double minimumdistance=20;
double z=Math.sqrt(Math.pow((x-otherboat.x),2)+
        Math.pow((y-otherboat.y),2));
if (z<minimumdistance) {System.out.print("**** too close:");}
return z;
} /*end distance method*/
```

```
/*method*/ void plotcourse(Graphics g) {
cpjxy.dline(oldx,oldy,x,y,g,boatcolor);
} /*end plotcourse*/
```

```
} /*end boatcl*/
```

Here is the program to write boat objects to the file:

```
import java.io.*;

import java.awt.*;

public class boatwrit {


static int numboats=4;

static boatcl boat[ ]=new boatcl[numboats+1];

public static void main(String arg[ ]) {

boatcl boat0=new boatcl(1.6, 0.3, 6.1, 10.4, Color.red);
boat[1]=boat0;
boat0=new boatcl(30.5, 46.8, -5.2, -1.4, Color.blue);
boat[2]=boat0;
boat0=new boatcl(15.8, 20.4, 7.2, -4.9, Color.green);
boat[3]=boat0;
boat0=new boatcl(7.4, 14.8, 0.2, 8.6, Color.magenta);
boat[4]=boat0;

try {
FileOutputStream boatfile = new FileOutputStream("BOATS.OBJ");
ObjectOutputStream bfs = new ObjectOutputStream(boatfile);

for (int i=1; i<=numboats; i++) {
bfs.writeObject(boat[i]);
} /*end for loop*/
} catch (Exception ex) {String err = e.toString();
                                   System.out.println(err);}

} /*end main*/

} /*end class boatwrit*/
```

We need to create a file object of the class **FileOutputStream** (we call it boatfile in this example). Then, we create an object of the class **ObjectOutputStream** (which we call bfs in this example) that is associated with the file called "BOATS.OBJ".

To write objects to the file, all we need is the **writeObject** method. Here's the segment of code that writes to the file:

```
FileOutputStream boatfile = new FileOutputStream("BOATS.OBJ");
ObjectOutputStream bfs = new ObjectOutputStream(boatfile);

for (int i=1; i<=numboats; i++) {
bfs.writeObject(boat[i]);
```

Following is the program that reads objects back from the file. (All this program does is display information; a more useful program would do further processing.)

```
import java.io.*;

import java.awt.*;

public class boatread {

static boatcl boat[ ]=new boatcl[21];
/*20 is max number of boats*/

public static void main(String arg[ ]) {
int numboats=0;

try {
FileInputStream boatfile = new FileInputStream("BOATS.OBJ");
ObjectInputStream bfs = new ObjectInputStream(boatfile);

/*Assume that the file contains at least one boat object.*/

int i=1;

/*The following while loop will be executed repeatedly until the
  end-of-file exception (EOFException) is thrown; then the
  catch block and following code will be executed.*/
try {
while (true) {
System.out.println("attempting to read boat "+i);
boat[i]=(boatcl)(bfs.readObject());
i++;
} /*end while loop*/
} catch (EOFException eofex)
{numboats=i-1;
System.out.println("number of boats read: "+numboats);
    }

} catch (Exception ex) {String err = ex.toString();
                                  System.out.println(err);}

/*Now, display information about the boats read in on the screen.*/
for (int i=1; i<=numboats; i++) {
System.out.println("Boat "+i+" x:"+boat[i].x+" y:"+boat[i].y+
" vx:"+boat[i].vx+" vy:"+boat[i].vy);

} /*end for loop*/
```

```
} /*end main*/
} /*end class boatread*/
```

Note the comparison of the input commands to the output commands:

Output to file:

bfs.**writeObject**(boat[i]);

Input from file:

boat[i]=(boatcl)(bfs.**readObject**());

The output method is **writeObject**, which takes as its argument the name of the object to write; the input method is **readObject()**, which has no argument but whose return value must be assigned to an object. The object returned by **readObject** has type **Object**, which is the most general kind of object. We need to cast this object into an object of class boatcl in order to use it; that is the purpose of the expression (boatcl) in the line above.

11.9   File Dialog Window

You are probably thinking that it is very primitive to require that the file names be typed at the command line, as we have done so far in this chapter. You have grown up with Windows-based systems, so you feel that you should be able to select files by pointing and clicking at a file dialog box. Although it would be very useful to add that capability to our programs, you might be daunted by the complexity of programming such a dialog box. There are many details that need to be covered: the dialog box needs to respond to mouse movements, it needs to be able to scroll through the file list, it needs to be able to jump to different directories to select files, and it must behave like a normal window (for example, you need to be able to move it around the screen).

Although some computer programming problems are hard, it is important to distinguish between hard standard problems and hard non-standard problems. If your program requires a solution to a hard problem that is unique to your situation, then you're on your own: you'll have to find a way to solve the problem. On the other hand, if a problem is hard but standard, it only needs to be solved once, and then it isn't really hard for subsequent programmers to use that solution. A file dialog box is in this category. Java comes with a built-in file dialog box capability (which, as you can probably guess, is defined as a class; you instantiate specific objects of it). All of the code for handling the dialog box comes with Java. Here is an example:

import java.awt.*;

import java.io.*;
import java.awt.event.*;

public class file8 **extends Frame** {

```
/*This program demonstrates a file dialog box. After the user selects
   a text file, the file will be displayed with System.out.println.*/


static file8 file8frame;

/*constructor*/
public file8(String title) {
super(title);

} /*end constructor*/

public void init() {
setBackground(Color.blue);
} /*end init*/

public void paint (Graphics g) {
/*This method doesn't do anything, since the only purpose of this
   program is to demonstrate file dialog boxes.*/

} /*end paint*/

/*to close the window:*/
static class winlis extends WindowAdapter {
public void windowClosing(WindowEvent e) {
System.exit(0);
} /*end windowClosing*/
} /*end winlis*/

public static void main(String args[ ]) {

file8frame = new file8("File Dialog Example Program");
file8frame.setBounds(20,20,400,400);
file8frame.addWindowListener(new winlis());
file8frame.init();
file8frame.setVisible(true);
FileDialog fd = new FileDialog(file8frame,
"File Dialog Box Example", FileDialog.LOAD);
fd.setVisible(true);
String filename = fd.getFile();
System.out.println("File name:"+filename);
try{
DataInput f1 = new DataInputStream(new FileInputStream(filename));
String textline=f1.readLine();

while (textline!=null) {
        System.out.println(textline);
        textline=f1.readLine();
    } /*end while*/

} catch (Exception ex) {String err = ex.toString();
                                    System.out.println(err);}
```

} /*end main*/

} /*end class file8*/

This program will let you select a file from the dialog box, and then it uses **System.out.println** to display the contents of that file on the screen. (This only works with text files.) You probably would prefer to see the file in a scrolling window, but that will have to wait for Chapter 15. Because the program is an application that will run in a window, it needs to include the code discussed on page 147.

The programming of the file dialog box itself is very simple:

```
FileDialog fd = new FileDialog(file8frame,
"File Dialog Box Example", FileDialog.LOAD);
fd.setVisible(true);
String filename = fd.getFile();
```

FileDialog is the name of the class. We will instantiate an object of this class called fd. The constructor we are using takes three arguments: the first is the name of the parent frame (which is file8frame in this example); the second is a string that will provide a title for the box; and the third can be either **FileDialog.LOAD** or **FileDialog.SAVE**, depending on whether the box will be used for reading in a file or writing a file to the disk.

The command fd.**setVisible(true)** makes the dialog box appear on the screen. The user can choose files with this box just as if it were any other file dialog box. (The box will look like typical file dialog boxes for the system you are working on.) After you've made your selection, the program will execute the command

```
filename=fd.getFile()
```

which assigns the file name chosen in the box to the string variable *filename*. We can then use this name to display the contents of the file on the screen, as we did in the program on page 176.

Now that we have seen how we can greatly increase the power of our programs by giving them the ability to read from and write to files, we will be able to create even more useful programs for the rest of this book.

EXERCISES

1. Look at the example programs involving character strings for Chapter 7. Convert all of the applicable programs into programs that operate on files (that is, they read in lines from an input file, perform a transformation on that string, and then write the result to an output file).

2. Write a program that directs all of its output to a method that can send output either to the screen, a file, or both.

3. Write a program that reads in a file of text lines and then creates an alphabetical list of all of the words that appear. Ignore all punctuation characters; assume that the words are separated by blanks.

4. Consider a file representing a dictionary, where each word in the dictionary is marked with * at the beginning of the word. Following the word itself is a definition, which may fill more than one line. (However, the definition is not allowed to contain *.) For example,

```
*dog
four-legged mammal that says "woof"; includes
golden retrievers and beagles.
*cat
four-legged mammal that says "meow"; cats often
own people (even if the people think they own
the cats).
```

Write a program that alphabetizes this dictionary, being sure that you keep all the lines in a definition together.

5. Write a program that reads in an HTML document file that is divided into sections marked by the headings <h1> and <h2>. Have the program create two tables of contents. The first table of contents only lists those headings at the <h1> level; the detailed table of contents includes headings at both the <h1> and <h2> levels. Finally, have the program automatically generate links, so that each line in the table of contents can be clicked on when you want to jump to the corresponding point in the document.

CHAPTER 12

MATHEMATICAL OPERATIONS

12.1 Square Root (**sqrt**) and Absolute Value (**abs**)

In the old days (before computers), mathematical subjects such as algebra and trigonometry were difficult to learn partly because the calculations were so tedious. Math concepts are still a challenge, but we can ease the burden considerably by using the computer to perform the calculations. In this chapter, it is assumed that you have some familiarity with algebra and trigonometry. We have seen a couple of mathematical functions already: square root (**sqrt**) (page 111) and power (**pow**) (page 13).

Suppose we need to know the diagonal distance across a field that is 100 yards long and 30 yards wide (see Figure 12–1). From the Pythagorean theorem, the distance will be the following:

$$\sqrt{100^2 + 30^2}$$

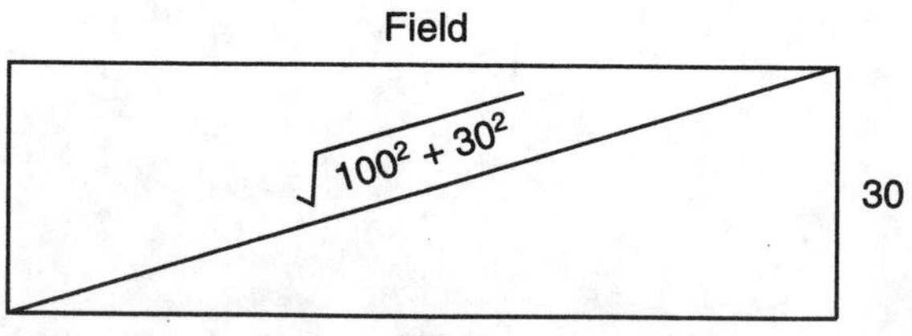

Field

FIGURE 12–1

In Java, this can be written as

System.out.println(Math.sqrt(100*100+30*30));

or as

190

System.out.println(Math.sqrt (Math.pow(100,2)+Math.pow(30,2)));

The result is 104.403.

Another useful function is the absolute value function, **abs**. The absolute value of a positive number is equal to itself; the absolute value of a negative number is found by taking its negative (which turns it into a positive).

For example, **Math.abs**(16) results in 16; **Math.abs**(-16) also results in 16. **Math.abs**(0) results in 0.

12.2 Trigonometric Functions (sin, cos, tan)

There are several kinds of problems for which trigonometric functions are very helpful.

Suppose you need to measure the distance to a rock that is located in the middle of a river. You can't very well swim across the river with a tape measure, but you can calculate the distance if you know trigonometry. First, stand along the riverbank directly opposite the rock (Point A in Figure 12–2). Then go to a point $a = 10$ yards away (Point B in Figure 12–2) and observe the rock from there. Next, measure the angle between the rock and point A (call it theta, θ). Suppose this angle is 65 degrees, which is the same as $65\pi/180 = 1.13446$ radians. The distance d to the rock can be found from this formula:

$$d = a \tan \theta$$

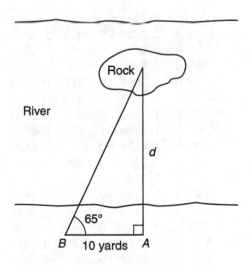

FIGURE 12–2

When translated into Java, the formula looks like this:

```
double a=10;
double theta=65*Math.PI/180;
double d=a*Math.tan(theta);
```

Since the value of π (pi) is used so frequently, Java provides the constant **Math.PI**, which has the value 3.141592653589793.

Here is a program that illustrates the **sin**, **cos**, and **tan** functions by creating a table of their values:

```
import java.io.*;

public class trigtab {
/*This program creates a file with a table of values of trigonometric
functions.*/

public static void main(String args[ ]) {
try{
DataOutput f1=new DataOutputStream(new
FileOutputStream("trigtab.doc"));
f1.writeBytes("␣Degrees␣␣Radians␣␣␣␣sin␣␣␣␣␣cos␣␣␣␣␣tan\r\n");
for (double x=0; x<=360; x+=15) {
double xr=x*Math.PI/180;
/*x is measured in degrees; xr is measured in radians.*/
String tanstring="␣␣␣␣␣...";
if (!((x==90.0)|(x==270.0))) {tanstring=cpj.nf(Math.tan(xr),8,4);}
f1.writeBytes(cpj.nf(x,8,1)+cpj.nf(xr,8,4)+
        cpj.nf(Math.sin(xr),8,4)+ cpj.nf(Math.cos(xr),8,4)+
        tanstring+"\r\n");
} /*end for loop*/
} catch (Exception ex) {String err = ex.toString();
        System.out.println(err);}
} /*end main*/
} /*end class trigtab*/
```

The program generates this output:

```
Degrees   Radians    sin      cos      tan
    0.0    0.0000   0.0000   1.0000   0.0000
   15.0    0.2618   0.2588   0.9659   0.2679
   30.0    0.5236   0.5000   0.8660   0.5774
   45.0    0.7854   0.7071   0.7071   1.0000
   60.0    1.0472   0.8660   0.5000   1.7321
   75.0    1.3090   0.9659   0.2588   3.7321
   90.0    1.5708   1.0000   0.0000      ...
  105.0    1.8326   0.9659  -0.2588  -3.7321
  120.0    2.0944   0.8660  -0.5000  -1.7321
  135.0    2.3562   0.7071  -0.7071  -1.0000
  150.0    2.6180   0.5000  -0.8660  -0.5774
  165.0    2.8798   0.2588  -0.9659  -0.2679
  180.0    3.1416   0.0000  -1.0000   0.0000
  195.0    3.4034  -0.2588  -0.9659   0.2679
  210.0    3.6652  -0.5000  -0.8660   0.5774
  225.0    3.9270  -0.7071  -0.7071   1.0000
  240.0    4.1888  -0.8660  -0.5000   1.7321
  255.0    4.4506  -0.9659  -0.2588   3.7321
  270.0    4.7124  -1.0000   0.0000      ...
  285.0    4.9742  -0.9659   0.2588  -3.7321
  300.0    5.2360  -0.8660   0.5000  -1.7321
  315.0    5.4978  -0.7071   0.7071  -1.0000
  330.0    5.7596  -0.5000   0.8660  -0.5774
  345.0    6.0214  -0.2588   0.9659  -0.2679
  360.0    6.2832   0.0000   1.0000   0.0000
```

Trigonometric functions are also useful for describing waves. We can write a program to graph the curve $y = \sin x$ by extending the curvegraph class as we did on page 159.

```java
import java.applet.*;

import java.awt.*;

public class singraph extends curvegraph {

public void init() {
setBackground(Color.white);
cpjxy.xscale=8;
cpjxy.yscale=2.5;
cpjxy.xaxisgridstep=.5;
cpjxy.yaxisgridstep=.5;
cpjxy.xc=3;
cpjxy.griddp=1;
} /*end init*/


/*method*/ double y(double x) {
return Math.sin(x);
} /*end y*/


} /*end class singraph*/
```

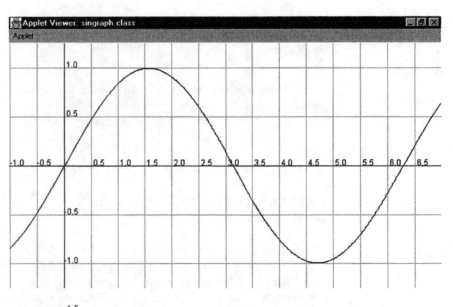

FIGURE 12–3

12.3   Polar Coordinates

So far, we have identified points on the screen with the rectangular (Cartesian) coordinate values (x, y). In some problems it helps to identify points with *polar* coordinates, where each point is identified by its distance from the origin (called r) and its direction (called theta, θ). In polar coordinates, the 0 degree direction is traditionally defined to point to the right (in the direction of the positive x axis) (see Figure 12–4).

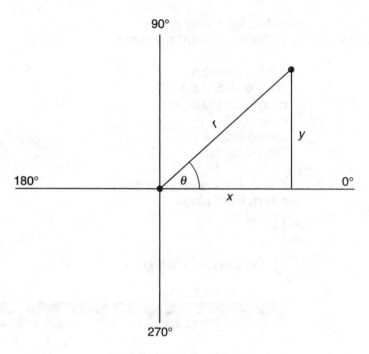

FIGURE 12–4

We can convert polar coordinates to rectangular coordinates with these formulas:

$$x = r \cos \theta$$

$$y = r \sin \theta$$

In Java, this transformation is written like this:

```
x=r*Math.cos(theta); /*theta is in radians.*/
y=r*Math.sin(theta);
```

For example, suppose $r = 10$, $\theta = 30$ degrees $= \pi/6$ radians. Then $x = 10 \cos(\pi/6) = 10 \times .866 = 8.66$ and $y = 10 \sin(\pi/6) = 10 \times .5 = 5$.

There will be other types of problems when we need to do the conversion in reverse; that is, we will know x and y and we will want to find r and θ. To do this, we can use these formulas:

$$r = \sqrt{x^2 + y^2}$$

$$\theta = \arctan(y, x)$$

The "arc" refers to the inverse of the tangent function. If $\tan \theta = y/x$, then $\arctan(y, x) = \theta$.

In Java, this transformation is written like this:

```
r=Math.sqrt(x*x+y*y);
theta=Math.atan2(y,x);
```

The function **atan2** takes two arguments, the y and x coordinates of a point, and calculates the angle θ whose arctangent value is y/x, and which is placed in the correct quadrant, according to these rules:

Quadrant	x	y	θ
1	positive	positive	0 to $\pi/2$ (0 to 90 degrees)
2	negative	positive	$\pi/2$ to π (90 to 180 degrees)
3	negative	negative	$-\pi/2$ to $-\pi$ (−90 to −180 degrees)
4	positive	negative	0 to $-\pi/2$ (0 to −90 degrees)

See Figure 12–5.

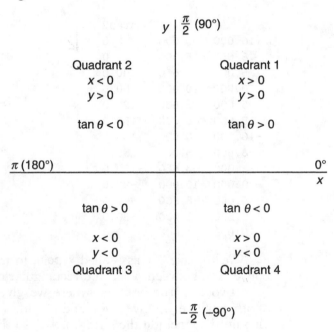

FIGURE 12–5

At first it seems confusing that the y coordinate is given first in the **atan2** function, since normally x is given first. The reason for giving y first is because it reminds you that the tangent value is y/x.

Here is a program that illustrates the use of **atan2**:

```
import java.io.*;

public class atan2ex {
/*This program illustrates the atan2 (arctangent) function.*/

public static void main(String args[ ]){
System.out.println("        x        y   atan2");
for (double theta=0; theta<=360; theta+=30) {
```

```
double thetarad=theta*Math.PI/180;
/*Theta is measured in degrees; thetarad is measured in radians.*/
double r=10;
double x=r*Math.cos(thetarad);
double y=r*Math.sin(thetarad);
double thetarad2=Math.atan2(y,x);
        /*thetarad2 will be the same as thetarad.*/
double theta2=thetarad2*180/Math.PI;
System.out.println(cpj.nf(x,8,3)+ cpj.nf(y,8,3)+ cpj.nf(theta2,8,1));
     } /*end for loop*/
} /*end main*/
} /*end class trigtab*/
```

This program is a bit silly, since it calculates θ first, then calculates x and y, and then uses x and y to calculate θ again. But it serves its purpose, which is to illustrate the operation of **atan2**. Here is the output:

```
       x         y     atan2
  10.000     0.000       0.0
   8.660     5.000      30.0
   5.000     8.660      60.0
   0.000    10.000      90.0
  -5.000     8.660     120.0
  -8.660     5.000     150.0
 -10.000     0.000     180.0
  -8.660    -5.000    -150.0
  -5.000    -8.660    -120.0
   0.000   -10.000     -90.0
   5.000    -8.660     -60.0
   8.660    -5.000     -30.0
  10.000     0.000       0.0
```

We'll create a class called **xypoint** to make it easy to handle the conversion between polar and rectangular coordinates. The class will have two constructors: one where we give the x and y values, and another where we give the r and θ values. (For that constructor, we also need to include the string "**polar**" so the computer knows which constructor to use.) Our class will only have two variables, the x and y values of the point, but it will also have two methods, **getrvalue** and **getthetavalue**, to retrieve the polar coordinate values. Here's the source code for the class:

```
public class xypoint {
        double x; double y;

/*constructor*/
/*This constructor takes the x and y values of the point.*/
public xypoint(int startx, int starty) {
            this.x=startx; this.y=starty;
} /*end constructor*/

/*constructor*/
```

```
/*This constructor takes the polar coordinates r and theta.
The third argument is the string "polar".*/
public xypoint(double r, double theta, String indicator) {
/*Theta is measured in degrees here.*/
if (indicator.equals("polar")) {
        this.x=r*Math.cos(theta*Math.PI/180);
        this.y=r*Math.sin(theta*Math.PI/180);
} /*end if*/
} /*end constructor*/

/*method*/ double getrvalue() {
return Math.sqrt(x*x+y*y);}

/*method*/ double getthetavalue() {
return Math.atan2(y,x)*180/Math.PI;}
/*return value is in degrees*/
} /*end class xypoint*/
```

We'll use this class in the next section.

12.4   Pie Charts

A pie chart is the best diagram when a quantity is divided up into different categories. To draw a pie chart, we need to draw a circle on the screen, and then draw lines identifying each pie slice. Each slice can be identified by two numbers: its startangle and its sliceangle (see Figure 12–6).

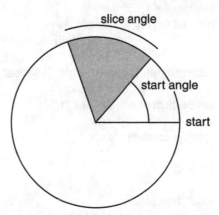

FIGURE 12–6

We need to calculate these two angles given the data, and then draw the slice. Clearly, polar coordinates are the easy way to represent the points along the circle that represent slice boundaries. However, we need to convert the coordinates in order to draw the line, so we will use our *xypoint* class from page 196. Here is the first version of a pie chart program:

import java.applet.*;

import java.awt.*;

```java
public class pie1 extends Applet {

double radius=120;

int maxarray=25; /*maximum number of pie chart values allowed*/
int numvals=maxarray-1;

double a[ ] = new double[maxarray];
double startangle[ ] = new double[maxarray];
double sliceangle[ ] = new double[maxarray];
double total=0;

/*method*/ void setvalues() {
numvals=5; /*actual number of values in pie chart*/
a[1]=20.0;
a[2]=30.0;
a[3]=40.0;
a[4]=15.0;
a[5]=25.0;
          } /*end setvalues*/

/*method*/ public void init() {
setvalues();
total=0;
for (int i=1; i<=numvals; i++) {
              total+=a[i];
          } /*end for loop*/
startangle[1]=0;
for (int i=1; i<=numvals; i++) {
              sliceangle[i]=360*a[i]/total;
              if (i<numvals)
{startangle[i+1]=startangle[i]+sliceangle[i];}
          } /*end for loop*/
setBackground(Color.black);
cpjxy.xscale=cpjxy.sw;
cpjxy.yscale=cpjxy.sh;

} /*end init*/

void drawpieslice
(double startangle, double sliceangle,
        Graphics g) {
xypoint p=new xypoint(radius,startangle,"polar");
cpjxy.dline(0, 0, p.x, p.y, g, Color.orange);
p=new xypoint(radius,(startangle+sliceangle),"polar");
cpjxy.dline(0, 0, p.x, p.y, g, Color.orange);
} /*end drawpieslice*/


public void paint(Graphics g) {
g.setColor(Color.orange);
cpjxy.dcircle(radius,0,0,g,Color.orange);
```

```
for (int j=1; j<=numvals; j++) {
        drawpieslice(startangle[j],sliceangle[j],g);
                                } /*end for loop*/
} /*end paint*/

} /*end class pie1*/
```

This program is not very satisfactory, however, because it does not include any labels for the slices. Here is a more elaborate version that includes labels:

```
import java.applet.*;

import java.awt.*;
import java.lang.Math;

public class pie extends Applet {

double radius=120;

int maxarray=25; /*maximum number of pie chart values allowed*/
int numvals=maxarray-1;

double a[ ] = new double[maxarray];
double startangle[ ] = new double[maxarray];
double sliceangle[ ] = new double[maxarray];
String pielabel[ ] = new String[maxarray];
String heading;
String notestring1;
String notestring2;
double total=0;

/*method*/ void setvalues() {
numvals=5; /*actual number of values in pie chart*/
a[1]=20.0; pielabel[1]="Slice 1";
a[2]=30.0; pielabel[2]="Slice 2";
a[3]=40.0; pielabel[3]="Slice 3";
a[4]=15.0; pielabel[4]="Slice 4";
a[5]=25.0; pielabel[5]="Slice 5";
heading="Sample Pie Chart";
notestring1="notestring1";
notestring2="notestring2";
        } /*end setvalues*/

/*method*/ public void init() {
setvalues();
total=0;
for (int i=1; i<=numvals; i++) {
            total+=a[i];
                } /*end for loop*/
startangle[1]=0;
for (int i=1; i<=numvals; i++) {
            sliceangle[i]=360*a[i]/total;
```

```
            if (i<numvals)
{startangle[i+1]=startangle[i]+sliceangle[i];}
                                              } /*end for loop*/
setBackground(Color.white);
cpjxy.xscale=cpjxy.sw;
cpjxy.yscale=cpjxy.sh;

} /*end init*/



/*method*/ String percentconvert(double a, double b) {
/*This method returns a string representing a/b converted to a percent.*/
return (cpj.nf((100*a/b),5,1)+"%");
            } /*end percentconvert*/


void drawpieslice
(double startangle, double sliceangle, double avalue,
        String label, Graphics g) {
xypoint p=new xypoint(radius,startangle,"polar");
cpjxy.dline (0, 0, p.x, p.y, g, Color.black);
p=new xypoint(radius,(startangle+sliceangle),"polar");
cpjxy.dline (0, 0, p.x, p.y, g, Color.black);
if (sliceangle>10) { /*To avoid clutter, the program
                        does not label very small slices.*/
    /*Draw percentages:*/
    double middleangle=startangle+sliceangle/2;
    p=new xypoint((radius/2),middleangle,"polar");
    String percentstring=percentconvert(avalue,total);
    cpjxy.dstring(percentstring, p.x-8, p.y, g, Color.black);
     /*Draw slice label:*/
    p=new xypoint((radius*1.2),middleangle,"polar");
     int dx=0;
     if ((middleangle>90)&(middleangle<270)) {dx=20;}
    cpjxy.dstring(label, p.x-dx, p.y, g, Color.black);
                    } /*end if sliceangle>10*/

} /*end drawpieslice*/

public void paint(Graphics g) {
g.setColor(Color.black);
g.drawString(heading,10,15);
g.drawString(notestring1,10,35);
g.drawString(notestring2,10,55);
cpjxy.dcircle(radius,0,0,g,Color.black);

for (int j=1; j<=numvals; j++) {
    drawpieslice(startangle[j],sliceangle[j],a[j],pielabel[j],g);
                            } /*end for loop*/
            } /*end paint*/
} /*end class pie*/
```

When we want to create a pie chart for real data, all we need to do is extend the pie class and overwrite the setvalues method, as we did on page 159. Here is an example:

```
public class natinc extends pie {

/*method*/ void setvalues() {
numvals=9; /*actual number of values in pie chart*/
a[1]=94.0; pielabel[1]="Agriculture";
a[2]=43.6; pielabel[2]="Mining";
a[3]=263.6; pielabel[3]="Construction";
a[4]=1026.3; pielabel[4]="Manufacturing";
a[5]=451.0; pielabel[5]="Transp/Utilities";
a[6]=327.0; pielabel[6]="Wholesale";
a[7]=478.6; pielabel[7]="Retail";
a[8]=991.9; pielabel[8]="Finance";
a[9]=1335.9; pielabel[9]="Services";

heading="U.S. National Income";
notestring1="by industry";
notestring2="1995";
/*values are in billion dollars*/

       } /*end setvalues*/
} /*end class natinc*/
```

Here is the screen output:

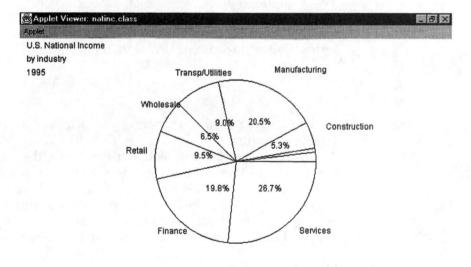

FIGURE 12–7

12.5   Logarithms and Exponential Functions

There are two more mathematical functions we will need: a logarithm function and an exponential function. If $y = a^x$, then y is an exponential function with base a. Then we can also say that $x = \log_a y$ (x is the logarithm of y to the base a).

Here is an application of these functions. If we start with some radioactive atoms, then the fraction (f) of our original sample that will remain at time t is

$$f = \left(\frac{1}{2}\right)^{t/t_2}$$

where t_2 is the *half-life* of the element. At the end of one half-life, only half of the original sample will be left. (The rest will have undergone radioactive decay and turned into something else.) At the end of two half-lives, one quarter of the original sample will be remaining, at the end of three half-lives, one eighth of the original sample will be remaining, and so on. The half-life of radium is 1,600 years, so we can use the following statements to calculate the fraction of radium that will be remaining at the end of 10,000 years:

```
t2=1600;
t=10000;
f=Math.pow(0.5,(t/t2));
```

The result is $f = .0131$.

Suppose we need to know how many years will pass until only one tenth of the original sample remains. We need to reverse our original formula, using logarithms to find that

$$t = \frac{t_2 \log f}{\log \frac{1}{2}}$$

Here, f represents the fraction of the original sample that will be remaining at time t.

In Java, the function **Math.log** represents the *natural logarithm* function, which uses the number e as its base; e is a special number used in calculus. Its value is given in Java by the constant **Math.EE**, which is 2.718281828459045. The natural logarithm of x tells you to what power e must be raised in order to produce x. In other words, if $e^a = x$, then $\log_e x = a$. Now we can solve the radium problem:

```
t2=1600;
f=.1;
t=t2*Math.log(f)/Math.log(.5);
```

The result is $t = 5315$. Therefore, after 5,315 years there will only be one tenth of the original sample of radium remaining.

Following is a program that graphs the function $y = \log_e x$. (This program uses the class on page 158.)

```
import java.applet.*;

import java.awt.*;
```

```
public class loggraph extends curvegraph {

public void init() {
setBackground(Color.white);
cpjxy.xscale=10;
cpjxy.yscale=4;
cpjxy.xaxisgridstep=0.5;
cpjxy.yaxisgridstep=0.5;
cpjxy.xc=4;
cpjxy.griddp=1;
} /*end init*/

/*method*/ double y(double x) {
return Math.log(x);
} /*end y*/



} /*end class loggraph*/
```

Here is the result:

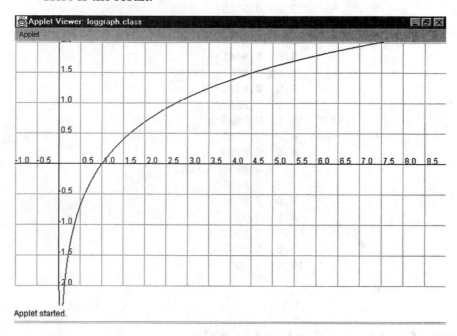

FIGURE 12–8

It also is convenient to find logarithms to the base 10 (called *common logarithms*), which can be found from this formula:

$$\log_{10} x = \frac{\log_e x}{\log_e 10}$$

Here's a program to display a table of common logarithms:

```
public class logtab {
/*This program displays a table of common (base 10) logarithms.*/
```

```
/*method*/ static double log10(double x) {
/*This method calculates the log to the base 10.*/
return Math.log(x)/Math.log(10);
} /*end log10*/


public static void main(String args[ ]) {
System.out.println("␣␣␣␣␣␣␣␣x␣log10(x)");
for (double x=0.5; x<=10; x+=0.5) {
        System.out.println(cpj.nf(x,8,1)+ cpj.nf(log10(x),8,4));
} /*end for loop*/
} /*end main*/
} /*end class logtab*/
```

Here is the output:

```
   x log10(x)
 0.5 -0.3010
 1.0  0.0000
 1.5  0.1761
 2.0  0.3010
 2.5  0.3979
 3.0  0.4771
 3.5  0.5441
 4.0  0.6021
 4.5  0.6532
 5.0  0.6990
 5.5  0.7404
 6.0  0.7782
 6.5  0.8129
 7.0  0.8451
 7.5  0.8751
 8.0  0.9031
 8.5  0.9294
 9.0  0.9542
 9.5  0.9777
10.0  1.0000
```

12.6   Numerical Integration

If you have studied the calculus technique called integration, you know how to find a formula for the area under a curve. However, there are many important curves whose areas cannot be found by a simple formula. The only possible method to find the area is a technique called *numerical integration*. Numerical integration requires a lot of tedious calculation, so it is the type of work perfectly suited for a computer. In fact, the first general purpose electronic computer was called the ENIAC, which stood for Electronic Numerical Integrator and Calculator.

For example, suppose we need to calculate the area of a quarter of a circle (see Figure 12–9). (You might know that the area is $\frac{1}{4}\pi r^2$, but for the moment pretend that you don't know the value of π.) We'll approximate the area by dividing it up into a series of small rectangles, as shown in Figure 12–10). The more rectangles we draw, the more accurate the approximation will be.

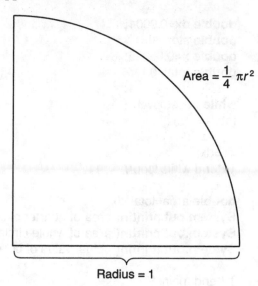

Area $= \frac{1}{4}\pi r^2$

FIGURE 12–9

Radius = 1

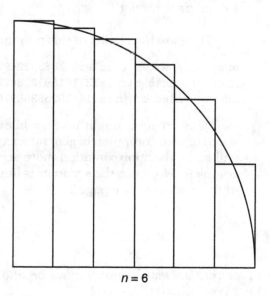

FIGURE 12–10

$n = 6$

Consider a circle of radius 1. If there are n rectangles, and the x coordinate of the midpoint of a particular rectangle is x, then the height of each rectangle is $y = \sqrt{1 - x^2}$ and the width of each rectangle is $1/n$. We need to create a loop to calculate the height of each rectangle, add up the heights, and then multiply by $1/n$. Here is the program:

public class numint {

/*This program uses numerical integration to find the area of a
    quarter circle with radius 1.*/

```
/*method*/ static double y(double x) {
return Math.sqrt(1-x*x);
} /*end method y*/

public static void main(String args[ ]){

double dx=0.0001;
double stopval=1;
double x=0.00005;
double total=0;

while (x<stopval) {
total+=y(x);

x+=dx;
} /*end while loop*/

double area=total*dx;
System.out.println("area of quarter circle:"+area);
System.out.println("area of whole circle:"+(4*area));
System.out.println("actual value of pi:"+Math.PI);

} /*end main*/
} /*end class numint*/
```

Here are the results of this program:

```
area of quarter circle:0.7853982495062283
area of whole circle:3.141592998024913
actual value of pi:3.141592653589793
```

This program might take a while to complete, depending on the speed of your computer. In general, increasing the number of rectangles will make the approximation more accurate, but it will take longer to complete. However, the accuracy is limited by the numerical precision of the computer (see page 22).

EXERCISES

For Exercises 1–6, translate the algebraic expression into Java.

1. $\sqrt{x^2 + y^2 + z^2}$

2. $\sqrt{(x - h)^2 + (y - k)^2}$

3. $\dfrac{-b + \sqrt{b^2 - 4ac}}{2a}$

4. $a^2 + b^2 - 2ab \cos C$

5. $b_1 \sin A / \sin B$

6. $\ln(a + b + c)$

7. Write methods for trigonometric functions that take their input measured in degrees.

8. Suppose that one day you bought what you thought was a very large triangle of land. It had dimensions of 200 miles, 101 miles, and 100 miles. It turned out that this triangle did not have as much area as you thought. Write a program that reads in the lengths of the three sides of a triangle and then calculates the area of the triangle.

9. Write a program that reads in two sides (a and b) of a triangle, as well as the angle between those two sides (C), then calculates the length of the third side (c) from the law of cosines:

$$c^2 = a^2 + b^2 - 2ab \cos C$$

10. Write a program that reads in three numbers a, b, and c (where a is not zero) and then calculates the value(s) of x that solve the quadratic equation

$$ax^2 + bx + c = 0$$

11. Write a class that represents numbers that can be expressed in either decimal or binary form. Include methods to convert between the two forms.

12. Write a polynomial class. This class has a constructor that reads in the coefficients of the polynomial, and a method that evaluates the polynomial for a particular x.

13. Add a method to the polynomial class (see previous exercise) that performs a polynomial division:

$$\frac{a_n x^n + a_{n-1} x^{n-1} + \ldots + a_3 x^3 + a_2 x^2 + a_1 x + a_0}{b_m x^m + b_{m-1} x^{m-1} + \ldots + b_3 x^3 + b_2 x^2 + b_1 x + b_0}$$

where $m < n$. The program needs to give both the quotient and remainder, if any.

14. Add a method to the polynomial class that multiplies two polynomials:

$$(a_n x^n + a_{n-1} x^{n-1} + \ldots + a_3 x^3 + a_2 x^2 + a_1 x + a_0) \times$$
$$(b_m x^m + b_{m-1} x^{m-1} + \ldots + b_3 x^3 + b_2 x^2 + b_1 x + b_0)$$

15. Add a method to the polynomial class that finds the derivative of the polynomial. If $f(x)$ represents the polynomial

$$f(x) = a_n x^n + a_{n-1} x^{n-1} + \ldots + a_3 x^3 + a_2 x^2 + a_1 x + a_0$$

then the derivative (represented by $f'(x)$) is found from this formula:

$$f'(x) = n a_n x^{n-1} + (n-1) a_{n-1} x^{n-2} + \ldots + 3 a_3 x^2 + 2 a_2 x + a_1$$

16. Add a method to the polynomial class that uses Newton's method to find a real root of the equation. If $f(x)$ represents the polynomial, then a root is a value of x that solves the equation $f(x) = 0$. First, make an initial guess x_1. Then, calculate a closer guess x_2 from the formula

$$x_2 = x_1 - \frac{f(x_1)}{f'(x)}$$

where $f'(x)$ is the derivative (use the method from the previous exercise). Keep repeating the process until you find an x that satisfies

$$|f(x)| < 0.00001$$

17. Add a constructor to the polynomial class that accepts an array of values that represent the roots of the equation, and then determines the polynomial. This can be found by using the polynomial multiplication method above. If $r_1, r_2, \ldots, r_n$ are the roots, then the polynomial can be found by performing this multiplication:

$$(x - r_1)(x - r_2)(x - r_3) \times \ldots \times (x - r_n)$$

(For this problem, we are assuming that all of the roots of the polynomial are real numbers.)

For Exercises 18–20, use rectangles to find an approximation for the area of the region.

18. the area under the curve $y = \sin x$ from $x = 0$ to $x = \pi/2$

19. the area of the ellipse $x^2/9 + y^2/16 = 1$

20. the area under the curve $y = e^{-x^2}$ from $x = 0$ to $x = 2$

21. Make a table that gives the area under the curve

$$y = \frac{1}{\sqrt{2\pi}} e^{-x^2/2}$$

to the right of the line $x = 0$ and to the left of the line $x = x_1$, for these values of x_1: 0.01, 0.02, 0.03, and so on, up to 3.00. This area is very important in statistics because it is the area of the normal probability curve.

22. Find the approximate volume of a sphere with radius 1 by using nested loops that find the volume of columns with square bases. Then find the area of the ellipsoid formed by rotating the ellipse $x^2/25 + y^2/9$ about the x axis.

23. Approximate the curve $y = \sin x$ from $x = 0$ to $x = \pi/2$ by a series of small straight segments. Then add up the lengths of all the straight segments to find an approximation for the total length of the curve.

24. Write a program that reads in a number x and calculates an approximation for e^x using the formula

$$e^x = 1 + x + \frac{x^2}{2!} + \frac{x^3}{3!} + \frac{x^4}{4!} + \ldots$$

25. Write a program that reads in a number x and then calculates an approximation for $\sin x$ using the formula

$$\sin x = x - \frac{x^3}{3!} + \frac{x^5}{5!} - \frac{x^7}{7!} + \frac{x^9}{9!} - \cdots$$

26. Write a program that reads in a number x and then calculates an approximation for $\cos x$ using the formula

$$\cos x = 1 - \frac{x^2}{2!} + \frac{x^4}{4!} - \frac{x^6}{6!} + \cdots$$

27. Create a matrix class. Include methods for multiplying two matrices; finding the determinant of a matrix; and finding the inverse of a matrix. Use the class in a program to solve a system of simultaneous linear equations.

28. Create a class to represent complex numbers. Include methods for adding, subtracting, multiplying, dividing, and raising to a power. Also include a method that evaluates a polynomial with a complex number argument. (A complex number has the form $a + bi$, where a and b can be any two real numbers, and $i = \sqrt{-1}$.)

29. Write a method that draws a regular polygon on the screen. Have the program take two arguments: the radius of the polygon and the number of sides. Assume that the polygon is centered in the middle of the screen. (In a regular polygon, all sides are the same length, and all angles are the same size.)

30. Write a program that displays a triangle of numbers such that each number in the triangle is equal to the sum of the two numbers above it. Use recursion. This arrangement is known as Pascal's triangle. The top part of the triangle looks like this:

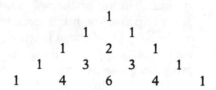

```
              1
           1     1
        1     2     1
     1     3     3     1
  1     4     6     4     1
```

CHAPTER 13

WINDOWS PROGRAMMING: MOUSE CLICKS AND BUTTONS

13.1 Windows, Events, and the Abstract Windowing Toolkit (AWT)

Most likely, you are very familiar with the operation of a computer that uses a graphical user interface (GUI), where text and graphics are displayed in windows on the screen, and you can use the mouse to call for commands and perform other operations. Because of the standardization of the way many features works, it is easy to learn a new program. You might even have been thinking, "I wish my programs could have all of those features," but you may well have been daunted when you stopped to imagine the complexity that must be needed to program those features.

Think again. Remember one key word in Java: reusability. Because windows interfaces are standard, we don't have to reinvent the wheel; we just need to use code that is already provided by Java. If you are truly beginning to think like a Java programmer, then you should even be able to anticipate how this is done: windows and other user interface elements are objects that have standard behavior. In order to standardize them for your program, all you need to do is inherit from certain classes, and then override the standard methods with your own methods. Then all of the standard windows behavior such as resizing, moving, maximizing, and minimizing will automatically be part of your program.

The second key concept necessary for programming a graphical user interface is the idea of event-driven programming. A windows program will just sit on the screen for a while, doing nothing, until some event happens (for example, you might click a button or select a

210

menu item). Then the program starts doing something in response to that event. However, while the program is working on that task, it also needs to be ready to respond in case another event happens. You might click on some other button, and then the computer needs to recognize that event and respond accordingly.

Therefore, your program needs to be able to pay attention to when events happen. It is said to be *listening* for events, which it does by implementing various kinds of listener interfaces. However, you don't want your program wasting time by listening for events that it doesn't need to respond to. Therefore, by selecting which listeners are implemented, you can determine what events your program will respond to.

In order to add a listener to a class, you need to include the statement

implements *specific listener*

Then, the **init** method needs to add the listeners where appropriate.

Here's a list of various attributes we want our Java windows programs to have:

- respond to mouse clicks at specific locations

- respond to keys being pressed

- include buttons that call for specific commands when they are clicked

- include menus of commands

- display and respond to dialog boxes

- transfer data to and from the clipboard

The feature of Java that implements these attributes is called the AWT (Abstract Windowing Toolkit). There is one problem with designing a language to be cross-platform like Java: different platforms work slightly differently. Although many of the general features of windows are standard, the exact appearance and operations of windows are different in Windows 95/98/NT than they are with the Macintosh or other platforms. The AWT is designed so that you can write a general windowing program without having to worry about the specific features of the platform. Then, each Java Virtual Machine (JVM) is responsible for implementing windowing behavior in the manner that is appropriate for that platform. The big advantage of this approach is that developers only have to write their Java program once, which is much easier than writing custom versions for different platforms. There is, however, a disadvantage: your Java programs are precluded from taking advantage of platform-specific features, such as the right mouse button.

Unfortunately, the situation with Java becomes complicated because even though it is a young language there are three different versions. Version 1.0 is still used often for applets because there is no guarantee that browsers will implement later versions. Version 1.1 made improvements to the way in which events are handled, which requires rewriting some of the code that was used in 1.0. Version 2 keeps the same event-handling model as version 1.1, but it adds a new set of components from the Java Foundations Classes (called swing). This chapter is written from the viewpoint of Java 1.1. To see the equivalent programs using the Java 1.0 event model, and for more about the swing components in Java 2, see the book's web page at *http://www.spu.edu/~ddowning/cpjava.html.*

The programs in this chapter are mostly very simple; their purpose is to illustrate how the Java code implements various features.

13.2   Mouse Clicks

We'll start with an applet that responds to mouse clicks. Whenever you click the mouse, this program will determine the location where the click occurred, then it will draw a blue circle on the screen with center at that point.

```java
import java.applet.*;

import java.awt.*;
import java.awt.event.*;


public class mouse1 extends Applet
implements MouseListener {

/*This program draws a blue circle on the screen, centered at the
  point where you click the mouse.*/


Color circlecolor=Color.blue;
int r=30; /*circle radius*/
int x=100; int y=100;

/*method*/ public void init() {
setBackground(Color.lightGray);


addMouseListener(this);
} /*end init*/

public void mouseMoved(MouseEvent e) {}
public void mouseDragged(MouseEvent e) {}
public void mouseReleased(MouseEvent e) {}
public void mouseClicked(MouseEvent e) {}
public void mouseEntered(MouseEvent e) {}
public void mouseExited(MouseEvent e) {}


/*method*/ public void paint(Graphics g) {
g.setColor(circlecolor);
g.fillOval(x-r,y-r,2*r,2*r);
} /*end paint*/
```

```
/*method*/ public void mousePressed(MouseEvent e) {
/*x and y will be the x and y screen coordinates of the point where
  the mouse was pressed, in pixels.*/
x=e.getX();
y=e.getY();
repaint();
} /*end mousePressed*/

} /*end mouse1*/
```

Here are some notes about this program:

- We need this import command: **import java.awt.event.*;**.

- We need to implement the interface **MouseListener** so the program will listen for mouse events.

- In the **init** method for the applet, we need to add the mouse listener.

- The **MouseListener** interface defines seven methods: **mousePressed**, **mouseMoved**, **mouseDragged**, **mouseReleased**, **mouseClicked**, **mouseEntered**, and **mouseExited**. In this particular program, the only one we are using is **mousePressed**. However, we must include empty declarations for the others, since when we implement an interface we must mention all of the methods it contains.

- The **mousePressed** method takes one argument, of class **MouseEvent**, that we will call **e**. (We choose **e** because it stands for event.) Because we have added a **MouseListener** to our applet, this method will be called whenever the user clicks the mouse over our applet. (There will be no effect if you click on a window belonging to some other application; remember that you might have more than one window showing on the screen at the same time.)

- We need to know the exact coordinates (in pixels) where the mouse click occurred; we get this from the **getX()** and **getY()** methods (which are part of the class **mouseEvent**). Our program then assigns these two values to the variables **x** and **y**.

- The **mousePressed** method needs to call the **repaint()** method; otherwise, our new circle will not be displayed on the screen. The **repaint()** method calls the **paint** method. In general, your program should call **repaint()** whenever something has changed that affects the visual display of the screen.

Try this program; it will be fun for a few seconds to watch the blue circle jump around the screen in response to your mouse clicks. (This will quickly become boring, but console yourself with the thought that this is only the beginning; you will be able to write much more interesting windows programs soon.)

Here is the same program as an application (instead of an applet):

import java.awt.*;

import java.awt.event.*;

```java
public class mouse2 extends Frame
implements MouseListener {
/*This Java application draws colored circles on the screen at the
  points where the mouse is clicked.*/

static mouse2 mouse2frame;

/*constructor method*/
public mouse2(String title) {
      super(title);
      addMouseListener(this);
} /*end constructor*/

Color circlecolor=Color.blue;
int r=30; /*circle radius*/
int x=100; int y=100;

public void init() {
      setBackground(Color.lightGray);
} /*end init*/

public void mouseMoved(MouseEvent e ) {}
public void mouseDragged(MouseEvent e ) {}
public void mouseReleased(MouseEvent e ) {}
public void mouseClicked(MouseEvent e ) {}
public void mouseEntered(MouseEvent e ) {}
public void mouseExited(MouseEvent e ) {}


/*method*/ public void paint(Graphics g) {
g.setColor(circlecolor);
g.fillOval(x-r,y-r,2*r,2*r);
} /*end paint*/


/*method*/ public void mousePressed(MouseEvent e) {
/*x and y will be the x and y screen coordinates of the point where
  the mouse was pressed, in pixels.*/
x=e.getX();
y=e.getY();
mouse2frame.repaint();
} /*end mousePressed*/

/*to close the window:*/
static class winlis extends WindowAdapter {
public void windowClosing(WindowEvent e) {
System.exit(0);
} /*end windowClosing*/
} /*end winlis*/


public static void main(String args[ ]) {
mouse2frame = new mouse2("Mouse Example Application");
```

```
mouse2frame.init();
mouse2frame.addWindowListener(new winlis());
mouse2frame.setBounds(10,10,300,300);
mouse2frame.setVisible(true);
} /*end main*/
} /*end class mouse2*/
```

13.3   Dynamic Graphs

We can now easily create a graph that changes in response to mouse clicks. We need a variable that keeps track of the state of the graph. A mouse click will advance this variable to the next number. The **paint** method needs to adjust the way it draws the diagram depending on the state variable. Here is an example that draws a simple spiral pattern on the screen. Once you see how this example works, you can easily adapt it to more complicated examples of dynamic graphs.

```
import java.applet.*;

import java.awt.*;
import java.awt.event.*;

public class dyngraph extends Applet
implements MouseListener {

/*This program draws a spiral pattern on the screen; each mouse click
  causes one more line to be drawn.*/

static int state=0;

/*method*/ public void init() {
setBackground(Color.lightGray);
addMouseListener(this);
cpjxy.xscale=30;
cpjxy.yscale=30;
} /*end init*/

/*When we implement the MouseListener interface, we need to list
   all of the following methods, even if we will not define
   any specific behavior for them.*/

public void mouseMoved(MouseEvent e) {}
public void mouseDragged(MouseEvent e) {}
public void mouseReleased(MouseEvent e) {}
public void mouseClicked(MouseEvent e) {}
public void mouseEntered(MouseEvent e) {}
public void mouseExited(MouseEvent e) {}


/*method*/ public void paint(Graphics g) {
```

```
        if (state>=1) {
                cpjxy.dline (0,0,1,0,g,Color.blue);
                        }

        if (state>=2) {
                cpjxy.dline (1,0,1,2,g,Color.blue);
                        }

        if (state>=3) {
                cpjxy.dline (1,2,-3,2,g,Color.blue);
                        }

        if (state>=4) {
                cpjxy.dline (-3,2,-3,-4,g,Color.blue);
                        }

        if (state>=5) {
                cpjxy.dline (-3,-4,5,-4,g,Color.blue);
                        }

        if (state>=6) {
                cpjxy.dline (5,-4,5,6,g,Color.blue);
                        }

        if (state>=7) {
                cpjxy.dline (5,6,-7,6,g,Color.blue);
                        }

        if (state>=8) {
                cpjxy.dline (-7,6,-7,-8,g,Color.blue);
                        }

} /*end paint*/

/*method*/ public void mousePressed(MouseEvent e) {
state++;
repaint();
} /*end mousePressed*/


} /*end dyngraph*/
```

Here is the screen:

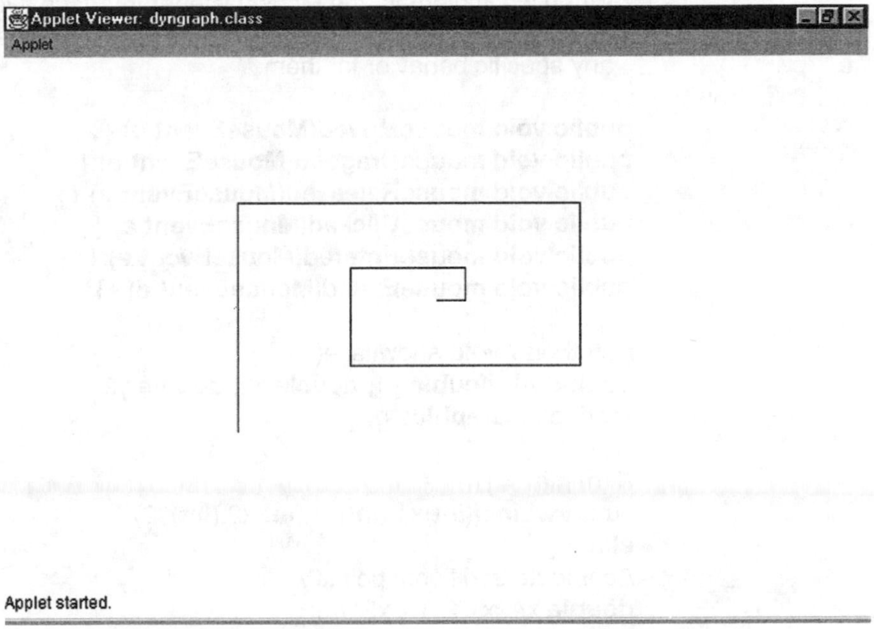

FIGURE 13–1   Applet started.

Here's an example that uses recursion (see page 101) to draw an interesting fractal pattern known as the Koch snowflake. To draw this pattern, start with a triangle. Then, replace each straight line _____ with a bent line like this _/_. The second stage of the picture is a six-pointed star. With each new stage, the picture looks more and more like a snowflake.

Here's the program:

```java
import java.applet.*;

import java.awt.*;
import java.awt.event.*;

public class fractal extends Applet
implements MouseListener {

/*This program uses recursion to draw a fractal image called the
   Koch snowflake on the screen. Each time the mouse is clicked,
   the depth of the recursion increases by 1. Technically, you have
   to click the mouse an infinite number of times and use a screen
   with infinitely fine resolution to see the full fractal image.*/


int depth;

/*method*/ public void init() {
setBackground(Color.white);
addMouseListener(this);
depth=1;
} /*end init*/
```

```java
/*When we implement the MouseListener interface, we need to list
  all of the following methods, even if we will not define
  any specific behavior for them.*/

public void mouseMoved(MouseEvent e) {}
public void mouseDragged(MouseEvent e) {}
public void mouseReleased(MouseEvent e) {}
public void mouseClicked(MouseEvent e) {}
public void mouseEntered(MouseEvent e) {}
public void mouseExited(MouseEvent e) {}


/*method*/ void snowflake(
double x1, double y1, double x2, double y2,
int depth, Graphics g) {

if (depth<=1)
{g.drawLine((int)x1,(int)y1,(int)x2,(int)y2);}
else {
/*compute additional points*/
double x4=x1*2/3 + x2*1/3;
double y4=y1*2/3 + y2*1/3;
double x5=x1*1/3 + x2*2/3;
double y5=y1*1/3 + y2*2/3;
double x6=(x4+x5)/2+(y4-y5)*Math.sqrt(3)/2;
double y6=(y4+y5)/2+(x5-x4)*Math.sqrt(3)/2;
/*call snowflake recursively*/
snowflake(x1,y1,x4,y4,depth-1,g);
snowflake(x4,y4,x6,y6,depth-1,g);
snowflake(x6,y6,x5,y5,depth-1,g);
snowflake(x5,y5,x2,y2,depth-1,g);

} /*end else*/
} /*end snowflake*/



/*method*/ public void paint(Graphics g) {
g.setColor(Color.black);
snowflake(280.0, 10.0, 164.5, 210.0, depth, g);
snowflake(164.5, 210.0, 395.5, 210.0, depth, g);
snowflake(395.5, 210.0, 280.0, 10.0, depth, g);

} /*end paint*/

/*method*/ public void mousePressed(MouseEvent e) {
depth++;
repaint();
} /*end mousePressed*/

} /*end fractal*/
```

Here is the screen after four repetitions:

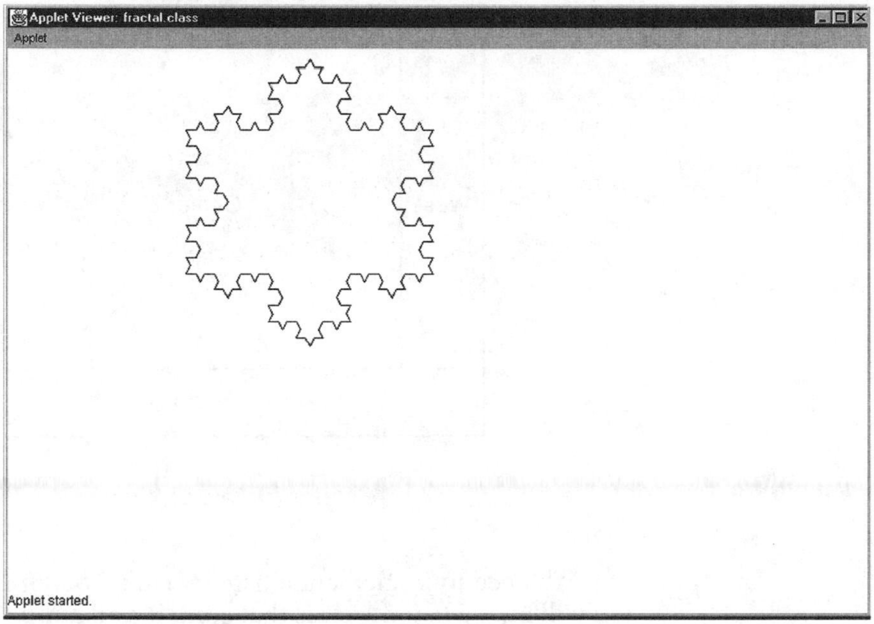

FIGURE 13–2

13.4   Buttons

Screen buttons are a very helpful way for users to call for commands in your programs. There are two general tasks we need to perform to add buttons to our Java programs: (1) design the location of the buttons; and (2) write the code that responds to a click on the button.

As you might expect, there is a button class in Java. To create a specific button, we need to create an instance of this class and then add it to our screen. However, we will often want to include more than one button, so it helps to group them together into an object called a panel.

There are several different ways of arranging the layout of a Java screen, but we will only look at one of the most convenient. Our layout will have one row of buttons at the top of the screen, and another row at the bottom. (If you have so many buttons that they won't fit on two rows, consider using menu items instead.)

We create two panels, one for the top row and one for the bottom row. We add the buttons to the panels; then we add the panels to the applet screen. To do this, our applet will have a layout called a border layout. In a border layout, the top of the screen is called "North," the bottom is called "South," and the center is called "Center" (see Figure 13–3). (There are also East and West sections, but we will not be using those.) We add the top panel to the North section, and the bottom panel to the South section, and then the center section is free for whatever else we want our program to do.

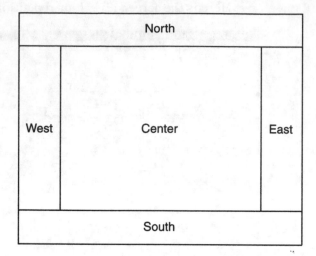

FIGURE 13–3   *Border Layout Regions*

We need to implement a listener called **actionListener**. Each button will have a listener class that contains an **actionPerformed** method that gives the action to take when the button is clicked.

13.5   Outline Code

Before we look at the Java code to create the buttons, we will sketch an outline of our program. The first line of our outline will contain our program name (button1 in this case). Then the outline will have seven sections:

1. `<VARS>`: a listing of variable and method declarations

2. `<INIT>`: code we want in the **init** method

3. `<BUTTONS>`: a list of button labels and their associated actions

4. `<MENU>`: a list of menu items and their associated actions; this will be covered in the next chapter

5. `<MOUSE>`: code we want to be executed when the mouse button is pressed

6. `<PAINT>`: code we want in the **paint** method

7. `<CLOSE>`: code we want to be executed when the program window is closed (if any)

We'll mark the beginning of each section with a marker like this:

`*:<sectionname>`

Then we'll mark the end of each section like this:

`*:</sectionname>`

The style of these markers should look familiar since they are the same style as HTML markers. The "*:" is included at the beginning of each marker so we can distinguish our outline code markers from actual HTML markers.

Since we will use this outline code several times in this book, it will help to create a template file with the section markers. When you start a new program, copy the template file to another file with extension '.OUT' whose name is the name of the program. Then fill in the spaces between the section beginning and end markers. Here is the blank template file:

```
programname

*:<VARS>
*:</VARS>

*:<INIT>
*:</INIT>

*:<BUTTONS>
*:</BUTTONS>

*:<MENU>
*:</MENU>

*:<MOUSE>
*:</MOUSE>

*:<PAINT>
*:</PAINT>

*:<CLOSE>
*:</CLOSE>
```

For more about this outline code, see Appendix E.

13.6   Programming with Buttons to Change Colors

Our example program will be quite simple; the only thing it will do is change the text or background colors. There will be four buttons on the top panel for text colors. For our outline code, we'll give the name of the button followed by a left brace; then we'll list the statements we want the computer to follow when that button is clicked; then we'll close the section for that button with a right brace on a new line. We'll use <BREAK> as a marker for the end of the top panel buttons and the beginning of the lower panel buttons, which will set the background color.

Here is the outline code for our program:

```
button1

*:<VARS>
Color textcolor=Color.black;
```

```
*:</VARS>

*:<INIT>
setBackground(Color.lightGray);
*:</INIT>

*:<BUTTONS>
White_Text{
textcolor=Color.white;
}
Red_Text{
textcolor=Color.red;
}
Green_Text{
textcolor=Color.green;
}
Blue_Text{
textcolor=Color.blue;
}
<BREAK>
White_background{
setBackground(Color.white);
}
Red_background{
setBackground(Color.red);
}
Green_background{
setBackground(Color.green);
}
Blue_background{
setBackground(Color.blue);
}
*:</BUTTONS>

*:<MENU>
*:</MENU>

*:<MOUSE>
*:</MOUSE>

*:<PAINT>
g.setColor(textcolor);
g.drawString("Hello",100,200);
*:</PAINT>

*:<CLOSE>
*:</CLOSE>
```

The outline code leaves out all of the standard code needed to make a Java program function, and it leaves out the code to actually implement the buttons. The latter code consists of the code to place the buttons on the screen (which goes in the **init** method), and the code describing the action to take when the button is clicked. Since all of this code will be standard in any of our Java programs with buttons, we might find it a bit tedious to translate our outline code into actual Java code, particularly if we will be writing many different programs with buttons.

The word "tedious" should ring a bell. We want to use the computer to save us from tedious work . . . so why not use the computer to save us from the tedious work of writing computer programs themselves? Of course, the computer cannot help you write the specific features that are unique to your program, because it would have no way to know what those would be. However, when there are standard features that will commonly be used by many programs, we can use a code generator program to create the actual Java code. The code generator program is included in appendix E. You don't have to understand all of the features of the code generator program to use it; all you need to do is understand the features of the outline code described on page 221.

The name of the input file with the outline code has the extension out; in our case, the file is (button1.out). To execute the code generator program, use this command line:

```
java codegen button1
```

When we run the program, it will generate the following code. (Actually, the code generator will also include some extra code to initialize items such as menus. Since we are not using that code in this example, those lines have been removed from the listing below, so that only those lines directly involved with buttons are included. You can look at this example to see how Java implements buttons.)

```java
import java .awt.*;

import java .awt.event.*;

public class button1 extends Frame {

public static button1 button1frame;

Color textcolor=Color.black;

/*constructor*/
public button1(String title) {
super(title);
} /*end constructor*/

public void init() {
setBackground(Color.lightGray);
Panel upperpanel = new Panel ();
Panel lowerpanel = new Panel ();
/*Button */ White_Textbtn= new Button ("White_Text");
        White_Textbtn.addActionListener (new White_Textbtnlis());
          upperpanel.add (White_Textbtn);
/*Button */ Red_Textbtn= new Button ("Red_Text");
        Red_Textbtn.addActionListener (new Red_Textbtnlis());
          upperpanel.add (Red_Textbtn);
/*Button */ Green_Textbtn= new Button ("Green_Text");
        Green_Textbtn.addActionListener (new Green_Textbtnlis());
```

```
            upperpanel.add (Green_Textbtn);
/*Button */ Blue_Textbtn= new Button ("Blue_Text");
        Blue_Textbtn.addActionListener (new Blue_Textbtnlis());
            upperpanel.add (Blue_Textbtn);
/*Button */ White_backgroundbtn= new Button ("White_background");
        White_backgroundbtn.addActionListener (new
        White_backgroundbtnlis());
        lowerpanel.add (White_backgroundbtn);
/*Button */ Red_backgroundbtn= new Button ("Red_background");
        Red_backgroundbtn.addActionListener (new
        Red_backgroundbtnlis());
        lowerpanel.add (Red_backgroundbtn);
/*Button */ Green_backgroundbtn= new Button ("Green_background");
        Green_backgroundbtn.addActionListener (new
        Green_backgroundbtnlis());
        lowerpanel.add (Green_backgroundbtn);
/*Button */ Blue_backgroundbtn= new Button ("Blue_background");
        Blue_backgroundbtn.addActionListener (new
        Blue_backgroundbtnlis());
        lowerpanel.add (Blue_backgroundbtn);
add(BorderLayout .NORTH,upperpanel);
add(BorderLayout .SOUTH,lowerpanel);
} /*end init*/

/*Here are the declarations for the buttons:*/
Button White_Textbtn;
Button Red_Textbtn;
Button Green_Textbtn;
Button Blue_Textbtn;
Button White_backgroundbtn;
Button Red_backgroundbtn;
Button Green_backgroundbtn;
Button Blue_backgroundbtn;

/*method*/ public void paint (Graphics g) {
g.setColor(textcolor);
g.drawString("Hello",100,200);
} /*end paint*/

/*inner*/ class White_Textbtnlis implements ActionListener {
public void actionPerformed(ActionEvent e) {
textcolor=Color.white;
button1frame.repaint ();
} /*end actionPerformed*/
} /*end inner class White_Textbtnlis*/

/*inner*/ class Red_Textbtnlis implements ActionListener {
public void actionPerformed(ActionEvent e) {
textcolor=Color.red;
button1frame.repaint ();
} /*end actionPerformed*/
} /*end inner class Red_Textbtnlis*/
```

```
/*inner*/ class Green_Textbtnlis implements ActionListener {
public void actionPerformed(ActionEvent e) {
textcolor=Color.green;
button1frame.repaint ();
} /*end actionPerformed*/
} /*end inner class Green_Textbtnlis*/

/*inner*/ class Blue_Textbtnlis implements ActionListener {
public void actionPerformed(ActionEvent e) {
textcolor=Color.blue;
button1frame.repaint ();
} /*end actionPerformed*/
} /*end inner class Blue_Textbtnlis*/

/*inner*/ class White_backgroundbtnlis implements ActionListener {
public void actionPerformed(ActionEvent e) {
setBackground(Color.white);
button1frame.repaint ();
} /*end actionPerformed*/
} /*end inner class White_backgroundbtnlis*/

/*inner*/ class Red_backgroundbtnlis implements ActionListener {
public void actionPerformed(ActionEvent e) {
setBackground(Color.red);
button1frame.repaint ();
} /*end actionPerformed*/
} /*end inner class Red_backgroundbtnlis*/

/*inner*/ class Green_backgroundbtnlis implements ActionListener {
public void actionPerformed(ActionEvent e) {
setBackground(Color.green);
button1frame.repaint ();
} /*end actionPerformed*/
} /*end inner class Green_backgroundbtnlis*/

/*inner*/ class Blue_backgroundbtnlis implements ActionListener {
public void actionPerformed(ActionEvent e) {
setBackground(Color.blue);
button1frame.repaint ();
} /*end actionPerformed*/
} /*end inner class Blue_backgroundbtnlis*/


/*To close the window:*/
static class winlis extends WindowAdapter {
public void windowClosing(WindowEvent e) {
System.exit(0);
} /*end windowClosing*/
} /*end winlis*/

public static void main (String args[ ]) {
button1frame = new button1("button1");
button1frame.addWindowListener(new winlis());
```

```
button1frame.init();
button1frame.setBounds (10,10,360,360);
button1frame.setVisible(true);
} /*end main*/
} /*end class button1*/
```

When we compile and run button1, we will see these buttons on the screen:

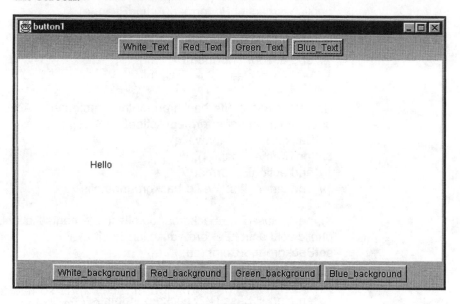

FIGURE 13–4

You can experiment with changing the text and background colors. (Notice how the text becomes invisible if you set it to be the same color as the background.) In reality, you will write programs with buttons that perform more elaborate commands.

EXERCISES

1. Write a program that draws lines on the screen. Each time the user clicks the mouse, a line is drawn connecting that point with the previous mouse click.

2. Write a program similar to the previous one, except include a grid system so that the endpoints of the lines are automatically moved to the closest point on the grid.

3. Write a question drill program that displays questions on the screen. After you click the mouse, the answer appears; click the mouse again and a new question appears. You can use this program to help you study; you will need to write the questions that are relevant for the subject you are learning.

4. Write a program that changes colors on the screen in response to the buttons you push. Have six buttons: three to increase the intensity level of red, green, and blue, and three to decrease the level of those three colors.

5. If **bt1** is a button object, then calling the method

   bt1.setEnabled(false);

   causes that button to become disabled, that is, it can't be clicked. Revise the color program in the chapter so that the button representing the current color is disabled. To enable the button again, call the method bt1.**setEnabled(true);**.

CHAPTER 14

WINDOWS PROGRAMMING: DIALOG BOXES AND MENUS

14.1 Message Boxes

Dialog boxes provide a way for a program to send a message to the user, or to receive input from the user. A dialog box is a special type of window that appears when it is needed and then disappears after the user has dealt with it. We have already seen one important type of dialog box: the file dialog box used to select files (see page 186).

As you might expect, Java already includes a **Dialog** class, which we can extend to create our own kind of dialog box. The first type we'll create is a simple message box that does nothing but display a message to the user. However, even a dialog box that simple needs to have an "OK" button so the user can tell the computer that the message has been read and the box is no longer needed.

Here is the code to create the message box:

```
import java.awt.*;

import java.awt.event.*;

public class mbox extends Dialog
implements ActionListener {

/*This class creates a message box, which other programs can use
   to display a message to the user.*/

Button okbtn; TextField msgtext;

/*constructor*/ public mbox(Frame parent,
          String msg) {
```

```
super(parent,"Message", true);
                    /*The previous line calls the constructor of the
                      superclass, which is Dialog.*/
                    /*Parent represents the frame that is the parent of this
                      dialog box, which is passed to the constructor as a
                      parameter in the calling program.*/
                    /*true means that this will be a modal dialog box,
                      which means that the user must clear it before other
                      processing will proceed.*/
setLayout(new BorderLayout());
okbtn = new Button("OK");
okbtn.addActionListener(this);
add(BorderLayout.SOUTH,okbtn);
msgtext = new TextField(50);
msgtext.setEditable(false);
msgtext.setText(msg);
add(BorderLayout.NORTH,msgtext);
pack(); /*make compact*/
} /*end constructor*/

public void actionPerformed(ActionEvent e) {
String btn=e.getActionCommand();

if (btn.equals("OK")) {
        setVisible(false);
} /*end if*/

} /*end actionPerformed*/
} /*end mbox*/
```

Here are some notes about this program:

- Our class, mbox, extends the class **Dialog**.

- The text of the message appears in an object we will call msgtext that is of class **TextField**.

- To use a **TextField**, first create it by giving the number of characters it may contain (in our case, 50):

```
msgtext = new TextField(50);
```

- Use the statement

```
msgtext.setEditable(false);
```

if you want the text field to display a message that the user cannot change, as in this example. (If you leave out msgtext.**setEditable(false)**, then the computer will assume that you wish to have **setEditable** be true, and the user can make changes.)

- Use the **setText** method to determine the string that the text field will contain. In our example, the string variable msg (which is supplied as an argument of the constructor) holds the string that will be displayed in the text box after this statement is executed:

msgtext.**setText**(msg);

- The **TextField** needs to be added to the dialog box with this statement:

add(BorderLayout.NORTH,msgtext);

We include "NORTH" because we want the text field added to the top of the box. See the diagram depicting the border layout on page 220.

- The commands describing the text field are added to the constructor for the dialog box. The constructor also defines one button: the "OK" button. We also need an **actionPerformed** method; all this method does is get rid of the dialog box with the

setVisible(false);

command when the "OK" button has been clicked.

- The constructor for mbox takes two parameters: the frame that is the parent window of the dialog box (which will be the frame in which the program is running); and a string that is the title of the dialog box (which is the simple string "Message" in our example). The word "parent" here does not refer to a class inheriting from another class. Instead, certain windows such as dialog boxes are not independent windows; they "belong" to another window that is said to be their parent. In general, the parent window of a dialog box will be the window containing the program that called the dialog box.

- The constructor for mbox calls the constructor of the superclass **Dialog** (see page 119). This constructor takes three parameters: the parent frame, the title, and the boolean value **true**. The value **true** tells the computer that this is a dialog box that will not allow the rest of your program to proceed until it has been taken care of. (Such a dialog box is called a *modal* dialog box.) This is normally the behavior you want, since the dialog box is there to provide a message to the user (which presumably should not be ignored) or else to receive input from the user (which presumably is required by the program before it can proceed). Even though the modal dialog box temporarily prevents any action from the program that calls it, you may still interact with windows that belong to other programs. You can create a non-modal dialog box by using the value **false** in the constructor; however, this is not the behavior one normally expects a dialog box to have. If you want your program to have more than one active window on the screen simultaneously, you can create other windows that are not dialog boxes.

- Although not exactly forbidden, dialog boxes are not intended to be used with applets. A normal applet is contained within the browser's window, but a dialog box is free to float around the screen, which potentially could confuse the user into thinking the box comes from some other program, rather than the applet. A malicious programmer could conceivably create a program with a dialog box that fools the user into typing in a password, and then sending that password back to the server from whence the web page came. Dialog boxes in applets do contain a warning, something like "Warning—Applet Window" to try to protect users from this possibility. Even if security were not an issue, dialog boxes with applets pose another problem because they cannot be modal, that is, they cannot freeze the browser until the user clears it, since the user could always move to another web page. You can include a non-modal dialog box in an applet, but that can have unpredictable effects on the operation of the applet. These restrictions on dialog boxes for applets are not much of a problem as long as applets are only small-scale programs (which is what the diminutive name "applet" implies). However, if it becomes common to distribute larger-scale programs as applets, then we must hope that future versions of Java will provide better support for dialog boxes in applets.

Now we need a program to illustrate the use of the message box. Here is a simple program that displays a counter on the screen; every time the counter advances 50 numbers it displays a dialog box informing the user of that fact.

```
import java.awt.*;

import java.awt.event.*;

public class dial1 extends Frame {

/*This program illustrates the use of the mbox (messagebox) class.*/

static dial1 dial1frame;
static mbox mb1;
static int i=0;

/*constructor*/
public dial1(String title) {
super(title);
} /*end constructor*/

public void init() {
setBackground(Color.white);
} /*end init*/

/*method*/ public void paint(Graphics g) {
g.drawString(""+i,100,200);
} /*end paint*/

/*to close the window:*/
static class winlis extends WindowAdapter {
public void windowClosing(WindowEvent e) {
System.exit(0);
} /*end windowClosing*/
} /*end WindowAdapter*/
```

```
public static void main(String args[ ]) {
dial1frame = new dial1("Dialog box Example Application");
dial1frame.addWindowListener(new winlis());
dial1frame.init();
dial1frame.setBounds(10,20,400,300);
dial1frame.setVisible(true);

while (i<1000000) {
        dial1frame.repaint();
        if ((i%50)==0) {
                /*The message will be shown whenever i is divisible
                        by 50.*/
                mb1=new mbox(dial1frame,("Counter has reached "+i));
                mb1.setVisible (true);
                        } /*end if*/
            i++;
                try{
                /*The program will rest for 200 milliseconds.*/
                Thread.currentThread().sleep(200);
                    } catch (InterruptedException ex) {}
        } /*end while*/
} /*end main*/
} /*end class dial1*/
```

Here is a view of the screen when this dialog box appears:

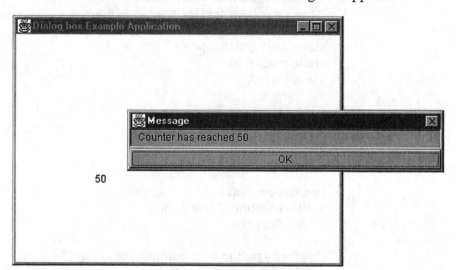

FIGURE 14–1

14.2   Input Boxes

Another type of dialog box allows the user to type in information. We'll create a new class called inbox:

```java
import java.awt.*;

import java.awt.event.*;

class inbox extends Dialog
implements ActionListener {

/*This class allows the user to type in one line of text.*/

Button okbtn; Button cancelbtn;
TextField msgtext;

/*constructor method*/ public inbox(Frame parent,
        String label) {

super(parent,label, true);
setLayout(new BorderLayout());
Panel buttonpanel = new Panel();
okbtn = new Button("OK");
okbtn.addActionListener(this);
buttonpanel.add(okbtn);
cancelbtn = new Button("Cancel");
cancelbtn.addActionListener(this);
buttonpanel.add(cancelbtn);
add(BorderLayout.SOUTH,buttonpanel);
msgtext = new TextField(50);
msgtext.setEditable(true);
msgtext.setText(" ");
add(BorderLayout.NORTH,msgtext);
pack();
} /*end public*/

public void actionPerformed(ActionEvent e) {
String btn=e.getActionCommand();

if (btn.equals("OK")) {
        setVisible(false);
} /*end if*/
else if (btn.equals("Cancel")) {
        setVisible(false);
        msgtext.setText(" ");
} /*end if*/

} /*end actionPerformed*/
} /*end inbox*/
```

This class is very similar to our mbox class on page 228. The differences follow:

- Since we have not included the command **setEditable(false)**, the user can type in text this time.
- The **TextField** is initially set to have a blank message.
- The dialog box contains a "Cancel" button in addition to the "OK" button.

   Following is a program that illustrates the use of this dialog box. This program has the user type in lines of text that are added to the screen.

```java
import java.awt.*;

import java.awt.event.*;

public class dial2 extends Frame {
/*This program illustrates the use of inbox (an input dialog box).*/

static dial2 dial2frame;

static inbox in1;

static int numlines=0;
static int startline=1;
static int lps=20; /*lines per screen*/
static String a[ ]=new String[100];

/*constructor*/
public dial2(String title) {
super(title);
} /*end constructor*/

public void init() {
setBackground(Color.white);
} /*end init*/

/*method*/ public void paint(Graphics g) {
for (int i=startline; i<=(numlines-1); i++) {
g.drawString(" "+i+": "+a[i],50,20*(i+1));
} /*end for loop*/
} /*end paint*/

public static void main(String args[ ]) {

dial2frame = new dial2("Input Dialog box Example Application");
dial2frame.init();
dial2frame.setBounds(10,20,400,300);
dial2frame.setVisible(true);
while (true) {
        numlines++;
          /*The next two lines display the dialog box.*/
        in1 = new inbox(dial2frame,("Enter line "+numlines));
        in1.setVisible(true);
        a[numlines]=in1.msgtext.getText();
```

```
                    dial2frame.repaint();
                } /*end while*/
        } /*end main*/
        } /*end class dial2*/
```

(There is no way to end this program directly, since a new dialog box keeps reappearing every time you close the previous one, and you cannot close the main window while the dialog box is on the screen. In Windows, you need to press Control-Alt-Delete to call for the task manager in order to end the program. Normally, you will not write a program that constantly keeps displaying dialog boxes on the screen like this.)

Here is a view of the screen:

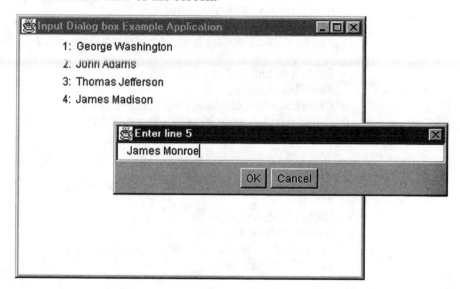

FIGURE 14–2

14.3   Check Boxes, Radio Buttons, and Choice Boxes

If you're familiar with Windows, you've likely used programs that obtained input with these features:

- a check box: a labeled square box that allows you to turn a feature on or off. A check appears in the box when the feature is on. Unlike with radio buttons, checking or unchecking a checkbox has no effect on any other checkboxes or buttons.

- a group of radio buttons: labeled circular buttons allowing you to make one selection. A marker always appears in one of these circles indicating which item is selected. When you click the mouse in one circle, then that circle becomes selected and the others are automatically deselected. The name radio button comes from early car radio buttons, where pushing one button to select a station would automatically make the other station buttons pop out.

- a choice box: a drop-down list that appears when you click on an arrow. You choose one of the items from the list by clicking on it with the mouse.

We'll create a new dialog box illustrating these features. This dialog box will have a text field allowing you to type in a line of text; two check boxes allowing you to select italic or bold type (you can select both if you want both italic and bold); three radio buttons allowing you to choose a font (serif, sans serif, or monospaced), and a choice box allowing you to choose one of three different type sizes.

Here is the code for the dialog box:

```
import java.awt.*;

import java.awt.event.*;

class inbox2 extends Dialog
implements ActionListener {
        /*This dialog box illustrates the use of radio buttons, check boxes,
            and a choice box, as well as a TextField.*/

Button okbtn; Button cancelbtn;
TextField msgtext;
Checkbox italiccb=new Checkbox("Italic");
Checkbox boldcb=new Checkbox("Bold");

        /*The next three buttons are radio buttons.*/
CheckboxGroup cbgroup1;
Checkbox serifrb, sanserifrb, monospacedrb;

        Choice choice1;

/*constructor method*/ public inbox2(Frame parent,
        String label) {

super(parent, label, true);
setLayout(new BorderLayout());
Panel buttonpanel=new Panel();
okbtn=new Button("OK");
okbtn.addActionListener(this);
buttonpanel.add(okbtn);
cancelbtn=new Button("Cancel");
cancelbtn.addActionListener(this);
buttonpanel.add(cancelbtn);
add(BorderLayout.SOUTH,buttonpanel);

Panel centerpanel=new Panel();
centerpanel.setLayout(new GridLayout(3,1));
                                          /*3 rows, 1 column*/
msgtext=new TextField(50);
msgtext.setEditable(true);
msgtext.setText(" ");
centerpanel.add(msgtext);

Panel middlerowpanel=new Panel();
italiccb=new Checkbox("Italic");
middlerowpanel.add(italiccb);
```

```
boldcb=new Checkbox("Bold");
middlerowpanel.add(boldcb);

        /*Define a choice list for different font sizes:*/
            choice1=new Choice();
            choice1.addItem("16 point");
            choice1.addItem("24 point");
            choice1.addItem("32 point");
            middlerowpanel.add(choice1);

        centerpanel.add(middlerowpanel);

/*Define three radio buttons for different fonts:*/
            Panel radiopanel=new Panel();
            cbgroup1=new CheckboxGroup();
            serifrb=new Checkbox("serif", true, cbgroup1);
            sanserifrb=new Checkbox("sanserif", false, cbgroup1);
            monospacedrb=new Checkbox("monospaced", false,
                        cbgroup1);
            radiopanel.add(serifrb);
            radiopanel.add(sanserifrb);
            radiopanel.add(monospacedrb);
            centerpanel.add(radiopanel);
    add(BorderLayout.CENTER,centerpanel);

    pack();
} /*end public*/

public void actionPerformed(ActionEvent e) {
String btn=e.getActionCommand();

if (btn.equals("OK")) {
        setVisible(false);
} /*end if*/
else if (btn.equals("Cancel")) {
        setVisible(false);
        msgtext.setText(" ");
} /*end if*/


} /*end actionPerformed*/
} /*end inbox*/
```

Here are some notes for this program:

- Creating a check box is easy. First, declare an object of type **Check-box**. (You need to do this outside the **init** method, so the value will be accessible elsewhere. Note the capitalization pattern in **Checkbox**.) In the **init** method, call the **Checkbox** constructor method, which takes one argument: a string that is the label for the box. Then, add the box (either to the dialog box itself, or to another panel as we do in this example):

```
italiccb=new Checkbox("Italic");
middlerowpanel.add(italiccb);
```

Here, italiccb is the name of our check box that turns italic on or off.

- Creating a choice box is easy. Create an object of type **Choice**. Add the different items (where each item is represented by a string). Finally, add the choice object to a panel:

```
choice1=new Choice();
choice1.addItem("16 point");
choice1.addItem("24 point");
choice1.addItem("32 point");
middlerowpanel.add(choice1);
```

- Creating a set of radio buttons is only slightly more complicated. Each radio button is in fact declared as a **Checkbox**. The only difference is that radio buttons are grouped together in an object called a **CheckboxGroup**. Also, when you call the constructor for the checkbox, use three arguments: the first is a string giving the label; the second is the value true or false, which determines which button is initially on (make sure that one and only one button is set to true); the third is the name of the check box group. Then, each individual radio button needs to be added to a panel. In our example we have the following:

```
Panel radiopanel=new Panel();
cbgroup1=new CheckboxGroup();
serifrb=new Checkbox("serif", true, cbgroup1);
sanserifrb=new Checkbox("sanserif", false, cbgroup1);
monospacedrb=new Checkbox("monospaced", false, cbgroup1);
radiopanel.add(serifrb);
radiopanel.add(sanserifrb);
radiopanel.add(monospacedrb);
centerpanel.add(radiopanel);
```

- Arranging the components can sometimes be tricky. Our example dialog box illustrates one way of doing it. The box itself has a border layout; the OK and cancel buttons are added to a panel that is added to the South part of the layout. The Center part of the layout contains a panel called *centerpanel*; this panel has a layout called a grid layout with three rows and one column. The first row is the text field; the second row is a panel containing the two check boxes and the choice box; the third row is a panel containing the radio buttons. By arranging the components in panels and then arranging the panels with a grid layout, we can make sure that the components we want side by side actually are side by side, and the components we want on top of each other actually are on top of each other.

Our next step is to write a program that uses our new dialog box:

```
import java.awt.*;
```

```
import java.awt.event.*;

public class dial3 extends Frame {

static dial3 dial3frame;

static inbox2 in2;
static int maxlines=100;

static int numlines=0;
static int startline=1;
static int lps=20; /*lines per screen*/
static String a[ ]=new String[maxlines];
static Font fontlist[ ]=new Font[maxlines];

/*constructor*/
public dial3(String title) {
super(title);
} /*end constructor*/

public void init() {
setBackground(Color.white);
} /*end init*/

/*method*/ public void paint(Graphics g) {
for (int i=startline; i<=(numlines-1); i++) {
Font f=fontlist[i];
g.setFont(f);
g.drawString(" "+i+": "+a[i],50,20*(i+1));
} /*end for loop*/
} /*end paint*/

public static void main(String args[ ]) {

dial3frame=new dial3("Input Dialog box Example Application");
dial3frame.init();
dial3frame.setBounds(10,20,400,300);
dial3frame.setVisible(true);
while (true) {
        numlines++;
        /*The next two lines cause the dialog box to be displayed.*/
        in2=new inbox2(dial3frame,("Enter line "+numlines));
        in2.setVisible(true);
        a[numlines]=in2.msgtext.getText();
        String fontname="";
        if (in2.cbgroup1.getCurrent()==in2.serifrb)
                    {fontname="serif";}
        if (in2.cbgroup1.getCurrent()==in2.sanserifrb)
                    {fontname="sanserif";}
        if (in2.cbgroup1.getCurrent()==in2.monospacedrb)
                    {fontname="monospaced";}

        int fontstyle=0;
```

```
                    if (in2.italiccb.getState())
                                {fontstyle+=Font.ITALIC;}
                    if (in2.boldcb.getState())
                                {fontstyle+=Font.BOLD;}
                    if (fontstyle==0) {fontstyle=Font.PLAIN;}

                    String fontsizestring=in2.choice1.getSelectedItem();
                    int fontsize=0;
                    if (fontsizestring.equals("16 point")) {fontsize=16;}
                    if (fontsizestring.equals("24 point")) {fontsize=24;}
                    if (fontsizestring.equals("32 point")) {fontsize=32;}

                fontlist[numlines]=new Font(fontname,fontstyle,fontsize);

                    dial3frame.repaint();
                } /*end while*/
        } /*end main*/
        } /*end class dial3*/
```

Here are some notes for this program:

- After the dialog box has been called, you can determine if a particular radio button is selected with the command

```
if (in2.cbgroup1.getCurrent()==in2.serifrb)
```

Recall that in2 is the name of the dialog box object; cbgroup1 is the name of the check box group in that dialog box. The **getCurrent()** method is a method for check box groups that determines which button is currently selected. The statement above will be true if the serifrb radio button is currently selected.

- You can determine whether or not a check box is checked with the **getState()** method, which will be true if the check box is checked.

```
int fontstyle=0;
if (in2.italiccb.getState())
        {fontstyle+=Font.ITALIC;}
if (in2.boldcb.getState())
        {fontstyle+=Font.BOLD;}
if (fontstyle==0) {fontstyle=Font.PLAIN;}
```

This segment of code also illustrates how font style constants can be added together. The Font.ITALIC and Font.BOLD constants are in fact integers (you don't ever need to know their values). If only the italic check box is on, then the code segment above will cause the integer variable fontstyle to take the value Font.ITALIC. If only the bold check box is on, fontstyle will take the value Font.BOLD. If both checkboxes are on, fontstyle will take the value Font.ITALIC+Font.BOLD, which, as you might guess, is the code for both italics and bold. If neither check box is on, then the final if statement will set fontstyle to Font.PLAIN.

- You can determine which item is selected in a choice box with the **getSelectedItem**() method, as in this example:

String fontsizestring=in2.choice1.**getSelectedItem**();

Here is a screen view showing this dialog box in action:

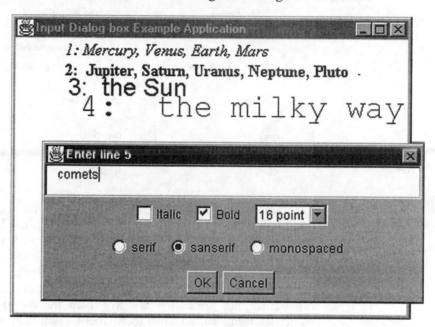

FIGURE 14–3

14.4   Menus

When your program features a large number of choices, it is best to arrange them in menus. You are probably familiar with menus in a graphical user interface. A menu bar at the top of the window contains menu names; clicking on one of these will expose a menu of choices. Some of those choices represent actions; others represent additional menus. This hierarchical arrangement of menus makes it possible to organize a large number of user choices in an efficient manner.

As you can guess, menus in Java are objects. Specifically, there is a **MenuBar** class, for the menu bar at the top of the screen; a **Menu** class, for menus chosen from the menu bar or other menus; and a **MenuItem** class, for menu items that call for commands. You need to create new **MenuItem** objects for each choice, then add these to **Menu** objects. Then add the **Menu** objects to other **Menu** objects or to the **MenuBar** object. Finally, add the **MenuBar** object to your window. As we did with the buttons in the previous chapter, you also need to add **ActionEventListeners**, and then include the code with the actions in the **actionPerformed** method.

Now we'll plan an example program, which will provide one menu for changing the background color; one for changing the text color; and one for changing the message the program will display. We'll arrange the menu items in a hierarchy:

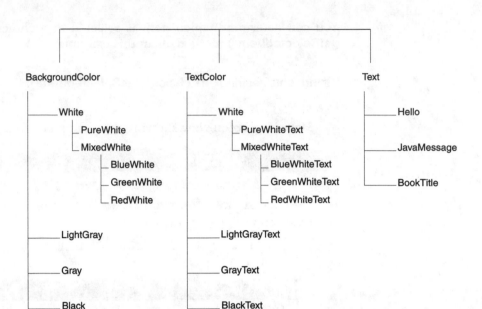

FIGURE 14–4

Now we'll prepare an outline code for this program. Our outline code will follow the same form as we used in the last chapter for the program with buttons, except that now we will use codes for Java menus. In the outline code, each menu item is preceded by a number of asterisks "*" to indicate the menu level. Menus from the menu bar are at the top level, so they will have one asterisk; items that appear on menus that are called directly from the menu bar will have two asterisks; items called from those menus will have three asterisks; and so on.

Here is the outline code:

```
menu1

*:<VARS>
Color c=Color.black;    /*text color*/
Color bc=Color.lightGray; /*background color*/
String textstring="Select from the menu";
*:</VARS>

*:<INIT>
setBackground(bc);
*:</INIT>

*:<BUTTONS>
*:</BUTTONS>

*:<MENU>
*BackgroundColor
**White
***PureWhite{
bc=new Color(255,255,255);
}
***MixedWhite
****BlueWhite{
```

```
bc=new Color(225,225,255);
}
****GreenWhite{
bc=new Color(225,255,225);
}
****RedWhite{
bc=new Color(255,225,225);
}
**LightGray{
bc=Color.lightGray;
}
**Gray{
bc=Color.gray;
}
**Black{
bc=Color.black;
}
*TextColor
**White
***PureWhiteText{
c=new Color(255,255,255);
}
***MixedWhite
****BlueWhiteText{
c=new Color(225,225,255);
}
****GreenWhiteText{
c=new Color(225,255,225);
}
****RedWhiteText{
c=new Color(255,225,225);
}
**LightGrayText{
c=Color.lightGray;
}
**GrayText{
c=Color.gray;
}
**BlackText{
c=Color.black;
}
*Text
**Hello{
textstring="Hello";
}
**JavaMessage{
textstring="this program was written in Java";
}
**BookTitle{
textstring="from the book Java Programming the Easy Way";
}
*:</MENU>
```

```
*:<MOUSE>
*:</MOUSE>

*:<PAINT>
setBackground(bc);
g.setColor(c);
g.drawString(textstring,100,200);
*:</PAINT>

*:<CLOSE>
*:</CLOSE>
```

Each menu item that calls a command (rather than another menu) ends with a left brace, which is followed on a new line by the actions to be taken when that menu is called. The command is concluded by a right brace on another new line. In this example, the actions are all only one line; in reality, they may be multiple lines (or they may be calls to other methods).

Now we need to use the code generator program from Appendix E to convert the outline code into true Java code. Following is the Java program that is generated; you can look at this listing to see the way to establish a menu in Java.

Each menu item is given a name beginning with m. The number of digits following the m indicates the level of the menu item: one digit for top level menus, two digits for the second level, and so on. The digit itself indicates the position at that level; for example, m2123 indicates the third item on the second menu that can be selected from the first menu that can be selected from the second menu on the menu bar.

```
import java .awt.*;

import java .awt.event.*;

public class menu1 extends Frame {

/*This program illustrates the use of menus.*/

public static menu1 menu1frame;

Color c=Color.black; /*text color*/
Color bc=Color.lightGray; /*background color*/
String textstring="Select from the menu";

/*constructor*/
public menu1(String title) {
super(title);
} /*end constructor*/

public void init() {
setBackground(bc);

MenuBar m0=new MenuBar();
/*Menu*/ m1=new Menu("BackgroundColor");
/*Menu*/ m11=new Menu("White");
```

```
/*MenuItem*/ m111=new MenuItem("PureWhite");
m111.addActionListener (new m111lis());
m11.add (m111);
/*Menu*/ m112=new Menu("MixedWhite");
/*MenuItem*/ m1121=new MenuItem("BlueWhite");
      m1121.addActionListener (new m1121lis());
m112.add (m1121);
/*MenuItem*/ m1122=new MenuItem("GreenWhite");
      m1122.addActionListener (new m1122lis());
m112.add (m1122);
/*MenuItem*/ m1123=new MenuItem("RedWhite");
      m1123.addActionListener (new m1123lis());
m112.add (m1123);
m11.add (m112);
m1.add (m11);
/*MenuItem*/ m12=new MenuItem("LightGray");
m12.addActionListener (new m12lis());
m1.add (m12);
/*MenuItem*/ m13=new MenuItem("Gray");
m13.addActionListener (new m13lis());
m1.add (m13);
/*MenuItem*/ m14=new MenuItem("Black");
m14.addActionListener (new m14lis());
m1.add (m14);
m0.add (m1);


/*Menu*/ m2=new Menu("TextColor");
/*Menu*/ m21=new Menu("White");
/*MenuItem*/ m211=new MenuItem("PureWhiteText");
m211.addActionListener (new m211lis());
m21.add (m211);
/*Menu*/ m212=new Menu("MixedWhite");
/*MenuItem*/ m2121=new MenuItem("BlueWhiteText");
      m2121.addActionListener (new m2121lis());
m212.add (m2121);
/*MenuItem*/ m2122=new MenuItem("GreenWhiteText");
      m2122.addActionListener (new m2122lis());
m212.add (m2122);
/*MenuItem*/ m2123=new MenuItem("RedWhiteText");
      m2123.addActionListener (new m2123lis());
m212.add (m2123);
m21.add (m212);
m2.add (m21);
/*MenuItem*/ m22=new MenuItem("LightGrayText");
m22.addActionListener (new m22lis());
m2.add (m22);
/*MenuItem*/ m23=new MenuItem("GrayText");
m23.addActionListener (new m23lis());
m2.add (m23);
/*MenuItem*/ m24=new MenuItem("BlackText");
m24.addActionListener (new m24lis());
m2.add (m24);
m0.add (m2);
```

```
/*Menu*/ m3=new Menu("Text");
/*MenuItem*/ m31=new MenuItem("Hello");
m31.addActionListener (new m31lis());
m3.add (m31);
/*MenuItem*/ m32=new MenuItem("JavaMessage");
m32.addActionListener (new m32lis());
m3.add (m32);
/*MenuItem*/ m33=new MenuItem("BookTitle");
m33.addActionListener (new m33lis());
m3.add (m33);
m0.add (m3);

setMenuBar(m0);
} /*end init*/

/*Declare the menus and menuitems:*/
Menu m1;
Menu m11;
MenuItem m111;
Menu m112;
MenuItem m1121;
        MenuItem m1122;
        MenuItem m1123;
MenuItem m12;
MenuItem m13;
MenuItem m14;
Menu m2;
Menu m21;
MenuItem m211;
Menu m212;
MenuItem m2121;
        MenuItem m2122;
        MenuItem m2123;
MenuItem m22;
MenuItem m23;
MenuItem m24;
Menu m3;
MenuItem m31;
MenuItem m32;
MenuItem m33;


/*method*/ public void paint (Graphics g) {
setBackground(bc);
g.setColor(c);
g.drawString(textstring,100,200);
} /*end paint*/


/*inner*/ class m111lis implements ActionListener {
/*action called by menu item PureWhite*/
public void actionPerformed(ActionEvent e) {
```

```
bc=new Color(255,255,255);
menu1frame.repaint ();
} /*end actionPerformed*/
} /*end inner class m111lis*/

/*inner*/ class m1121lis implements ActionListener {
/*action called by menu item BlueWhite*/
public void actionPerformed(ActionEvent e) {
bc=new Color(225,225,255);
menu1frame.repaint ();
} /*end actionPerformed*/
} /*end inner class m1121lis*/

/*inner*/ class m1122lis implements ActionListener {
/*action called by menu item GreenWhite*/
public void actionPerformed(ActionEvent e) {
bc=new Color(225,255,225);
menu1frame.repaint ();
} /*end actionPerformed*/
} /*end inner class m1122lis*/

/*inner*/ class m1123lis implements ActionListener {
/*action called by menu item RedWhite*/
public void actionPerformed(ActionEvent e) {
bc=new Color(255,225,225);
menu1frame.repaint ();
} /*end actionPerformed*/
} /*end inner class m1123lis*/

/*inner*/ class m12lis implements ActionListener {
/*action called by menu item LightGray*/
public void actionPerformed(ActionEvent e) {
bc=Color.lightGray;
menu1frame.repaint ();
} /*end actionPerformed*/
} /*end inner class m12lis*/

/*inner*/ class m13lis implements ActionListener {
/*action called by menu item Gray*/
public void actionPerformed(ActionEvent e) {
bc=Color.gray;
menu1frame.repaint ();
} /*end actionPerformed*/
} /*end inner class m13lis*/

/*inner*/ class m14lis implements ActionListener {
/*action called by menu item Black*/
public void actionPerformed(ActionEvent e) {
bc=Color.black;
menu1frame.repaint ();
} /*end actionPerformed*/
} /*end inner class m14lis*/
```

```
/*inner*/ class m211lis implements ActionListener {
/*action called by menu item PureWhiteText*/
public void actionPerformed(ActionEvent e) {
c=new Color(255,255,255);
menu1frame.repaint ();
} /*end actionPerformed*/
} /*end inner class m211lis*/

/*inner*/ class m2121lis implements ActionListener {
/*action called by menu item BlueWhiteText*/
public void actionPerformed(ActionEvent e) {
c=new Color(225,225,255);
menu1frame.repaint ();
} /*end actionPerformed*/
} /*end inner class m2121lis*/

/*inner*/ class m2122lis implements ActionListener {
/*action called by menu item GreenWhiteText*/
public void actionPerformed(ActionEvent e) {
c=new Color(225,255,225);
menu1frame.repaint ();
} /*end actionPerformed*/
} /*end inner class m2122lis*/

/*inner*/ class m2123lis implements ActionListener {
/*action called by menu item RedWhiteText*/
public void actionPerformed(ActionEvent e) {
c=new Color(255,225,225);
menu1frame.repaint ();
} /*end actionPerformed*/
} /*end inner class m2123lis*/

/*inner*/ class m22lis implements ActionListener {
/*action called by menu item LightGrayText*/
public void actionPerformed(ActionEvent e) {
c=Color.lightGray;
menu1frame.repaint ();
} /*end actionPerformed*/
} /*end inner class m22lis*/

/*inner*/ class m23lis implements ActionListener {
/*action called by menu item GrayText*/
public void actionPerformed(ActionEvent e) {
c=Color.gray;
menu1frame.repaint ();
} /*end actionPerformed*/
} /*end inner class m23lis*/

/*inner*/ class m24lis implements ActionListener {
/*action called by menu item BlackText*/
public void actionPerformed(ActionEvent e) {
c=Color.black;
menu1frame.repaint ();
```

```
} /*end actionPerformed*/
} /*end inner class m24lis*/

/*inner*/ class m31lis implements ActionListener {
/*action called by menu item Hello*/
public void actionPerformed(ActionEvent e) {
textstring="Hello";
menu1frame.repaint ();
} /*end actionPerformed*/
} /*end inner class m31lis*/

/*inner*/ class m32lis implements ActionListener {
/*action called by menu item JavaMessage*/
public void actionPerformed(ActionEvent e) {
textstring="this program was written in Java";
menu1frame.repaint ();
] /*ond actionPerformed*/
} /*end inner class m32lis*/

/*inner*/ class m33lis implements ActionListener {
/*action called by menu item BookTitle*/
public void actionPerformed(ActionEvent e) {
textstring="from the book Java Programming the Easy Way";
menu1frame.repaint ();
} /*end actionPerformed*/
} /*end inner class m33lis*/

/*to close the window:*/
static class winlis extends WindowAdapter {
public void windowClosing(WindowEvent e) {
System.exit(0);
} /*end windowClosing*/
} /*end winlis*/

public static void main (String args[ ]) {
menu1frame=new menu1("menu1");
menu1frame.addWindowListener(new winlis());
menu1frame.init();
menu1frame.setBounds (10,10,360,360);
menu1frame.setVisible(true);
} /*end main*/
} /*end class menu1*/
```

Following is a view of the screen with some of the menus selected:

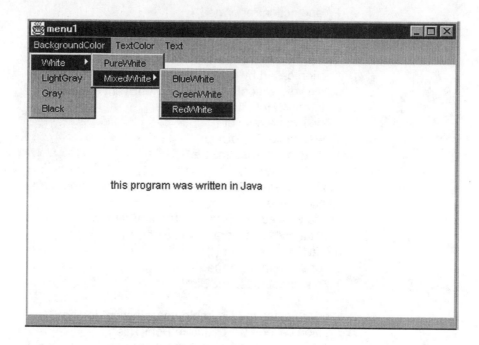

FIGURE 14–5

14.5   Including a Menu in an Applet

Since menus provide a convenient way for users to make choices, you likely will want to include menus with your applets. However, this is slightly more complicated because Java 1.0 and 1.1 do not allow you to include a menu on an applet window. Fortunately, the applet can create another frame, which can include a menu (see the web page at *http://www.spu.edu/~ddowning/cpjava.html* for information on menus in Java 2).

Here is how we can adapt our previous menu program so that it runs in an applet. Start with the source code for that program and make these changes:

1. Include the line **import java.applet.*** at the start of the file.

2. Include the definition for an applet class in the source code. This must be a public class (we'll call it menuapp for our example), so the name of the entire source code file needs to be changed to menuapp.java.

3. The applet defines a variable menu1frame of class menu1. The applet's **init** method does three things: (a) instantiate menu1frame; (b) set its bounds; and (c) cause it to become visible. We don't even need a **paint** method for this applet. Since we haven't defined a **paint** method, a blank applet window will appear on the screen. We'll ignore this, since we're only interested in the frame with the menu. (However, when you're done with the program, you need to close the applet window, not the window with the menu.)

4. The menu1 class is almost the same as it was in our previous program when it was a Java application. Here are the changes you

must make: (a) remove the line **public static** menu1 menu1frame, since the variable menu1frame is now declared inside the applet; (b) remove the entire **main** method; (c) remove the window closing method; (d) change each reference to menu1frame in the program to menuapp.menu1frame (since the variable menu1frame is now defined as a member of the applet's class).

In this case we have kept menu1 as the name of the class with the menu. If you will be using this program as both an applet and an application, and need both class files available at the same time, then you will have to give the applet version of this class a different name.

If you want, you can also make use of the applet window itself to display some useful information to the user. However, if you do this, then the applet version of the program will no longer function in the same manner as the application version (since the application version will only run in one window, not two windows).

The procedure described here can be used to convert any windows-based Java application to an applet that will look the same. Actually, the two versions won't be exactly the same—the applet version will contain a warning at the bottom reminding people that this is an applet window. This is a security feature to prevent programmers from creating applets that trick the user into entering their password, which can then be sent back to the computer from whence the applet was loaded. Another difference is that file reading and writing commands will not work with the applet version because of security restrictions.

Following is the applet version of the program. To make the example more concise, the number of menu choices is smaller than it was in the previous version.

```java
import java .awt.*;

import java .awt.event.*;
import java.applet.*;

class menu1 extends Frame {

/*This program illustrates the use of menus in an applet.*/

Color c=Color.black; /*text color*/
Color bc=Color.lightGray; /*background color*/
String textstring="Select from the menu";

/*constructor*/
public menu1(String title) {
super(title);
} /*end constructor*/

public void init() {
setBackground(bc);

MenuBar m0=new MenuBar();
/*Menu*/ m1=new Menu("BackgroundColor");
/*MenuItem*/ m12=new MenuItem("LightGray");
```

```
        m12.addActionListener (new m12lis());
        m1.add (m12);
        /*MenuItem*/ m14=new MenuItem("Black");
        m14.addActionListener (new m14lis());
        m1.add (m14);
        m0.add (m1);

        /*Menu*/ m2=new Menu("TextColor");
        /*MenuItem*/ m22=new MenuItem("WhiteText");
        m22.addActionListener (new m22lis());
        m2.add (m22);
        /*MenuItem*/ m24=new MenuItem("BlueText");
        m24.addActionListener (new m24lis());
        m2.add (m24);
        m0.add (m2);

        setMenuBar(m0);
        } /*end init*/

        /*declare the menus and menuitems:*/
        Menu m1;
        MenuItem m12;
        MenuItem m14;
        Menu m2;
        MenuItem m22;
        MenuItem m24;

        /*method*/ public void paint (Graphics g) {
        setBackground(bc);
        g.setColor(c);
        g.drawString(textstring,100,200);
        } /*end paint*/


        /*inner*/ class m12lis implements ActionListener {
        /*action called by menu item LightGray*/
        public void actionPerformed(ActionEvent e) {
        bc=Color.lightGray;
        menuapp.menu1frame.repaint ();
        } /*end actionPerformed*/
        } /*end inner class m12lis*/

        /*inner*/ class m14lis implements ActionListener {
        /*action called by menu item Black*/
        public void actionPerformed(ActionEvent e) {
        bc=Color.black;
        menuapp.menu1frame.repaint ();
        } /*end actionPerformed*/
        } /*end inner class m14lis*/

        /*inner*/ class m22lis implements ActionListener {
        /*action called by menu item WhiteText*/
        public void actionPerformed(ActionEvent e) {
```

```
c=Color.white;
menuapp.menu1frame.repaint ();
} /*end actionPerformed*/
} /*end inner class m22lis*/

/*inner*/ class m24lis implements ActionListener {
/*action called by menu item BlueText*/
public void actionPerformed(ActionEvent e) {
c=Color.blue;
menuapp.menu1frame.repaint ();
} /*end actionPerformed*/
} /*end inner class m24lis*/

} /*end class menu1*/

public class menuapp extends Applet {

static menu1 menu1frame;

public void init() {
menu1frame=new menu1("Applet Menu Example");
menu1frame.init();
menu1frame.setBounds(10,10,360,360);
menu1frame.setVisible(true);
} /*end init*/
} /*end menuapp*/
```

Now that you know how to program for mouse clicks, buttons, dialog boxes, and menus, you can create very powerful windows programs. And there are more windows features to come: printing, responding to keystroke events, and using the clipboard.

Notes

Sometimes you will wish to disable a menu item if it would be inappropriate for the user to select it at a particular time. The command **m234.setEnabled(false)**; will disable the menu item m234; the command m234.**setEnabled(true)**; will enable it again.

EXERCISES

1. In Chapters 2 to 7 we wrote several programs that took input from keyboard parameters. You can now revise these programs so that they take input from a dialog box.

2. Adjust the color selection program in the chapter so that the menu representing the currently selected color is disabled.

3. Adjust the wage calculation programs in Chapter 4 so that the messages to the user appear in message boxes (instead of through **System.out.println** commands).

4. Write a program that changes the colors on the screen through choices made with a choice box.

5. Write a program that changes the colors on the screen through choices made with radio buttons.

6. Write a program that displays a calendar on the screen, allowing the user to use menu items to select the month and year to display.

7. Write a program that creates dynamic diagrams with symbols that can move around the screen. One menu item allows you to create a new symbol, so that you can choose the shape and color of the symbol. Then, click on the mouse at the location where the symbol should appear at first. Another menu item will save the current position of all of the symbols in the diagram. Then another menu item will allow you to click on a symbol and move it to a new location for the next stage of the diagram. The diagram could have several different stages, where in each case you can track the movement of a particular symbol from one stage to the next. Once you have finished creating the dynamic diagram, provide a menu item to save the diagram to a file, and then another menu item that allows you to load a previously stored dynamic diagram and then replay it. One possible use for this program would be to present diagrams of sports plays; a coach could create these diagrams and then show them to the team.

CHAPTER 15

WINDOWS PROGRAMMING: KEYBOARD INPUT, PRINTING, SCROLLING, AND THE CLIPBOARD

15.1 Text Fields

Many programs require input from the keyboard, and Java provides several options for how to accomplish this. One option is to call for a dialog box whenever keyboard input is needed (see page 233). (However, dialog boxes do not work well with applets; see page 230.) We can also add text fields directly to our window. Here is an example:

```java
import java.applet.*;

import java.awt.*;
import java.awt.event.*;

public class textf1 extends Applet {
/*This program demonstrates the use of TextFields for simple
  calculations.*/
TextField tf1, tf2;

/*method*/ public void init() {
setBackground(Color.lightGray);
Label l1=new Label("Enter x:");
add(l1);
tf1=new TextField(10);
add(tf1);
```

```
tf1.requestFocus();
Label l2=new Label("x squared:");
add(l2);
tf2=new TextField(10);
tf2.setEditable(false);
add(tf2);
Button btn1=new Button("Calculate");
btn1.addActionListener(new btn1lis());
add(btn1);
} /*end init*/

/*inner*/ class btn1lis implements ActionListener {
public void actionPerformed(ActionEvent e) {
int x= Integer.parseInt(tf1.getText());
int x2=x*x;
tf2.setText(""+x2);
tf1.requestFocus();
} /*end actionPerformed*/
} /*end inner class btn1list*/


/*method*/ public void paint(Graphics g) {

} /*end paint*/

} /*end textf1*/
```

The **init** method for this applet creates two text fields, **tf1** and **tf2**, and a button. The first text field is editable. After typing a number into this first text field, the user clicks on the "Calculate" button and then the result of the calculation appears in the second text field. Also, when the button is clicked it returns the focus to the first text field. When the focus is on a particular component, then that component is waiting for input. You could also return the focus to the first text field by clicking on the mouse over that field, but having the program request the focus for you saves the user one mouse click. The user can also shift between text fields with the tab key (which is a common feature of many user interfaces).

15.2   Key Events

The third alternative to receiving keyboard input is to add a **KeyListener**, which is similar to a **MouseListener**, and then respond to keyboard events. Here is a simple program that reads whatever characters are typed and then displays them on the screen:

```
import java.applet.*;

import java.awt.*;
import java.awt.event.*;

public class key1 extends Applet
```

```
implements KeyListener {

/*This applet displays the characters that the user types.*/

String textstring="";

/*method*/ public void init() {
setBackground(Color.lightGray);
addKeyListener(this);
requestFocus();
} /*end init*/

/*Because the KeyListener interface is implemented, the following
  two methods must be declared even if they will not be used:*/
public void keyReleased(KeyEvent e) {}
public void keyPressed(KeyEvent e) {}

/*method*/ public void paint(Graphics g) {
g.drawString(textstring,100,100);
} /*end paint*/

/*method*/ public void keyTyped(KeyEvent e) {
char c=e.getKeyChar();
textstring=textstring+c;
repaint();
} /*end keyTyped*/

} /*end key1*/
```

Following is a more elaborate key event program that also uses a **MouseListener**. This program allows the user to use the mouse to click on a point, then type characters that will appear at that point. It uses a red vertical line to indicate where the characters will appear. (The string currently being typed appears in red; the strings previously typed appear in black.) It also helps to implement a backspace key whenever keyboard input is received, since few people are infallible and never make typing mistakes. The program also defines the escape key to mean clear the current string.

```
import java.applet.*;

import java.awt.*;
import java.awt.event.*;


public class key2 extends Applet
implements MouseListener, KeyListener {

/*This program draws text on the screen, at the point where you
  click the mouse.*/

int numlines=0;
```

```
textclass textarray[ ]=new textclass[30];

/*method*/ public void init() {
setBackground(Color.lightGray);
addMouseListener(this);
addKeyListener(this);
requestFocus();
} /*end init*/

public void mouseMoved(MouseEvent e) {}
public void mouseDragged(MouseEvent e) {}
public void mouseReleased(MouseEvent e) {}
public void mouseClicked(MouseEvent e) {}
public void mouseEntered(MouseEvent e) {}
public void mouseExited(MouseEvent e) {}

public void keyPressed(KeyEvent e) {}
public void keyReleased(KeyEvent e) {}


/*method*/ public void paint(Graphics g) {
textclass text0;
g.setColor(Color.black);
for (int i=1; i<=(numlines-1); i++) {
text0=textarray[i];
g.drawString(text0.textline, text0.x, text0.y);
} /*end for loop*/
text0=textarray[numlines];
g.setColor(Color.red);
if (text0!=null) {
g.drawString(text0.textline+"|", text0.x, text0.y);
} /*end if*/
} /*end paint*/


/*method*/ public void mousePressed(MouseEvent e) {
/*x and y will be the x and y screen coordinates of the point
  where the mouse was pressed, in pixels.*/
int x=e.getX();
int y=e.getY();
textclass text0=new textclass(x,y);
numlines++;
textarray[numlines]=text0;
repaint();
} /*end mousePressed*/

/*method*/ public void keyTyped(KeyEvent e) {
String z=textarray[numlines].textline;
char c=e.getKeyChar();
char bspace=(char)(8); /*backspace key*/
char escape=(char)(27); /*escape key*/
```

```
if (c==escape) {z="";}
else { /*not escape key*/
if (c==bspace) {int len=z.length();
                    if (len>0) {z=z.substring(0,(len-1));}
                } /*end backspace key*/
else { /*not backspace key*/
            z+=c;
        } /*end not backspace key*/
} /*end else not escape key*/
textarray[numlines].textline=z;
repaint();
} /*end keyTyped*/


/*inner*/ class textclass {
/*This inner class has three variables: a text string and the
  x and y coordinates of where it will be drawn on the screen.*/
int x=0; int y=0;
String textline="";

/*constructor*/ public textclass(int x, int y) {
this.x=x; this.y=y;
} /*end constructor*/
} /*end textclass*/

} /*end class key2*/
```

15.3 A Printing Example: A Curve Graphing Program with an Adjustable Scale

Here is one way to print the results of a Java program, one screen at a time. Whenever the screen shows a result you want to print, hit the "PrintScreen" key (for Windows computers). Although this key doesn't actually print the screen directly, it will create a bitmap image of the screen and store it on the clipboard. Then you can enter any program that can read in a bitmap (the paint program that comes with Windows will do). Paste the contents of the clipboard into the paint program, and then print it using the normal procedure for that program. This is a very versatile way to produce screen printouts that works for anything, including Java programs. However, this method may seem slightly cumbersome, so you naturally wonder if Java provides a more direct way to print.

If you're using an applet with a web browser, you would think that you should be able to use the browser print button to print the applet, just as it prints everything else on a web page. Unfortunately, many browsers have not implemented this feature, so in order to print an applet screen you need to follow the procedure described in the previous paragraph.

Java 1.1 implemented a procedure for printing a frame from a Java application (which doesn't work for applets because of the security restrictions). Here's an example of how this works. In Chapter 10 (page 158) we developed a program that would draw curves on the screen. This program allowed you to adjust the scale of the diagram, but these adjustments had to be done in the source code, which had to be recompiled before you could see the result. Now that we have created programs with menus, we can provide menu commands to adjust the scale of the diagram. We can also provide a menu command to print the diagram. And, as one added bonus, since we now know how to program mouse events, we can arrange the diagram so that the user can center the diagram on any point by clicking with the mouse.

We'll first set up the outline code for our program. The menu items are mostly concerned with adjusting the scale of the graph. (There are several options, so the viewer can adjust the scale of the graph and the scale of the grid separately.) We'll call the program graphz, short for graph zoom.

graphz

```
*:<VARS>
Color c=Color.black;    /*curve color*/
Color bc=Color.white; /*background color*/
boolean blackonwhite=true;
  /*The following numbers are included so the grid
     spacing is always either 2, 5, or 10, multiplied
     by a power of 10.*/
double upmultiplier[]={2.5, 2, 2};
double downmultiplier[]={0.5, 0.4, 0.5};
int xaxispos=2;
int yaxispos=2;


/*method*/ void xscaleadjust(double sfactor) {
cpjxy.xscale/=sfactor;
}


/*method*/ void yscaleadjust(double sfactor) {
cpjxy.yscale/=sfactor;
}


/*method*/ void scaleadjust(double sfactor) {
xscaleadjust(sfactor);
yscaleadjust(sfactor);
} /*end scaleadjust*/


/*method*/ void xgridadjustup() {
cpjxy.xaxisgridstep*=upmultiplier[xaxispos];
xaxispos++;
if (xaxispos>2) {xaxispos=0;}
}


/*method*/ void xgridadjustdown() {
cpjxy.xaxisgridstep*=downmultiplier[xaxispos];
xaxispos--;
if (xaxispos<0) {xaxispos=2;}
}
```

```
/*method*/ void ygridadjustup() {
cpjxy.yaxisgridstep*=upmultiplier[yaxispos];
yaxispos++;
if (yaxispos>2) {yaxispos=0;}
}


/*method*/ void ygridadjustdown() {
cpjxy.yaxisgridstep*=downmultiplier[yaxispos];
yaxispos--;
if (yaxispos<0) {yaxispos=2;}
}


/*method*/ void bothadjustup() {
xgridadjustup();
ygridadjustup();
}


/*method*/ void bothadjustdown() {
xgridadjustdown();
ygridadjustdown();
}



*:</VARS>

*:<INIT>
setBackground(bc);
cpjxy.xscale=100;   /*width of screen, mathematical units*/
cpjxy.yscale=100;   /*height of screen, mathematical units*/



*:</INIT>

*:<BUTTONS>
*:</BUTTONS>

*:<MENU>
*File
**Print{
PrintJob pj = getToolkit().getPrintJob(graphzframe,
     "Graph Print Job",null);
Graphics pg= pj.getGraphics();
if (pg != null) {
graphzframe.paintAll(pg);
pg.dispose();
  } /*end if*/
pj.end();
}
*View
**ZoomIn
***2.0{
scaleadjust(2.0);
}
```

```
***5.0{
scaleadjust(5.0);
}
***10.0{
scaleadjust(10.0);
}
**ZoomOut
***0.5{
scaleadjust(0.5);
}
***0.2{
scaleadjust(0.2);
}
***0.1{
scaleadjust(0.1);
}
**AdjustHorizontalScale
***10.0h{
xscaleadjust(10.0);
}
***2.0h{
xscaleadjust(2.0);
}
***0.5h{
xscaleadjust(0.5);
}
***0.1h{
xscaleadjust(0.1);
}
**AdjustVerticalScale
***10.0v{
yscaleadjust(10.0);
}
***2.0v{
yscaleadjust(2.0);
}
***0.5v{
yscaleadjust(0.5);
}
***0.1v{
yscaleadjust(0.1);
}
**ReverseColor{
if (blackonwhite) {bc=Color.black;  c=Color.white;
                   cpjxy.gridcolor=Color.darkGray;}
           else {bc=Color.white;  c=Color.black;
                   cpjxy.gridcolor=Color.lightGray;}
blackonwhite=!blackonwhite;
}
**Adjust_Decimal_Places
***Increase_Horizontal_dp{
cpjxy.gridxdp++;
}
```

```
***Decrease_Horizontal_dp{
if (cpjxy.gridxdp>=1) {cpjxy.gridxdp--;}
}
***Increase_Vertical_dp{
cpjxy.gridydp++;
}
***Decrease_Vertical_dp{
if (cpjxy.gridydp>=1) {cpjxy.gridydp--;}
}
**Adjust_grid_spacing
***x_axis
****more_space{
xgridadjustup();
}
****less_space{
xgridadjustdown();
}
***y_axis
****more_space{
ygridadjustup();
}
****less_space{
ygridadjustdown();
}
***both_axes
****more_space{
bothadjustup();
}
****less_space{
bothadjustdown();
}
*:</MENU>

*:<MOUSE>
cpjxy.xc=cpjxy.x(mx);
cpjxy.yc=cpjxy.y(my);
*:</MOUSE>

*:<PAINT>
setBackground(bc);
double oldx1=0;  double oldy1=0;
cpjxy.drawaxes(g);
g.setColor(c);
/*xs is in screen coordinates;
x1 and y1 are mathematical coordinates.*/

for (int xs=1; xs<=cpjxy.sw; xs++) {
double x1=cpjxy.x(xs);
double y1=graphzy.y(x1);

if (xs>1) {cpjxy.dline(oldx1,oldy1,x1,y1,g,c);}
oldx1=x1;
oldy1=y1;
```

```
} /*end for loop*/

*:</PAINT>

*:<CLOSE>
*:</CLOSE>
```

In order to convert the outline into Java source code, we need to use the code generator program in Appendix E. Here is the program that results:

```java
import java .awt.*;

import java .awt.event.*;
import java .awt.datatransfer.*;
import java .io.*;
import java .util.*;
import java .text.*;
public class graphz extends Frame
implements MouseListener {
public static graphz graphzframe;

Color c=Color.black; /*curve color*/
Color bc=Color.white; /*background color*/
boolean blackonwhite=true;
/*The following numbers are included so the grid spacing is
  always either 2, 5, or 10, multiplied by a power of 10.*/
double upmultiplier[ ]={2.5, 2, 2};
double downmultiplier[ ]={0.5, 0.4, 0.5};
int xaxispos=2;
int yaxispos=2;

/*method*/ void xscaleadjust(double sfactor) {
cpjxy.xscale/=sfactor;
}

/*method*/ void yscaleadjust(double sfactor) {
cpjxy.yscale/=sfactor;
}

/*method*/ void scaleadjust(double sfactor) {
xscaleadjust(sfactor);
yscaleadjust(sfactor);
} /*end scaleadjust*/

/*method*/ void xgridadjustup() {
cpjxy.xaxisgridstep*=upmultiplier[xaxispos];
xaxispos++;
if (xaxispos>2) {xaxispos=0;}
}

/*method*/ void xgridadjustdown() {
cpjxy.xaxisgridstep*=downmultiplier[xaxispos];
xaxispos−;
```

```
if (xaxispos<0) {xaxispos=2;}
}

/*method*/ void ygridadjustup() {
cpjxy.yaxisgridstep*=upmultiplier[yaxispos];
yaxispos++;
if (yaxispos>2) {yaxispos=0;}
}

/*method*/ void ygridadjustdown() {
cpjxy.yaxisgridstep*=downmultiplier[yaxispos];
yaxispos–;
if (yaxispos<0) {yaxispos=2;}
}

/*method*/ void bothadjustup() {
xgridadjustup();
ygridadjustup();
}

/*method*/ void bothadjustdown() {
xgridadjustdown();
ygridadjustdown();
}



/*constructor*/
public graphz(String title) {
super(title);
} /*end constructor*/

public void init() {
setBackground(bc);
cpjxy.xscale=100; /*width of screen, mathematical units*/
cpjxy.yscale=100; /*height of screen, mathematical units*/


Panel upperpanel=new Panel ();
Panel lowerpanel=new Panel ();
add(BorderLayout .NORTH,upperpanel);
add(BorderLayout .SOUTH,lowerpanel);
MenuBar m0=new MenuBar();
/*Menu*/ m1=new Menu("File");
/*MenuItem*/ m11=new MenuItem("Print");
m11.addActionListener (new m11lis());
m1.add (m11);
m0.add (m1);

/*Menu*/ m2=new Menu("View");
/*Menu*/ m21=new Menu("ZoomIn");
/*MenuItem*/ m211=new MenuItem("2.0");
m211.addActionListener (new m211lis());
```

```
m21.add (m211);
/*MenuItem*/ m212=new MenuItem("5.0");
m212.addActionListener (new m212lis());
m21.add (m212);
/*MenuItem*/ m213=new MenuItem("10.0");
m213.addActionListener (new m213lis());
m21.add (m213);
m2.add (m21);
/*Menu*/ m22=new Menu("ZoomOut");
/*MenuItem*/ m221=new MenuItem("0.5");
m221.addActionListener (new m221lis());
m22.add (m221);
/*MenuItem*/ m222=new MenuItem("0.2");
m222.addActionListener (new m222lis());
m22.add (m222);
/*MenuItem*/ m223=new MenuItem("0.1");
m223.addActionListener (new m223lis());
m22.add (m223);
m2.add (m22);
/*Menu*/ m23=new Menu("AdjustHorizontalScale");
/*MenuItem*/ m231=new MenuItem("10.0h");
m231.addActionListener (new m231lis());
m23.add (m231);
/*MenuItem*/ m232=new MenuItem("2.0h");
m232.addActionListener (new m232lis());
m23.add (m232);
/*MenuItem*/ m233=new MenuItem("0.5h");
m233.addActionListener (new m233lis());
m23.add (m233);
/*MenuItem*/ m234=new MenuItem("0.1h");
m234.addActionListener (new m234lis());
m23.add (m234);
m2.add (m23);
/*Menu*/ m24=new Menu("AdjustVerticalScale");
/*MenuItem*/ m241=new MenuItem("10.0v");
m241.addActionListener (new m241lis());
m24.add (m241);
/*MenuItem*/ m242=new MenuItem("2.0v");
m242.addActionListener (new m242lis());
m24.add (m242);
/*MenuItem*/ m243=new MenuItem("0.5v");
m243.addActionListener (new m243lis());
m24.add (m243);
/*MenuItem*/ m244=new MenuItem("0.1v");
m244.addActionListener (new m244lis());
m24.add (m244);
m2.add (m24);
/*MenuItem*/ m25=new MenuItem("ReverseColor");
m25.addActionListener (new m25lis());
m2.add (m25);
/*Menu*/ m26=new Menu("Adjust_Decimal_Places");
/*MenuItem*/ m261=new MenuItem("Increase_Horizontal_dp");
m261.addActionListener (new m261lis());
```

```
m26.add (m261);
/*MenuItem*/ m262=new MenuItem("Decrease_Horizontal_dp");
m262.addActionListener (new m262lis());
m26.add (m262);
/*MenuItem*/ m263=new MenuItem("Increase_Vertical_dp");
m263.addActionListener (new m263lis());
m26.add (m263);
/*MenuItem*/ m264=new MenuItem("Decrease_Vertical_dp");
m264.addActionListener (new m264lis());
m26.add (m264);
m2.add (m26);
/*Menu*/ m27=new Menu("Adjust_grid_spacing");
/*Menu*/ m271=new Menu("x_axis");
/*MenuItem*/ m2711=new MenuItem("more_space");
        m2711.addActionListener (new m2711lis());
m271.add (m2711);
/*MenuItem*/ m2712=new MenuItem("less_space");
        m2712.addActionListener (new m2712lis());
m271.add (m2712);
m27.add (m271);
/*Menu*/ m272=new Menu("y_axis");
/*MenuItem*/ m2721=new MenuItem("more_space");
        m2721.addActionListener (new m2721lis());
m272.add (m2721);
/*MenuItem*/ m2722=new MenuItem("less_space");
        m2722.addActionListener (new m2722lis());
m272.add (m2722);
m27.add (m272);
/*Menu*/ m273=new Menu("both_axes");
/*MenuItem*/ m2731=new MenuItem("more_space");
        m2731.addActionListener (new m2731lis());
m273.add (m2731);
/*MenuItem*/ m2732=new MenuItem("less_space");
        m2732.addActionListener (new m2732lis());
m273.add (m2732);
m27.add (m273);
m2.add (m27);
m0.add (m2);

setMenuBar(m0);
addMouseListener(this);
} /*end init*/

public void mouseMoved(MouseEvent e) {}
public void mouseDragged(MouseEvent e) {}
public void mouseReleased(MouseEvent e) {}
public void mouseClicked(MouseEvent e) {}
public void mouseEntered(MouseEvent e) {}
public void mouseExited(MouseEvent e) {}

/*method*/ public void mousePressed(MouseEvent e) {
/*mx and my are the mouse coordinates.*/
int mx=e.getX();
```

```
int my=e.getY();
cpjxy.xc=cpjxy.x(mx);
cpjxy.yc=cpjxy.y(my);
repaint();
} /*end mousePressed*/


/*Here are the declarations for the buttons:*/

/*Declare the menus and menuitems:*/
Menu m1;
MenuItem m11;
Menu m2;
Menu m21;
MenuItem m211;
MenuItem m212;
MenuItem m213;
Menu m22;
MenuItem m221;
MenuItem m222;
MenuItem m223;
Menu m23;
MenuItem m231;
MenuItem m232;
MenuItem m233;
MenuItem m234;
Menu m24;
MenuItem m241;
MenuItem m242;
MenuItem m243;
MenuItem m244;
MenuItem m25;
Menu m26;
MenuItem m261;
MenuItem m262;
MenuItem m263;
MenuItem m264;
Menu m27;
Menu m271;
MenuItem m2711;
        MenuItem m2712;
Menu m272;
MenuItem m2721;
        MenuItem m2722;
Menu m273;
MenuItem m2731;
        MenuItem m2732;


/*method*/ public void paint (Graphics g) {
setBackground(bc);
double oldx1=0; double oldy1=0;
cpjxy.drawaxes(g);
```

```
g.setColor(c);
/*xs is in screen coordinates; x1 and y1 are mathematical coordinates.*/

for(int xs=1; xs<=cpjxy.sw; xs++) {
double x1=cpjxy.x(xs);
double y1=graphzy.y(x1);

if (xs>1) {cpjxy.dline(oldx1,oldy1,x1,y1,g,c);}
oldx1=x1;
oldy1=y1;
} /*end for loop*/

} /*end paint*/


/*inner*/ class m11lis implements ActionListener {
/*action called by menu item Print*/
public void actionPerformed(ActionEvent e) {
PrintJob pj=getToolkit().getPrintJob(graphzframe,"Graph Print Job",null);
Graphics pg=pj.getGraphics();
if (pg !=null) {
graphzframe.paintAll(pg);
pg.dispose();
} /*end if*/
pj.end();
graphzframe.repaint ();
} /*end actionPerformed*/
} /*end inner class m11lis*/

/*inner*/ class m211lis implements ActionListener {
/*action called by menu item 2.0*/
public void actionPerformed(ActionEvent e) {
scaleadjust(2.0);
graphzframe.repaint ();
} /*end actionPerformed*/
} /*end inner class m211lis*/

/*inner*/ class m212lis implements ActionListener {
/*action called by menu item 5.0*/
public void actionPerformed(ActionEvent e) {
scaleadjust(5.0);
graphzframe.repaint ();
} /*end actionPerformed*/
} /*end inner class m212lis*/

/*inner*/ class m213lis implements ActionListener {
/*action called by menu item 10.0*/
public void actionPerformed(ActionEvent e) {
scaleadjust(10.0);
graphzframe.repaint ();
} /*end actionPerformed*/
} /*end inner class m213lis*/
```

```
/*inner*/ class m221lis implements ActionListener {
/*action called by menu item 0.5*/
public void actionPerformed(ActionEvent e) {
scaleadjust(0.5);
graphzframe.repaint ();
} /*end actionPerformed*/
} /*end inner class m221lis*/

/*inner*/ class m222lis implements ActionListener {
/*action called by menu item 0.2*/
public void actionPerformed(ActionEvent e) {
scaleadjust(0.2);
graphzframe.repaint ();
} /*end actionPerformed*/
} /*end inner class m222lis*/

/*inner*/ class m223lis implements ActionListener {
/*action called by menu item 0.1*/
public void actionPerformed(ActionEvent e) {
scaleadjust(0.1);
graphzframe.repaint ();
} /*end actionPerformed*/
} /*end inner class m223lis*/

/*inner*/ class m231lis implements ActionListener {
/*action called by menu item 10.0h*/
public void actionPerformed(ActionEvent e) {
xscaleadjust(10.0);
graphzframe.repaint ();
} /*end actionPerformed*/
} /*end inner class m231lis*/

/*inner*/ class m232lis implements ActionListener {
/*action called by menu item 2.0h*/
public void actionPerformed(ActionEvent e) {
xscaleadjust(2.0);
graphzframe.repaint ();
} /*end actionPerformed*/
} /*end inner class m232lis*/

/*inner*/ class m233lis implements ActionListener {
/*action called by menu item 0.5h*/
public void actionPerformed(ActionEvent e) {
xscaleadjust(0.5);
graphzframe.repaint ();
} /*end actionPerformed*/
} /*end inner class m233lis*/

/*inner*/ class m234lis implements ActionListener {
/*action called by menu item 0.1h*/
public void actionPerformed(ActionEvent e) {
xscaleadjust(0.1);
graphzframe.repaint ();
```

```
} /*end actionPerformed*/
} /*end inner class m234lis*/

/*inner*/ class m241lis implements ActionListener {
/*action called by menu item 10.0v*/
public void actionPerformed(ActionEvent e) {
yscaleadjust(10.0);
graphzframe.repaint ();
} /*end actionPerformed*/
} /*end inner class m241lis*/

/*inner*/ class m242lis implements ActionListener {
/*action called by menu item 2.0v*/
public void actionPerformed(ActionEvent e) {
yscaleadjust(2.0);
graphzframe.repaint ();
} /*end actionPerformed*/
} /*end inner class m242lis*/

/*inner*/ class m243lis implements ActionListener {
/*action called by menu item 0.5v*/
public void actionPerformed(ActionEvent e) {
yscaleadjust(0.5);
graphzframe.repaint ();
} /*end actionPerformed*/
} /*end inner class m243lis*/

/*inner*/ class m244lis implements ActionListener {
/*action called by menu item 0.1v*/
public void actionPerformed(ActionEvent e) {
yscaleadjust(0.1);
graphzframe.repaint ();
} /*end actionPerformed*/
} /*end inner class m244lis*/

/*inner*/ class m25lis implements ActionListener {
/*action called by menu item ReverseColor*/
public void actionPerformed(ActionEvent e) {
if (blackonwhite) {bc=Color.black; c=Color.white;
                            cpjxy.gridcolor=Color.darkGray;}
                   else {bc=Color.white; c=Color.black;
                            cpjxy.gridcolor=Color.lightGray;}
blackonwhite=!blackonwhite;
graphzframe.repaint ();
} /*end actionPerformed*/
} /*end inner class m25lis*/

/*inner*/ class m261lis implements ActionListener {
/*action called by menu item Increase_Horizontal_dp*/
public void actionPerformed(ActionEvent e) {
cpjxy.gridxdp++;
graphzframe.repaint ();
} /*end actionPerformed*/
```

```
} /*end inner class m261lis*/

/*inner*/ class m262lis implements ActionListener {
/*action called by menu item Decrease_Horizontal_dp*/
public void actionPerformed(ActionEvent e) {
if (cpjxy.gridxdp>=1) {cpjxy.gridxdp--;}
graphzframe.repaint ();
} /*end actionPerformed*/
} /*end inner class m262lis*/

/*inner*/ class m263lis implements ActionListener {
/*action called by menu item Increase_Vertical_dp*/
public void actionPerformed(ActionEvent e) {
cpjxy.gridydp++;
graphzframe.repaint ();
} /*end actionPerformed*/
} /*end inner class m263lis*/

/*inner*/ class m264lis implements ActionListener {
/*action called by menu item Decrease_Vertical_dp*/
public void actionPerformed(ActionEvent e) {
if (cpjxy.gridydp>=1) {cpjxy.gridydp--;}
graphzframe.repaint ();
} /*end actionPerformed*/
} /*end inner class m264lis*/

/*inner*/ class m2711lis implements ActionListener {
/*action called by menu item more_space*/
public void actionPerformed(ActionEvent e) {
xgridadjustup();
graphzframe.repaint ();
} /*end actionPerformed*/
} /*end inner class m2711lis*/

/*inner*/ class m2712lis implements ActionListener {
/*action called by menu item less_space*/
public void actionPerformed(ActionEvent e) {
xgridadjustdown();
graphzframe.repaint ();
} /*end actionPerformed*/
} /*end inner class m2712lis*/

/*inner*/ class m2721lis implements ActionListener {
/*action called by menu item more_space*/
public void actionPerformed(ActionEvent e) {
ygridadjustup();
graphzframe.repaint ();
} /*end actionPerformed*/
} /*end inner class m2721lis*/

/*inner*/ class m2722lis implements ActionListener {
/*action called by menu item less_space*/
public void actionPerformed(ActionEvent e) {
```

```
ygridadjustdown();
graphzframe.repaint ();
} /*end actionPerformed*/
} /*end inner class m2722lis*/

/*inner*/ class m2731lis implements ActionListener {
/*action called by menu item more_space*/
public void actionPerformed(ActionEvent e) {
bothadjustup();
graphzframe.repaint ();
} /*end actionPerformed*/
} /*end inner class m2731lis*/

/*inner*/ class m2732lis implements ActionListener {
/*action called by menu item less_space*/
public void actionPerformed(ActionEvent e) {
bothadjuotdown();
graphzframe.repaint ();
} /*end actionPerformed*/
} /*end inner class m2732lis*/

/*to close the window:*/
static class winlis extends WindowAdapter {
public void windowClosing(WindowEvent e) {
System.exit(0);
} /*end windowClosing*/
} /*end winlis*/

public static void main (String args[ ]) {
graphzframe=new graphz("graphz");
graphzframe.addWindowListener(new winlis());
graphzframe.init();
graphzframe.setBounds (10,10,360,360);
graphzframe.setVisible(true);
} /*end main*/
} /*end class graphz*/
```

Here is the code that actually handles the printing (in the program, it appears as one of the menu items):

```
PrintJob pj=
getToolkit().getPrintJob(graphzframe,"Graph Print Job",null);
Graphics pg=pj.getGraphics();
if (pg !=null) {
graphzframe.paintAll(pg);
pg.dispose();
```

First, we have to create a **PrintJob** object (called pj in this example). To do this, we need to call a method called **getPrintJob**, which is part of the class **getToolkit**. We need to call a constructor with three arguments: the first is the frame to be printed (which is graphzframe in our case); the second is a string to identify the print job; and the third makes it possible to send additional configuration information to the printer (which we will not use in this book, so we set this third argument to **null**).

Second, we have to create a **Graphics** object, which we have called pg in this example. (Recall that we usually call the graphics object g; here we'll call it pg to remind us that this graphics object applies to a printer.) To print the graphics and text in the frame, use the command

graphzframe.**paintAll**(pg);

(The program also checks to make sure that pg is not null, as would be the case if there were a printer problem.) Finally, when the print job is done, the graphics object pg should be disposed of. (In the next chapter we will learn how the Java garbage collector helps us by disposing of objects no longer needed in memory. However, there are a few hardware-related items like printer graphics objects that cannot be handled by the garbage collector, so the program needs to dispose of these explicitly.)

The function to be graphed is in a separate class:

```
public class graphzy {

/*The following method can be changed to display different curves:*/

/*method*/ static double y (double x) {
return Math.sin(x);
} /*end y*/
} /*end graphzy*/
```

Here are a couple of screen views showing the graph of the curve $y = \sin x$, with different levels of magnification.

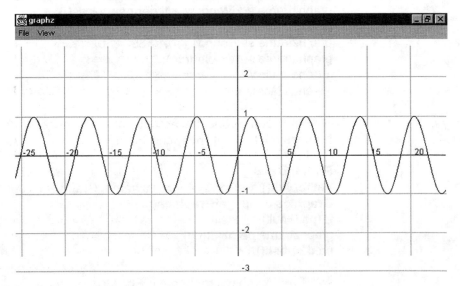

FIGURE 15–1

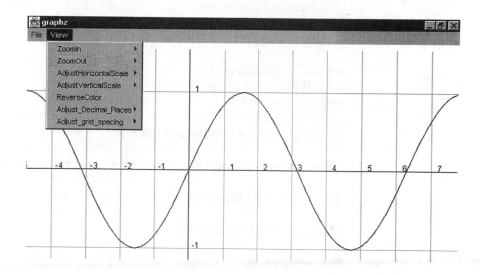

FIGURE 15–2

15.4   Scrolling

If you wish to draw something on the screen that is too big to be seen all at once, you need to be able to scroll (that is, move the screen vertically or horizontally using scrollbars). Java 1.1 allows you to create a **ScrollPane** object, with scrolling built in.

For example, following is a program that displays a text file on the screen, allowing for scrolling. We'll create two classes. The first, scrollfi, contains the **main** method. It reads the file into a vector object. Its application window is called scrollfileframe. To this window we add a **ScrollPane** object, which we'll call sp1. The **ScrollPane** object automatically has scrolling built in, but there is one catch: you can only add one object to the scroll pane. The object that we will add is called a **Canvas**, which is a drawing surface (just like an oil painter paints on a canvas). Our second class, scroll1, contains a **paint** method to display the file on the screen. Note that the scroll1 class looks just like the graphics classes we have done before. It uses a **Graphics** object g with our standard **drawString** method. (You could also use **drawLine** or any of the other graphics methods we have seen.) The only difference between class scroll1 and previous graphics programs is that scroll1 extends **Canvas** instead of **Frame**. A **Canvas** object does not have a border, as does a **Frame** object. Also, a **Canvas** object can be added to a **ScrollPane** object, which is what we want. (The reason we don't need a border around our **Canvas** object is because the border is supplied by class scrollfi, which does extend **Frame**.)

Here is the program:

```
import java.awt.*;

import java.awt.event.*;
import java.io.*;
import java.util.*;

public class scrollfi extends Frame {

/*This program displays a text file on the screen in a scrolling window.*/

static scrollfi scrollfileframe;

static scroll1 scroll1canvas;

ScrollPane sp1;

/*constructor method*/
public scrollfi(String title) {
        super(title);
} /*end constructor*/

public void init() {
        sp1=new ScrollPane(ScrollPane.SCROLLBARS_ALWAYS);
        scroll1canvas=new scroll1();
        scroll1canvas.setBounds(1,1,600,1200);
        sp1.add(scroll1canvas);
        add(sp1);
        scroll1canvas.init();
} /*end init*/

/*to close the window:*/
static class winlis extends WindowAdapter {
public void windowClosing(WindowEvent e) {
System.exit(0);
} /*end windowClosing*/
} /*end winlis*/


public static void main(String args[ ]) {
scrollfileframe=new scrollfi("Scrolling File Viewer");
scrollfileframe.init();
scrollfileframe.addWindowListener(new winlis());
FileDialog fd=new FileDialog(scrollfileframe,
"Scrolling File Viewer", FileDialog.LOAD);
fd.show();
String filename=fd.getFile();
try{
DataInput f1=
        new DataInputStream(new FileInputStream(filename));
String textline=f1.readLine();
while (textline!=null) {
```

```
            scroll1canvas.a.addElement(textline);
            textline=f1.readLine();
      } /*end while*/
            scroll1canvas.a.trimToSize();


} catch (Exception ex) {String err=ex.toString();
                                    System.out.println(err);}



scroll1canvas.setBounds
      (1,1,500,scroll1canvas.pixelsperline* (1+scroll1canvas.a.size()));
scrollfileframe.setBounds(10,10,500,300);
scrollfileframe.setVisible(true);




} /*end main*/
} /*end class scrollfi*/


class scroll1 extends Canvas {
Vector a;
int pixelsperline=25;

public void init() {
      setBackground(Color.black);
      a=new Vector(100,20);
            /*The initial size of the vector is 100.*/
            /*20 elements will be added whenever more size
               is needed.*/
} /*end init*/

public void paint(Graphics g) {
       g.setColor(Color.orange);
      int i=0;
      while (i<=(a.size()-1)) {
            String str=(String)a.elementAt(i);
            g.drawString(str, 1, pixelsperline*(i+1));
            i++;
      } /*end i loop*/
} /*end paint*/

} /*end class scroll1*/
```

15.5   Using the Clipboard in a Small Word Processing Program

We've seen most of the pieces we need to put together a word processing program. This program will work for relatively short notes. Even though you will normally use your regular word processing program, it is interesting to see how you can put these pieces together in Java.

Our word processing program will use a **TextArea**, which is like a **TextField** except that it allows for more than one line. A **TextArea** automatically comes with these important features:

- As you type, the backspace, insert, and delete keys work as you expect they would.

- You can click on the mouse to move the cursor to a new location.

- Scrolling is supported.

- You can use the mouse to highlight text.

Our word processing program will have a File menu that supports opening a new file, saving the current file, and printing the current file. It will have an Edit menu that supports copying selected text to the clipboard, copying all text to the clipboard, cutting text (that is, sending it to the clipboard and also deleting it), and pasting text from the clipboard. The only operations we have not seen before are those involving the clipboard; this program illustrates how clipboard actions work.

Here is the outline code for the program:

```
notes

*:<VARS>
Color c=Color.black;   /*text color*/
Color bc=Color.lightGray; /*background color*/
TextArea t;
Clipboard cb;
String textstring="";
public void lostOwnership(Clipboard cb,
    Transferable contents) { }
*:</VARS>

*:<INIT>
setBackground(bc);
t=new TextArea(8,60);
notesframe.add(t);
cb=getToolkit().getSystemClipboard();
*:</INIT>

*:<BUTTONS>
*:</BUTTONS>

*:<MENU>
*File
**Open{
```

```
FileDialog fd=
    new FileDialog(notesframe,"Open",FileDialog.LOAD);
fd.show();
String fn=fd.getFile();
try {
  DataInput f1=new DataInputStream(new FileInputStream(fn));
  String textline=f1.readLine();
  while (textline!=null) {
    t.appendText(textline+"\n");
    textline=f1.readLine();
    } /*end while*/
  } catch (Exception ex) {String err=ex.toString();
      System.out.println(err);}
}
**Save{
FileDialog fd=
    new FileDialog(notesframe,"Save",FileDialog.SAVE);
fd.show();
String fn=fd.getFile();
try {
DataOutput f2=new DataOutputStream(new FileOutputStream(fn));
f2.writeBytes(t.getText());
  } catch (Exception ex) {String err=ex.toString();
      System.out.println(err);}
}
**Print{
printframe pf=new printframe("Print frame");
pf.s=t.getText();
int numlines=pf.countlines(pf.s);
int pixelsperpage=pf.pixelsperline*pf.linesperpage;
int totalpixels=numlines*pf.pixelsperline;
int lastpixelline=pixelsperpage;
int maxpage=5;
int pagewidth=500;
pf.setBounds(1, 1, pagewidth, maxpage*pixelsperpage);

while (lastpixelline>totalpixels) { /*print each page*/
pf.topofpage=lastpixelline- -pixelsperpage;
/**pf.g2.setClip(1, (lastpixelline- -pixelsperpage), pagewidth,
    pixelsperpage);**/
pf.repaint();
pf.setVisible(true);
System.out.println("in print:"+pf.s);
PrintJob pj=
  getToolkit().getPrintJob(notesframe,"Notes Print Job",null);
Graphics pg=pj.getGraphics();
if (pg !=null) {
pf.paintAll(pg);
pg.dispose();
/*pf.setVisible(false);*/
  } /*end if*/
pj.end();
  lastpixelline+=pixelsperpage;
```

```
        } /*end while*/
}
*Edit
**Copy{
String selection=t.getSelectedText();
StringSelection clipString=new StringSelection(selection);
cb.setContents(clipString, clipString);
}
**CopyAll{
String selection=t.getText();
StringSelection clipString=new StringSelection(selection);
cb.setContents(clipString, clipString);
}
**Cut{
int selectionstart=t.getSelectionStart();
int selectionend=t.getSelectionEnd();
t.replaceText("",selectionstart,selectionend);
}
**Paste{
Transferable transfertext=cb.getContents(this);
if (transfertext!=null) {
  try {
    String pastestring=(String)
      transfertext.getTransferData(DataFlavor.stringFlavor);
    int selectionstart=t.getSelectionStart();
    int selectionend=t.getSelectionEnd();
    t.replaceText(pastestring,selectionstart,selectionend);
  } catch (Exception ex) {String err=ex.toString();
      System.out.println(err);}
  } /*end if transfertext!=null*/
}
*:</MENU>

*:<MOUSE>
*:</MOUSE>

*:<PAINT>
setBackground(bc);
g.drawString("***",1,1);
*:</PAINT>

*:<CLOSE>
*:</CLOSE>
```

Here is the complete program after being processed by the code generator (see Appendix E):

```
import java .awt.*;

import java .awt.event.*;
import java .awt.datatransfer.*;
import java .io.*;
import java .util.*;
import java .text.*;
```

```
public class notes extends Frame
implements MouseListener {
public static notes notesframe;

Color c=Color.black; /*text color*/
Color bc=Color.lightGray; /*background color*/
TextArea t;
Clipboard cb;
String textstring="";
public void lostOwnership(Clipboard cb, Transferable contents) { }

/*constructor*/
public notes(String title) {
super(title);
} /*end constructor*/

public void init() {
setBackground(bc);
t=new TextArea(8,60);
notesframe.add(t);
cb=getToolkit().getSystemClipboard();
Panel upperpanel=new Panel ();
Panel lowerpanel=new Panel ();
add(BorderLayout .NORTH,upperpanel);
add(BorderLayout .SOUTH,lowerpanel);
MenuBar m0=new MenuBar();
/*Menu*/ m1=new Menu("File");
/*MenuItem*/ m11=new MenuItem("Open");
m11.addActionListener (new m11lis());
m1.add (m11);
/*MenuItem*/ m12=new MenuItem("Save");
m12.addActionListener (new m12lis());
m1.add (m12);
/*MenuItem*/ m13=new MenuItem("Print");
m13.addActionListener (new m13lis());
m1.add (m13);
m0.add (m1);

/*Menu*/ m2=new Menu("Edit");
/*MenuItem*/ m21=new MenuItem("Copy");
m21.addActionListener (new m21lis());
m2.add (m21);
/*MenuItem*/ m22=new MenuItem("CopyAll");
m22.addActionListener (new m22lis());
m2.add (m22);
/*MenuItem*/ m23=new MenuItem("Cut");
m23.addActionListener (new m23lis());
m2.add (m23);
/*MenuItem*/ m24=new MenuItem("Paste");
m24.addActionListener (new m24lis());
m2.add (m24);
m0.add (m2);
```

```
setMenuBar(m0);
addMouseListener(this);
} /*end init*/

public void mouseMoved(MouseEvent e) {}
public void mouseDragged(MouseEvent e) {}
public void mouseReleased(MouseEvent e) {}
public void mouseClicked(MouseEvent e) {}
public void mouseEntered(MouseEvent e) {}
public void mouseExited(MouseEvent e) {}

/*method*/ public void mousePressed(MouseEvent e) {
/*mx and my are the mouse coordinates.*/
int mx=e.getX();
int my=e.getY();
repaint();
} /*end mousePressed*/


/*Here are the declarations for the buttons:*/

/*Declare the menus and menuitems:*/
Menu m1;
MenuItem m11;
MenuItem m12;
MenuItem m13;
Menu m2;
MenuItem m21;
MenuItem m22;
MenuItem m23;
MenuItem m24;


/*method*/ public void paint (Graphics g) {
setBackground(bc);
g.drawString("***",1,1);
} /*end paint*/


/*inner*/ class m11lis implements ActionListener {
/*action called by menu item Open*/
public void actionPerformed(ActionEvent e) {
FileDialog fd=new FileDialog(notesframe,"Open",FileDialog.LOAD);
fd.show();
String fn=fd.getFile();
try {
DataInput f1=new DataInputStream(new FileInputStream(fn));
String textline=f1.readLine();
while (textline!=null) {
        t.appendText(textline+"\n");
        textline=f1.readLine();
    } /*end while*/
} catch (Exception ex) {String err=ex.toString(); System.out.println(err);}
```

```
notesframe.repaint ();
} /*end actionPerformed*/
} /*end inner class m11lis*/

/*inner*/ class m12lis implements ActionListener {
/*action called by menu item Save*/
public void actionPerformed(ActionEvent e) {
FileDialog fd=new FileDialog(notesframe,"Save",FileDialog.SAVE);
fd.show();
String fn=fd.getFile();
try {
DataOutput f2=new DataOutputStream(new FileOutputStream(fn));
f2.writeBytes(t.getText());
} catch (Exception ex) {String err=ex.toString(); System.out.println(err);}
notesframe.repaint ();
} /*end actionPerformed*/
} /*end inner class m12lis*/

/*inner*/ class m13lis implements ActionListener {
/*action called by menu item Print*/
public void actionPerformed(ActionEvent e) {
printframe pf=new printframe("Print frame");
pf.s=t.getText();
int numlines=pf.countlines(pf.s);
int pixelsperpage=pf.pixelsperline*pf.linesperpage;
int totalpixels=numlines*pf.pixelsperline;
int lastpixelline=pixelsperpage;
int maxpage=5;
int pagewidth=500;
pf.setBounds(1, 1, pagewidth, maxpage*pixelsperpage);

while (lastpixelline>totalpixels) { /*Print each page.*/
pf.topofpage=lastpixelline-pixelsperpage;
/**pf.g2.setClip(1, (lastpixelline-pixelsperpage), pagewidth,
pixelsperpage);**/
pf.repaint();
pf.setVisible(true);
System.out.println("in print:"+pf.s);
PrintJob pj=getToolkit().getPrintJob(notesframe,"Notes Print Job",null);
Graphics pg=pj.getGraphics();
if (pg !=null) {
pf.paintAll(pg);
pg.dispose();
/*pf.setVisible(false);*/
} /*end if*/
pj.end();
lastpixelline+=pixelsperpage;
} /*end while*/
notesframe.repaint ();
} /*end actionPerformed*/
} /*end inner class m13lis*/

/*inner*/ class m21lis implements ActionListener {
```

```
/*action called by menu item Copy*/
public void actionPerformed(ActionEvent e) {
String selection=t.getSelectedText();
StringSelection clipString=new StringSelection(selection);
cb.setContents(clipString, clipString);
notesframe.repaint ();
} /*end actionPerformed*/
} /*end inner class m21lis*/

/*inner*/ class m22lis implements ActionListener {
/*action called by menu item CopyAll*/
public void actionPerformed(ActionEvent e) {
String selection=t.getText();
StringSelection clipString=new StringSelection(selection);
cb.setContents(clipString, clipString);
notesframe.repaint ();
} /*end actionPerformed*/
} /*end inner class m22lis*/

/*inner*/ class m23lis implements ActionListener {
/*action called by menu item Cut*/
public void actionPerformed(ActionEvent e) {
int selectionstart=t.getSelectionStart();
int selectionend=t.getSelectionEnd();
t.replaceText("",selectionstart,selectionend);
notesframe.repaint ();
} /*end actionPerformed*/
} /*end inner class m23lis*/

/*inner*/ class m24lis implements ActionListener {
/*action called by menu item Paste*/
public void actionPerformed(ActionEvent e) {
Transferable transfertext=cb.getContents(this);
if (transfertext!=null) {
try {
        String pastestring=(String)
            transfertext.getTransferData(DataFlavor.stringFlavor);
        int selectionstart=t.getSelectionStart();
        int selectionend=t.getSelectionEnd();
        t.replaceText(pastestring,selectionstart,selectionend);
} catch (Exception ex) {String err=ex.toString(); System.out.println(err);}
} /*end if transfertext!=null*/
notesframe.repaint ();
} /*end actionPerformed*/
} /*end inner class m24lis*/

/*to close the window:*/
static class winlis extends WindowAdapter {
public void windowClosing(WindowEvent e) {
System.exit(0);
} /*end windowClosing*/
} /*end winlis*/
```

```
public static void main (String args[ ]) {
notesframe=new notes("notes");
notesframe.addWindowListener(new winlis());
notesframe.init();
notesframe.setBounds (10,10,360,360);
notesframe.setVisible(true);
} /*end main*/
} /*end class notes*/
```

In order to access the clipboard, we create an object *cb* of class **Clipboard** (and we need to import the package **java.awt.datatransfer.***). We use the command

cb=getToolkit().getSystemClipboard();

to assign the object **cb** to the actual system clipboard.

Here are the commands that will write the text that has been selected by the mouse to the clipboard (in the program, these lines appear as one of the menu items):

String selection=t.**getSelectedText**(); /*t is the text area.*/
StringSelection clipstring=**new StringSelection**(selection);
cb.**setContents**(clipString, clipString);

In the first line, replace **getSelectedText**(); with **getText**(); if you want to write the entire contents of the text area (not just the selected text) to the clipboard.

In order to transfer text from the clipboard to the selected location in the text area, use these commands (which again appear as one of the menu items):

Transferable transfertext=cb.**getContents(this)**;
if (transfertext!=**null**) {
try {
    String pastestring=(**String**)
        transfertext.**getTransferData(DataFlavor.stringFlavor)**;
    int selectionstart=t.**getSelectionStart**();
    int selectionend=t.**getSelectionEnd**();
    t.**replaceText**(pastestring,selectionstart,selectionend);
} **catch** (**Exception** ex) {**String** err=ex.**toString**();
    System.out.println(err);}
} /*end if transfertext!=null*/

We also need another class called printframe, since we need to copy the text from the **TextArea** to a frame in order to print it.

import java.awt.*;

class printframe **extends Frame** {
String s;

int pixelsperline=25;
int linesperpage=28;

```java
int topofpage=0;

/*constructor method*/
public printframe(String title) {
super(title);
} /*end constructor*/

/*method*/ int countlines(String s) {
int z=0;
for (int i=0; i<=(s.length()-1); i++)
{if (s.charAt(i)=='\n') {z++;}}
return z;
} /*end countlines*/

/*method*/ public void paint(Graphics g2) {
int pixelsperpage=pixelsperline*linesperpage;
int pagewidth=500;
g2.setClip(1,topofpage,pagewidth,pixelsperpage);

System.out.println("in printframe paint:"+s);

int ylocation=pixelsperline;
int lm=10; /*left margin*/

char linebreak=(char)(10);
s+=linebreak;
g2.setColor(Color.black);

while (s.length()>0) {
        int L=s.indexOf(linebreak);
        String s2=s.substring(0,L);
        System.out.println("|"+s2+"|");
        ylocation+=pixelsperline;
        g2.drawString(s2,lm,ylocation);
        s=s.substring(L+1);
} /*end while*/

} /*end paint*/
} /*end class printframe*/
```

These last three chapters have inevitably been complex because they focus on taking advantage of the features of a windows-based graphical user interface. Even though GUI's are easy to use, they are a bit difficult to program. However, you will be well-rewarded for learning Java's methods for programming windows, since then your programs will become very easy to use, earning you the everlasting gratitude of your users.

We have now covered most of the elements of the Java language that we will look at in this book. The next chapter will focus on some general strategies to help you develop your programs. The last two chapters give some examples of different applications of Java.

EXERCISES

1. Revise the graphics programs in Chapter 10 so that they can print graphs.

2. In Chapters 2 to 7 we wrote several programs that took input from a command line parameter. Revise these programs so they take input from a text field that is added directly to the window.

3. Revise the graphics programs in Chapter 10 so that the graphs appear in a **ScrollPane**.

4. Write a program that allows the user to type a list of words that appear on the screen. (Use a **KeyListener**.) Make it possible for the user to swap the positions of two words. If the user clicks on one word, then that word changes color; if the user then clicks on a second word, then the second word swaps position with the first word.

5. It is common for a program to have menus labeled File, Edit, and View. Prepare an outline code which has a File menu with options to load or save data. Have the outline call for file dialog boxes for each of these cases. You can't fill in the rest of the code until you're working on a specific example, but preparing a generic outline like this for code that will be used many times makes it easier for you to develop future applications.

6. Write a program that draws a map that shows the outline of the 48 contiguous states in the United States. Design the program so the user can zoom in or out and can adjust the center of the map by clicking the mouse.

CHAPTER 16

PROGRAMMING STRATEGY

16.1   Computers and Programming Languages

Now that we've seen many of the building blocks of Java programming, we'll discuss some general issues involving computer programming, answering questions such as "Why program in Java rather than some other language?" and "How do you plan a complicated computer programming project?"

A computer is a machine that stores data and instructions for acting on those data. A computer consists of physical devices that can represent abstract quantities, such as numbers. Modern computers represent data with electronic components known as *transistors*, which are grouped together in silicon chips known as *integrated circuits*. These data storage components only have two states, like a light switch that is either on or off. A switch can store one binary digit, or bit. It sounds like it would be very difficult to represent data with this kind of device, but as long as you have enough of these devices you can represent whatever data you want. For example, if you have 16 bits, you have 2^{16} possible patterns that can be represented, which is more than enough to represent all of the unicode characters for most of the world's languages.

A computer's native language is known as *machine language*, in which all instructions are represented as a pattern of bits (1's and 0's). Machine languages are different for computers with different central processing units. Early computers in the late 1940s had to be programmed directly in machine language. Since it is very difficult for people to accurately write machine language code, better ways were developed. One improvement is *assembly language*, in which the commands available are almost the same as machine language, but it is easier to give commands because they are given with simple codes rather than patterns of 1's and 0's.

Programming languages were developed to make it easier for people to give instructions for computers. Two early computer languages of note were FORTRAN, designed for scientific and engineering problems, and COBOL, designed for business data processing. These languages were much easier to use than assembly language, and the power of computers increased greatly as more and more programs were written in these (and other) languages. However, writing computer programs for complicated problems turned out to be very difficult. Over the last few decades, considerable effort has been invested in developing computer programming languages that will ease this process. Language developers learned from the experience of early programmers and created languages such as Algol and Pascal (designed to promote well-structured programs). Another notable language was BASIC, which was designed to be very easy to use for simple programs (although original versions were not well-suited for complicated problems). More recently, the programming language C became widely used.

Another important advance was the concept of object-oriented programming, which was included in the language Smalltalk and extended to other languages. A new language, C++, was created to add object-oriented programming to C. (You should be able to guess why the ++ was used in the name. Hint: ++ means the same in C++ as it does in Java.) C++ became the most popular language for writing many application programs. Because C++ was so popular, the designers of Java adopted much of the same syntax. However, their goal was for Java to be much-improved over C++, and the languages are different in important ways that will be discussed in the next section.

16.2   Why Program in Java?

Since you are reading this book, you probably have heard it said that Java is a good language for writing computer programs. Following is a list of some of these important reasons.

1. Java's design is completely object oriented. For reasons to be discussed below, the object-oriented approach to programming is helpful when you are creating complicated computer programs. Previous generations of programmers have grown up with non-object-oriented languages, so they will need to change their thinking to take advantage of object-oriented programming. If you're learning Java as your first programming language, you will have an advantage because you will learn how to think in terms of objects when you first learn programming. You may, however, also need to learn the non-object-oriented procedural approach to programming if you will be working with other languages during your programming career. For example, C++ was designed to be backward-compatible with the older language C. That means that any program that works in C will also work in C++. However, since C is not object-oriented, that means that non-object-oriented approaches can be used in C++. Java, by contrast, was designed as a completely new language when it was first released in 1995. That is an advantage because Java did not have to include any language features for backward-compatibility. Also, the language was designed to force programmers to work with objects. You may protest about having your freedom as a programmer restricted in this manner, but in the long run it is in your best interests to work with a language that disciplines you.

2. A Java program that works on one computer will also work on any computer with a Java system. There are several ways of saying this: Java is *platform neutral*; Java is *architecture neutral*; Java programs are *portable*. One of the slogans Sun has adopted for Java is "Write Once, Run Anywhere." This is a big advantage if you need to write programs that will work for Windows systems, Macintosh systems, Unix systems, and Solaris systems, among others. By contrast, a C++ program will need to be compiled separately for each platform, and there could be platform differences in the way the program is executed.

Unfortunately, the Java world is not quite perfect. First is the difficulty with making "Write Once, Run Anywhere" a reality. Some features are inherently different on different computers, such as the resolution of the monitor, the size of the memory, or the speed of execution. These factors can make programs behave differently on different computers.

Although platform neutrality is one of Java's greatest strengths, it is also one of its greatest weakness. The way that platform neutrality is achieved is this: Java programs are compiled into Java bytecodes. This is a special language that is not exactly like a machine language, but it is more like a machine language than it is like a programming language that will be used by people. The bytecode version of a program is the same for all machines. However, the machine itself only understands its own machine language, not Java bytecode. Therefore, it needs an interpreter, called the *Java Virtual Machine* (JVM), to interpret the bytecodes for it. This inevitably slows the program down a bit. Imagine you are talking with a citizen of a different country. If that person knows your language, you will be able to understand what they say more quickly than you will if you have to speak through an interpreter. The interpretation process slows the conversation down, just as the JVM interpreter slows down the program execution process compared to what it would have been if the computer were executing a program in its native machine language.

There are several possible solutions that might reduce the concern about Java performance:

- As computers become faster, concern about the speed of program execution fades away. Java is already fast enough on most platforms to perform a wide variety of tasks; this situation should only improve as computer hardware improves. If your Java program is fast enough for the programs you use, then you don't have a performance problem.

- Improved versions of the JVM can improve execution speed. One technique is to use what is called a *Just In Time* compiler (JIT). When the JIT comes to a block of Java bytecode, it translates it into machine language. If the code is only used once, then this doesn't help performance because the computer has to spend the time doing the translation. If, however, that code is executed often (for example, it might be in the middle of a loop, or it might be part of a method that is called repeatedly), then the JIT approach can noticeably improve program execution speed so that it is almost as good as if the program itself were compiled to machine language.

- Java programs will execute very fast if they are running on a computer with a microprocessor (CPU) whose native machine language is the Java bytecode. This type of microprocessor is called a Java chip. These are not common as of 1998, but they may well become more common in the future.

- A Java program can call a block of code written in the native machine language. Such a block of code most likely will have been written first in C++, and then compiled to machine language. A method written in the computer's machine language, rather than Java bytecode, is called a *native method*. By using native methods, you can sometimes improve the performance of the program. However, you lose the advantage of platform compatibility, since the native methods will not work on other machines unless they are recompiled. This book only covers pure Java programs, so we will not discuss native methods further.

If your program will not need to run on more than one platform, then you don't need to be concerned about platform compatibility issues.

Java is also intended for platforms beyond the traditional desktop computer. More and more electronic devices have embedded microprocessors, and Java is being used as the programming environment for an increasing number of these.

3. Java has effective memory management regarding garbage collection. When a new object is created, the computer needs to allocate space for it in its memory. When you no longer need the object, then the computer should release that memory so it is available for other objects. If the program repeatedly fails to release memory from objects that are no longer needed, there is a risk that the program will fail due to lack of memory. That is one problem that can occur with C++ programs, since the program needs to explicitly release unneeded memory. The designers of Java solved that problem by providing for an automatic garbage collection process. Although garbage collection does not sound like a very high-tech term, in fact the garbage collection process is very important because the garbage collector periodically scans the memory and releases memory that is no longer needed. Since you don't have to think about this process when you are writing Java programs, your job is much easier.

4. Java is secure. Java is designed with security in mind, a sad necessity of life given the number of malicious computer hackers in the world. In particular, Java applets face severe security restrictions (see page 31). Applets downloaded from the Internet cannot read from or write to the local disk, and they cannot connect to web servers other than the server from where the applet was loaded. This security is carefully enforced by the compiler, which carefully checks the validity of the code before it creates a class file, and the Java Virtual Machine, which runs a verification routine before it

loads and executes a Java class.

Applets written with newer versions of Java have fewer security restrictions if they come from a trusted source. A digital signature is used to verify where the applet came from, and the user can decide if that source is trustworthy and thereby decide the degree of security restrictions that should apply to it.

Java also provides other security measures such as built-in encryption methods that are beyond the scope of this book.

5. Java has the capability for multi-threaded programs. Java provides built-in support for programs that will run more than one thread (task) at the same time (see the book's web page for more information: *http://www.spu.edu/~ddowning/cpjava.html*).

6. Network capability is built in. See the book's web page.

7. Java is designed to make the programmer's job easier. A key feature we have seen before is reusability. There are many problems that recur again and again in programming projects; the more you can reuse previously written code, rather than create new code, the easier your job will be.

8. The Java development kit is available for free from Sun Microsystems. There are also other Java development environments that you can purchase from other vendors.

Despite all the advantages, there are a few disadvantages with Java.

1. Execution speed slowed with use of JVM (discussed previously).

2. By being platform neutral, Java is limited to a "least common denominator" approach. That is, it is limited to include only those features that are available on all platforms, and it is prevented from taking advantages of the unique benefits of any platform. The **swing** components in Java 2 are a step toward easing these difficulties (see the web page for the book).

3. The version confusion of Java is a problem. There are enough differences between Java 1.0 (released in 1995), Java 1.1 (released in 1997), and Java 2 (released in 1998) that you can face a serious problem if you have to support multiple Java platforms. This problem will not go away unless all JVM installations (including web browsers) support the Java 2 standard, and even then there will be a lot of legacy code left from earlier versions. Fortunately, most code written in Java 1.1 will also work in Java 2, but code written for Java 1.0 will often include "deprecated methods," that is, old methods that are still supported but not recommended. (Versions of Java also have a third digit, such as 1.02 or 1.15. A change in the last digit is made when minor revisions are made; there is only a significant change if the digit immediately after the decimal point is changed. Normally, you don't have to worry about differences between two versions if the first two digits are the same.)

Fortunately, the programs in the first nine chapters of the book will work with all versions of Java. The differences between 1.0

and 1.1 or 2 only become significant when you are dealing with events, such as mouse clicks. Also, there are some features such as printing that are supported in versions 1.1 and 2 but not in 1.0. The book's web page gives examples of how the same program will be different when it is written in different versions.

16.3 Guidelines for Writing Java Programs

You need to learn the building blocks (that is, the basic elements of a language) in order to write computer programs. You also need practice with the process of developing a program. Here are some general guidelines to help you.

1. Think in terms of classes and objects. Programming in many ways is more of an art than a science. You need to use your own judgment about what objects are best for your program. Your skill about making these judgments will increase with experience. In general, your program should not have one giant class or many small classes; try to find a balance where each class has a clear, valuable purpose. Each class should be an abstraction of some part of your program. As you design your classes, keep these ideas in mind:

   • *encapsulation:* Each class should keep its data and methods internal to itself, so you can use the class in programs without having to know about its internal details.

   • *inheritance:* Find patterns where there is the same method that applies in different forms to different objects that are subsets of a larger class. Then create a superclass and subclasses to implement this relationship.

   • *polymorphism:* Recall that an object declared to be of a superclass can also be assigned to represent an object of any of the subclasses of that superclass. Another aspect of polymorphism is that different subclasses might have the same method that accomplishes roughly the same thing but with different details. In that case, the superclass can declare an abstract method and the subclasses declare specific methods, all with the same name, to implement the desired behavior.

2. Know the basic building blocks and language syntax. As you gain more experience, then more features of the language will stick in your memory. Also know where to look up features that you might need. The index of this book provides a good start; you can also find information on the web, at the Sun JavaSoft site (*http://www.javasoft.com*) and others (see the web page for this book for more links).

3. Don't think about too much at one time. It is hard to think of the overall design of a program at the same time you are thinking of the specific details of how a particular method will be implemented. Fortunately, the design of Java allows you to plan the details of your objects without having to worry about how they will be used, and

you can plan the program that uses your objects without having to worry about the details of their implementation.

4. Make your programs readable by humans as well as computers. Imagine that you will be kidnapped by aliens who will completely erase your memory and then return you to Earth a year later. When you try to read your program code, will it make any sense to you? (Even if that scenario is far-fetched, you will almost certainly have to look back on code you wrote in the past after you have forgotten exactly what you were thinking of when you wrote it.) The next three suggestions help you write more person-friendly codes.

5. Use names that help you remember what a variable represents. It's not worth going overboard and using variable names that are extremely long, but you generally will find that the little bit of extra typing required for longer variable names is worth it because of the improvement in readability. Also, it helps to follow consistent patterns. You will often use variables for similar purposes, so it helps to use consistent names. For example, in this book we always use g for a graphics object, and we often use *i* and *j* as counter variables in loops (see Appendix D).

6. Usually, use variables instead of literal numbers. For example, consider these two program segments:

```
/*version 1*/
offavg=offpoint/14;
defavg=defpoints/14;
```

```
/*version 2*/
int numgames=14;
offavg=offpoint/numgames;
defavg=defpoints/numgames;
```

Both of these code segments will accomplish the same thing. The second version is superior for two reasons: (1) it makes it clear what the number 14 stands for; and (2) it will be much easier to update the program if the value of *numgames* changes. For example, if you had written a program to calculate NFL statistics in the early 1970s when teams played 14 games, you would have had to change every 14 to 16 when the number of games played changed. This would be much easier to do if the 14 only occurred in one place. Since you can never know what might change in the future, you are better off using variable names where one change to the assignment at the beginning will change all references to that variable in your program. (In shorter programs, this rule becomes less important.)

You can use a number in an expression when you are sure that the number will not change and you are sure that the reader of the program will know the meaning. For example, in the expression $\sqrt{a^2 + b^2}$ from the Pythagorean theorem, you can be sure that the

2's will not change, so you can use those in an expression.

7. Include comments where it will help you understand what is going on. Don't include pointless comments like this:

x=2*y; /*The value of x will be twice the value of y.*/

However, do include comments that explain what a variable represents, like this:

d=56; /*d is the distance between Centerville and Rivertown.*/

In this book we have generally used comments to identify right braces }, and comments are often used at the beginning of a method to explain what the method does.

You can also use comments to temporarily block out a section of code. There are times while you are developing a program when you would like a section of code to be ignored, but you know you will want that code later, so you don't want to erase it. Putting comment markers /* and */ around that block will temporarily disable it. (Make sure that the block you are commenting out does not itself contain an end of comment symbol */, because then the computer would treat that as ending the comment sooner than you intended.)

8. Keep variables as local as possible. If a variable is only to be used inside a method or a loop, then declare it in that block. This protects you from some other block accidentally changing the value.

9. In large programs, use the **private** access modifier to prevent other classes from accessing the data in an object. In that case, use set and get methods to allow other classes to reach the data when they need it (see page 131).

10. Remember that one reason programming is difficult is that people can seldom envision all of the ways in which their work might be generalized. You might have written a program that works fine for the problem it was originally intended to solve, but later you realize it would also be nice to use the program for a slightly different problem. However, it might be very difficult to change the program to solve the new problem, even if the new problem doesn't seem much different than the original problem. If you had anticipated the possibility of the new problem, then you could have originally written the program to make it easier to adapt. Although there is no way to anticipate every possible future problem for which your program might be applied, it does help when you are first designing the program to think about making it easier to generalize in case you later wish to apply it to different problems.

11. Distinguish between standard problems and program-specific problems. If a problem is a standard problem that arises with

many different problems, then you should be able to find a solution in a standard Java library, or in one of the routines in this book or another book. Once you have a solution to a standard problem, then you should be able to reuse that code when that problem arises again in another problem. Viewed in this light, a standard problem should never be hard to solve; it is just a matter of finding a solution that already exists. Of course, each program will have its own idiosyncratic problems. For those, you're on your own for finding solutions, and you have no guarantee that you will be able to reuse your solution anywhere else. That is the kind of problem that might be a hard problem.

12. If possible, test pieces of your program as you are developing it. If you have to wait until the entire program is written before you start testing, it will be more complicated to track down the locations of any errors that might occur. Also, there is an important psychological motivation: you will enjoy being able to see your progress if you can watch part of the program work while it is under construction.

16.4   Fixing Compiler Errors

Writing a complicated program that will work correctly is a challenge. If your program is well designed, then the process of eliminating errors should go more smoothly, but most likely there will always be some kind of error to fix before the program is ready for users. (Alas, all too often there are still errors to fix after the program has been released to users . . . .) We'll look at three types of errors: compiler errors, exceptions, and program logic errors.

If your program does not follow the syntax of the Java language, the compiler will display an error message for you, and it will not create the class file. Although annoying, this is the easiest kind of error to track down, because the compiler will give you an indication of the kind of error and the location (line number) where the error occurred. If you think of your program as a sea voyage, then you can imagine that a compiler error is a problem that prevents you from leaving the harbor.

Here are some kinds of errors the compiler will catch, and some suggestions of what might cause them:

- *Variable not found error.* Recall that all variables must be declared before they can be used. This requirement helps you a lot because it means that if you misspell a variable name the compiler will catch it for you. (Unless, by bad luck, you misspell a variable name so that it has the same name as another variable you are already using—then the compiler won't complain and the error won't show up until a later time when it will be harder to track down. If possible, it helps to avoid using variables names that are too similar.) Also recall that miscapitalization counts as misspelling. Since you are used to English, where a different capitalization does not change one word into another word, in the early days of your Java career you will likely make some mistakes due to incorrect capitalization.

- *Can't convert int to boolean.* A common cause of this error is to use only one equal sign in a comparison, that is, for example, writing **if** (a=b) instead of **if** (a==b).

- *Method not found.* If you're using a method that you know to be correct, such as **drawString**, then the error is likely caused because you have failed to include the appropriate **import** statement at the top of the class. (Or it might be a spelling error; check the code carefully.)

- *Variable may not have been initialized.* The compiler will check to make sure that every variable used has been assigned an initial value. A common source of errors in other programming languages is a failure to set initial values correctly. For example, this program:

```
class test {
public static void main(String args[ ]) {
double x;
System.out.println(x);
} /*end main*/
} /*end test*/
```

will generate a compiler error message because *x* is not initialized. You will also see this error message with this program:

```
class test {
public static void main(String args[ ]) {
String a=args[0];
double x;
if (a.equals("2")) {x=2;}
System.out.println(x);
} /*end main*/
} /*end test*/
```

The compiler has no way of knowing what value will be used for the command line parameter args[0], but it can tell there is a possibility that x ends up with no initial value.

- *Class or interface definition expected.* This can be one of the trickier compiler errors to track down, because the message and the location given do not clearly indicate the nature of the problem. Look at this program and see if you find the error:

```
class test {
public static void main(String args[ ]) {
double x=2;
System.out.println("HI");}
} /*end main*/
} /*end test*/
```

Did you spot the unneeded right brace } after the **System.out.println** statement? It would help if the compiler recognized that as an error, but there is no way for it to know that. It will assume that the first right brace ends the **main** method, and the next right brace it comes to ends the class. Then it comes to another right brace, which it knows shouldn't be there. Since it has just finished with a class, the only thing it should see now would be a new class or interface definition (or else the end of the program file). Therefore, the compiler gives the error message "class or interface definition expected." for the last line of the program. It is not too difficult to track down the actual location of the error in a program this short, but in a longer program the error message may be many lines after the stray right brace.

This example illustrates another thing to be careful of: although we include comments next to right braces indicating what the right brace marks the end of, there is no guarantee that the comments are actually placed correctly. (The compiler, of course, ignores whatever is in the text of the comment.)

- } *expected.* If you include a stray left brace { in your program, then the compiler will notice at some point that the braces do not match, and it will tell you that it expects a right brace. Here's an example program with this error; try to find the exact location of the problem:

```
class test {
public static void main(String args[ ]) {
double x=2;
{System.out.println("HI");
} /*end main*/
} /*end test*/
```

Here is one method to help you make sure that the braces match: whenever you type a left brace, at the same time also type the corresponding right brace (with its comment). Then, insert some blank lines between the two braces; then type the lines that go between them. That way, you will be sure that you don't forget to include the right brace.

- *Can't make a static reference to a nonstatic variable.* See if you can determine the nature of the compiler error in this program:

```
class test {
int x=10;
public static void main(String args[ ]) {
for (int i=1; i<=10; i++) {
System.out.println(i+" "+x);
} /*end for loop*/
} /*end main*/
} /*end test*/
```

Look carefully at the variable x. It is not declared in a method, which means it belongs to the class *test*. Now ask, "Is it a static or nonstatic variable?" Since it does not include the **static** modifier, it must be a nonstatic variable. But recall that nonstatic variables can only be accessed through an object that is instantiated of that class. Since we have not created any objects of the class **test**, there is no way to access the variable **x**. The solution in this case would be to declare **x** with this statement: **static int** x. In a real problem, you need to decide whether **x** really should be static (that is, it will have the same value for all objects of that class) or if you should create an object in order to access it.

See if you can find the error here:

```
class test {
static int x;

/*method*/ static void init() {
int y=20;
int x=10;
} /*end init*/

public static void main(String args[ ]) {
init();
for (int i=1; i<=10; i++) {
System.out.println(i+" "+x+" "+y);
} /*end for loop*/
} /*end main*/
} /*end test*/
```

The problem is that the variable y is only declared within the **init** method, not within the class itself. That means it cannot be accessed outside the **init** method. This type of problem can commonly arise if you are not careful, because you will often wish to assign the initial value to a variable in the **init** method. However, you need to declare the variable outside the **init** method so it will be accessible elsewhere.

We can fix the problem like this (but look at this program closely):

```
class test {
static int x=30;
static int y;

/*method*/ static void init() {
y=20;
int x=10;
} /*end init*/

public static void main(String args[ ]) {
init();
for (int i=1; i<=10; i++) {
System.out.println(i+" "+x+" "+y);
} /*end for loop*/
} /*end main*/
} /*end test*/
```

The compiler won't complain about this program. However, the program probably doesn't do what we intend; the **init** method presumably intends to assign the value 10 to the same variable **x** that is defined in the second line of the program. However, because the **x** variable is declared inside the **init** method, this means that the x receiving the value 10 in the init method is a local variable that is different from the x variable for the class. The solution is to remove the **int** in front of the x in the **init** method, so the x will not be redeclared as a local variable.

Other kinds of compiler errors come from using language elements incorrectly, for example, using commas instead of semicolons while describing a **for** loop; using a \ (backslash) instead of a forward slash / in a comment definition; or incorrect capitalization.

Another complication to keep in mind is that a single error might generate more than one error message. For example, if you forget to declare a variable that is used 50 times, you will see 50 "variable not found" errors. Therefore, don't panic when you see a large number of error messages. As soon as you have identified one of the errors, it is best to fix it right away and recompile the program to see if there still are errors. Unfortunately, the number of error messages is not guaranteed to go down each time you fix one error, since sometimes the compiler is so confused by one error that it does not see the remaining errors in the program. However, with appropriate care on your part it should be possible to come up with a program that generates no compiler errors and is ready to run—where it faces its next hurdle: exceptions that occur while the program is being executed.

16.5   Exceptions

After your program has made it out of the harbor (compiler) and is ready to run on the open ocean, the next hazard it faces are exceptions, which are error conditions that happen while the program is being executed.

Try to find the problem with this program:

```
class test {

public static void main(String args[ ]) {
int a[ ]=new int[6];
a[6]=10;
System.out.println(a[6]);
} /*end main*/
} /*end test*/
```

If you run this program, you will receive this message:

```
ArrayIndexOutofBoundsException.
```

You might fall into this trap often in your early days as a Java programmer. The array **a** has been declared to have 6 elements, but recall that array subscripts start at 0. Therefore, the allowable subscripts are 0, 1, 2, 3, 4, 5. Attempting to find a[6] creates the exception. It is actually good that Java always catches out-of-range array indexes. Some languages don't check array subscripts, which means that an out-of-range subscript can access some other area of memory where it's not supposed to be. This will inevitably lead to an error at some point, but it likely will be much harder to track down the location of the error.

(Another problem with failing to check for array subscripts is a security problem: malicious programmers in some other languages can use out-of-range array subscripts to tamper with other memory locations. This is another reason to be glad you're programming in Java.)

In general, if your program will ever use a user-entered value as an array subscript, you should check to make sure it is in the appropriate range before the statement where it is used as a subscript.

Look for the errors in this program:

```
class test {
static double x=0;
public static void main(String args[ ]) {
System.out.println(1/x);
System.out.println(Math.sqrt(-2));
System.out.println(Math.acos(1.2));
System.out.println(Math.log(-5));
} /*end main*/
} /*end test*/
```

This program could be the poster child for bad mathematical behavior: dividing by 0, taking the square root and logarithm of negative numbers, and looking for the arccosine for a number greater than 1. Java will treat 1/0 as infinity, and the other results will have a special value called NaN, which stands for Not a Number. Although none of these will crash the program, they will not give any sensible result.

Another exception that can arise is NumberFormatException, which occurs when you are trying to convert a string to a number but the string does not represent a number. Here's an example:

```
class test {
public static void main(String args[ ]) {
String x="345a";
int n=Integer.parseInt(x);
System.out.println(n);

} /*end main*/
} /*end test*/
```

This type of error is more likely to occur in a program where the user has entered the string to convert. Remember that you have no control over what input a user might give to your program, so in order for your program to be robust you need to check for invalid input. Here's a more robust version:

```
class test {
public static void main(String args[ ]) {
String x="345a";
try{
int n=Integer.parseInt(x);
System.out.println(n);
} catch (NumberFormatException ex) {
System.out.println("not a number");
}
```

```
} /*end main*/
} /*end test*/
```

In general, if you suspect that a block of code might generate an exception, then enclose it within a **try** block. Following the **try** block, include a **catch** block that gives the name of the exception and then what to do if the exception arises. In the example above, the program will display the message "not a number." In some cases, the Java compiler will force you to include statements within a **try** block; for example, when you include file input/output operations, the code will not compile if those statements are not in a **try** block.

Here is another program that will cause an exception:

```
class test {
public static void main(String args[ ]) {
String s=null;
System.out.println(s.length());
} /*end main*/
} /*end test*/
```

This program generates the exception

```
java.lang.NullPointerException
```

because the String s has a null value.

16.6   Logic Errors

After making it safely out of the harbor (the compiler), and then avoiding storms (exceptions), you'll make it to the other shore (your program will run without any complaints from the computer). However, you're not guaranteed that you've arrived at the right destination. Your program may contain logic errors that prevent it from doing what it was supposed to do. You will need to test the program for data for which you know the correct result. As a general rule, don't believe results just because they have come from a computer.

When you're running the program, it is as if you are on the surface while the program is on a submarine journey. You know where it starts (that is, you know the input it receives) and you can see where the journey ends (that is, the results of the program). If the results are not what they are supposed to be, then the program must have taken a wrong turn somewhere. The question is "Where?" One possibility would be to follow the program every step of the journey and determine by hand where it is supposed to be at each point. If the result is incorrect, then sooner or later you will come across a point where the program has veered away from the course it is supposed to be on. Once you have found the location of the error, then often you're halfway to fixing it. However, this approach seems like a terrible amount of work. You are having the computer work on the problem precisely because you don't want to work on it in detail.

Another approach is to check the position of the program only at carefully selected intervals of the journey. Choose a strategic point in the program, and then insert an extra **System.out.println** statement to check on the value of one or more variables at that point. (Another option is to write this extra diagnostic output to a file; you will need to use this approach if the diagnostic output will be too large to be conveniently viewed on the screen.) When the program is run, you can observe the way the variables change at that strategic point. If the values are correct, then you know (approximately) that the error must occur after that point. If they're incorrect, then the error must occur earlier. The trick is to develop a good feel for where to put these checkpoints, so you are not inundated with too much information by having too many checkpoints. (You can use your editor program's search feature when you need to look through a source code file to find all occurrences of a particular variable.)

Java development environments often contain debugging aids. For example, the debugger could trace the history of a particular variable and prepare a report telling you each time the value of the variable changes. The details of how to use these aids vary for different environments. These aids may help you track down certain kinds of errors; it is up to you to decide if they are helpful for you.

One of the basic problems with writing a computer program is designing the program so it can respond to different user input. Try to design your program to be able to handle all possible types of input safely. Although you don't want to insult your users deliberately, while you are designing these input checks it is best to imagine the users as being very stupid and capable of creating any kind of erroneous input.

This chapter has included some general ideas about how to develop your programs, but there are few absolute rules that give the best strategy in every case. The best way for your programming skill to grow is to practice with different kinds of problems. The next two chapters give some examples of some different Java applications. You can look at these programs to see examples of using different features of Java; you should also be thinking of ways you would like to change and improve these programs to adapt them in the best way for your own circumstances. You can also find more Java examples on the disc that comes with this book, and on the web page at *http://www.spu.edu/~ddowning/cpjava.html.*

CHAPTER 17

GAMES

17.1 Types of Computer Games

Computers can play many different types of games. Many computer games allow you to move pictures around the artificial worlds on the screen by using a special input device, such as a joystick. We won't write any complicated game programs in this book, but future versions of Java will provide greater three-dimensional drawing capabilities that will be useful for such games.

In another type of computer game, known as an adventure game, the computer places the player in an imaginary situation with some objective, such as finding a treasure buried in a cave. The player can type in commands such as "Look around" or "Walk forward," and the computer will tell what will happen. These programs will be very complicated because the program will need to keep track of many different possible actions by the player.

Computers can help you keep track of statistics for non-computer games as well. The web page for the book contains programs you can use to keep score and statistics for a baseball game and a football game.

Computers have been taught to play strategy games. Some games, such as tic-tac-toe, are simple enough that it is possible to develop an unbeatable strategy. For very complicated games, such as chess, there is no unbeatable strategy. Computer chess programs cannot always beat human chess players. Computer scientists have put a lot of effort into writing chess strategy programs, but they do not do this just for fun. Studying the strategy for a game such as chess helps scientists understand how to make a computer "think" (and they can also learn the limitations that prevent a computer from ever thinking like a person). The field that studies computer thought is known as *artificial intelligence*. Computer chess programs that are competitive with human chess masters must perform a large number of calculations as they look ahead to evaluate various board positions, so they usually need to run on supercomputers.

17.2   Scoreboard Timer

If you're playing a game that requires keeping track of the time, the computer can help. Following is a program that creates a scoreboard timer. You can stop the clock at any time with a mouse click, then restart the clock with a mouse click when you are ready to resume play. In addition to displaying the clock digitally, this program will display a pie-slice-shaped sector of a circle that gradually shrinks as time expires. You can change the program so it runs for the length of time you want.

```
import java.applet.*;

import java.awt.*;
import java.awt.event.*;

public class timer extends Applet
implements MouseListener {

/*This program displays a scoreboard timer on the screen.*/

long starttime=0;
long totaltime=4*60*1000; /*timer runs for 4 minutes,
                                   or 240,000 milliseconds*/
String timestring="4:00";
Font font1;
boolean timeron=false;
long timeleft=totaltime;
long endtime;
int angle=0;
/*The next two lines are needed for double-buffering.*/
Image offscreenimage;
Graphics g2; /*offscreen graphics*/
Color circlecolor=Color.red;

/*method*/ public void update(Graphics g) {
/*This method is included to override the standard method update
   so that the screen is not automatically cleared each time
   repaint is called.*/
paint(g);
}


/*method*/ public void init() {
setBackground(Color.lightGray);
addMouseListener(this);
starttime=System.currentTimeMillis();
font1=new Font("TimesRoman", Font.BOLD, 64);
/*The next two lines are needed for double-buffering.*/
offscreenimage=createImage(size().width,size().height);
g2=offscreenimage.getGraphics();
} /*end init*/
```

```
/*When we implement the MouseListener interface, we need to list
  all of the following methods, even if we will not define any
  specific behavior for them.*/

public void mouseMoved(MouseEvent e) {}
public void mouseDragged(MouseEvent e) {}
public void mouseReleased(MouseEvent e) {}
public void mouseClicked(MouseEvent e) {}
public void mouseEntered(MouseEvent e) {}
public void mouseExited(MouseEvent e) {}




/*method*/ public void paint(Graphics g) {
g2.setColor(Color.lightGray);
g2.fillRect(0,0,size().width,size().height);
g2.setColor(Color.black);
g2.setFont(font1);
g2.drawString(timestring,100,100);
g2.setColor(Color.white);
g2.fillArc(200,120,240,240,0,360);
g2.setColor(circlecolor);
g2.drawArc(200,120,240,240,0,360);
g2.fillArc(200,120,240,240,90-angle,angle);
/*The next line is needed for double-buffering.*/
g.drawImage(offscreenimage,0,0,this);
drawscreen();
} /*end paint*/




/*method*/ void drawscreen() {

if (timeron) {timeleft=endtime-System.currentTimeMillis();}
timestring="0:00";
if (timeleft>=0) {
long seconds=(timeleft/1000);
long minutes=seconds/60;
seconds=seconds-60*minutes;
if (seconds<10) {timestring=""+minutes+":0"+seconds;}
               else {timestring=""+minutes+":"+seconds;}
} /*end if timeleft>0*/
angle=(int)(360-360*timeleft/totaltime);
if (timeleft<=0) {circlecolor=Color.black;}
else {
if (timeron) {circlecolor=new Color(0,100,0);}
             else {circlecolor=Color.red;}
} /*end else*/

repaint();
try{
Thread.currentThread().sleep(200);
} catch (InterruptedException ex) {}
```

```
} /*end drawscreen*/


/*method*/ public void mousePressed(MouseEvent e) {
timeron=!timeron;
if (timeron) {endtime=System.currentTimeMillis()+timeleft;}
repaint();
} /*end mousePressed*/

public void destroy() {
g2.dispose();
} /*end destroy*/


} /*end timer*/
```

If a Java program will repaint the screen too often, it sometimes develops an annoying flicker. The timer program above reduces the flicker through a process called double-buffering. This means that the graphical output is first drawn on an offscreen image; then the offscreen image is copied to the actual screen. This allows the drawing process to be faster, so the flicker is reduced.

Part of the flicker problem is that normally the computer will clear the screen whenever it comes to a **repaint()** command. (It clears the screen by filling the screen with the current background color.) If you don't want the screen cleared each time **repaint()** is called, include this method in your program:

```
public void update(Graphics g) {
paint(g);
} /*end update*/
```

Here is why this works: Normally, when a program executes a **repaint()** command, it calls a standard method called **update**, which first clears the screen and then executes the **paint** method. When you define an **update** method in your program, it then overrides the standard **update** method. Our new version of **update** does not clear the screen; instead, it simply calls the **paint** method. Sometimes including this method is all you need to end the flicker problem. However, this does not work if you really do need the screen to be cleared each time **repaint** is called, since images left over from previous **repaint** commands will never disappear.

The double-buffering process works first by creating an offscreen image with these two statements in the **init** method:

```
offscreenimage=createImage(size().width,size().height);
g2=offscreenimage.getGraphics();
```

We normally call our graphics object g; in this example, we will call our offscreen graphics object g2. The **paint** command uses g2 for all its graphics commands. Then, after it has finished drawing the image to the offscreen graphics image, it uses the command

```
g.drawImage(offscreenimage,0,0,this);
```

to transfer the image from the offscreen image to the actual screen.

17.3   Quick Trivia Quiz Game

Now we'll write a quick trivia game program in which the computer acts as the referee for two human players. The computer displays a question on the screen. The first player to signal the computer is allowed to answer the question. To do well at this game you have to be quick as well as knowledgeable.

At the start of the game, the players type their names. Also, each player is assigned a key to press; the person on the left will press "z" and the person on the right will press "/". (These keys are chosen because they are on opposite ends of the keyboard; you can choose different keys if you desire.)

The questions are stored in files of 20 questions each. Each question consists of two lines for the question and one line for the answer, so there are 60 lines per file. The disc that accompanies this book contains many different files of questions for this game. They can be identified with the extension ".qz". You need to select a file of questions to load at the start of the game.

The program will ask the questions in random order. Java includes a random number generator that is very helpful with many types of games. For example, if you wanted to write a program to simulate a card game or a dice game, you would need a random number generator. (In reality, these numbers are determined by an algorithm, so they are not truly random; however, the algorithm is designed so that for practical purposes they seem to be random.)

To use a random number generator, first declare an object of class **Random**:

static Random rnumgen;

Then, use a constructor with no argument to instantiate the random number generator:

rnumgen=**new Random**();

(You can also include a **long** value as the argument. Do this if you would like the random number generator to generate the same sequence of values each time.)

When you want the program to generate an integer random value, use this command: rnumgen.**nextInt**();. This statement will generate a random variable chosen so that all integer values are equally likely. Most of the time, you would rather have the values confined to a particular positive range. To do this, take the absolute value of the random number, and then take the remainder with respect to the maximum number in your range. For example, this statement will generate a random number between 1 and 20:

x=1+**Math.abs**(rnumgen.**nextInt**()) % 20;

When the players are ready, the computer displays the question on the screen. The first player to signal can answer. (Press "&" if neither player wants to answer). After you state your answer, you need to declare how confident you are in your answer. If you choose positive, then you will gain 50 points if you are correct but you will lose 100 points if you are wrong. If you choose guess, then you will gain 20 points if you are correct but you will only lose 20 points if you are wrong. After the computer displays the answer, you indicate whether the response was correct or not; then the computer displays the updated score and is ready for the next question.

Here is the program:

```java
import java.awt.*;

import java.awt.event.*;
import java.util.Random;
import java.io.*;



public class quizgame extends Frame
implements KeyListener {

static quizgame quizgameframe;

static int state=0; /*state variable controlling appearance of screen*/
static int numquestionsasked=0;
static int qnum=0;
static int maxquestions=20;
static int signalplayer=0;
static int confidencecode=0;
static int pointlist[ ][ ]={{0,0,0},{0,50,-100},{0,20,-20}};
static boolean advanceok=true;
static Random rnumgen;
static boolean alreadyasked[ ]=new boolean [maxquestions+1];


        /*The classes player and question are defined at the end of
          this file.*/
static player player0;
static player playerlist[ ]=new player[3];
        /*Element 0 of this array will be ignored.*/
static question questionlist[ ]=new question[51];
        /*Element 0 of these arrays will be ignored.*/
        /*The question files have 20 questions, but the array allows
          space for 50.*/

int sh=400; int sw=800; /*screen height, screen width*/

/*constructor*/
public quizgame(String title) {
        super(title);
        addKeyListener(this);
} /*end constructor*/
```

```
/*method*/ public void init() {
setBackground(Color.black);
rnumgen=new Random();
for (int i=1; i<=maxquestions; i++) {
        alreadyasked[i]=false;}
requestFocus();
} /*end init*/

public void keyPressed(KeyEvent e) {}
public void keyReleased(KeyEvent e) {}


/*method*/ public void paint(Graphics g) {
g.setColor(Color.orange);
Font f1=new Font ("serif",Font.PLAIN,20);
g.setFont(f1);

if (state==1) {
for (int i=1; i<=2; i++) {
        g.drawString(playerlist[i].name,80*i,100);
        g.drawString(""+playerlist[i].getscore(),80*i,125);
        } /*end for loop*/
if (numquestionsasked<maxquestions) {
g.drawString("Press a key to continue",50,200);
} else {g.drawString("Game over",50,200);
                        numquestionsasked++;}
} /*end if state==1*/


if (state==2) {
if (advanceok) {
numquestionsasked++;
if (numquestionsasked<=maxquestions) {
g.drawString("Get ready",50,200);
try{
Thread.currentThread().sleep(2000); /*Pause 2 seconds.*/
} catch (InterruptedException ex) {}
g.setColor(Color.black);
g.fillRect(1,1,sw,sh);
g.setColor(Color.orange);

/*The next line will generate a random integer from 1 to maxquestions
  (=20).*/
qnum=1+Math.abs(rnumgen.nextInt()) % maxquestions;
while (alreadyasked[qnum]) {
/*Keep drawing new random numbers until a question that has not been
  asked is found.*/
        qnum=1+Math.abs(rnumgen.nextInt()) % maxquestions;
            }
        alreadyasked[qnum]=true;
                } /*end if advanceok*/
g.drawString(""+numquestionsasked+".␣"+
    questionlist[qnum].line1,20,100);
```

```
g.drawString("␣␣␣"+questionlist[qnum].line2,20,125);
} /*end if (numquestionsasked<=maxquestions)*/


} /*end if state==2*/


if (state==3) {
g.drawString(""+numquestionsasked+".␣"+
        questionlist[qnum].line1,20,100);
g.drawString("␣␣␣␣"+questionlist[qnum].line2,20,125);
g.drawString("Answer:␣"+playerlist[signalplayer].name,20,200);
g.drawString("state answer, then enter p for positive, g for
guess",20,250);
} /*end state==3*/


if (state==4) {
g.drawString(""+numquestionsasked+".␣"+
        questionlist[qnum].line1,20,100);
g.drawString("␣␣␣␣"+questionlist[qnum].line2,20,125);
g.drawString("␣␣␣␣"+questionlist[qnum].answer,20,150);
If (signalplayer>0) {
g.drawString("Answer:␣"+playerlist[signalplayer].name,20,200);
if (confidencecode==1)
{g.drawString("confidence level: positive: right +50, wrong
-100",20,225);}
if (confidencecode==2)
{g.drawString("confidence level: guess: right +20, wrong -20",20,225);}
g.drawString("Enter r for right, w for wrong",20,250);
        } /*end if signalplayer>0*/
} /*end state==4*/


} /*end paint*/


/*method*/ public void keyTyped(KeyEvent e) {
if (numquestionsasked>maxquestions) {state=1;}
else {
char c=e.getKeyChar();
if (state==1) {state=2; advanceok=true;}
else if (state==2) {advanceok=false;
                        if (c==playerlist[1].signalkey)
                                {signalplayer=1; state=3;
                                    advanceok=true;}
                        if (c==playerlist[2].signalkey)
                                {signalplayer=2; state=3;
                                    advanceok=true;}
                        if (c=='&')
                            /*If the & key is typed, neither
                                player wishes to answer.*/
                                {signalplayer=0; state=4;
                                    advanceok=true;}
                        } /*end state==2*/
else if (state==3) {

                        if (signalplayer==0)
                                {state=1;}
```

```
                                    else {
                                      if (c=='p')
                                        {confidencecode=1; state=4;}
                                    if (c=='g')
                                        {confidencecode=2; state=4;}
                                              } /*end else*/
                                  } /*end state==3*/
        else if (state==4) {
                    if (signalplayer==0) {state=1;}
                    else {
                    if (c=='r')
                  {playerlist[signalplayer].newscore(pointlist[confidencecode][1]);
                      state=1;}
                                if (c=='w')
                  {playerlist[signalplayer].newscore(pointlist[confidencecode][2]);
                      state=1;}
                                } /*end else*/
                              } /*end state==4*/
            } /*end else*/
quizgameframe.repaint();
} /*end keyTyped*/


/*method*/ static void readquestions() {
FileDialog fd=new FileDialog(quizgameframe,
"Choose file of questions to load (extension 'qz'", FileDialog.LOAD);
fd.setVisible(true);
String filename=fd.getFile();
try{
DataInput f1=new DataInputStream(new FileInputStream(filename));
int qnum=0;
String qline1=f1.readLine();
while (qline1!=null) {
        String qline2=f1.readLine();
        String answerline=f1.readLine();
          qnum++;
          question q0=new question(qline1,qline2,answerline);
          questionlist[qnum]=q0;
          qline1=f1.readLine();
        } /*end while*/

} catch (Exception ex) {String err=ex.toString();
                                        System.out.println(err);}

} /*end readquestions*/

/*to close the window:*/
static class winlis extends WindowAdapter {
public void windowClosing(WindowEvent e) {
System.exit(0);
} /*end windowClosing*/
} /*end winlis*/
```

```
public static void main(String args[ ]) {

quizgameframe=new quizgame("Trivia Quiz Game");
quizgameframe.init();
quizgameframe.addWindowListener(new winlis());
quizgameframe.setBounds(10,10,300,300);
quizgameframe.setVisible(true);
quizname quiznamebox=new quizname(quizgameframe,"Enter player
names");
quiznamebox.setBounds(10,10,300,300);
quiznamebox.setVisible(true);
player0=new player(quiznamebox.name1,'z');
playerlist[1]=player0;
player0=new player(quiznamebox.name2,'/');
playerlist[2]=player0;
readquestions();
state=1;
quizgameframe.repaint();
} /*end main*/

} /*end class quizgame*/


class player {
String name;
private int score;
char signalkey;

/*constructor*/ public player(
String name, char signalkey) {
this.name=name;
this.signalkey=signalkey;
this.score=0;
} /*end constructor*/

/*method*/ void newscore(int x) {
/*This method adds the given value to the score.*/
score+=x;
} /*end newscore*/

/*method*/ int getscore() {
return score;
} /*end getscore*/

} /*end class player*/

class question {
String line1;
String line2;
String answer;

/*constructor*/ public question(
```

```
String line1, String line2, String answer) {
this.line1=line1;
this.line2=line2;
this.answer=answer;
} /*end constructor*/

} /*end class question*/
```

This program also needs a dialog box to read in the player's names at the beginning of the game; here is the code for the dialog box:

```
import java.awt.*;
import java.awt.event.*;

public class quizname extends Dialog
implements ActionListener {

Button okbtn; Button cancelbtn;
TextField name1tf;
String name1;
TextField name2tf;
String name2;

/*constructor method*/ public quizname(Frame parent,
        String label) {

super (parent,label,true);
setLayout(new GridLayout(3,1));
Panel panel1=new Panel();
Label label1 =new Label("Enter Player 1 name");
panel1.add(label1);
name1tf=new TextField (40);
name1tf.setEditable (true);
name1tf.setText (" ");
panel1.add(name1tf);
add(panel1);
Panel panel2=new Panel();
Label label2 =new Label("Enter Player 2 name");
panel2.add(label2);
name2tf=new TextField (40);
name2tf.setEditable (true);
name2tf.setText (" ");
panel2.add(name2tf);
add(panel2);
Panel buttonpanel=new Panel();
okbtn=new Button ("OK");
okbtn.addActionListener(this);
buttonpanel.add (okbtn);
cancelbtn=new Button ("Cancel");
cancelbtn.addActionListener(this);
buttonpanel.add (cancelbtn);
add(buttonpanel);
pack();} /*end constructor*/
```

```
public void actionPerformed(ActionEvent e) {
String btn=e.getActionCommand ();

if (btn.equals ("OK")) {
name1=name1tf.getText();
name2=name2tf.getText();
      setVisible(false);
} /*end if*/
else if (btn.equals ("Cancel")) {
name1tf.setText(" ");
name2tf.setText(" ");
      setVisible(false);
} /*end if*/


} /*end actionPerformed*/
} /*end quizname*/
```

17.4 Football Strategy Game

Another type of game is a strategy game where you try to predict what the other player will do. Here's an example of a football strategy game, where the offensive player chooses from a list of plays and the defensive player chooses from a list of defenses. If the offense play goes to the left side, and the defense is stacked on the right side, then the play will go for a large gain. On the other hand, if the defense is stacked on the side where the offense runs, the play will not go far. A "prevent" defense is good for stopping a long pass, but it will give up yards on other plays.

To make it more interesting, each player will also decide on how many execution points they want to use on a given play. The more points they use, the greater the chance of success. Each player starts with 100 execution points, and they get 5 more after each play. However, if you use up execution points too quickly, then the other player will gain an advantage by being able to use more execution points than you the rest of the game. You will want to use up more execution points on a critical play, but then you know your opponent will also want to use more execution points on a critical play.

The program calls for a dialog box that reads in information from the offensive player and the defensive player. (The players will have to write choices on a card in advance, because it is not fair if one of the players knows the other player's choices before entering his or her own choices.)

The program shown below is simplified in some ways: there are no kickoffs (the receiving team always starts at the 30 yard line); extra points are automatically good; and there are no interceptions or fumbles. You can add more interesting features to the program if you like. Also, the program as written only runs for one simulated quarter of 15 minutes; you can enhance the program by making it run for four quarters if you would like.

Here is the program:

```
import java.awt.*;

import java.awt.event.*;

public class ftbgame extends Frame {

static ftbgame ftbgameframe;

static ftbin ftbinbox;

static ftbplay currplay;

static fbteam t1;
static fbteam t2;

static int prevgain=0;

/*constructor*/
public ftbgame(String title) {
super(title);
} /*end constructor*/

public void init() {
setBackground(Color.lightGray);
t1=new fbteam("Home",0,100,1);
t2=new fbteam("Visitor",0,100,-1);

} /*end init*/


/*method*/ public void paint(Graphics g) {
currplay.showscoreboard(g);
} /*end paint*/

/*method*/ static int playresult(
        int offplay, int defplay,
        int offex, int defex) {

int gain=0;

/*a is an array that stores play results, in yards.*/
int a[ ][ ]=

/*defenses: Stand Left Right Center Blitz Nickel Prevent*/
/*offense plays*/
/*SweepLeft*/ {{ 4, -6, 15, 3, 3, 4, 5 },
/*OffTacLeft*/ { 3, -2, 8, 2, 3, 4, 5 },
/*Center*/ { 2, 3, 3, -1, 3, 4, 5 },
/*OffTacRight*/{ 3, 8, -2, 2, 3, 4, 5 },
/*SweepRight*/ { 4, 15, -6, 3, 3, 4, 5 },
/*ScreenPass*/ { 5, 5, 5, 5, 20, 4, 5 },
```

```
/*QuickPass*/ { 4, 4, 4, 10, 20, 2, 5 },
/*LeftPass*/ { 7, -9, 25, 6, 6, 4, 5 },
/*RightPass*/ { 7, 25, -9, 5, 6, 4, 5 },
/*LongPass*/ { 15, 15, 15, 30, -12, 4, -1 }};

if (offplay==10) { /*punt*/ gain=40+4*(offex-defex);
                                if (gain<0) {gain=0;}
                                if (gain>55) {gain=55;}}
if (offplay==11) { /*field goal*/ gain=35+3*(offex-defex);
                                    if (gain>50) {gain=50;}}
if (offplay<=9) { /*regular scrimmage play*/
        gain=a[offplay][defplay];
        if (offplay<=4) { /*running play*/
                    gain+=(offex-defex);
                    if (gain<-4) {gain=-4;}}
        else { /*passing play*/
                if (gain>=0) {
                        if (gain>=20) {if ((offex-defex)<8)
                                                {gain=0;}}
                        else if (gain>=10) {if ((offex-defex)<4)
                                                {gain=0;}}
                        else If (offex<defex) {gain=0;}
                                } /*end if gain>=0*/
                } /*end passing play*/
} /*end regular scrimmage play*/

prevgain=gain;
If (prevgain>currplay.yttd) {prevgain=currplay.yttd;}
return gain;

} /*end playresult*/

public static void main(String args[ ]) {

ftbgameframe=new ftbgame("Football");
ftbgameframe.init();
ftbgameframe.setBounds(100,150,400,300);
ftbgameframe.setVisible(true);


currplay=new ftbplay(30,t1,t2,1,10,15*60);

while (currplay.timeleft>0) {
        ftbgameframe.repaint();
        ftbinbox=new ftbin(ftbgameframe,"Enter strategies");
        ftbinbox.setVIsible(true);
        int gain=playresult(ftbinbox.offplay, ftbinbox.defplay,
                    ftbinbox.offexpoints, ftbinbox.defexpoints);
        currplay.offteam.expoints+=(5-ftbinbox.offexpoints);
        currplay.defteam.expoints+=(5-ftbinbox.defexpoints);
        currplay=currplay.advanceball(gain, ftbinbox.offplay);

    } /*end while*/
```

```
} /*end main*/
} /*end class ftbgame*/


class fbteam {
String name;
int score=0;
int expoints=0;
int direction=0;

/*constructor*/ public fbteam(
String name, int score, int expoints,
int direction) {
this.name=name;
this.score=score;
this.expoints=expoints;
this.direction=direction;
} /*end constructor*/

} /*end fbteam*/


class ftbplay {

int yardline, down, ytg /*yards to go*/, timeleft,
yttd /*yards to touchdown*/;

fbteam offteam; fbteam defteam;

/*constructor*/ public ftbplay(
int yardline, fbteam offteam, fbteam defteam,
int down, int ytg, int timeleft) {
this.yardline=yardline;
this.offteam=offteam;
this.defteam=defteam;
this.down=down;
this.ytg=ytg;
this.timeleft=timeleft;
if (offteam.direction==1) {yttd=100-yardline;}
                          else {yttd=yardline;}
if (ytg>yttd) {this.ytg=yttd;}
} /*end constructor*/


/*method*/ void showscoreboard(Graphics g) {
g.drawString((offteam.name+"  "+offteam.score+"␣␣␣"+
                  defteam.name+"␣␣"+defteam.score),10,40);
g.drawString(("Down:  "+down+"␣␣Yards to gain:␣"+ytg),10,60);
String yardlinestring=ftbgame.t1.name+"␣"+yardline;
if (yardline>50) {yardlinestring=ftbgame.t2.name+"␣"+(100-yardline);}
g.drawString(offteam.name+"␣ball at␣"+yardlinestring+
      "␣yard line",10,80);
```

```
g.drawString("Time left:"+timeleft,10,100);
g.drawString(("Execution
points:␣"+offteam.name+"␣"+offteam.expoints+
        "␣␣␣␣"+defteam.name+"␣"+defteam.expoints),10,120);
g.drawString("Previous play gain:"+ftbgame.prevgain,10,140);
} /*end showscoreboard*/


/*method*/ ftbplay advanceball(int gain, int offplay) {
                            /*dummy initialization*/
ftbplay newplay=new ftbplay(20,offteam,defteam,1,10,timeleft);

int newyardline=0;
if (offplay==10) { /*punt*/
newyardline=yardline+offteam.direction*gain;
if (newyardline<=0) {newyardline=20;}
if (newyardline>=100) {newyardline=80;}
newplay=new ftbplay(newyardline, defteam, offteam, 1, 10,
timeleft-30);
} /*end punt*/
else if (offplay==11) { /*field goal attempt*/
int fgdist=yttd+17;
if (gain>=fgdist) { /*field goal is good*/
offteam.score+=3;
if (offteam.direction==1) {newyardline=70;}
                    else {newyardline=30;}
newplay=new ftbplay(newyardline, defteam, offteam, 1, 10,
        timeleft-30);
        } /*end field goal is good*/
else { /*field goal attempt fails*/
newyardline=yardline;
if ((offteam.direction==1)&(yardline>80)) {newyardline=80;}
if ((offteam.direction==-1)&(yardline<20)) {newyardline=20;}
newplay=new ftbplay(newyardline, defteam, offteam, 1, 10,
        timeleft-30);
        } /*end field goal attempt fails*/
} /*end field goal attempt*/
else { /*scrimmage play*/
        newyardline=yardline+offteam.direction*gain;
if ((newyardline>=100)|(newyardline<=0)) { /*safety or td*/
        if (gain>=yttd) { /*td scored*/
                offteam.score+=7;
if (offteam.direction==1) {newyardline=70;}
                        else {newyardline=30;}
        newplay=new ftbplay(newyardline, defteam, offteam, 1, 10,
                timeleft-30);
                } /*end td scored*/
else if (((offteam.direction==1)&(newyardline<=0))|
        ((offteam.direction==-1)&(newyardline>=100)))
                { /*safety scored*/
        defteam.score+=2;
        newplay=new ftbplay(50, defteam, offteam, 1, 10,
                timeleft-30);
```

```
                        } /*end safety scored*/
                  } /*end safety or td*/
else { /*not safety or td*/
int newdown=down+1;
int newytg=ytg-gain;
fbteam newoffteam=offteam; fbteam newdefteam=defteam;
if (newytg<=0) {newytg=10; newdown=1;}
else {if (newdown>4) {newoffteam=defteam;
                                        newdefteam=offteam;
                                        newdown=1;
                                        newytg=10;
                              } /*end turn over on 4th down*/
                  }
newplay=new ftbplay(newyardline, newoffteam,
            newdefteam, newdown, newytg, timeleft-30);
      } /*end not safety or td*/
   } /*end scrimmage play*/
return newplay;
} /*end advanceball*/
} /*end ftbplay*/

class ftbin extends Dialog
implements ActionListener {
Button okbtn;
Choice offplaychoice;
int offplay;
TextField offexpointstf;
int offexpoints;
Choice defplaychoice;
int defplay;
TextField defexpointstf;
int defexpoints;

/*constructor*/ public ftbin(Frame parent,
         String label) {

super(parent,label,true);
setLayout(new GridLayout(5,2));

      offplaychoice=new Choice();
      offplaychoice.addItem("SweepLeft");
      offplaychoice.addItem("OffTackleLeft");
      offplaychoice.addItem("RunOverCenter");
      offplaychoice.addItem("OffTackleRight");
      offplaychoice.addItem("SweepRight");
      offplaychoice.addItem("ScreenPass");
      offplaychoice.addItem("QuickPass");
      offplaychoice.addItem("RolloutLeftPass");
      offplaychoice.addItem("RolloutRightPass");
      offplaychoice.addItem("LongPass");
      offplaychoice.addItem("Punt");
      offplaychoice.addItem("FieldGoalAttempt");
```

```
        add (new Label("Offense play:"));
        add(offplaychoice);

        add (new Label("Offense ex points:"));
        offexpointstf=new TextField(" ");
        offexpointstf.setForeground(Color.orange);
        offexpointstf.setBackground(Color.black);
        add(offexpointstf);

        defplaychoice=new Choice();
        defplaychoice.addItem("Standard");
        defplaychoice.addItem("StackLeft");
        defplaychoice.addItem("StackRight");
        defplaychoice.addItem("CrowdCenter");
        defplaychoice.addItem("Blitz");
        defplaychoice.addItem("Nickel");
        defplaychoice.addItem("Prevent");

        add (new Label("Defense formation:"));
        add(defplaychoice);

        add (new Label("Defense ex points:"));
        defexpointstf=new TextField(" ");
        defexpointstf.setForeground(Color.orange);
        defexpointstf.setBackground(Color.black);
        add(defexpointstf);

        okbtn=new Button("OK");
        okbtn.addActionListener(this);
        add(okbtn);

pack();
} /*end constructor*/

public void actionPerformed(ActionEvent e) {
String btn=e.getActionCommand();

if (btn.equals("OK")) {
        String offplaystring=offplaychoice.getSelectedItem();
        if (offplaystring.equals("SweepLeft")) {offplay=0;}
        if (offplaystring.equals("OffTackleLeft")) {offplay=1;}
        if (offplaystring.equals("RunOverCenter")) {offplay=2;}
        if (offplaystring.equals("OffTackleRight")) {offplay=3;}
        if (offplaystring.equals("SweepRight")) {offplay=4;}
        if (offplaystring.equals("ScreenPass")) {offplay=5;}
        if (offplaystring.equals("QuickPass")) {offplay=6;}
        if (offplaystring.equals("RolloutLeftPass")) {offplay=7;}
        if (offplaystring.equals("RolloutRightPass")) {offplay=8;}
        if (offplaystring.equals("LongPass")) {offplay=9;}
        if (offplaystring.equals("Punt")) {offplay=10;}
        if (offplaystring.equals("FieldGoalAttempt")) {offplay=11;}

        String defplaystring=defplaychoice.getSelectedItem();
```

```
        if (defplaystring.equals("Standard")) {defplay=0;}
        if (defplaystring.equals("StackLeft")) {defplay=1;}
        if (defplaystring.equals("StackRight")) {defplay=2;}
        if (defplaystring.equals("CrowdCenter")) {defplay=3;}
        if (defplaystring.equals("Blitz")) {defplay=4;}
        if (defplaystring.equals("Nickel")) {defplay=5;}
        if (defplaystring.equals("Prevent")) {defplay=6;}

        try {
          offexpoints=Integer.parseInt(offexpointstf.getText().trim());
        } catch (NumberFormatException ex) {offexpoints=0;}

        try {
          defexpoints=Integer.parseInt(defexpointstf.getText().trim());
        } catch (NumberFormatException ex) {defexpoints=0;}

        setVisible(false);
    } /*end if*/
  } /*end actionPerformed*/
} /*end ftbin*/
```

The web page for the book includes a more elaborate football statistics program that is designed to be used while you are watching a game.

17.5   Bouncing Balls

Computer games often involve objects that move along the screen. Most of these games require very elaborate programming, so we will look at a very simple game. Three balls move around the screen: a blue ball, representing you; a green ball, which is good, and a red ball, which is bad. If you bounce against the green ball, you gain 10 points; if you bounce against the red ball, you lose 20 points. If a ball hits a wall, then it bounces back. After you have hit one of the other balls, you need to bounce against a wall before you can gain or lose any points by hitting the other balls. If you click the mouse, then your blue ball will change its direction of motion so that it starts moving toward the point you clicked.

Here is the program:

```
import java.applet.*;

import java.awt.*;
import java.awt.event.*;

public class ballgame extends Applet
implements MouseListener {
ballclass ball1, ball2, ball3;
/*The next two lines are needed for double-buffering.*/
Image offscreenimage;
Graphics g2; /*offscreen graphics*/
```

```
static int score=0;


/*method*/ public void init() {
setBackground(Color.lightGray);
addMouseListener(this);
ball1=new ballclass (25,100,100,2,2,Color.blue);
ball2=new ballclass (25,200,200,-2,2,Color.green);
ball3=new ballclass (25,300,300,-2,-2,Color.red);
ball1.otherballlist[0]=ball2; ball1.otherballlist[1]=ball3;
ball2.otherballlist[0]=ball1; ball2.otherballlist[1]=ball3;
ball3.otherballlist[0]=ball1; ball3.otherballlist[1]=ball2;
/*The next two lines are needed for double-buffering.*/
offscreenimage=createImage(size().width,size().height);
g2=offscreenimage.getGraphics();

} /*end init*/
```

/*When we implement the MouseListener interface, we need to list
   all of the following methods, even if we will not define
   any specific behavior for them.*/

```
public void mouseMoved(MouseEvent e) {}
public void mouseDragged(MouseEvent e) {}
public void mouseReleased(MouseEvent e) {}
public void mouseClicked(MouseEvent e) {}
public void mouseEntered(MouseEvent e) {}
public void mouseExited(MouseEvent e) {}

/*method*/ public void update(Graphics g) {
/*This method is included to overrride the standard method update
   so that the screen is not automatically cleared each time
   repaint is called.*/
paint(g);
}

/*method*/ public void paint(Graphics g) {
g2.setColor(Color.lightGray);
g2.fillRect(0,0,size().width, size() .height);
g2.setColor(Color.black);
g2.drawRect(1,1,605,405);
g2.drawString("Score: "+score,50,50);
ball1.moveball();
ball1.drawball(g2);
ball2.moveball();
ball2.drawball(g2);
ball3.moveball();
ball3.drawball(g2);
/*The next line is needed for double-buffering.*/
g.drawImage(offscreenimage,0,0,this);
try{
Thread.currentThread().sleep(10);
} catch (InterruptedException ex) {}
```

```
    repaint();
} /*end paint*/

/*method*/ public void mousePressed(MouseEvent e) {
/*x and y will be the x and y screen coordinates of the point where
   the mouse was pressed, in pixels.*/
double v1=ball1.v()+1; /*initial velocity magnitude+1*/
ball1.vx=e.getX()-ball1.x;
ball1.vy=e.getY()-ball1.y;
double v2=ball1.v();
ball1.vx=ball1.vx*v1/v2+1;
ball1.vy=ball1.vy*v1/v2+1;
repaint();
} /*end mousePressed*/

public void destroy() {
g2.dispose();
} /*end destroy*/

} /*end ballgame*/

class ballclass {
Color circlecolor;
int r; /*circle radius*/
int x; int y;
double vy; double vx;
int minx=10+r/2; int miny=10+r/2;
int maxx=595-r/2; int maxy=395-r/2;
boolean recentlybouncedoffwall=false;

/*constructor*/ public ballclass(
int r, int x, int y, int vx, int vy,
Color circlecolor)
{this.r=r; this.x=x; this.y=y;
this.vx=vx; this.vy=vy;
this.circlecolor=circlecolor;
} /*end constructor*/

ballclass otherballlist[ ]=new ballclass[2];

/*method*/ double distance(ballclass otherball) {
/*This method calculates the distance between the center of this
   ball and the other ball.*/
return (Math.sqrt(Math.pow((x-otherball.x),2)+
                         Math.pow((y-otherball.y),2)));
} /*end distance*/

/*method*/ double v() {
/*This method calculates the magnitude of the velocity vector.*/
return Math.sqrt(vx*vx+vy*vy);
} /*end v*/

/*method*/ double angle(double x1, double y1,
```

```
                double x2, double y2) {
/*This method returns the angle between the (x1,y1) vector and the
   (x2,y2) vector.*/
double dotproduct=x1*x2+y1*y2;
double costheta=dotproduct/(Math.sqrt(x1*x1+y1*y1)*
       Math.sqrt(x2*x2+y2*y2));
return Math.acos(costheta);
} /*end angle*/


/*method*/ void moveball() {
x+=(int)vx;
y+=(int)vy;
/*The balls gradually move faster.*/
if (vx>=vy) {vx+=0.1;}
else {vy+=0.1;}


if ((x<=minx)|(x>=maxx))
       {vx= (vx+0.1),
          x+=(int)vx; recentlybouncedoffwall=true;}
if ((y<=miny)|(y>=maxy))
          {vy=-(vy+0.1);
          y+=(int)vy; recentlybouncedoffwall=true;}
for (int i=0; i<=1; i++) {
if (distance(otherballlist[i])<(2*r)) { /*close enough to bounce*/
ballclass b=otherballlist[i];
if (this.circlecolor==Color.blue) {
if (recentlybouncedoffwall) {
if (b.circlecolor==Color.red) {ballgame.score-=20;}
else {if (b.circlecolor==Color.green) {ballgame.score+=10;}}
             recentlybouncedoffwall=false;}
                                  }
double angle0=angle(vx,vy,1,0);
          /*angle0 is the initial velocity vector angle for this ball.*/
double angle1=angle(vx,vy,(b.x-x),(b.y-y));
             /*angle1 is the angle between the velocity vector and the vector
                that points from the center of this ball to the center of the
                other ball.*/
double angle2=2*(Math.PI/2-angle1);
             /*angle2 is the angle between the initial velocity vector
                and the new velocity vector.*/
double angle3=angle0-angle2;
vx=(v()+0.5)*Math.cos(angle3);
vy=(v()+0.5)*Math.sin(angle3);
} /*end if*/
} /*end for loop*/
} /*end moveball*/


/*method*/ void drawball(Graphics g) {
g.setColor(circlecolor);
g.fillOval(x-r,y-r,2*r,2*r);


} /*end drawball*/
} /*end ballclass*/
```

There are plenty of enhancements you can add to this program. For example, you can add a timer, add more balls, or change the way that the balls speed up.

EXERCISES

1. Write a tic-tac-toe strategy program. The computer will play against a human player. The game of tic-tac-toe is simple enough that it is possible to make a chart showing every possible game outcome, so your task will be translating this information into a form that allows the computer to know how to respond to each possible move.

2. Write a program that simulates the shuffle and deal of a deck of cards, and then use this program to simulate a card game of your choice.

3. Write a program to play the game Hangman.

4. Write a program that allows two people to play a checkers game. The screen displays the checkerboard. To make a move, a player clicks on the piece to move, and then clicks on the square to move to.

5. Write a StarShip program. Have the program keep track of the position of your starship in the galaxy, the position of the other obstacles, and the amount of power your ship has left. Think of a creative objective for the game to make it interesting.

6. Write a program that tries to predict the outcomes of major league baseball games by reading in information about the batting averages of the two teams and then simulating a series of games between them.

7. Write a program that keeps track of the scores during a bowling game.

8. Write a program that can be used during a baseball game to keep track of the scoring and statistics.

9. Write a program that can be used during a football game to keep track of the scoring and statistics.

CHAPTER 18

SCIENTIFIC APPLICATIONS

18.1   Scientific Models

Computers help scientists in many different ways. In many cases computers are used for calculations, such as numerical integration or statistical analysis. Computers are also often used to create models of physical systems. A model is any kind of a relatively simple system that can be used to represent a more complicated system. (Models are not necessarily simple; they are just simpler than the real system they represent.) Computers are very helpful in creating models because they can include abstract representations of physical objects. If you know enough science to understand how those objects interact, and you know programming, you can write a program in which the objects in your program interact in the same way as do the objects in the real world.

Here are some examples where computer programs can be written to create scientific models:

- A model of the solar system can predict how the planets will move under the influence of the sun's gravity. A sample of such a program is included on the disc with this book.

- A model of Earth's atmosphere needs to keep track of pressure, temperature, water vapor, wind speed, and so on, at different points. These models can forecast the weather. The forecasts are not perfect, because the model cannot represent all of the relevant variables, but the forecasts can still be very useful.

- A model of the sun (or other stars) can be programmed by representing the pressure, temperature, and other variables at different points. This allows scientists to learn more about the behavior of the sun.

- A model can represent complex molecules from organic chemistry, and represent the interactions between those molecules. As these models are improved, they will help discover new medicines.

- A model of an ecosystem can predict future changes in animal and plant populations.

- Computer models are used increasingly in engineering. For example, the Boeing 777 airplane was designed entirely by computer. (Previous airplanes were designed on paper, and wooden mock-ups needed to be constructed to make sure the parts would fit together.)

- Economic forecasting firms create models of the economy that represent the total spending in different sectors of the economy. These models can help predict the effects of different policies, but the predictions are not perfect because the model cannot represent all relevant variables.

18.2   Navigating Across the Surface of the Earth

Here is an example of a scientific problem with important practical applications. If you are planning to fly an airplane or sail a ship between two cities, you would like to know the shortest possible distance between them. Because the Earth is a sphere, the shortest distance between two cities is not always obvious. For example, the shortest route between cities in the United States and cities in Europe sometimes involves flying over the North Pole.

Our program will need to know the latitude and longitude of the two cities. We can define a triangle consisting of the North Pole and the two cities. However, this is not an ordinary triangle in a plane; we want to look at a *spherical* triangle because we want the sides of the triangle to follow the surface of the Earth. We'll assume that the Earth is a perfect sphere (see Figure 18–1).

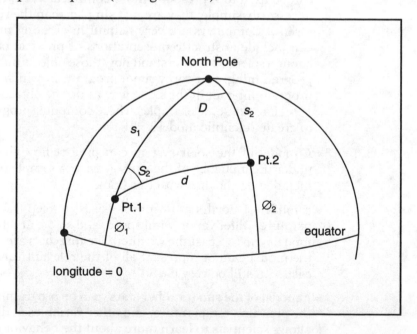

FIGURE 18–1

Let s_1 represent the angular distance between the North Pole and City 1, which is 90 degrees minus the latitude of City 1. Likewise, s_2 is the angular pole distance for City 2. (The diagram shows two cities in the northern hemisphere, but it also works for the southern hemisphere if you use negative numbers for southern latitudes.) Let D be the difference in longitudes between the two cities, and let d be the angular distance between the two cities along the shortest course. This course is called a *great circle* course. A great circle is a circle that intersects a sphere so that the center of the circle is at the center of the sphere. For example, the equator is a great circle, but the circle of all points at latitude 40 degrees is not a great circle. A circle connecting all points of constant longitude and all points with the opposite longitude is a great circle. Let S_2 be the angle the initial course from City 1 makes with the North Pole. For example, if S_2 is 30 degrees, it means that your initial course starts out at 30 degrees East of the North Pole, assuming City 2 is further East. The names of these angles follow the convention in spherical trigonometry that the name of a side of a triangle is the same as the opposite angle, except the angle is uppercase and the side is lowercase. However, in the program we will use longer, more descriptive names for the variables. Spherical triangles are slightly more confusing than plane triangles because the lengths of the sides in a spherical triangle are also measured in degrees (whereas in a plane triangle, the sides are measured in linear units like meters or inches).

We can now use some formulas from spherical trigonometry, assuming that we know the pole distances s_1 and s_2, and the difference in longitudes D:

$$\cos d = \cos s_1 \cos s_2 + \sin s_1 \sin s_2 \cos D$$

Once we know $\cos d$, we can use the arcosine function (**acos** in Java) to find d. If we know d in radians, then the distance between the two cities is rd, where r is the radius of the Earth.

We can use this formula to find the course angle S_2:

$$\sin S_2 = \frac{\sin s_2 \sin D}{\sin d}$$

Finally, we can find formulas that give us the latitude of a particular point along the course between the two cities, assuming we know the longitude of that point. This allows us to track the course (D^* is the difference in longitude between City 1 and the point on the course).

$$\cos k = - \cos S_2 \times \cos D^* + \sin S_2 \sin D^* \cos s_1$$

$$\cos h = \frac{\cos S_2 + \cos D^* \cos k}{\sin D^* \sin k}$$

$$\text{latitude } = 90 \text{ degrees} - h$$

Our program will illustrate the course on the screen by drawing a globe with grid lines for latitude and longitude. It will respond to mouse events that allow the globe to rotate. If you click near the top of the screen, the globe will rotate in that direction; if you click on the right side the globe will rotate in that direction; and so on. The program only shows the course for one pair of cities; you can add a dialog box that reads in the city information if you would like to make it more general.

```java
import java.applet.*;

import java.awt.*;
import java.awt.event.*;

public class course extends Applet
implements MouseListener {

static int rs=200;
        /*rs is the radius of the Earth on the screen, in pixels.*/
static int sw=500; /*screen width*/
static int sh=440; /*screen height*/

static double angle1=0;
static double downangle=0;


double city1lat=0; double city1lon=0;
double city2lat=0; double city2lon=0;


/*method*/ public void init() {
setBackground(Color.black);
addMouseListener(this);

city1lon=0; city1lat=51; /*London*/
city2lon=118; city2lat=34; /*Los Angeles*/
        /*In this example, longitudes are measured to the West.*/
        /*You also could measure longitudes to the East, but you need
          to measure the same direction for both cities, and you need to
          measure longitude in the direction of travel between the two
          cities. In this example, we will travel to the West from London
          to Los Angeles. Also, city1 must have a smaller longitude than
          city2 in the direction you are traveling.*/

} /*end init*/


/*method*/ public void paint(Graphics g) {
Color darkblue=new Color(0,0,100);
g.setColor(darkblue);
g.fillOval(sw/2-rs, sh/2-rs, 2*rs, 2*rs);

/*Draw latitude and longitude grid lines.*/
for (double lat1=60; lat1>=-60; lat1-=30) {
for (double lon1=0; lon1<=360; lon1+=10) {
        globepoint p=new globepoint(lon1,lat1);
        globepoint p2=new globepoint(lon1+1, lat1);
        p.coordinatecalc(angle1,downangle);
        p2.coordinatecalc(angle1,downangle);
        p.drawcourse(p2,Color.yellow,g);
} /*end lon for loop*/
} /*end lat for loop*/
```

```
for (double lon1=0; lon1<=360; lon1+=30) {
for (double lat1=90; lat1>=-90; lat1-=10) {
        globepoint p=new globepoint(lon1,lat1);
        globepoint p2=new globepoint(lon1,lat1+1);
        p.coordinatecalc(angle1,downangle);
        p2.coordinatecalc(angle1,downangle);
        p.drawcourse(p2,Color.yellow,g);
} /*end lat for loop*/
} /*end lon for loop*/

        /*add labels:*/
g.setColor(Color.lightGray);
for (double lat=-60; lat<=60; lat+=30) {
globepoint lp1=new globepoint(0,lat);
lp1.coordinatecalc(angle1,downangle);
if (lp1.y3>0) {g.drawString(cpj.nf(lat,4,0),lp1.xs,lp1.ys);}
globepoint lp2=new globepoint(180,lat);
lp2.coordinatecalc(angle1,downangle);
if (lp2.y3>0) {g.drawString(cpj.nf(lat,4,0),lp2.xs,lp2.ys);}
} /*end for loop*/

for (double lon=0; lon<=300; lon+=60) {
globepoint lp3=new globepoint(lon,0);
lp3.coordinatecalc(angle1,downangle);
if (lp3.y3>0) {g.drawString(cpj.nf(lon,4,0),lp3.xs,lp3.ys);}
} /*end for loop*/


/*now plot course*/
globepoint oldpoint=new globepoint(city1lon,city1lat);
double courselon=city1lon;

        /*The next two quantities give the angles from each city
        to the North Pole, in radians.*/
double city1poleangle=(90-city1lat)*Math.PI/180;
double city2poleangle=(90-city2lat)*Math.PI/180;

double londiff=(city2lon-city1lon)*Math.PI/180;
double distancecosine=
        Math.cos(city1poleangle)*Math.cos(city2poleangle)+
        Math.sin(city1poleangle)*Math.sin(city2poleangle)*
        Math.cos(londiff);
/*The next quantity is the distance between the two cities measured in
  radians.*/
double distanceradians=Math.acos(distancecosine);

double courseanglecosine=
        (Math.cos(city2poleangle)-Math.cos(city1poleangle)*
        Math.cos(distanceradians))/
        (Math.sin(city1poleangle)*Math.sin(distanceradians));
/*courseangle is the initial angle the course makes with the North Pole.*/
double courseangle=Math.acos(courseanglecosine);
```

```
/*courselon and courselat are the coordinates of the points along the
   course between the two cities.*/

while (courselon<city2lon) {
courselon+=2;

double londiff2=(courselon-city1lon)*Math.PI/180;
double kcosine=-Math.cos(courseangle)*Math.cos(londiff2)+
      Math.sin(courseangle)*Math.sin(londiff2)*
      Math.cos(city1poleangle);
double k=Math.acos(kcosine);
double hcosine=(Math.cos(courseangle)+Math.cos(londiff2)*
      kcosine)/(Math.sin(londiff2)*Math.sin(k));
double courselat=90-180*Math.acos(hcosine)/Math.PI;
globepoint newpoint=new globepoint(courselon,courselat);
newpoint.coordinatecalc(angle1,downangle);
oldpoint.coordinatecalc(angle1,downangle);
newpoint.drawcourse (oldpoint,Color.white,g);
oldpoint=newpoint;
} /*end while*/


} /*end paint*/


/*method*/ public void mousePressed(MouseEvent e) {
/*mx and my will be the x and y screen coordinates of the
point where the mouse was pressed, in pixels.*/
int mx=e.getX();
int my=e.getY();
int mx2=mx-sw/2;
int my2=sh/2-my;
if (Math.abs(mx2)>=Math.abs(my2)) {
      if (mx2>0) {angle1+=5;}
                  else {angle1-=5;}
      }
else {
      if (my2>0) {downangle-=5;}
                  else {downangle+=5;}
      }
repaint();
} /*end mousePressed*/


/*When we implement the MouseListener interface, we need to list
   all of the following methods, even if we will not define any
   specific behavior for them.*/

public void mouseMoved(MouseEvent e) {}
public void mouseDragged(MouseEvent e) {}
public void mouseReleased(MouseEvent e) {}
public void mouseClicked(MouseEvent e) {}
public void mouseEntered(MouseEvent e) {}
public void mouseExited(MouseEvent e) {}
```

```
} /*end course*/


class globepoint {
private double lat=0; /*measured in radians*/
private double lon=0; /*measured in radians*/
private int r=3813; /*radius of Earth in kilometers*/

private double x=0;
private double y=0;
private double z=0;
        /*x, y, z are rectangular coordinates of the point with the
            origin at the center of the earth, the z axis pointing to
            the North Pole, and the x axis pointing along the equator
            to 0 degrees longitude.*/
double y3=0;

int xs=0;
int ys=0;
        /*xs and ys give the screen coordinates of the point.*/

/*constructor method*/ public globepoint(
double londeg, double latdeg) {
lat=Math.PI*latdeg/180; /*input to constructor is in degrees*/
lon=Math.PI*londeg/180;
x=r*Math.cos(lon)*Math.cos(lat);
y=r*Math.sin(lon)*Math.cos(lat);
z=r*Math.sin(lat);
} /*end constructor method*/

/*method*/ void coordinatecalc(
double angle1deg, double downangledeg) {
double angle1=angle1deg*Math.PI/180;
double downangle=downangledeg*Math.PI/180;


        /*This method draws a line connecting this point to another point
            (secondpoint), which is given as a parameter. angle1 tells how
            much the globe has been rotated about its axis, and downangle
            tells how much the North Pole has been rotated downward.*/

double x2=x;
double y2=y*Math.cos(downangle)+z*Math.sin(downangle);
double z2=z*Math.cos(downangle)-y*Math.sin(downangle);

double x3=x2*Math.cos(angle1)+y2*Math.sin(angle1);
y3=y2*Math.cos(angle1)-x2*Math.sin(angle1);
double z3=z2;

xs=course.sw/2+(int)(course.rs*x3/r);
ys=course.sh/2-(int)(course.rs*z3/r);
```

```
} /*end coordinatecalc*/

/*method*/ void drawcourse(
globepoint secondpoint, Color c, Graphics g) {
if (y3>=0) {g.setColor(c);
g.drawLine(secondpoint.xs,secondpoint.ys,xs,ys);}
} /*end drawcourse*/

} /*end class globepoint*/
```

Here is the screen:

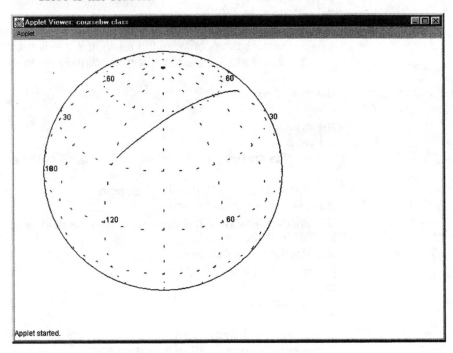

FIGURE 18–2

18.3 This Is Only the Beginning

By now you have seen some examples of the many tasks that can be performed by Java programs. Your skill with programming will grow even more with further practice. Once you have a computer to spare you from having to do boring work, you are free to concentrate on much more creative and interesting tasks, both at home and at work.

There are many advanced features of Java that we have not been able to consider in this book. Now that you've mastered the basic concepts of Java, you may proceed to learn how to use Java to perform such tasks as these:

- include animations in web pages

- write programs with multiple threads running at the same time

- connect Java applets together over a network

- connect Java programs to databases (called JDBC)

- execute methods on other networked computers (called remote method invocation (RMI))

- write programs with reusable components called JavaBeans

- include encryption and other security features in your programs

Although this is the end of the print version of the book, be sure to check the book's disc and the web page at

http://www.spu.edu/~ddowning/cpjava.html

for more examples of what you can do with Java.

This is only the beginning of what you might be able to accomplish.

EXERCISES

1. Suppose P is a one-dimensional array in which $P(I)$ is the number of people in the country of age I. On the internet you can find information about the current age distribution of the U.S. population, as well as birth and death rates. Write a program that calculates what the age distribution of the population will look like each year for the next 20 years. Use the program to determine how changes in the assumptions about birth and death rates will affect the future development of the population age distribution.

2. Write a program that reads in the size of an object and its distance and then computes its apparent angular size. Here are some sample objects:

Object	Size	Distance
Mt. Rainier, seen from Seattle	2.7 miles	60 miles
Width of Central Park, seen from the Empire State Building	3,000 feet	8,000 feet
Moon	3,500 kilometers	384,000 kilometers
Sun	864,000 miles	93 million miles
Saturn	75,000 miles	800 million miles
Star Antares	5.5×10^8 miles	2.3×10^{15} miles
Andromeda galaxy	130,000 light-years	2.2 million light-years

3. Suppose an economy is governed by these three equations:

$$Y_t = C_t + I_t$$

$$C_t = 50 + 0.5 Y_t$$

$$I_t = 0.5 \times (Y_{t-1} - Y_{t-2})$$

Here Y_t is national income in year t, Y_{t-1} is national income in year $t-1$, Y_{t-2} is national income in year $t-2$, C_t is consumption spending in year t, and I_t is investment spending in year t. If $Y = 105$ in the year 2000 and $Y = 95$ in 1999, what will Y be each year for the next 20 years? In economics, this type of model is called a *multiplier-accelerator* model. It is a vastly simplified version of models used to predict the economy. How will the results change if the third equation becomes as below?

$$I_t = 0.65 \times (Y_{t-1} - Y_{t-2})$$

4. When parallel light rays strike a parabolic mirror, they will be reflected back. Write a program that reads in the distance of a particular light ray from the axis of the parabola and then calculates where that light ray will cross the axis after it has been reflected. (This is the concept used to build a telescope.)

5. Write a program similar to the one for Exercise 6, but have the light rays strike a spherical mirror.

6. Ohm's law says that $I = V/R$, where V is the voltage in an electronic circuit, R is the resistance (in ohms), and I is the current (in amperes). Write a program that reads in values for V and R and then calculates I.

7. Write a program that calculates the total impedance in an AC electrical circuit that has frequency f, a resistor of resistance R, a capacitor of capacitance C, and an inductor with inductance L. (Refer to an electronics book.)

8. Some gases obey the van der Waals equation of state, which gives the temperature of one mole of gas if the pressure is P and the volume is V:

$$\left(P + \frac{a}{V^2}\right)(V - b) = RT$$

R is the gas constant, which has the value 8.31 joules/mole-degree kelvin), and a and b are constants that depend on the type of gas. Write a program that reads in values of P, V, a, and b and then calculates the temperature.

9. The magnitude system used to measure the brightness of stars is based on common (base 10) logarithms. The faintest stars visible to the eye have magnitude 6. If a star is b times as bright as a sixth magnitude star, its magnitude is given by this formula:

$$m = 6 - 2.5 \log_{10} b$$

Brighter stars have smaller magnitudes. Very bright stars and planets have negative magnitudes. Write a program that reads in b and then calculates the magnitude.

10. Write a program that reads in the distance to a star (d) in parsecs and the absolute magnitude of the star (M), then calculates the apparent magnitude (that is, the brightness of the star as seen from Earth). Use this formula:

$$magnitude = M + 5 \log \frac{d}{10}$$

11. Write a program that reads in the mass of an object in grams and then calculates the equivalent energy from the formula $E = mc^2$. Here c is the speed of light, which is 3×10^{10} cm/sec. The result for energy will be measured in a unit called the erg.

12. The theory of relativity says that, if an object is traveling past you at a high speed, it will appear shorter to you than it would if you observed it when it was at rest. If the length of a rod at rest is L and it is moving with velocity v, then its length as it will look to you is given by the following formula:

$$\frac{L}{\sqrt{1 - \frac{v^2}{c^2}}}$$

(Here c represents the speed of light; see the previous exercise.) Write a program to calculate the apparent length of the rod.

13. Write a program that calculates how much the frequency (that is, the color) of light shifts because of the Doppler effect when the light source is moving away from you at velocity v.

14. Write a program that reads in the mass of two objects, m_1 and m_2 (in kilograms), and their distance apart, d (in meters), and then calculates the force of gravity between them from the following formula:

$$F = \frac{Gm_1m_2}{d^2}$$

Here $G = 6.67 \times 10^{-11} m^3/(kg - sec^2)$. Use the program to calculate the gravitational force of attraction between two people, if they each weigh 200 kilograms and they are two meters apart.

15. Write a program that demonstrates one of Kepler's laws of planetary motion, which states that the ratio of the cube of a planet's mean distance from the Sun divided by the square of its orbital period is the same for all nine planets in the solar system.

16. Write a program that illustrates one of Kepler's laws of planetary motion, which states that planets move in an ellipse. This program will use the same x acceleration as in the program on the disc:

$$a_x = \frac{\frac{xF}{r}}{m} = -\frac{\frac{xGmM}{r^3}}{m} = -\frac{GMx}{r^3}$$

However, instead of automatically assuming that the planet moves in an ellipse (as does the program on the disc), use this formula to calculate the acceleration in the y direction:

$$a_y = \frac{\frac{yF}{r}}{m} = -\frac{\frac{yGmM}{r^3}}{m} = -\frac{GMy}{r^3}$$

Then calculate the change in the position in the y direction in the same manner as you calculate the change in the x position. For this program, have the program use these initial values: $x = (1 + e)a$, where a is the semimajor axis of the planet's orbit and e is the eccentricity (both given in the program on the disc); $v_x = 0$; and $y = 0$. Experiment with different initial values of v_y to see what happens. As the planet moves, have the program illustrate the elliptical course on the screen.

17. Write a program that illustrates how four bodies move in response to their mutual gravitational attraction. For example, you could use this program to illustrate how the stars in a four-star system behave, or you could use the program to illustrate a trip to Mars (to do this, the four objects you need to include are Mars, Earth, the spaceship, and the Sun).

18. (a) Write a class called $xyrotate$ that contains two values: the x and y coordinates of a point, and two methods: $x2(\theta)$ and $y2(\theta)$, which

calculate what the coordinates of the point would become when the coordinate axes are rotated by an angle θ, found from these formulas:

$$x_2 = x \cos \theta + y \sin \theta$$

$$y_2 = y \cos \theta - x \sin \theta$$

(b) Write a class *xyline* that contains two *xyrotate* points (representing the two endpoints of the line), a variable for the color of the line, and a method for drawing the line on the screen. The method takes one argument: the angle by which the coordinate system is rotated.

(c) Write a class *xyobject* that consists of a group of *xyline* objects. It has one method to draw itself; this method calls the draw method for each of the lines.

19. This is similar to the previous exercise, except now create a class *xyzpoint* that represents points in three-dimensional space. This class allows the coordinate system to be rotated in two ways, measured by these angles: θ, the angle that describes how much the xy plane has been rotated counterclockwise (if you look down from the positive z axis); and ϕ (phi), which gives the amount by which the z axis has been rotated in the direction of the x axis. Use x, y, and z to represent the coordinates of the point in the original coordinate system, and x_2, y_2, and z_2 to represent the coordinates in the rotated coordinate system. Use these formulas:

$$x_2 = x \cos \theta \cos \phi + y \sin \theta \cos \phi - z \sin \phi$$

$$y_2 = y \cos \theta - x \sin \theta$$

$$z_2 = z \cos \phi + x \cos \theta \sin \phi + y \sin \theta \sin \phi$$

Now create a class representing line segments in three-dimensional space, where each endpoint is an object of class *xyzpoint*. Then create wireframe objects that consist of some lines; then rotate the objects so you can view them from different angles.

SUMMARY OF JAVA KEYWORDS AND STANDARD PACKAGES AND CLASSES

Keywords

These words are reserved keywords in Java; you cannot use them as names of any variables you create:

abstract	default	if	private	throw
boolean	do	implements	protected	throws
break	double	import	public	transient
byte	else	instanceof	return	try
case	extends	int	short	void
catch	final	interface	static	volatile
char	finally	long	super	while
class	float	native	switch	
const	for	new	synchronized	
continue	goto	package	this	

It is also recommended that you do not use the following words as variable names: true, false, null.

Standard Packages and Classes

The rest of this appendix describes a few of the standard Java classes and packages. For a complete list of packages, check this web address:

http://www.javasoft.com/products/jdk/1.1/docs/api/packages.html

For the complete class hierarchy, check this web address:

http://www.javasoft.com/products/jdk/1.1/docs/api/tree.html

(These provide documentation for the Java 2 Software Development Kit version 1.2, which was the latest available as this book was written.)

java.lang package

The **java.lang** package contains many standard classes, including the **Integer** and **Double** classes, and the **Math** class, which contains the methods listed in Chapter 12. To see the complete list of methods in the **Math** class, check this web address:

http://www.javasoft.com/products/jdk/1.1/docs/api/java.lang.Math.html

The **java.lang** package is automatically available to your programs, so you don't need to import it explicitly.

java.awt package

The **java.awt** package contains classes used for graphical user interfaces, including **BorderLayout, Button, Canvas, Checkbox, Checkbox-Group, Choice, Color, Component, Container, Dialog, Event, FileDialog, FlowLayout, Font, FontMetrics, Frame, Graphics, Image, Label, List, Menu, MenuBar, MenuItem, Panel, Polygon, ScrollPane, TextArea, TextComponent, TextField, Toolkit,** and **Window**.

The **Component** class is a general class for windows objects; some of its methods include **paint(Graphics), setBackground(Color), setBounds(int, int, int, int), setEnabled(boolean), setFont(Font), setForeground(Color),** and **setVisible(boolean)**. (For each method, the type of argument is listed in parentheses.)

The classes that extend the **Component** class include **Button, Canvas, Checkbox, Choice,** and **TextComponent** (**TextArea** and **TextField** extend **TextComponent**).

The class **Container** extends **Component**; it is used to collect other components together. The **Container** class includes the **add(Component)** method, which is used to include other components in the container.

The class **Panel** extends **Container**; it can be used to group components such as buttons together, and then one or more panels can be added to another container.

The **Window** class, which also extends **Container**, provides a window that can be moved independently around the screen. Instead of using the class **Window** directly, usually your program will use a class such as **Dialog** or **Frame**, which both extend **Window** and add more features to the window. The **Frame** class provides a generic window with a title and a border. The windows applications in this book all run in a frame. If your program uses a menu bar, the bar needs to be added to a frame. The **Dialog** class provides a dialog box (also available is **FileDialog**, which extends **Dialog**).

Another class that extends **Container** is **ScrollPane**.

The **Color** class contains variables representing the standard colors, such as **Color.blue**, and it provides a constructor, **Color(int, int, int)**, where you can specify the values of red, green, and blue, respectively, to include in this color (the values are between 0 and 255).

The **Graphics** class includes the methods **setColor(Color)** and **setFont(Font)** to control the characteristics of items that are drawn. It also includes the drawing methods such as **drawLine(int, int, int, int)**, **drawRect(int, int, int, int)**, **fillRect(int, int, int, int)** and **drawString (String, int, int)**. For the complete list, see this web address:

http://www.javasoft.com/products/jdk/1.1/docs/api/java.awt.Graphics.html

Other Packages

- **java.applet** contains one class: **Applet**. (Note that the class name is capitalized; the package name is not.) The **Applet** class extends **Panel** (which extends **Container**, which extends **Component**); it includes all of the functionality needed by an applet window.

- **java.awt.event** is used for implementing **MouseListener**, **KeyListener**, and other event-driven program features.

- **java.awt.datatransfer** is used for transferring data to and from the clipboard.

- **java.io** is used for file input and output.

- **java.util** is a package of utilities that includes the classes **Gregorian-Calendar**, **Random**, and **Vector**, among others.

APPENDIX B

HTML

Hypertext Markup Language, or HTML, provides a set of codes that can be inserted into text files to indicate special typefaces, inserted images, and links to other hypertext documents. The main use of HTML is to publish information on the World Wide Web.

HTML features are indicated by special codes, called *tags*. If there was an HTML tag called ZZZ, then the characters <ZZZ> would mark the beginning of this feature, and </ZZZ> would mark the end. For example, the keywords <TITLE> and </TITLE> mark the beginning and end of the title. The tag <P> marks a paragraph break, and <IMG SRC=*filename*> embeds an image in the document. Many image formats are supported by HTML, but GIF is the most popular. Codes for special typefaces include the following:

<H1> ... </H1>	Heading, size 1 (largest)
<H6> ... </H6>	Heading, size 6 (smallest)
<B> ... </B>	Boldface
<I> ... </I>	Italics
<U> ... </U>	Underline
<T> ... </T>	Typewriter type

The tag <BR> inserts a line break; without this tag, the line breaks on the displayed web page will not necessarily match the line breaks on the original HTML text. The tag <HR> inserts a horizontal rule.

An unnumbered list of items can be inserted as follows:

```
<UL>
<LI> put first item in list here </LI>
<LI> put second item here </LI>
<LI> put third item here </LI>
</UL>
```

An ordered (numbered) list is created in the same manner, except with OL used in place of UL.

A link to another document looks like this:

```
<A HREF="XXXX.HTML"> Click here.</A>
```

This means "Jump to file XXXX.HTML (another HTML document) if the user clicks on the words 'Click here.' " A web address (URL) can appear in place of the file name. A link to another place in the same document looks like this:

```
<A HREF="#XXXX"> This is the text that will display the
    link</A>
```

When the user clicks on this link, the browser will jump to the location in the current document marked with

```
<A NAME="XXXX"> This is the target of the link</A>
```

Comments (to be ignored by the HTML system) look like this:

```
<! This is a comment>
```

HTML also provides features to accept data from a form filled out by the user and sent to the server.

The applet tag makes it possible to include a Java applet in an HTML document. Here is an example of a complete HTML document with an applet:

```
<HTML><HEAD><TITLE>Applet example</TITLE></HEAD>
<BODY>
<APPLET CODE="appletname.class", HEIGHT=300, WIDTH=400>
a Java compatible browser is needed for this
</APPLET>
</BODY>
</HTML>
```

There also is a language associated with HTML called JavaScript. The name comes from the fact that there is some similarity between the syntax of JavaScript and Java, but they work quite differently. JavaScript is a scripting language that allows a web page author to program various activities to happen when the user of a browser performs actions such as clicking on a button. Java, as you know, is a full-featured programming language that can be used for applications as well as web-page applets.

(This description is excerpted from *Dictionary of Computer and Internet Terms*, by Michael Covington, Melody Covington, and Douglas Downing, and published by Barron's Educational Series, Inc.)

APPENDIX C

ABOUT THE DISC

Here is a list of the items included on the compact disc that comes with the book. (To find your way around the disc, point your web browser to the file `about_the_disc.html`.)

1. Java Development Kit 1.2, from Sun Microsystems. This software includes the Java compiler, a set of standard classes, and the appletviewer software. Sun makes it available for free on its web page; it is included here with Sun's permission to make it more convenient for you since you don't need to download it. All of the files are in a single compressed self-extracting executable file; all you need to do is run this file and it will guide you through the installation process. (See the disc for additional notes.) This version of the software was released in December 1998; it is also called the Java 2 platform. See Sun's Java web site at *http://www.javasoft.com* for the latest information on the different versions of Java.

2. The programs that appear in the text of the book. Both the Java source code and the compiled class files are included. You are free to copy the programs to your disk and modify them as you wish.

3. Sample answers to selected exercises from the book. Check the web page of the book for answers to additional exercises and additional suggestions for Java projects.

4. Java code generator program. This is the program described in the book and included as Appendix E; you can use it to convert the outline code into Java source code.

5. Quick trivia game. This is the program for the question-answering game described in the book. The disc also contains 32 files of 20 questions each covering a variety of different topics.

6. Planetary motion program. The disc includes a program for predicting the positions and rising and setting times for the four planets Venus, Mars, Jupiter, and Saturn. This provides an example of a

345

scientific application of Java. The disc also contains a description of how the program works and a sample of the output.

7. Sample images. Since Java applets can include images, you will probably want to experiment with including different images in your applets. Most of the time you will want to obtain your own images with a digital camera or scanner, or else you can download images available on the web. The disc includes some sample scenery images (in *jpg* format) that you can use to experiment with. These photographs were all taken by the author; if you've purchased this book, you're free to use these photographs in any of your programs or web pages. A Java program is included that allows you to select from the sample images by clicking on the description of the photograph. If memory limitations make it difficult to run this program with a web browser, try running it with the appletviewer. Or you can include images directly in an *html* document; here's an example:

```
<html><head><title>Milky Way</title></head>
<body>
<img src="milky_way.jpg" align=right>
</body></html>
```

APPENDIX D

STANDARD VARIABLE NAMES USED IN THIS BOOK

- *bc*: background color
- *c*: color
- *cpj*: standard class used in this book including some useful methods for formatting numbers
- *cpjxy*: standard class used in this book including some graphics methods
- *e*: event
- *ex*: exception
- *f1, f2*, etc: files
- *frame*: The windows-based Java application programs in this book create a variable whose name begins with the name of the program and ends with the word "frame;" the program runs in this frame.
- *g*: graphics element
- *h*: height of screen element
- *i*: index or counter
- *inbox*: dialog box that accepts one line of text from user
- *j*: index or counter
- *k*: index or counter
- *lis*: The letters "lis" at the end of a name indicate that this is a listener class.
- *lm*: left margin (in pixels)
- *m0, m1*, etc: menubar, menu, or menu item

- *mbox*: message box
- *nf*: number format method (part of *cpj* class)
- *sh*: screen height (in pixels)
- *sw*: screen width (in pixels)
- *tm*: top margin (in pixels)
- *w*: width of screen element
- *x*: x coordinate or generic variable
- *xc*: mathematical x coordinate of center of screen
- *xscale*: width of screen, mathematical units
- *y*: y coordinate or generic variable
- *yc*: mathematical y coordinate of center of screen
- *yscale*: height of screen, mathematical units
- *z*: z coordinate or generic variable

CODE GENERATOR

This program generates Java source code for an application from an outline code. The outline code has this general form:

```
programname
```

```
*:<VARS>
```

[Put code for variable and method declarations here.]

```
*:</VARS>
```

```
*:<INIT>
```

[Put code for the init method here (the init method will be called by the main method before other methods are called).]

```
*:</INIT>
```

```
*:<BUTTONS>
```

[Include code for buttons here, in this general form:

name_of_button {
code to be executed when this button is clicked
}

(Mark the end of the code for the buttons with a right brace as the first character on a line by itself; don't put any right braces as the first character of a line in the middle of the button code.) All buttons before <BREAK> will be put on a panel at the top of the screen; all buttons after <BREAK> will be put on a panel at the bottom of the screen.]

```
*:</BUTTONS>
```

```
*:<MENU>
```

[Put code for menu items here, in this general form:

menu1
**menuitem1* {
code to be executed when menuitem 1 is clicked
}

(Close the code for menuitem 1 with a right brace on a line by itself; do not put a right brace as the first character on a line in the middle of the code for the menu.) The number of asterisks before the name of the menuitem indicates how deep it is in the hierarchy of menus. One asterisk means that the menu item will appear on the menu bar; two asterisks means it will appear on a menu that can be selected from the menu bar; and so on. If a menuitem has action code associated with it (not another menu), then put a right brace after the menuitem name. If a menuitem has further menus below it, then don't put a right brace after the name; instead, have it followed by other menu items (which must be lower in the hierarchy—that is, they have more asterisks in front of their names.)]

```
*:</MENU>
```

```
*:<MOUSE>
```

[Put code to be executed when the mouse is clicked here.]

```
*:</MOUSE>
```

```
*:<PAINT>
```

[Put code to be executed when the paint method is to be executed here.]

```
*:</PAINT>
```

```
*:<CLOSE>
```

[Put any code to be executed when the application window is closed here.]

```
*:</CLOSE>
```

See the book's web site at

http://www.spu.edu/~ddowning/cpjava.html

for more examples of code generating programs.
Here is the code generator program:

```
import java.io.*;

public class codegen {
/*This code generator program reads in an input file with outline code
  menus, then it generates the Java source code file.*/

static DataInput f1;
static DataOutput f2;
```

```
static DataOutput f3;
static DataOutput f4;

static String programname=" ";

/*method*/ static void initbuttons() {
/*This method generates the code for creating the buttons in the file f2;
   then it generates the code for the inner classes that will
   listen for the button events and generate the action in the file f3.*/

try{
f2.writeBytes("Panel upperpanel=new Panel();\r\n");
f2.writeBytes("Panel lowerpanel=new Panel();\r\n");
String currentpanel="upperpanel";

f4.writeBytes("\r\n");
f4.writeBytes("/*Here are the declarations for the buttons:*/ \r\n");

/*Read lines from the input file starting with <BUTTONS> and ending
   with </BUTTONS>.*/
String x=f1.readLine(); /*BUTTONS*/
while (!(x.startsWith("*:<BUTTONS>"))) {x=f1.readLine();}
System.out.println("starting to read "+x);
x=f1.readLine();
while (!(x.startsWith("*:</BUTTONS>"))) {

x=x.substring(0,x.indexOf("{"));
System.out.println("     new  button:   "+x);
String btname=x+"btn";
        /*The file f4 holds the declarations.*/

f4.writeBytes("Button "+btname+"; \r\n");
f2.writeBytes("/*Button*/ "+btname+"=newButton(""+x+"");\r\n");
f2.writeBytes("     "+btname+".addActionListener(new "+
        btname+"lis());\r\n");
f2.writeBytes(" "+currentpanel+".add("+btname+");\r\n");

        /*Write the code for the listener class. The name of
          the listener class will be the name of the button,
          followed by "lis". The actual action code that
          goes in the listener class is read from the input file.*/
f3.writeBytes("/*inner*/ class "+btname+
        "lis implements ActionListener { \r\n");
f3.writeBytes("public void actionPerformed(ActionEvent e) { \r\n");
        x=f1.readLine();
        while (!(x.startsWith("}"))) {
            f3.writeBytes(x+"\r\n");
            x=f1.readLine();
        } /*end while*/
f3.writeBytes(programname+"frame.repaint();\r\n");
        f3.writeBytes("} /*end actionPerformed*/ \r\n");
        f3.writeBytes("} /*end inner class "+btname+"lis */ \r\n");
        f3.writeBytes(" \r\n");
```

```
            x=f1.readLine();

        /*The symbol <BREAK> in the input file means that the end of
          the top panel buttons has been reached; the remaining buttons
          will be placed on the bottom panel.*/

    if (x.startsWith("<BREAK>")) {currentpanel="lowerpanel";
                                    x=f1.readLine(); }
    } /*while*/

    f2.writeBytes("add(BorderLayout.NORTH,upperpanel);\r\n");
    f2.writeBytes("add(BorderLayout.SOUTH,lowerpanel);\r\n");

    } catch (Exception ex) {String err=ex.toString();
                                    System.out.println(err);}
    } /*end initbuttons*/


/*method*/ static void readlines(String x1, String x2) {
/*This method reads through the input file until it reaches a line that
  starts with the string x1. Then it keeps reading through the input file
  while also writing the result to the output file until it reaches a
  line that begins with the string x2.*/

try{
String x=f1.readLine();
while (!(x.startsWith(x1))) {x=f1.readLine();}
System.out.println("starting to read:␣"+x);
x=f1.readLine();
while (!(x.startsWith(x2))) {f2.writeBytes(x+"\r\n"); x=f1.readLine();}
} catch (Exception ex) {String err=ex.toString();
                                    System.out.println(err);}
} /*end readlines*/

/*method*/ static int countstars(String x) {
int k=0;
while (x.charAt(k)=='*') {k++;}
return k;
} /*end countstars*/

/*method*/ static String blank (int n) {
String x=" ";
return x.substring(0,(n-1));
}

/*method*/ static void initmenu() {
/*This method reads in the outline code for a menu and generates
  the Java code to implement the menu. It also creates a listener
  inner class for each menu item.*/

String parentitem="␣";
String thisitem="␣";
int maxlevel=7; /*maxmimum depth of menu levels*/
```

```
int a[ ]={0,0,0,0,0,0,0,0};

try{
String x=f1.readLine(); String x2="";
while (!(x.startsWith("*:<MENU>"))) {x=f1.readLine();}
System.out.println("start reading"+x);
boolean continue1=true;
int oldlevel=0; int level=0;

f2.writeBytes("MenuBar m0=new MenuBar(); \r\n");
f4.writeBytes("\r\n");
f4.writeBytes(" /*Declare the menus and menuitems:*/ \r\n");

while (continue1) {
        x=f1.readLine();
        if (x.startsWith("*:</MENU>")) {continue1=false; level=0;}
        else {
           System.out.print("␣␣␣␣reading menuitem:"+x+"␣␣␣");
           if (x.indexOf("{")<0) {System.out.println("␣");}
           level=countstars(x);
           x=x.substring(level);
                  }

        if (level<oldlevel) {
              for (int level2=oldlevel-1; level2>=level; level2- -) {
              if (level2>0) {
                     f2.writeBytes(blank(level2)+"m");
                     if (level2==1) {f2.writeBytes("0"); }
                        else {
                          for (int k=1; k<=(level2-1); k++)
                              {f2.writeBytes(""+a[k]);}
                          } /*end else*/
                     f2.writeBytes(".add(m");
                     for (int k=1; k<=level2; k++)
                          {f2.writeBytes(""+a[k]);}
                     f2.writeBytes("); \r\n");
                     if (level2==1) {f2.writeBytes(" \r\n");}
                              } /*end if level2>0*/
              } /*end level2 for loop*/
           } /*end level<oldlevel*/

if (continue1) {
        int L=x.indexOf("{");
      if (L>0) {
           x2= x.substring(0,L);
           a[level]=a[level]+1;
           parentitem="m";
           for (int k=1; k<=(level-1); k++)
                {parentitem+=a[k];}
           thisitem=parentitem+a[level];
           System.out.println(thisitem);
               /*The declaration of the menu item is written to file
               f4.*/
```

```
f4.writeBytes(blank(level)+"MenuItem␣"+thisitem+";
    \r\n␣");
f2.writeBytes(blank(level)+"/*MenuItem*/␣"+thisitem+" =
    new MenuItem(""+x2+""); \r\n␣");
f2.writeBytes(blank(level)+thisitem+"
    .addActionListener(new "+thisitem+"lis()); \r\n");
f2.writeBytes(blank(level)+parentitem+".add("+thisitem+");
    \r\n");

/*The listener class that contains the action to be
  performed by this menu item is written to file f3.
  The action statements are read from the input file.*/
f3.writeBytes(" \r\n");
f3.writeBytes("/*inner*/ class "+thisitem+
    "lis implements ActionListener { \r\n");
f3.writeBytes("/*action called by menu item "+x2+"*/ \r\n");
f3.writeBytes("public void actionPerformed(ActionEvent e)
    { \r\n");

x=f1.readLine();

while (!(x.startsWith("}"))) {f3.writeBytes(x+" \r\n");
                                    x=f1.readLine();
                             }
f3.writeBytes(programname+"frame.repaint();\r\n");
f3.writeBytes("} /*end actionPerformed*/ \r\n");
f3.writeBytes("} /*end inner class "+thisitem+"lis*/ \r\n");

    } /*end if L>0*/
else {
    a[level]=a[level]+1;
    for (int k=(level+1); k<=maxlevel; k++) {a[k]=0;}
    String thismenu="m";
    for (int k=1; k<=level; k++) {thismenu+=a[k];}
    f4.writeBytes("Menu "+thismenu+"; \r\n");
    f2.writeBytes("/*Menu*/ "+thismenu+
        "= new Menu(""+x+""); \r\n");
    } /*end else*/

oldlevel=level;
    } /*else*/
} /*while continue1*/

f2.writeBytes("setMenuBar(m0); \r\n");

} catch (Exception ex) {String err=ex.toString();
                            System.out.println(err);}

} /*end initmenu*/
```

```
public static void main(String args[ ]) {
String f0n=args[0]; /*Read in name from command line parameter.*/

try{
String f1n=f0n+".out"; /*input file with outline code*/
String f2n=f0n+".j1"; /*output file: Java source code*/
String f3n=f0n+".temp"; /*temporary file*/
String f4n=f0n+".temp2"; /*temporary file*/

f1=new DataInputStream(new FileInputStream(f1n));
f2=new DataOutputStream(new FileOutputStream(f2n));
f3=new DataOutputStream(new FileOutputStream(f3n));
f4=new DataOutputStream(new FileOutputStream(f4n));

programname=f1.readLine();
System.out.println("program name:ᵤ"+programname);

f2.writeBytes("import java.awt.*;\r\n");
f2.writeBytes("import java.awt.event.*;\r\n");
f2.writeBytes("import java.awt.datatransfer.*;\r\n");
f2.writeBytes("import java.io.*;\r\n");
f2.writeBytes("import java.util.*;\r\n");
f2.writeBytes("import java.text.*;\r\n");


f2.writeBytes("public class "+ programname+ " extends Frame \r\n");
f2.writeBytes("implements MouseListener { \r\n");

f2.writeBytes("public static "+ programname+" "+programname+"frame;
          \r\n");
f2.writeBytes(" \r\n");

readlines("*:<VARS>","*:</VARS>");

f2.writeBytes(" \r\n");


f2.writeBytes("/*constructor*/\r\n");
f2.writeBytes("public "+ programname+"(String title) {\r\n");
f2.writeBytes("super(title);\r\n");
f2.writeBytes(" } /*end constructor*/\r\n");

f2.writeBytes(" \r\n");

f2.writeBytes("public void init() {\r\n");

readlines("*:<INIT>","*:</INIT>");

initbuttons();

initmenu();

f2.writeBytes("addMouseListener(this); \r\n");
```

```
f2.writeBytes("} /*end init*/\r\n");

f2.writeBytes(" \r\n");

f2.writeBytes("public void mouseMoved(MouseEvent e) {}\r\n");
f2.writeBytes("public void mouseDragged(MouseEvent e) {}\r\n");
f2.writeBytes("public void mouseReleased(MouseEvent e) {}\r\n");
f2.writeBytes("public void mouseClicked(MouseEvent e) {}\r\n");
f2.writeBytes("public void mouseEntered(MouseEvent e) {}\r\n");
f2.writeBytes("public void mouseExited(MouseEvent e) {}\r\n");

f2.writeBytes(" \r\n");

f2.writeBytes("/*method*/
        public void mousePressed(MouseEvent e) { \r\n");
f2.writeBytes("/*mx and my are the mouse coordinates.*/ \r\n");

f2.writeBytes("int mx=e.getX(); \r\n");
f2.writeBytes("int my=e.getY(); \r\n");

readlines("*:<MOUSE>","*:</MOUSE>");

f2.writeBytes("repaint(); \r\n");
f2.writeBytes(" } /*end mousePressed*/ \r\n");
f2.writeBytes(" \r\n");

/*Rename temporary file f4 as f4b and insert into file f2.*/
DataInput f4b=new DataInputStream(new FileInputStream(f4n));
String x4=f4b.readLine();
while (x4!=null) {f2.writeBytes(x4+"\r\n");
                        x4=f4b.readLine();}

f2.writeBytes(" \r\n");

f2.writeBytes("/*method*/ public void paint(Graphics g) {\r\n");

readlines("*:<PAINT>","*:</PAINT>");

f2.writeBytes("} /*end paint*/\r\n");

f2.writeBytes(" \r\n");

/*Rename temporary file f3 as f3b and insert into file f2.*/
DataInput f3b=new DataInputStream(new FileInputStream(f3n));
String x3=f3b.readLine();
while (x3!=null) {f2.writeBytes(x3+"\r\n");
                        x3=f3b.readLine();}

f2.writeBytes(" \r\n");

f2.writeBytes(" /*to close the window:*/ \r\n");
f2.writeBytes("static class winlis extends WindowAdapter { \r\n");
```

```
f2.writeBytes("public void windowClosing(WindowEvent e) { \r\n");

readlines("*:<CLOSE>","*:</CLOSE>");

f2.writeBytes("System.exit(0); \r\n");
f2.writeBytes("} /*end windowClosing*/ \r\n");
f2.writeBytes("} /*end winlis*/ \r\n");

f2.writeBytes(" \r\n");

f2.writeBytes("public static void main(String args[ ]) {\r\n");

f2.writeBytes(programname+"frame=new "+programname+"
                        (""+programname+"");\r\n");
f2.writeBytes(programname+"frame.addWindowListener(new winlis());
        \r\n");
f2.writeBytes(programname+"frame.init(),\r\n");
f2.writeBytes(programname+"frame.setBounds(10,10,360,360); \r\n");
f2.writeBytes(programname+"frame.setVisible(true);\r\n");
f2.writeBytes(" } /*end main*/\r\n");
f2.writeBytes("} /*end class "+programname+"*/\r\n");

} catch (Exception ex) {String err=ex.toString();
                                    System.out.println(err);}

} /*end main*/
} /*end codegen*/
```

INDEX

Sun Microsystems, Inc.

Binary Code License Agreement

READ THE TERMS OF THIS AGREEMENT AND ANY PROVIDED SUPPLEMENTAL LICENSE TERMS (COLLECTIVELY "AGREE-MENT") CAREFULLY BEFORE OPENING THE SOFTWARE MEDIA PACKAGE. BY OPENING THE SOFTWARE MEDIA PACKAGE, YOU AGREE TO THE TERMS OF THIS AGREEMENT.
IF YOU ARE ACCESSING THE SOFTWARE ELECTRONICALLY, IN-DICATE YOUR ACCEPTANCE OF THESE TERMS BY SELECTING THE "ACCEPT" BUTTON AT THE END OF THIS AGREEMENT. IF YOU DO NOT AGREE TO ALL THESE TERMS, PROMPTLY RETURN THE UNUSED SOFTWARE TO YOUR PLACE OF PURCHASE FOR A REFUND OR, IF THE SOFTWARE IS ACCESSED ELECTRONI-CALLY, SELECT THE "DECLINE" BUTTON AT THE END OF THIS AGREEMENT.

1. **LICENSE TO USE.** Sun grants you a non-exclusive and non-trans-ferable license for the internal use only of the accompanying soft-ware and documentation and any error corrections provided by Sun (collectively "Software"), by the number of users and the class of computer hardware for which the corresponding fee has been paid.

2. **RESTRICTIONS.** Software is confidential and copyrighted. Title to Software and all associated intellectual property rights is retained by Sun and/or its licensors. Except as specifically authorized in any Supplemental License Terms, you may not make copies of Soft-ware, other than a single copy of Software for archival purposes. Unless enforcement is prohibited by applicable law, you may not modify, decompile, reverse engineer Software. You acknowledge that Software is not designed or licensed for use in on-line control of aircraft, air traffic, aircraft navigation or aircraft communica-tions; or in the design, construction, operation or maintenance of any nuclear facility. Sun disclaims any express or implied warranty of fitness for such uses. No right, title or interest in or to any trade-mark, service mark, logo or trade name of Sun or its licensors is granted under this Agreement.

3. **LIMITED WARRANTY.** Sun warrants to you that for a period of ninety (90) days from the date of purchase, as evidenced by a copy of the receipt, the media on which Software is furnished (if any) will be free of defects in materials and workmanship under normal use. Except for the foregoing, Software is provided "AS IS." Your exclusive remedy and Sun's entire liability under this limited warranty will be at Sun's option to replace Software media or refund the fee paid for Software.

4. DISCLAIMER OF WARRANTY. UNLESS SPECIFIED IN THIS AGREEMENT, ALL EXPRESS OR IMPLIED CONDITIONS, REPRESENTATIONS AND WARRANTIES, INCLUDING ANY IMPLIED WARRANTY OF MERCHANTABILITY, FITNESS FOR A PARTICULAR PURPOSE, OR NON-INFRINGEMENT, ARE DISCLAIMED, EXCEPT TO THE EXTENT THAT THESE DISCLAIMERS ARE HELD TO BE LEGALLY INVALID.

5. LIMITATION OF LIABILITY. TO THE EXTENT NOT PROHIBITED BY LAW, IN NO EVENT WILL SUN OR ITS LICENSORS BE LIABLE FOR ANY LOST REVENUE, PROFIT OR DATA, OR FOR SPECIAL, INDIRECT, CONSEQUENTIAL, INCIDENTAL OR PUNITIVE DAMAGES, HOWEVER CAUSED REGARDLESS OF THE THEORY OF LIABILITY, ARISING OUT OF OR RELATED TO THE USE OF OR INABILITY TO USE SOFTWARE, EVEN IF SUN HAS BEEN ADVISED OF THE POSSIBILITY OF SUCH DAMAGES. In no event will Sun's liability to you, whether in contract, tort (including negligence), or otherwise, exceed the amount paid by you for Software under this Agreement. The foregoing limitations will apply even if the above stated warranty fails of its essential purpose.

6. Termination. This Agreement is effective until terminated. You may terminate this Agreement at any time by destroying all copies of Software. This Agreement will terminate immediately without notice from Sun if you fail to comply with any provision of this Agreement. Upon Termination, you must destroy all copies of Software.

7. Export Regulations. All Software and technical data delivered under this Agreement are subject to US export control laws and may be subject to export or import regulations in other countries. You agree to comply strictly with all such laws and regulations and acknowledge that you have the responsibility to obtain such licenses to export, reexport, or import as may be required after delivery to you.

8. U.S. Government Rights. If Software is being acquired by or on behalf of the U.S. Government or by a U.S. Government prime contractor or subcontractor (at any tier), then the Government's rights in Software will be only as set forth in this Agreement; this is in accordance with 48 CFR 227.7201 through 227.7202-4 (for Department of Defense (DOD) acquisitions) and with 48 CFR 2.101 and 12.212 (for non-DOD acquisitions).

9. Governing Law. Any action related to this Agreement will be governed by California law and controlling U.S. federal law. No choice of law rules of any jurisdiction will apply.

10. Severability. If any provision of this Agreement is held to be unenforceable, this Agreement will remain in effect with the provision omitted, unless omission would frustrate the intent of the parties, in which case this Agreement will immediately terminate.

11. Integration. This Agreement is the entire agreement between you and Sun relating to its subject matter. It supersedes all prior or contemporaneous oral or written communications, proposals, representations and warranties and prevails over any conflicting or additional terms of any quote, order, acknowledgment, or other communication between the parties relating to its subject matter during the term of this Agreement. No modification of this Agreement will be binding, unless in writing and signed by an authorized representative of each party.

For inquiries please contact: Sun Microsystems, Inc., 901 San Antonio Road, Palo Alto, California 94303.

JAVA™2 SOFTWARE DEVELOPMENT KIT VERSION 1.2

SUPPLEMENTAL LICENSE TERMS

These supplemental terms ("Supplement") add to the terms of the Binary Code License Agreement (collectively the "Agreement"). Capitalized terms not defined herein shall have the same meanings ascribed to them in the Agreement. The Supplement terms shall supersede any inconsistent or conflicting terms in the Agreement above, or in any license contained within the Software.

1. **Limited License Grant.** Sun grants to you a non-exclusive, non-transferable limited license to use the Software without fee for evaluation of the Software and for development of Java applets and applications provided that you: (i) may not re-distribute the Software in whole or in part, either separately or included with a product; and (ii) may not create, or authorize your licensees to create additional classes, interfaces, or subpackages that are contained in the "java" or "sun" packages or similar as specified by Sun in any class file naming convention. Refer to the Java Runtime Environment Version 1.2 binary code license (http://java.sun.com/products/jdk/1.2/jre/index.html) for the availability of runtime code which may be distributed with Java applets and applications.

2. **Java Platform Interface.** In the event that Licensee creates an additional API(s) which: (i) extends the functionality of a Java Environment; and, (ii) is exposed to third party software developers for the purpose of developing additional software which invokes such additional API, Licensee must promptly publish broadly an accurate specification for such API for free use by all developers.

3. **Trademarks and Logos.** Licensee acknowledges as between it and Sun that Sun owns the Java trademark and all Java-related trademarks, logos and icons including the Coffee Cup and Duke ("Java Marks") and agrees to comply with the Java Trademark Guidelines at http://www.sun.com/policies/trademarks.

4. **Source Code.** Software may contain source code that is provided solely for reference purposes pursuant to the terms of this Agreement.

Java™ Programming the Easy Way
CD-ROM Documentation

Use of this software is subject to the Binary Code License terms and conditions on pages 362–365. Read the license carefully. By opening this package, you are agreeing to be bound by the terms and conditions of this license from Sun Microsystems, Inc.

HARDWARE/SOFTWARE REQUIREMENTS

You may read the files on the disc with any computer that has a CD-ROM drive. You need a web browser to look at the HTML files that describe the contents of the disc. You may copy the Java source code files to your hard disk and then edit them with a text editor. The Java source code is the same for any computer environment.

To use the Java Development Kit (JDK) software on this disc, you need a computer that runs the Windows 95/98/NT operating system. You may download the JDK for other environments directly from the Sun web page. This disc includes version 1.2.1 of the JDK.

INSTALLATION

Point your web browser at the file *about_the_disc.html* to see a description of the files on the disc. The JDK software can be installed by executing the file *jdk1_2_1-win.exe*; executing this file will automatically lead you through the installation process. Additional installation information is on the disc.

BARRON'S LICENSING AGREEMENT/
DISCLAIMER OF WARRANTY

1. **Ownership of Rights.** The CD-ROM in this envelope was created for Barron's Educational Series, Inc. Users of the CD-ROM may not reproduce it, authorize or permit its reproduction, transmit it, or permit any portion thereof to be transmitted for any purpose whatsoever.

2. **License.** Barron's hereby grants to the consumer of this product the limited license to use same solely for personal use.

3. **Limited Warranty: Disclaimer of Implied Warranties.** If this CD-ROM fails to function in a satisfactory manner, Barron's sole liability to any purchaser or user shall be limited to refunding the price paid for the same by said purchaser or user. Barron's makes no further warranties, express or implied, with respect to the CD-ROM. *Barron's specifically disclaims any warranty of fitness for a particular purpose or of merchantability.*

4. **Consequential Damages.** Barron's shall not be liable under any circumstances for indirect, incidental, special, or consequential damages resulting from the purchase or use of the CD-ROM.

NOTES

NOTES

NOTES

NOTES